Lecture Notes in Computer Science 9750

Commenced Publication in 1973
Founding and Former Series Editors:
Gerhard Goos, Juris Hartmanis, and Jan van Leeuwen

More information about this series at http://www.springer.com/series/7409

Theo Tryfonas (Ed.)

Human Aspects of Information Security, Privacy, and Trust

4th International Conference, HAS 2016
Held as Part of HCI International 2016
Toronto, ON, Canada, July 17–22, 2016
Proceedings

 Springer

Editor
Theo Tryfonas
University of Bristol
Bristol
UK

ISSN 0302-9743   ISSN 1611-3349   (electronic)
Lecture Notes in Computer Science
ISBN 978-3-319-39380-3   ISBN 978-3-319-39381-0   (eBook)
DOI 10.1007/978-3-319-39381-0

Library of Congress Control Number: 2016939922

LNCS Sublibrary: SL3 – Information Systems and Applications, incl. Internet/Web, and HCI

Printed on acid-free paper

This Springer imprint is published by Springer Nature
The registered company is Springer International Publishing AG Switzerland

Foreword

The 18th International Conference on Human-Computer Interaction, HCI International 2016, was held in Toronto, Canada, during July 17–22, 2016. The event incorporated the 15 conferences/thematic areas listed on the following page.

A total of 4,354 individuals from academia, research institutes, industry, and governmental agencies from 74 countries submitted contributions, and 1,287 papers and 186 posters have been included in the proceedings. These papers address the latest research and development efforts and highlight the human aspects of the design and use of computing systems. The papers thoroughly cover the entire field of human-computer interaction, addressing major advances in knowledge and effective use of computers in a variety of application areas. The volumes constituting the full 27-volume set of the conference proceedings are listed on pages IX and X.

I would like to thank the program board chairs and the members of the program boards of all thematic areas and affiliated conferences for their contribution to the highest scientific quality and the overall success of the HCI International 2016 conference.

This conference would not have been possible without the continuous and unwavering support and advice of the founder, Conference General Chair Emeritus and Conference Scientific Advisor Prof. Gavriel Salvendy. For his outstanding efforts, I would like to express my appreciation to the communications chair and editor of *HCI International News*, Dr. Abbas Moallem.

April 2016   Constantine Stephanidis

HCI International 2016 Thematic Areas and Affiliated Conferences

Thematic areas:

- Human-Computer Interaction (HCI 2016)
- Human Interface and the Management of Information (HIMI 2016)

Affiliated conferences:

- 13th International Conference on Engineering Psychology and Cognitive Ergonomics (EPCE 2016)
- 10th International Conference on Universal Access in Human-Computer Interaction (UAHCI 2016)
- 8th International Conference on Virtual, Augmented and Mixed Reality (VAMR 2016)
- 8th International Conference on Cross-Cultural Design (CCD 2016)
- 8th International Conference on Social Computing and Social Media (SCSM 2016)
- 10th International Conference on Augmented Cognition (AC 2016)
- 7th International Conference on Digital Human Modeling and Applications in Health, Safety, Ergonomics and Risk Management (DHM 2016)
- 5th International Conference on Design, User Experience and Usability (DUXU 2016)
- 4th International Conference on Distributed, Ambient and Pervasive Interactions (DAPI 2016)
- 4th International Conference on Human Aspects of Information Security, Privacy and Trust (HAS 2016)
- Third International Conference on HCI in Business, Government, and Organizations (HCIBGO 2016)
- Third International Conference on Learning and Collaboration Technologies (LCT 2016)
- Second International Conference on Human Aspects of IT for the Aged Population (ITAP 2016)

Conference Proceedings Volumes Full List

1. LNCS 9731, Human-Computer Interaction: Theory, Design, Development and Practice (Part I), edited by Masaaki Kurosu
2. LNCS 9732, Human-Computer Interaction: Interaction Platforms and Techniques (Part II), edited by Masaaki Kurosu
3. LNCS 9733, Human-Computer Interaction: Novel User Experiences (Part III), edited by Masaaki Kurosu
4. LNCS 9734, Human Interface and the Management of Information: Information, Design and Interaction (Part I), edited by Sakae Yamamoto
5. LNCS 9735, Human Interface and the Management of Information: Applications and Services (Part II), edited by Sakae Yamamoto
6. LNAI 9736, Engineering Psychology and Cognitive Ergonomics, edited by Don Harris
7. LNCS 9737, Universal Access in Human-Computer Interaction: Methods, Techniques, and Best Practices (Part I), edited by Margherita Antona and Constantine Stephanidis
8. LNCS 9738, Universal Access in Human-Computer Interaction: Interaction Techniques and Environments (Part II), edited by Margherita Antona and Constantine Stephanidis
9. LNCS 9739, Universal Access in Human-Computer Interaction: Users and Context Diversity (Part III), edited by Margherita Antona and Constantine Stephanidis
10. LNCS 9740, Virtual, Augmented and Mixed Reality, edited by Stephanie Lackey and Randall Shumaker
11. LNCS 9741, Cross-Cultural Design, edited by Pei-Luen Patrick Rau
12. LNCS 9742, Social Computing and Social Media, edited by Gabriele Meiselwitz
13. LNAI 9743, Foundations of Augmented Cognition: Neuroergonomics and Operational Neuroscience (Part I), edited by Dylan D. Schmorrow and Cali M. Fidopiastis
14. LNAI 9744, Foundations of Augmented Cognition: Neuroergonomics and Operational Neuroscience (Part II), edited by Dylan D. Schmorrow and Cali M. Fidopiastis
15. LNCS 9745, Digital Human Modeling and Applications in Health, Safety, Ergonomics and Risk Management, edited by Vincent G. Duffy
16. LNCS 9746, Design, User Experience, and Usability: Design Thinking and Methods (Part I), edited by Aaron Marcus
17. LNCS 9747, Design, User Experience, and Usability: Novel User Experiences (Part II), edited by Aaron Marcus
18. LNCS 9748, Design, User Experience, and Usability: Technological Contexts (Part III), edited by Aaron Marcus
19. LNCS 9749, Distributed, Ambient and Pervasive Interactions, edited by Norbert Streitz and Panos Markopoulos
20. LNCS 9750, Human Aspects of Information Security, Privacy and Trust, edited by Theo Tryfonas

Human Aspects of Information Security, Privacy and Trust

Program Board Chair: **Theo Tryfonas,** *UK*

- Esma Aïmeur, Canada
- Claudio Agostino Ardagna, Italy
- Stefan Bauer, Austria
- Pam Briggs, UK
- Michael Carter, Canada
- Charlie Catlett, USA
- Yee-Yin Choong, USA
- Nathan Clarke, UK
- Lizzie Coles-Kemp, UK
- Lynne Coventry, UK
- Marc Dacier, USA
- Simone Fischer-Huebner, Sweden
- Steven Furnell, UK
- Tyrone Grandison, USA
- Ulrike Hugl, Austria
- Kevin Jones, UK
- Vasilis Katos, UK
- Kaido Kikkas, Estonia
- Dong-Seong Kim, New Zealand
- Gabriele Lenzini, Luxembourg
- Steve Marsh, Canada
- Noluntu Mpekoa, South Africa
- Masakatsu Nishigaki, Japan
- Jason Nurse, UK
- M. Maina Olembo, Germany
- Joon S. Park, USA
- Aljosa Pasic, Spain
- Joachim Posegga, Germany
- Sören Preibusch, UK
- Damien Sauveron, France
- Mary Frances Theofanos, USA
- Kerry-Lynn Thomson, South Africa
- Egdar Weippl, Austria
- Steffen Wendzel, Germany

The full list with the program board chairs and the members of the program boards of all thematic areas and affiliated conferences is available online at:

http://www.hci.international/2016/

HCI International 2017

The 19th International Conference on Human-Computer Interaction, HCI International 2017, will be held jointly with the affiliated conferences in Vancouver, Canada, at the Vancouver Convention Centre, July 9–14, 2017. It will cover a broad spectrum of themes related to human-computer interaction, including theoretical issues, methods, tools, processes, and case studies in HCI design, as well as novel interaction techniques, interfaces, and applications. The proceedings will be published by Springer. More information will be available on the conference website: http://2017.hci.international/.

General Chair
Prof. Constantine Stephanidis
University of Crete and ICS-FORTH
Heraklion, Crete, Greece
E-mail: general_chair@hcii2017.org

http://2017.hci.international/

Contents

Security Technologies

Human Factors of Authentication

User Identification Using Games

Oliver Buckley[⊠] and Duncan Hodges

Centre for Cyber Security and Information Systems, Cranfield University,
Defence Academy of the United Kingdom, Shrivenham, Swindon SN6 8LA, UK
{o.buckley,d.hodges}@cranfield.ac.uk

Abstract. There is a significant shift towards a digital identity and yet
the most common means of user authentication, username and password
pairs, is an imperfect system. In this paper we present the notion of
using videogames, specifically Tetris, to supplement traditional authentication methods and provide an additional layer of identity validation.
Two experiments were undertaken that required participants to play a
modified version of Tetris; the first experiment with a randomly ordered
set of pieces and the second with the pieces appearing in a fixed order.
The results showed that even simple games like Tetris demonstrate significant complexity in the available game states and that while some
users displayed repeatable strategic behaviour, others were effectively
random in their behaviours exhibiting no discernible strategy or repeatable behaviour. However, some pieces and gameboard scenarios encouraged users to exhibit behaviours that are more unique than others.

1 Introduction

Society has an increasing reliance on cyberspace as progressively more of our
lives transition to the digital world, whether it be interacting with friends right
through to the delivery of core government services. As a result of this shift the
notion of our digital identity is becoming increasingly important. Traditionally,
our digital identity has been secured with the use of a username and password
pair. However, this approach to identification places the cognitive load onto the
individual as they are required to remember a wide-range of security credentials.
In addition to this, users will rarely follow the guidelines for generating a strong
passwords [1]. Security credentials are easily compromised through a wide variety
of attack vectors, for example, phishing [2], hacking [3] or the credentials simply
being written down and lost [4].

In this paper, we hypothesise that videogames can be used as a means of
user validation, that relies on how an individual responds to scenarios within
the game, rather than the security credentials that they remember. We posit
that videogames provide an opportunity for a user to demonstrate a rich, multi-
dimensional and unique behaviour which can be used to validate an individual is
who they claim to be. In this work we specifically focus on the use of Tetris [5],
a popular single-screen puzzle game that presents players with an empty gameboard (a grid of 20-by-10). A sequence of 'tetrominoes' is generated and fall

© Springer International Publishing Switzerland 2016
T. Tryfonas (Ed.): HAS 2016, LNCS 9750, pp. 3–14, 2016.
DOI: 10.1007/978-3-319-39381-0_1

into the gameboard, players can rotate and move these shapes, with the aim of filling horizontal lines within the gameboard. Once a line is complete it will be removed from the gameboard and the rest of the board shuffles downwards. A player loses the game when the maximum height of the shapes exceeds the height of the gameboard.

The remainder of this paper is structured as follows: Sect. 2 provides a review of the related work covering alternative authentication and identification techniques. Section 3 details the methodology used to conduct the investigation. Section 4 provides an analysis of the collected data and the results of the study. Finally, in Sect. 5 we conclude by providing a reflection on our analysis and a discussion of further work in this area.

2 Background

Traditional approaches to user authentication, which rely on username and password pairs, are an imperfect system. The emphasis is placed on the individual to create a password that is both meaningful and memorable to them but that is also not easily guessed by a third-party. The strength of a password can be linked to the security expertise of the individual, with those with significant expertise typically choosing more secure passwords [6]. However, the choice of a password that is memorable and difficult to infer is hard to achieve, with a large percentage of passwords directly relating to personal characteristics and the reuse of passwords highly prevalent [7]. Additionally, it is becoming increasingly common for individuals to participate in risky security practices such as password sharing [8]. Once a user has successfully passed the authentication process there are typically no further challenges to their identity, which leads to the question of just how much confidence we can have that an individual is who their credentials claim them to be.

A significant amount of work has been undertaken investigating the use of graphical passwords [9] as an alternative means of authentication. Broadly speaking graphical passwords can be broken down into two broad groups: recognition based techniques and recall based techniques [10,11]. Recognition based techniques rely on a user recognising and selecting a set of images that they selected during the enrolment phase. Recall based techniques require a user to recall something that they had created at the enrolment phase, for example, a set of points on a particular image. However, users will typically choose similar spots on an image when creating a graphical password, thus creating hotspots around points of interest [12], this increases the guessability of these schemes. An alternative to passwords, graphical or textual, is the use of biometrics, which are measurable characteristics that can be used to describe an individual. Biometrics fall into two categories, physiological and behavioural [13]. Physiological traits are related to characteristics of the body of an individual, for example, fingerprints. Behavioural biometrics relate to the innate traits displayed by individuals, for example, keystroke dynamics. Traditional authentication methods rely on testing something that the individual knows, whereas biometrics place the emphasis on something that the person 'is'. This shift in focus from something known to some intrinsic characteristics, displayed naturally in response to the environment makes biometrics potentially harder to spoof [14,15].

In this work we present the use of videogames, specifically Tetris, as a behavioural biometric. We propose that individuals will display identifiable behaviours based on the state of the game. This approach will not rely on the individual remembering security credentials but will instead analyse their response to the context provided by the game they are playing.

3   Method

In this paper we focus on the use of Tetris to identify individuals based on the way in which they interact with the game. Tetris was chosen as it is a game that is both simple and intuitive for someone who does not have experience with videogames. However, Tetris also provides a consistent challenge that allows players to continually develop and refine their skills and strategies. Despite the depth of complexity of the demonstrable behaviours, the game board itself has a finite and manageable set of states and there is a limited set of pieces available to the player, as shown in Fig. 1.

Fig. 1. The pieces available (from left to right: 'L', 'J', 'S', 'Z', 'O', 'T', 'I')

To conduct this study a website was developed and deployed to play a modified version of Tetris, the modifications are required to allow data collection; the aim of the game and way the game is played remain entirely unchanged. During the study there were four key data dimensions that were collected:

- Current board state
- Current piece
- Next piece
- Keystrokes for the current piece

The study comprised of two experiments, the first required participants to simply play a game of Tetris with a random selection of pieces (i.e. there was no predetermined ordering to the shapes). Participants were required to play the game until they 'lost' the game, by the height of the pieces exceeding the height of board, or until they had played for three minutes. The second experiment again required participants to play the game for three minutes, or until they 'lost' the game but in this instance all participants were using a fixed set of pieces. That is to say, all of the participants would have exactly the same set of pieces, appearing in the same order, where the order was: 'S', 'S', 'T', 'Z', 'O', 'J', 'J', 'L', 'S', 'T', 'Z', 'Z', 'O', 'J', 'O', 'I', 'L', 'I', 'I'. This sequence of shapes was randomly generated prior to the start of the second experiment and remained constant throughout, with the sequence beginning again once the player had reached the end.

Recruitment for the survey was carried out using social-media networks as well as making use of the student population at Cranfield University. In total there were 50 unique participants who played 73 games during the first experiments and 75 unique participants who played 117 games during the second experiment.

4   Analysis and Results

It was hypothesised that there were two top-level approaches to playing Tetris: one approach only considers solving shorter-term problems whilst the other is based on longer-term problems. In the short-term approach the user only considers the current piece and the profile of the top of the current board state, however in the longer-term approach the user also considers the next piece in addition to any 'holes' that are trapped in the current board state. In the research presented in this paper the focus is on the short-term approach, in essence, the state of the game (i.e. the stimulus to the user) is entirely characterised by the board state and the current piece.

Initially the board state is characterised as the gradient of the profile of the pieces in the board, an example is shown in Fig. 2 along with the array defining this board state.

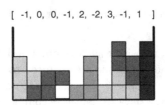

[-1, 0, 0, -1, 2, -2, 3, -1, 1   ]

Fig. 2. An example of the codification of the board state

An initial analysis explores the dimensionality associated with these profiles. Principle Components Analysis (PCA) was used to explore the set of board states that appeared in every game, that was played as part of both the experiments involving random and ordered play. The plot of the first two components is shown in Fig. 3a.

As can be seen there is some discrete structure in the first component, which can be expected given the discrete nature of the elements of the state vector. As expected the states associated with random play demonstrate a greater spread of states, the unconstrained nature of the piece order enabling a broader set of profiles.

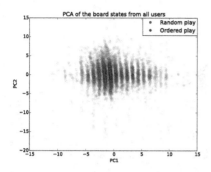

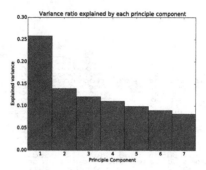

(a) The PCA of the board states for the two experiments

(b) The variances of the various principle components

Fig. 3. A principle components analysis of the board states in Tetris.

The variance described by each of the first 7 components is shown in Fig. 3b. As is consistent with Fig. 3a the first component describes around 25 % of the variance, however there is also significant variance contained in the other components. This implies that dimensionality reduction techniques will loose a significant amount of information within the state vector and the board state should be used as complete vector as the information content of the higher dimensions is significant.

The previous analysis considered each 'turn' in the game as an individual discrete state, given that a game is a time-ordered flow of these game states it is intuitive to plot the users 'journey' through these states as the game is played. Intuitively this can be represented as a directed graph, with the board states represented by the nodes and the type of the current piece representing the edges.

One game from each of the participants was randomly selected and the directed graph of the board states associated with the experiment with ordered play is shown in Fig. 4. In this graph the width of the transitions is proportional to the number of times an edge is used in play, with all edges that are used by one or more different users coloured red.

As can be seen the graph in Fig. 4 there are a number of common approaches to the early game phase — this is not surprising given the ordered nature of the pieces and the initial empty board state. There are two main approaches most users took for the first three or four pieces at which point the graph begins to diverge quickly. Once the graph has begun to diverge there are only three times a users' game reaches the same board state as that of another user, at which point the games immediately diverge again (i.e. the indegree of the node is greater than 1 and the indegree and outdegree are identical). Two examples of this are shown in Fig. 5 which shows a cropped and zoomed area of Fig. 4.

This implies that even in the ordered play experiment within a few pieces the games become relatively unique, the same graph analysis is shown in Fig. 6 for the random play experiment. Due to the more unconstrained nature of the

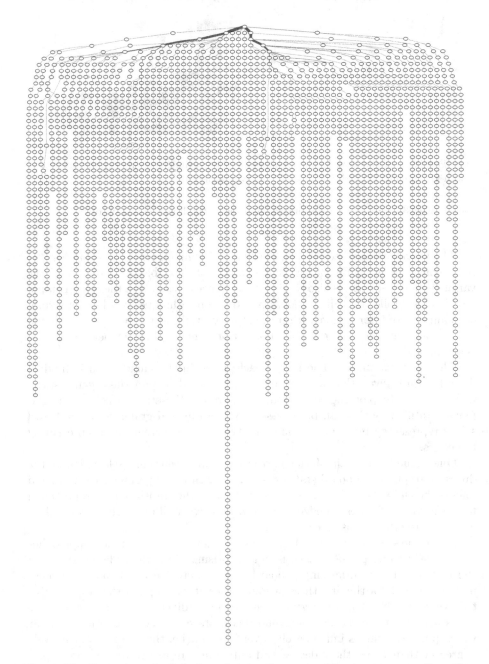

Fig. 4. The directed graph of the board states for one random game per user from the experiment in ordered play

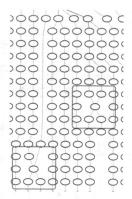

Fig. 5. Two examples of different users transitioning through the same game state.

game it is clearer that the board state diverges quicker than the ordered play, also of note is that the number of times board states are revisited is also small.

In addition to the uniqueness between users it is also important to assess the repeatability of users' play. In order to examine the repeatability of users behaviour the graphs associated with users who played multiple games were extracted from the ordered play experiment.

The first interesting characteristic is that it is apparent that a number of users exhibit little repeatable behaviour, with every game effectively taking a unique path, examples are shown in Fig. 7a and b. The games are also relatively short with few pieces placed during the three minute length of the game. This can be contrasted with other users such as those in Fig. 7c, d and e which demonstrate significantly more repeatable strategy for much longer. It is also notable the number of pieces placed in the same time-frame is significantly higher.

This difference in overall strategy is maybe not surprising as, although Tetris is a popular and common game, there will be differing degrees of experience with the game. This implies the users whose games are shown in Fig. 7a and b have not yet had enough experience in order to develop strategies for play. This also implies that an individual's strategies will evolve over time — in the same way that over time other behavioural biometrics (such as keystroke dynamics) will evolve, although the rate of this change is likely to decrease as the user becomes more experienced and their strategies stabilise. In solo games these strategies are likely to be more stable than in adversarial games where a users' strategy will evolve with respect to an opponent's.

Moving to a 'piece-centric' view it is possible to explore whether certain pieces result in more unique behaviours. In order to explore this question the board state at a given time is less important, what is more important is the change in the board state caused by a given piece. In this study the board state transition caused by a given piece is simply the change in the height of the board, as demonstrated in the two examples shown in Fig. 8.

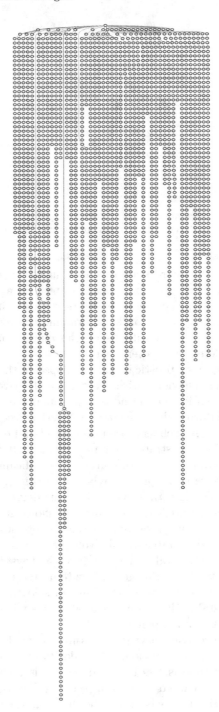

Fig. 6. The directed graph of the board states for one random game per user from the experiment in random play

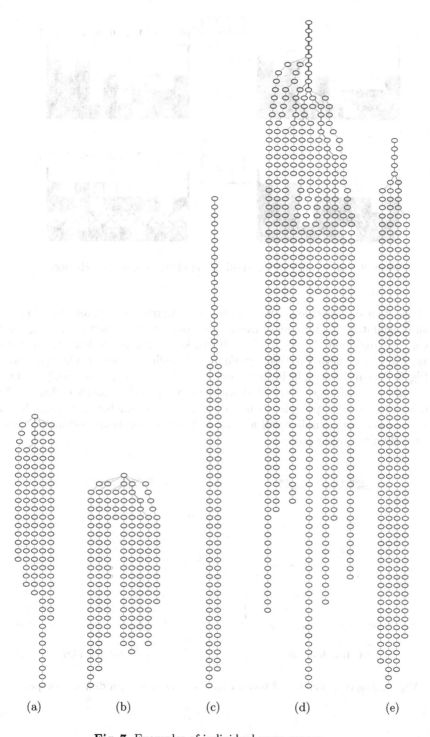

Fig. 7. Examples of individual users games.

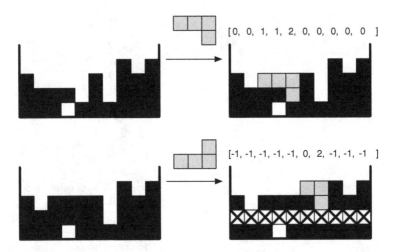

Fig. 8. An example of the codification of the board state changes

These board state changes were assessed for all participants and for all pieces, before calculating the number of times each board state change was seen for each piece. This highlighted very common board state changes which were seen per piece, the Cumulative Distribution Function (CDF) of these counts are shown in Fig. 9. As can be seen in both the graphs in Fig. 9, the commonality between the board state changes associated with the 'O' piece[1] is much higher — this indicates that the 'O' piece is less useful for discriminating between users. In this case the piece commonality will also be affected by rotational symmetry being greater than the other pieces.

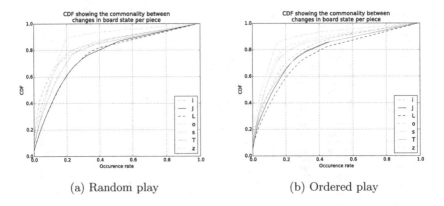

(a) Random play   (b) Ordered play

Fig. 9. The commonality of board changes associated with different shapes.

---

[1] The 2 × 2 square piece.

Also of note in Fig. 9a is the similarity between the curves associated with pieces that are mirror images of each other (e.g. 'J'/'L' and 'S'/'Z'). The 'J'/'L' pair also represent pieces that have a wider diversity of use than other pieces, this implies that using these pieces to discriminate between users will potentially provide more discriminatory power than other pieces.

Considering the ordered play, where the order of pieces is predetermined and all players receive the same pieces in the same order, the same analysis results in the plot shown in Fig. 9b. This plot shares several characteristics with that from random play, most notably that the 'O' piece has the greatest commonality in use. However, a number of the profiles for pieces differ from that of random play.

This indicates that by controlling the order of pieces it is possible to control the discriminatory power of individual pieces, in this example the 'J' piece has become less discriminatory whilst the 'Z' piece has become more discriminatory. The ability to control the discriminatory power of individual pieces by changing the order in which they appear is key to creating a system that can leverage gaming to aid user identification.

5 Conclusion and Future Work

In this paper we have investigated the use of videogames, specifically Tetris, and the associated strategies as a means of user validation. The findings have shown that some individuals exhibit repeatable strategies, although conversely there are those who appear to exhibit no notable, repeatable strategies. We posit that the degree of strategy that a player displays is linked to their experience with Tetris and is something that will be investigated in future work.

The other key finding from this work is that within Tetris there are certain states of the game board that are more divisive than others when trying to validate the identity of individuals. Similarly, some of the pieces are more useful when trying to discriminate between users, for example, it was discovered that the 'O' piece (as seen in Fig. 1) is less useful for determining individuals. This suggests that it will be possible to manufacture scenarios that allows users to exhibit more unique behaviours. Further experimentation will allow this idea to explored in more depth, and will help to determine those board states and pieces that are better suited to discriminating between individuals.

References

1. Gehringer, E.F.: Choosing passwords: security and human factors. In: 2002 International Symposium on Technology and Society (ISTAS 2002), pp. 369–373. IEEE (2002)
2. TechRadar: Hackers using advanced phishing attack to steal Google passwords (2014). http://www.techradar.com/news/internet/web/hackers-using-advanced-phishing-attack-to-steal-google-passwords-1248188. Accessed on 21 Jan 2016
3. Welivesecurity: Secure password: CyberVor hoard of 1.2 billion details 'used in attack' (2014). http://www.welivesecurity.com/2014/09/02/secure-password/. Accessed on 21 Jan 2016

4. Naked Security: Prince William photos accidentially reveal RAF password (2012). https://nakedsecurity.sophos.com/2012/11/21/prince-william-photos-password/. Accessed on 21 Jan 2016
5. Tetris (2016). http://tetris.com/about-tetris/. Accessed on 02 Feb 2016
6. Dodson, J., Hodges, D., Witty, M., Creese, S.: Does personality and security expertise predict password strength? Selected Papers of Internet Research 4 (2014)
7. Brown, A.S., Bracken, E., Zoccoli, S., King, D.: Generating and remembering passwords. Appl. Cogn. Psychol. **18**, 641–651 (2004)
8. Whitty, M., Doodson, J., Creese, S., Hodges, D.: Individual differences in cyber security behaviors: an examination of who is sharing passwords. Cyberpsychology Behav. Soc. Networking **18**(1), 3–7 (2015)
9. Jermyn, I., Mayer, A.J., Monrose, F., Reiter, M.K., Rubin, A.D., et al.: The design and analysis of graphical passwords. In: USENIX Security (1999)
10. Suo, X., Ying Zhu, G., Owen, S.: Graphical passwords: a survey. In: 21st Annual Computer Security Applications Conference, p. 10. IEEE (2005)
11. Biddle, R., Chiasson, S., Van Oorschot, P.C.: Graphical passwords: learning from the first twelve years. ACM Comput. Surv. (CSUR) **44**(4), Article no. 19 (2012)
12. Devlin, M., Nurse, J.R.C., Hodges, D., Goldsmith, M., Creese, S.: Predicting graphical passwords. In: Tryfonas, T., Askoxylakis, I. (eds.) HAS 2015. LNCS, vol. 9190, pp. 23–35. Springer, Heidelberg (2015)
13. Delac, K., Grgic, M.: A survey of biometric recognition methods. In: 2004 Proceedings of the 46th International Symposium on Electronics in Marine, Elmar 2004, pp. 184–193. IEEE (2004)
14. Rebera, A.P., Bonfanti, M.E., Venier, S.: Societal and ethical implications of anti-spoofing technologies in biometrics. Sci. Eng. Ethics **20**(1), 155–169 (2013)
15. Rodrigues, R.N., Ling, L.L., Govindaraju, V.: Robustness of multimodal biometric fusion methods against spoof attacks. J. Vis. Lang. Comput. **20**, 169–179 (2009)

Hermes: Hands-Free Authentication in Physical Spaces

Kulpreet Chilana[✉] and Federico Casalegno

MIT Design Lab, 77 Massachusetts Avenue, Cambridge, USA
{kulpreet,casalegno}@mit.edu

Abstract. This paper presents Hermes, a hands-free authentication system that makes use of credentials stored on a users smartphone to authenticate them when they enter a physical space or the vicinity of a physical object. By combining Bluetooth LE and Kerberos, Hermes is a novel system that makes use of existing technology available in today's internet-connected devices. This makes a system like Hermes suitable for widespread adoption for a number of applications in kiosks, shared printers and access control systems.

A prototype was developed to assess how such a system could improve interactions with connected objects and reduce the friction before a user can interact with the object. Based on our preliminary user studies and performance tests, we show a considerable improvement in the time required to authenticate via Hermes, as opposed to traditional authentication methods. We also evaluate the accuracy of Bluetooth LE for use in such a system.

Keywords: Authentication · Kiosk · Intelligent environment · Security · Smartphones · Physical interaction

1 Introduction

The internet is increasingly being used as a medium for developing new interactions with physical objects. With this *internet of things* paradigm growing increasingly popular, it becomes critical to rethink legacy infrastructure and implement new systems that better fit the model of the interactions being developed. One system that directly impacts user experience is authentication. Most user authentication mechanisms involve typing a username and password on a virtual keyboard. This can be both insecure and cumbersome [9]. In physical interactions, a system is required that considers the tradeoffs between security and convenience to authenticate users when they enter a physical space or the vicinity of a physical object. Such a system should seamlessly integrate into the experience of the interaction and make use of existing infrastructure. Doing so significantly reduces friction for the user by decreasing the time it takes for them to interface with the physical interaction.

In this paper we present Hermes, a novel hands-free authentication system that uses a smartphone to authenticate a user when they enter a physical space.

© Springer International Publishing Switzerland 2016
T. Tryfonas (Ed.): HAS 2016, LNCS 9750, pp. 15–24, 2016.
DOI: 10.1007/978-3-319-39381-0_2

As a starting point, aspects of architecture and technology were considered to develop a prototype with the goal of allowing users to simply walk up to a public kiosk and automatically be authenticated. There are a number of applications to this technology beyond the kiosk. For example, one can imagine restricting a bank teller's access to an account-holders records until the account-holder is in the physical branch or walking up to a personal computer and automatically log the user into the correct account.

By combining Bluetooth LE and Kerberos, we have developed a system that makes use of existing infrastructure. This makes the system suitable for widespread adoption for a number of applications. Based on our preliminary user studies and performance tests, we show a considerable improvement in the time required to use Hermes, as opposed to traditional authentication systems and show that Bluetooth LE is accurate enough for use in such a system.

2 Background

Current systems depend on existing authentication paradigms, which was observed in a preliminary study analyzing physical authentication systems around a college campus. The primary means of physical authentication involve RFID cards [10]. These cards, used more for access control than for authentication, were used by students to access dormitories and various buildings of the campus. However, the cards were not used when logging into campus computers or when interacting with other computer-based interactions such as point-of-sale terminals. Often times users had to input their username and a password. An example of an alternative approach to this interaction is being undertaken Knock, a system where the user is able to login to their OS X computer by walking up to their laptop and knocking on their iOS device[1].

Another physical system studied was the campus-wide printing system, which allowed students to print to a global print queue and release their print jobs at a small kiosk connected to the printer. While this system did use ID card for authentication, it required the user to print using their username and release the job using their ID card, making an otherwise simple process of printing directly to a printer unnecessarily complicated. A better experience could allow the user to simply walk into the vicinity of the printer and tap a button on the kiosk to release their print jobs, or automatically release the print jobs when the user is within range of the printer.

2.1 Prior Work

Using smartphones as a medium for authentication has been explored in different capacities in numerous studies. Hesselmann et al. explain how smartphones could be used as mediators between users and interactive tabletops to accomplish tasks such as authentication and information sharing. In doing so, they explain

---

[1] http://www.knocktounlock.com.

the shortcomings of wireless communications technologies to accomplish two-way communication between the smartphone and the tabletop, citing that they often require complex coupling procedures to establish the communication channel and are vulnerable to packet sniffing attacks [6]. Mayrhofer et al. describe a cryptographic approach to authentication based on accelerometer data and shaking two devices together to avoid the cumbersome task of inputting a PIN [8]. Greene et al. describe different authentication schemes in the context of password requirements. They conclude that device constraints must be considered before porting password requirements from one system to another (i.e. desktop to mobile). From this work, it makes sense that device constraints must also be considered when porting traditional authentication schemes to that of a physical interaction [5].

Most relevant to this publication is the work of Roalter et al., who also developed a smartphone-based authentication system for public kiosks [9]. Their work discusses a number of trends in authentication schemes used in industry today. In many ways, Hermes is an extension and improvement on their work in that it addresses many of the shortcomings of their system. Namely, that it requires active use of the smartphone rather than passively using the smartphone in the background. Hermes is a tested implementation that make use of existing infrastructure (Bluetooth LE and Kerberos) to accomplish something very similar with even less friction on the part of the user.

2.2   Technologies

Bluetooth LE (BLE) broadcasters or beacons can be used to detect proximity of a nearby device with an accuracy of $\approx 1m$. A number of studies have depicted the potential for vast applications of micro-location technologies such as BLE in enabling new experiences when interacting with physical spaces [4, 7]. Apple's CLBeacon API documentation categorizes beacon proximity into four categories: immediate, near, far and unknown. [3] These classifications are used to determine how far a user is from a beacon device, such as a kiosk, and will be used to describe various steps in the user flow and the design of the system below.

During the initial design stages several authentication schemes were considered, taking into account ease-of-use, reliability and security. Traditional authentication schemes that were considered include LDAP and Kerberos protocols. Additionally, less clean approaches were explored such as session-hijacking and cookie-forwarding. Kerberos is the most widely deployed computer network authentication protocol used on the internet and makes use of tickets to allow users to prove their identity to a service or application. The system described below outlines one approach to a hands-free authentication system that uses Kerberos with the added benefit of never sending a user's password over the air during authentication.

3 System Components

The system consists of three main components as shown in Fig. 1 above: a server, kiosk device, and the user's personal smartphone. First, the user stores their login credentials securely on their device when they download and install and mobile application. The kiosk device runs an application that connects to the server via a socket connection. Upon connecting to the server, the server supplies the kiosk with a UUID and a major and minor value. These three values are broadcast by the kiosk over Bluetooth LE and can be used by the server to uniquely identify the kiosk.

When the user enters the far field of any kiosk with that particular UUID, their smartphone authenticates them using their stored credentials against the authentication scheme. The result is an authentication credential (e.g. a Kerberos

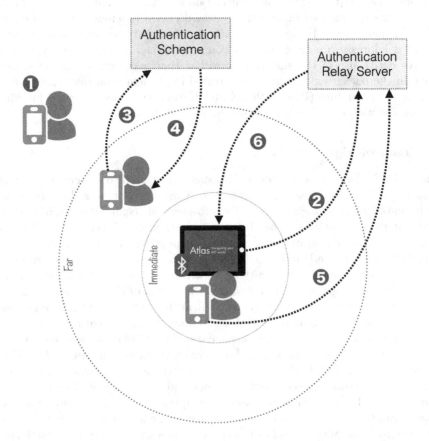

Fig. 1. A high-level overview of Hermes. (1) The user *logs in* and effectively stores their credentials on their smartphone. (2) The kiosk connects to the authentication relay server (3) The user enters the *far* field and (4) exchanges the stored credentials for a token. (5) The user enters the immediate field posting the token to the authentication relay server. (6) The server relays the token to the kiosk.

ticket, certificate, or session cookie) stored on the user's device. This secure information remains on the user's device until they enter the immediate field of a kiosk, at which point the authentication credential is forwarded to the server along with the major and minor value of the nearby kiosk. The authentication relay server uses this information to forward the authentication credential to the right kiosk, which can use the token to pose as the user until the user walks away from the kiosk or leaves the immediate field.

4 Design and Implementation

A prototype was developed that made use of the Bluetooth and Kerberos APIs included in the Apple iOS SDK. The kiosk was developed as a tablet application and a mobile client was written for the user to store their username and password. To sidestep the security issues with wireless communication outlined by Hesselmann et al. [6], the kiosks and the mobile client interfaced with each other through an authentication relay server. This server was written as a simple TCP socket, using the Python Twisted library and maintained connections to kiosks and clients separately.

An alternative approach could have the tablet and the mobile device communicating directly over Bluetooth LE link-layer, but this would require an additional mechanism to verify the identity of the kiosk to the mobile device to prevent an adversary from broadcasting the same UUID as the kiosks and intercepting the user's authentication credential. The iOS SDK provides such a mechanism to establish a secure link-layer connection, but it requires pairing the two devices. This additional step creates another level of friction in the user experience and defeats the purpose of hands-free authentication:

> If the central and the peripheral are iOS devices, both devices receive an alert indicating that the other device would like to pair. The alert on the central device contains a code that you must enter into a text field on the peripheral device's alert [2].

An authentication relay server acts as an effective mediator between the kiosk and client, with many mechanisms already existing to establish secure connections and verifying the identity of connected clients over TCP without requiring pairing. In our tests, the added time required to reroute through the authentication relay server as opposed to establishing a direct link-layer connection is negligible.

The kiosk and the client made use of the Generic Security Service Application Program Interface (GSS-API) for Kerberos authentication. The GSS-API is an IETF standard that provides a common API for authenticating against a large number of authentication schemes including Kerberos, NTLM, DCE, SESAME, SPKM and LIPKEY. This API makes adjusting a prototype built around one of these schemes easily adaptable to any of the others. Despite being a low-level API, the GSS-API comes bundled with the iOS SDK and is also written in C.

Two particular APIs can conveniently be used in this system: `gss_export_cred` and `gss_import_cred` [1].

The authentication process starts in a callback that is triggered when the user enters the far field of the kiosk with their mobile device. The mobile device uses the stored username and password to acquire an initial credential, in this case a forwardable Kerberos Ticket Granting Ticket (TGT). When the user enters the immediate field, another callback is called which serializes the acquired credential using `gss_export_cred` and send the credential to the authentication relay server over the TCP socket along with the major and minor value of the nearby kiosk. The server then blocks any other requests to authenticate to that kiosk and forwards the credential. The kiosk can import the credential using `gss_import_cred`. When the user exits the immediate field, another callback is triggered which signals the server to stop blocking requests and signal the kiosk to log out the user and destroy the imported credentials.

The TGT on the kiosk can be used to authenticate to any service that supports Kerberos authentication. Once the user is authenticated to this service on the kiosk, the TGT is no longer needed. For this reason, it makes sense for the mobile device to acquire and forward a TGT with a short expiration time as an added security measure in case the TGT gets intercepted. The use of the GSS-API greatly simplifies the process of acquiring, destroying, exporting, and importing Kerberos credentials, abstracting away complicated lower-level Kerberos APIs. The credentials acquired using the GSS-API can also be stored in the sandboxed application Keychain and integrates well with NSURLSession and its higher-level APIs such as UIWebView in the iOS SDK. This comes in handy for web authentication, as the imported TGT can be used to easily authenticate via the HTTP-Negotiate protocol to access secure corporate websites, for example.

5   Performance Tests

This section discusses several tests that were performed to determine the system's reliability and performance. The first set of measurements was taken in a large open space to get a sense of the broadcast range of the tablet kiosk. This range was measured to be between 40 and 50 m, greatly exceeding the 30 m described in the Bluetooth LE specification. This is most likely due to the higher power and frequency of broadcast of the tablet device as opposed to the much lower-power Bluetooth peripherals or beacon devices.

At the lower extreme, with default parameters and conditions, the immediate field callback was triggered when the subject walked within approximately 80 cm of the tablet. Being able to adjust this parameter is important for a system of this sort: since the user is logged in when they enter the immediate field, it should be feasible to adjust this parameter from 0.8 m to 2.0 m if the physical setup of the interaction requires it. Every beacon broadcasts a measured power value with each advertisement. This measured power value corresponds with the received signal strength indication (RSSI) of the beacon calibrated to be one meter away from the device. This calibration process can be used to adjust the distance at which the immediate field is triggered. A set of measurements were taken to determine the granularity of the RSSI signal at different distances and how well the measured power of a tablet placed at desk-level and face-level could be adjusted. The results are summarized in the Fig. 2.

These results show a similar signal strength measurement for a tablet at face-level and desk-level and a linear relationship between RSSI and distance. In collecting this data, a small anomaly was also discovered. One subject placed the mobile device used to measure RSSI into their back pocket. For this subject, shown by the yellow line in the figure above, the RSSI reading was much lower than the subjects who put the device in their front pocket. As the subject walked closer to the kiosk, the immediate field was not triggered; thus they were not authenticated. Upon further investigation we learned that the human body is a source of interference for Bluetooth LE signals and the subject's body was effectively shielding the signal. This presents a usability issue as many smartphone users prefer to keep their device in their back pocket. However, we also consider a future where wearable technology is more prevalent. Existing smartwatches on

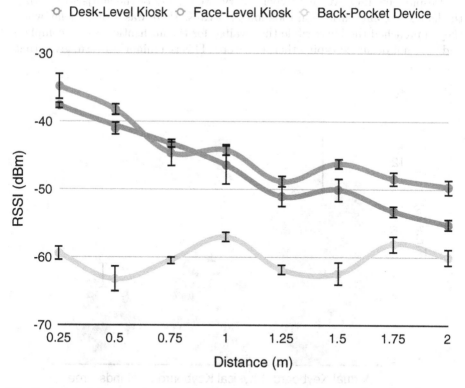

Fig. 2. A plot of distance from the kiosk and measured signal strength at that distance. Such a plot could be used to calibrate the distance that triggers the *immediate* field and thus the authentication. The yellow plot depicts the result of shielding that occurs when the user keeps their smartphone in their back pocket. (Color figure online)

the market today are equipped with the necessary technology to perform all the operations required by the mobile device in this system, so users could theoretically use them to authenticate from their exposed wrists rather than their back pockets.

5.1 User Study

A user study was also conducted, using a technique similar to that of Greene et al., to compare the time taken to authenticate through this hands-free system with that of a conventional password-based system [5]. Subjects were given an 8-character password comprised of letters, numbers and special characters to memorize. They were then timed from a starting position four meters away from the tablet device until they were successfully authenticated on the device. This was measured using a virtual keyboard on the tablet device, a physical keyboard attached to the tablet, and using the Hermes hands-free system developed in this paper. The results shown in Fig. 3 show a marked improvement from both the virtual and physical keyboard:

Despite this improvement, when interviewed many of the subjects felt that the hands-free authentication took longer because there was a short delay when they approached the kiosk while they waited for the authentication to complete and were not occupied typing their password. This is a minor concern, given that

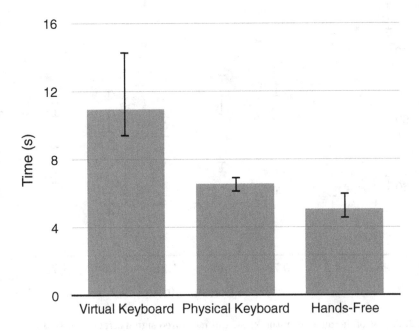

Fig. 3. Hermes, hands-free authentication performs markedly better than traditional authentication systems that use a keyboard, reducing the friction before a user can interface with an interaction.

this is an early prototype and the system design and network configurations could be further optimized to improve latency.

The final user study involved multiple subjects approaching and attempting to authenticate at the same kiosk. In this case, the subject who approached the kiosk first was authenticated on the kiosk at almost every trial. This situation could present some awkwardness in a deployed system but could easily be remedied with the two-factor authentication extension described in the next section.

6   Limitations and Extensions

There remain several limitations and areas for exploration. One of the first concerns is whether walking up to a physical device should be sufficient to authenticate a user. Other proposed models include a two-factor authentication model that requires the user to walk up to the physical interaction and also confirm their intention to authenticate by tapping on a smartwatch, scanning an ID card, or providing some other quick form of identification such as a thumbprint or facial scan. Another model proposes splitting the data in an application or service so that the user only be prompted for the second authentication factor when they need to access sensitive or secure information.

There are also several considerations concerning security and privacy. An authentication system involving beacons placed all around a campus could also be used to triangulate a user's location. While there are many interesting use cases such as tracking when a worker physically arrives at work and when they leave to get a more accurate clock in and clock out, the assumption is that a large majority of users would not be fond of allowing an organization to track their position. The final consideration is infrastructure, as this system requires all users to have a smartphone. There is no way of knowing with certainty if enough users of a particular physical system have smartphones to justify requiring it in this system; thus, the assumption is that a majority of systems will have a fallback method of authentication.

7   Contributions

In this paper, we have developed Hermes, a novel authentication system for physical interactions and demonstrated how it quantitatively and qualitatively performs better than traditional authentication systems. Hermes was developed mainly as a proof-of-concept prototype to show it's possible to build such a system and assess how well it performs in a variety of different scenarios. While it was shown that the system performs much better in certain situations than others, it remains a promising option for a future where remembering passwords and password-based security vulnerabilities are a thing of the past.

References

1. MIT Kerberos Documentation, Chapter Developing with GSSAPI, 20 March 2015
2. Core Bluetooth Programming Guide, chapter Best Practices for Setting Up Your Local Device as a Peripheral. Apple, Inc. (2013)
3. CoreLocation Framework Reference, chapter CLBeacon Class Reference. Apple, Inc. (2013)
4. Casado-Mansilla, D., Foster, D., Lawson, S., Garaizar, P., López-de Ipiña, D.: 'close the loop': An ibeacon app to foster recycling through just-in-time feedback. In: Proceedings of the 33rd Annual ACM Conference Extended Abstracts on Human Factors in Computing Systems, CHI EA 2015, pp. 1495–1500. ACM, New York (2015)
5. Greene, K.K., Gallagher, M.A., Stanton, B.C., Lee, P.Y.: I can't type that! P@$$word entry on mobile devices. In: Tryfonas, T., Askoxylakis, I. (eds.) HAS 2014. LNCS, vol. 8533, pp. 160–171. Springer, Heidelberg (2014)
6. Hesselmann, T., Henze, N., Boll, S.: Flashlight: Optical communication between mobile phones and interactive tabletops. In: ACM International Conference on Interactive Tabletops and Surfaces, ITS 2010, pp. 135–138, New York, NY, USA. ACM (2010)
7. Jamil, S., Basalamah, A., Lbath, A.: Crowdsensing traces using bluetooth low energy (ble) proximity tags. In: Proceedings of the 2014 ACM International Joint Conference on Pervasive and Ubiquitous Computing: Adjunct Publication, UbiComp 2014 Adjunct, pp. 71–74, New York, NY, USA. ACM (2014)
8. Mayrhofer, R., Gellersen, H.-W.: Shake well before use: authentication based on accelerometer data. In: LaMarca, A., Langheinrich, M., Truong, K.N. (eds.) Pervasive 2007. LNCS, vol. 4480, pp. 144–161. Springer, Heidelberg (2007)
9. Roalter, L., Kranz, M., Möller, A., Diewald, S., Stockinger, T., Koelle, M., Lindemann, P.: Visual authentication: a secure single step authentication for user authorization. In: Proceedings of the 12th International Conference on Mobile and Ubiquitous Multimedia, MUM 2013, pp. 30:1–30:4, New York, NY, USA. ACM (2013)
10. Walton, C.: Portable radio frequency emitting identifier, 17 May 1983. US Patent 4,384,288

Implicit Authentication for Mobile Devices Using Typing Behavior

Jonathan Gurary[1]([✉]), Ye Zhu[1], Nahed Alnahash[2], and Huirong Fu[2]

[1] Cleveland State University, Cleveland, USA
j.gurary@vikes.csuohio.edu, y.zhu61@csuohio.edu
[2] Oakland University, Rochester, USA
{nalnahas,fu}@oakland.edu

Abstract. An attacker that compromises the unlock mechanism of a mobile device can fundamentally use the device as if it were their own, with access to a large portion of the user's sensitive data and communications. We propose a secondary implicit authentication scheme which monitors typing behavior to detect unauthorized use and lock down the mobile device. We build a basic implementation of our scheme on the Android operating system. Our user studies on the implementation show that we can achieve an accuracy of up to 97 % identifying one user out of a set of fifteen, with an FAR of $< 3\%$ and an FRR of $< .5\%$.

1 Introduction and Related Work

For most smartphones in use today, the sole defense against intrusion is the unlock mechanism that allows use of the device. An attacker who breaks the device's unlock authentication can gain access to the device. Access to a victim's cell phone allows an attacker to read sensitive communications, reset account passwords, and potentially access sensitive applications like those used for banking. A second level of real time authentication is desirable- even if an attacker gains access to the device, they will eventually be detected and locked out while attempting to use it. In order to remain viable, a real time authentication scheme must be accurate enough not to lock out legitimate users. In this paper, we propose an implicit authentication scheme based on soft keyboard typing behaviors which can identify users with a high degree of accuracy.

We choose to identify users with the touch screen because using the touch screen is a core behavior of any meaningful smartphone use. Physical biometrics such as gait [8] can be used as implicit authentication, however the attacker can merely refrain from walking while the device is powered on. Voice recognition schemes such as [2,4] can identify implicitly if the owner of the device is speaking nearby, but cannot help if the attacker stays silent. Interaction with the touch screen is required to place calls, write text messages, or access secure accounts and applications. A behavioral biometric that depends on touch behavior is difficult for the attacker to avoid if they wish to use the device.

Various authors have proposed schemes to authenticate users based on their touch screen gestures, touch patterns, and readings from on-device sensors during a touch [1,3,5–7,9–11]. Unlike previous research such as Feng et al. [6], which

© Springer International Publishing Switzerland 2016
T. Tryfonas (Ed.): HAS 2016, LNCS 9750, pp. 25–36, 2016.
DOI: 10.1007/978-3-319-39381-0_3

identifies users based on their touch screen gestures, we focus specifically on identifying users based on their typing patterns with the soft keyboard. Many users type small amounts of characters regularly on their smartphones, for example to send text messages, write emails, or dial phone numbers. An attacker that steals the device and attempts to use it for any of these tasks may be locked out, or they may discretely trigger an alert to a location schemes such as Apple's "Find my iPhone." Users may also type passwords on their mobile devices. An attacker that has compromised a user's account password[1] and attempts to enter that password into the device may be detected, locking the account.

Previous works such as Draffin et al. [5] have utilized typing behavior to authenticate users. Unlike previous works, our scheme utilizes all features that can be collected on modern smartphones, including device acceleration data, for an increased rate of accuracy. We also present several approaches for implementing touch classification, based on efficient statistical classifiers, and compare them using the same data. Our results show that by utilizing the large amount of data available on touch screen devices, we can achieve a 97 % rate of accuracy identifying users after only 15 touches.

In the next section, we present background and related work on keystroke dynamics and implicit mobile authentication using the touch screen. We continue by describing our implementation the data we collect in detail in Sect. 2. We present our user study and details about our classification approaches in Sect. 3, and we discuss our planned future work and extensions in Sect. 4. We conclude the paper in Sect. 5.

2   Scheme

We designed a basic implementation of the soft keyboard on the Android operating system. The built-in soft keyboard intentionally disallows recording of touch information to avoid various misuse such as keyloggers, and we found it was easier to build a basic keyboard than to attempt to override this security feature. A screenshot of our implementation is presented in Fig. 1. We use the built in Android class MotionEvent to collect data from touches on the keyboard buttons, and the SensorEvent class to collect accelerometer data. With these classes, we were able to record the following information about each touch:

Duration of Touch and Time Since Last Touch: The use of these values by themselves is sometimes called *keystroke dynamics*. We record the duration of touches and time between touches, in milliseconds. The duration of a touch is considered the time between the press and release of a button (eventtime-downtime in the MotionEvent class). The time since the last touch is considered the time from one press to the next (downtime-previous downtime in the MotionEvent class). For the first touch in every trace, the time since last touch is set to zero.

---

[1] We assume that the account utilizes trusted devices, and the attacker cannot simply enter the account information on another device.

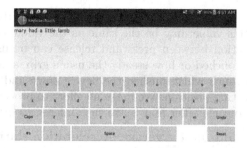

Fig. 1. A screenshot of our Android keyboard implementation.

Relative x and y Location of Press: The location of the center of the touch at the time the button was pressed, relative to the button, is recorded in pixel units. The top left corner of any button is (0,0) and the bottom right corner is the maximum, which varies by device.

Size of Touch on Press: The size of the touch is recorded on a scale from 0 to 1, where 1 is the maximum touch size the system will recognize, which varies by device. The system interprets all touches as a circle where size determines the radius of that circle. Size of a touch roughly correlates with finger size and touch pressure, which can be used to identify a user. The number of sizes supported by each device is not infinite; most devices support between 20 and 100 discrete touch sizes.

Magnitude of Acceleration on Press: The magnitude of acceleration is read in m/s^2 from the accelerometer, a sensor which the vast majority of devices on the market have today. Different devices update their sensors at different rates. We take the last known accelerometer reading before the press occurs, which may be several milliseconds before the touch itself.

Relative x and y Location of Release: The location of the center of the touch as the the button is let go. By taking the x and y locations of the press and release, we can determine how far, and in which direction, the user moves their finger during a touch. We do not use touch distance or direction in this paper directly because we are seeking to minimize computation requirements, though an intelligent classifier may utilize these features indirectly.

Size of Touch on Release: The size of the touch as the button is let go. We can infer pressure from the difference in sizes between press and release. If the press size is very large, and the release size is much smaller, then it is likely the user pushed their finger down hard on the device and increased the surface area that was making contact with the screen. We do not calculate pressure in this paper directly, though a classifier may indirectly take advantage of this relationship. Physical properties of the finger may also play into this feature, for example the amount an individual's finger yields when making contact with a hard surface.

Magnitude of Acceleration on Release: As with a press, the magnitude of acceleration on release is the last known accelerometer reading at the time the user releases the button. If a touch is short enough and the device's sensor is slow to update, this value may be the same as the value for the press. The difference in acceleration between press and release can be used to infer how hard the device was touched or how steady the user's grip is. A large difference can indicate a hard touch which pushed the device down and and caused it to recoil back to its starting position. We make no effort to process acceleration in this paper, however our classifier may make such inferences indirectly.

Maximum, Minimum, and Average Acceleration during the Touch: We take as many readings as possible from the accelerometer between the press and release of a touch, recording the max, min, and average of the magnitudes of acceleration. Depending on the speed of the touch and the rate at which the accelerometer updates on that particular device, it is possible to obtain zero readings between the press and release, in which case we set all three values to some default value.

Although we are able to collect pressure from the MotionEvent class, we found that on most modern mobile devices pressure is either (1) set a default value which does not change or (2) scaled linearly with touch size. Capacitive touch screens like those found in most modern mobile devices are not able to sense the pressure of a touch directly. Many previous works that utilize the pressure reading from the MotionEvent class are actually utilizing touch size indirectly instead, and in works where both touch size and pressure were used, the use of pressure can be considered double-counting of touch size. Some manufacturers such as Apple and Huawei are currently developing phones which have touch pressure sensors, and some devices such as the Samsung Note feature a touch pen which can report pressure based on how hard the tip of the pen is pushed down.

Another feature frequently used in previous works is orientation, defined as the angle that the pointing device (e.g. a finger) makes with the screen. Orientation is also not reported by the MotionEvent class in many modern devices: it is either set to a single static value or one of two values depending on whether the device is held in portrait or landscape mode.

2.1   Future Implementation

We envision a scheme that collects touch data anonymously from a large pool of users and stores the anonymous data on some server. Periodically, touch data from random users is sent from the server to each client and the client generates a classifier for that data by combining it with their own data. Typing behavior from the user is analyzed by the classifier using one of the approaches described in Sect. 3. The user will have a high rate of accuracy matching with themselves, however the attacker will have a much higher chance of matching other users, with a very low chance to match the actual user several times consecutively. For example with 15 users, an attacker who has an equal chance to be behaviorally matched to any of those users has a $1/15 = 7\%$ chance to be authenticated as the user per attempt. If three consecutive failures cause a lockout, the attacker has a $14/5^3 = 81\%$ chance to be locked out in the first three authentication attempts. We will also show that 15 touches or less can suffice for an authentication attempt. We will also demonstrate that we can attain high accuracy using a computationally simple classifier that can run in the background on a mobile device, with small sets of data that will require only minimal amounts of network use and device storage.

3   Experiment

3.1   Devices Used

We used a Galaxy Tab 3 tablet and a Google Nexus 4 smartphone for our experiments in order to ensure our results are consistent across different devices. The Galaxy Tab 3 has an 8 inch screen with a resolution of 1280 by 800, and the Nexus 4 has a 4.7 inch screen with a similar resolution of 1280 by 768.

There are several distinctions between the devices. We note that the Nexus 4 appears to report accelerometer readings more quickly, often enough that almost every touch reports a value for each of the acceleration features described in Sect. 2. In contrast, the accelerometer on the Tab 3 reports slowly. While it can collect information quickly enough for slow typists, for our faster typists as little as 5 % of touches report all the acceleration values described in Sect. 2. The Tab 3 reports the x and y location of touches to a precision of five decimal places, while the Nexus 4 uses only whole numbers. It is not clear to what digit the Tab 3's values are significant. Both devices report a large number of discrete touch sizes. The Tab 3 reports size on a scale from 0 to 1, while typical finger sizes on the Nexus 4 range from 9 to 11. We conclude that any implementation of our proposed authentication scheme will need to be device specific.

3.2   Experiment Setup

We recruited 15 volunteer participants to type the phrase "mary had a little lamb" on our tablet device and an additional 15 participants to type the phrase "maryhadalittlelamb" on our smartphone device. The space character is omitted for the second set of volunteers to determine if using the space character has a detrimental impact on identification accuracy. For example, we hypothesize that touches consecutive to space will consistently have a low time since last touch, since space is easy to find and reach on the keyboard, and this may make the time since last touch data point less useful in classification for those touches.

Participants typed the phrase a minimum of 20 times, though some participants chose to type the phrase up to 25 times. To ensure consistent acceleration data, participants were asked to sit in a stationary chair while typing, holding the device in landscape mode with their non-dominant hand and typing with their dominant hand. The particular grip participants used and the manner in which they typed were not specified, but participants could not use the hand holding the device to type or rest the device against any stationary surface. Participants were allowed to choose their stance and adjust it as they typed, for example they could lean forward or back in the chair.

3.3 Typographical Correction

We employed some typological correction similar to Draffin's approach [5]. Typographical mistakes were treated as follows: (1) if more than three typographical errors were present, the trace was discarded, (2) if a character was typed incorrectly, e.g. "msry had a little lamb," the incorrect letter was treated as correct (treating "s" as an "a" in the example), (3) if a character was missing, e.g. "mry had a little lamb," the previous character would be duplicated, e.g. "mmry had a little lamb," and the typo ignored as in (2) and (4) if an extra character was typed, e.g. "masry had a little lamb," the extra character was simply removed. We hypothesize that some users make the same typographical mistakes consistently, and keeping these mistakes may actually help to identify them. For example, if the user attempts to press "a" and consistently hits "s," we expect the x-coordinate of the mistaken touch on the "s" key, after we correct it to an "a," to be more leftwards than for other users. We plan to analyze feasibility of identifying these mistakes in real time and the impact of keeping these mistakes in our future work. On average, users made approximately 10 typos in all of their 20 traces combined, though many of these typos are concentrated on specific users. Due to typo correction, some participants ended up with fewer than 20 traces, with a minimum of 15.

3.4 Classification and Analysis

We processed our data using computationally efficient classifiers- K nearest neighbors (KNN), binary decision tree, and naive Bayes. As smartphones have reached a high level of computational power, our hope is that these classifiers could run on the device itself in the future. In this paper we present only the binary decision tree results, as they were the most favorable for our experiments. We measure the success of our classification with (1) Accuracy: the percentage of authentication attempts from a user correctly matched to that user, (2) False Acceptance Rate (FAR): the percentage of authentication attempts matched to a user that do not belong to that user, and (3) False Rejection Rate (FRR): the percentage of authentication attempts from a user matched incorrectly to other users or rejected outright. We will define the meaning of an authentication attempt for each of our approaches later on.

3.5 Character Independent Classification

For this experiment, touches are grouped together and classified without considering the character being touched. We split touches evenly into testing and training sets at random, with approximately 200 touches per user in each set. All character information is stripped, that is an "a" is treated the same as a "b" or any other character. Training sets from all users are combined and fed to the classifier. Note that for participants typing on the Tab 3, this also means that the "space" character is treated the same as any other character, even though the space bar is significantly larger than other buttons and thus has a wider

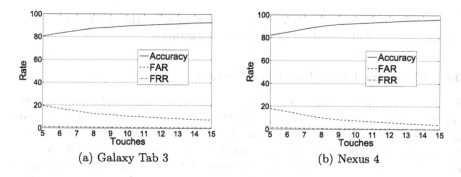

Fig. 2. Touches vs Accuracy and FAR/FRR for character independent data.

range of position values. We hypothesize including space will reduce accuracy in the Tab 3's results.

An authentication attempt is begun by taking n touches for each user from the testing set at random and applying the classifier to each touch individually. The identity of the user is determined by taking the plurality of the n chosen touches. For example, n is equal to five touches and user a's trace contains two touches identified as user a, one as user b, one as user c, and one as user d. The authentication attempt is marked as successful for user a, even though the majority of the touches were attributed to other users, because the plurality of touches were identified as user a's. An authentication attempt using n touches is taken from users b, c, and d in the same manner. A tie does not authenticate any user and is automatically considered a false reject. To ensure consistency, we take 2000 samples from each user for each value of n, and the overall accuracy, FAR, and FRR are calculated by averaging the results for all users. Figure 2 demonstrates our results from n = 5 to n = 15.

Figure 2 shows we can achieve an acceptance rate of 93 % after 15 touches with an FAR of 7 % and an FRR of .5 % for the Tab 3 and an acceptance rate of 96 % with an FAR of 4 % and an FRR of .25 % for the Nexus 4. Thus a user can be authenticated after typing a short text message, using a training set that can easily be built in as little as two or three text messages. Our hypothesis that the space character will worsen results has held for this data set, though other factors such as screen size may also influence the different in metrics.

We theorize this approach could be used to dynamically monitor all typing on the device. Assuming a generous allowance of three incorrect authentication attempts before device lockout, a legitimate user will have a near zero chance of lockout ($7\%^3 = .0343\%, 4\%^3 = .0064\%$), while an attacker will face a substantial chance of lockout after only 45 touches. Because all characters are treated identically, classification data from other users utilizing the authentication application can easily be anonymously collected and distributed, allowing each user of the application to be compared against other anonymous users, potentially against different users for each authentication attempt. This further reduces the chance of a legitimate user being mismatched with another user with similar typing behavior but serves no advantage to an attacker.

3.6   Character Dependent Classification

For this experiment, each character receives its own separate classification. We classify the characters "a," "space," and "l" as these are the most common characters in our typed phrase. We split touches evenly into testing and training sets at random, with approximately 40 touches for "a" and "space" and 30 touches for "l" in each set. An authentication attempt for this experiment is defined the same way as in the previous experiment, with n touches taken at random from each user and a plurality-wins model for each authentication attempt. Once again we take 2000 samples from each user for each value of n.

Figures 3, 4, and 5 show our results for each character from $n = 5$ to $n = 15$. We achieve an accuracy of 97 % after 15 touches of the letter "a," with an FAR of 2.6 % and an FRR of .2 % for the Tab 3 and an accuracy of 90 %, with an FAR of 10 % and an FRR of .7 % for the Nexus 4. For the letter "l," we achieve an accuracy of 92 % after 15 touches with an FAR of 7 % and an FRR of .4 % for the Tab 3 and an accuracy of 90 % with an FAR of 11 % and an FRR of .6 % for the Nexus 4. We note that for both characters, the Nexus 4 results are confounded by a single user who was consistently misidentified as one other user. Excluding this user puts the accuracy of the Nexus 4 above that of the Tab 3. Comparing against different users for each authentication attempt can reduce the probability of two users with very similar touch behavior getting confused with each other. Results for the "space" character on the Tab 3 are in line with other characters, achieving an accuracy of 95 % after 15 touches, with an FAR of 5 % and an FRR of .3 %.

This approach can be applied to frequent characters like vowels and space for reliable authentication with reduced overhead. As with the previous approach, the content and order of an individual's typed text do not matter, so anonymous classification data can easily be collected for different users. Comparing to different anonymous users for each authentication attempt can reduce the chances of

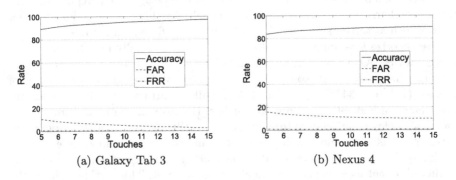

(a) Galaxy Tab 3   (b) Nexus 4

Fig. 3. Touches vs Accuracy and FAR/FRR for the Character "a"

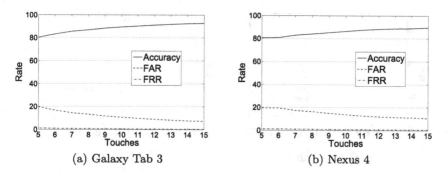

(a) Galaxy Tab 3   (b) Nexus 4

Fig. 4. Touches vs Accuracy and FAR/FRR for the Character "l"

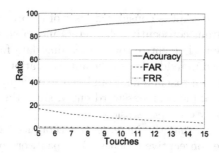

Fig. 5. Touches vs Accuracy and FAR/FRR for the Character "Space"

a consistent misidentification such as the one we encountered with the Nexus 4. While the success metrics for this approach are similar to the previous approach, applying classification only to popular characters can reduce the processing and memory overhead of the scheme.

3.7   Order Dependent

In our final approach, we consider how a user's typing behavior may change between different characters. In other words, a user may type the character "a" in a different way if "m" precedes it rather than "h," and this logic can further be extended to groups of 3, 4, or more characters. We believe this approach can be used for additional security on static text such as passwords. We keep the order of all touches and group them into pairs, threes, fours, and so forth, where n is the size of the group. The number of available traces depends on the size of n, for example there are 13 possible ordered letter pairs in our 22 character long phrase, and each user has approximately 20 traces, for a total of $13 * 20 = 260$ traces per user. Although success metrics may be different for certain letter combinations, e.g. for "ma" the results may be worse than for "ar," we combine the results and take their average for the purpose of condensing our results. We randomly select 60 % of the traces for training and 40 % for testing.

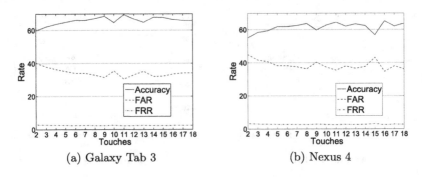

Fig. 6. Touches vs Accuracy and FAR/FRR for multiple consecutive touches

An authentication attempt is considered a set of n correctly ordered characters. We merge data from consecutive characters into a single row of data for purposes of classification. The entire row, containing data for each character in the sequence, is classified individually, so the authentication attempt is based on a single decision in this approach. This would be the only practical approach for a scheme designed to supplement password entry, since the user will generally enter their password only once per session.

From Fig. 6, it is clear that the increase in acceptance rate is actually quite minimal by using more consecutive touches. On a password of five of more characters, an accuracy of approximately 65 % is possible. Collecting classification data for an approach such as this one may be problematic, since other users will need to type precisely the same text. This approach may be applied to the entry of phone numbers rather than passwords, since phone numbers are also static. The number would not need to identical as the authentication can be done in three parts based on the area code, first set of digits, and final set of digits. Collecting classification data for phone numbers would be easier as many users will enter, at least, the same area code.

4   Discussion

There are two significant issues that our scheme faces before it could be applied to commercial use.

First, a smartphone is not a stationary object, and users frequently use their smartphone in different places and positions. In our experiment, we placed all users in a similar stance. Though most participants shifted stances slightly during the experiment, they still remained in largely the same positions. Different stances, e.g. walking, sitting, or lying down, must be identified, each with their own corresponding classification, because typing behavior will likely be different for the same user between these stances. Additionally being present in a moving object, for example a car, will affect acceleration results and potentially disrupt classification. While the scheme may work for the user most of the time without regard to the user's stance, intelligent stance and acceleration detection will be required to use the proposed scheme in all situations.

Second, user behavior can change in accordance with mood, injury, time of day, sleepiness, etc. We collect test and training data in the same session to simplify our experiment. In our future work, we plan to take several samples of from users at different times and on different days to verify that our scheme can maintain accuracy despite day to day behavioral changes.

As gyroscopes have now become more prolific, we plan to include gyroscope data in our future work. Various other sensors, such as those that detect touch pressure, may also become more popular and ultimately justify further study. We also plan to experiment with derived values, such as distance traveled (calculated as vector between the start and end point of the touch), and force of touch (calculated based on differences in acceleration during touch) to see if a significant improvement in accuracy can be obtained.

We plan to investigate the performance of our scheme on user generated text input rather than preassigned text. We believe that some degradation of performance may occur because users frequently pause to think about the text they are writing and thus alter the nature of timing data to measure thinking speed as opposed to typing speed. The degradation in performance may be counterbalanced by the differences in text. For the order-independent approaches in our experiment, having users type different text increases the chance that their typing behaviors are dissimilar, decreasing the chance that two users will be confused with each other. We expect that challenges like typo detection will be significantly more difficult to implement on user generated text.

We note that in the first two approaches, the time since last touch feature may be considered as noise, since no information about the last touch is known, and each touch is treated as independent. We attempted our experiments without the time since last touch and found that the results worsened. We hypothesize that the time since last touch is proportional to overall typing speed and helps the classifier to identify users.

The data used in our experiments required about 1.6 MB and 375 kB for the first and second approaches respectively. Simple fast zip compression can reduce the file size to 475 kB and 90 kB respectively, so the scheme can have negligible impact on network use and device storage.

Lastly we plan to develop a method for the automatic anonymizing and transferring of classification data between users, for the purpose of building unauthorized classification samples for each user frequently and on the fly.

5   Conclusion

In this paper, we proposed an implicit authentication scheme for mobile devices that relies on touch behavior. We presented three approaches for classifying touch behavior on a mobile device: character and order independent, character dependent and order dependent, and character and order dependent.The first two approaches yielded an accuracy of up to 97 % with only 15 touches, using statistical classifiers that are computationally cheap enough for implementation directly on the mobile device. Our third approach can be used as additional security for password entry, with an accuracy of approximately 65 % at five or more consecutive characters.

References

1. Antal, M., Szabó, L.Z., László, I.: Keystroke dynamics on android platform. Procedia Technol. **19**, 820–826 (2015)
2. Brunelli, R., Falavigna, D.: Person identification using multiple cues. IEEE Trans. Pattern Anal. Mach. Intell. **17**(10), 955–966 (1995)
3. Buchoux, A., Clarke, N.L.: Deployment of keystroke analysis on a smartphone. In: Australian Information Security Management Conference, p. 48 (2008)
4. Campbell Jr., J.P.: Speaker recognition: a tutorial. Proc. IEEE **85**(9), 1437–1462 (1997)
5. Draffin, B., Zhu, J., Zhang, J.: KeySens: passive user authentication through micro-behavior modeling of soft keyboard interaction. In: Memmi, G., Blanke, U. (eds.) MobiCASE 2013. LNICST, vol. 130, pp. 184–201. Springer, Heidelberg (2014)
6. Feng, T., Liu, Z., Kwon, K.-A., Shi, W., Carbunar, B., Jiang, Y., Nguyen, N.K.: Continuous mobile authentication using touchscreen gestures. In: 2012 IEEE Conference on Technologies for Homeland Security (HST), pp. 451–456. IEEE (2012)
7. Frank, M., Biedert, R., Ma, E.-D., Martinovic, I., Song, D.: Touchalytics: on the applicability of touchscreen input as a behavioral biometric for continuous authentication. IEEE Trans. Inf. Forensics Secur. **8**(1), 136–148 (2013)
8. Gafurov, D., Helkala, K., Søndrol, T.: Biometric gait authentication using accelerometer sensor. J. Comput. **1**(7), 51–59 (2006)
9. Maiorana, E., Campisi, P., González-Carballo, N., Neri, A.: Keystroke dynamics authentication for mobile phones. In: Proceedings of the 2011 ACM Symposium on Applied Computing, pp. 21–26. ACM (2011)
10. Saevanee, H., Bhattarakosol, P.: Authenticating user using keystroke dynamics and finger pressure. In: 2009 6th IEEE Consumer Communications and Networking Conference, CCNC 2009, pp. 1–2. IEEE (2009)
11. Trojahn, M., Ortmeier, F.: Biometric authentication through a virtual keyboard for smartphones. Int. J. Comput. Sci. Inf. Technol. **4**(5), 1 (2012)

Fraud Protection for Online Banking

A User-Centered Approach on Detecting Typical Double-Dealings Due to Social Engineering and Inobservance Whilst Operating with Personal Login Credentials

Verena M.I.A. Hartl[✉] and Ulrike Schmuntzsch

Department of Psychology and Ergonomics, Chair of Human-Machine Systems,
Technical University Berlin, Marchstr. 23, Sekr. MAR 3-1, 10587 Berlin, Germany
{verena.hartl,ulrike.schmuntzsch}@mms.tu-berlin.de

Abstract. Online-banking is becoming increasingly popular. Immense damage is done, however, by illegal actions also rising, such as unauthorized access to online-banking accounts. A project funded by the German Federal Ministry of Education and Research explores in a holistic approach, how fraud protection for online-banking can be improved. The focus is inter alia the user-end fraud detection and protection guiding, particularly for private customers, in online-banking and especially in the non-technical area of Social Engineering. Thereby the study examines the perceptibility of three different cases of fraudulent assaults, which showed that users know little about them. The comparison of two different two-factor methods of online-banking authentication and the analysis of verbal informations via the method of thinking aloud during the second experiment give initial hints which aspects should be changed in order to increase secure user behavior. Whichever, this is quite necessary regarding the high ratio of falling for assaults in the second experiment.

Keywords: Online-banking · Fraud protection · Social engineering · Secure transaction techniques

1 Introduction

1.1 Present Situation

Checking the account balance or making a transfer via the Internet - for 40 million people in Germany online-banking is now a matter of course and a indispensable part of every-days life [1]. Registered banking transactions are made conveniently from anywhere daily through various devices such as computer, laptop, tablet or smartphone. Besides various advantages, such as spatial and temporal independence of branch banks, online-banking also salvages some dangers. Illegal actions, such as unauthorized access to bank accounts, cause immense damage. The German Bundeskriminalamt estimated the amount of loss through phishing attacks in online-banking on 27.9 million euros in 2014, representing an increasing annual percentage change of 11.5 % [2]. Even though approximately halving the number to 3,440 cases in 2012 through the use of various protective

© Springer International Publishing Switzerland 2016
T. Tryfonas (Ed.): HAS 2016, LNCS 9750, pp. 37–47, 2016.
DOI: 10.1007/978-3-319-39381-0_4

measures as for instance the mTAN method (delivery of a transaction authentication number, which is necessary for making a transfer, via SMS), the number of cases till 2014 have more than doubled with 6,984 cases in total [1]. This fact indicates that the perpetrators have technically adapted to the changed framework conditions and developed new, even better malware to bypass the transaction process considered safe [2]. Especially after the introduction of authorization mechanisms, which require a positive action of the account beneficiary, the so-called two-factor authentication, other non-technical attack routes are chosen to get to the personal login data and transaction numbers (TAN) of bank customers and used for the perpetrators purposes. These types of attacks are summarized under the concept of *Social Engineering*, which in wider sense describes the manipulation of a person at predetermined purposes. The term Social Engineering initially sketches not directly a criminal influence of another person, only the urged change in action of a individual for own purposes [3].

1.2   Social Engineering and Current Transaction Techniques

However, Social Engineering in conjunction with online-banking describes selective damaging assaults on the trust of users, e.g. with a manipulated, confidential appearing login page, which prompts customers in an unauthorized way to enter their TAN [3]. Since no personal contact with the user is necessary, assaults on sensitive information via various electronic channels can be carried out. The scenarios can be distinguished as followes [4]:

- Phishing emails (query of personal identification data such as PIN[1] or TAN)
- Spam emails (attachments with links to malicious software ridden pages)
- Manipulation of well visited sites (installation of malicious software on randomly visited pages)
- Falsified web page appearance (simulation of a variation of the original page to get transaction data)

To carry out successfully attacks one has to attain the users`confidence. For this, various factors of social interaction between people can be considered. Therefore, perpetrators lay primarily focus on similarities (e.g. native language), sympathy (e.g. personalized approach), context (e.g. layout and logo) or feigned authorities (e.g. imitating official news) [4]. By means of these various factors, attackers attempt to collect informations about a person via the virtual path in order to influence their victim into divulging personal customer data. On the opposite side IT specialists are working on various authentication methods, which impede perpetrators using the captured customer data without active user actions. In this context, however, three concomitant problem areas occur, which are closely interwoven. On the one hand, verification systems are buildt to ensure, that the customer has to be proactive to guarantee, that not only a computer performs a transaction with stolen login keys. Near by, it is of paramount importance, that the customer checks the transaction data in two places: once when inserting the transaction data in the online-banking transaction form and repeatedly on

---

[1] PIN = Personal Identification Number.

the TAN-indicating device before entering the TAN for transaction completion. As we have already seen in a previous user study [5], this fact is closely associated with poor basic skills in relation to a safe use of personal identification information, a secure established connection, various types of online-banking fraud cases and a few other important aspects regarding online-banking. On the other side, since no studies dealing with mTAN or Sm@rtTAN authentication techniques (see next paragraph for explanation) have been documented yet, the unknown problem of acceptance and usability of using the transaction processes should be investigated. Therefore, as part of a research project funded by the German Federal Ministry of Education and Research we concentrate on how fraud protection for online banking can be improved. Thus, we focus on enquiring the usability of the two banking transaction techniques, which are predominantly used in Germany at the moment [6]: First, a transaction authentication number (TAN) transmission via SMS (the so-called mTAN technique) and second via flickering barcode on the computer screen (the so-called Sm@rtTAN technique using a TAN generator along with a banking card for generating the TAN). Both browser-based techniques are used as a form of single use one-time password to authorize financial transactions [7].

1.3 Aspired Goal

As there is an ongoing challenge between system developers and hackers, we see the need to consult the private customer as a resource to increase the online-banking security. The underlying intention focuses thereby on developing primal configuration guidelines to enhance the usability of the two authentication techniques. Furthermore, it shall be investigated how users (re-)act while executing a financial transaction to identify specific ways how to enable customers to increase their online-banking security. To investigate this issue the users behavior was observed in two user-centered studies, which were conducted in a laboratory setting. Therefore, the usability of these transaction techniques and matters of detecting different cases of fraudulent assaults were analyzed in two explorative approaches.

2 Methods for Both Experiments

2.1 Materials

Since it was an experiment, that should reflect as closely as possible the everyday use of the transaction process, a virtual database environment was created with the help of which transactions could be carried out in real form. The database environment was created by our federated project partners, modeled after the online banking environment of Raiffeinsenbanken and Volksbanken. In an account with personalized login (user name and password, same for all respondents) all services of a real bank could be handled, but the actions carried out ran only within the virtual environment - there were no real jobs executed. To execute a transfer, two transaction methods have been made available for the participants: the mTAN method and the Sm@rtTAN process. To perform a transaction via mTAN process participants have been handed over a mobile phone (Nokia 6233) on which the SMS with the transaction data and the TAN have been sent. To perform a transfer with the Sm@rtTAN process participants have been handed over a TAN generator with optical sensor for the flicker code and a debit card, which was only active within the virtual environment. To compare the two transaction processes several questionnaires were applied. To investigate the user acceptance, questions similar to the acceptance categories according to Pousttchi, Selk and Turovsky [8] were used. The user-friendliness of the transaction process has been interrogated with an questionnaire on technology acceptance [9]. In addition, the assessment of suitability for use was based on the international standard DIN EN ISONORM 9241/110-S (short version) by Prümper [10]. In order to assess, whether more technology-affine or technology-averted subjects participated in the study, a technology affinity questionnaire [11] was used as control variable. The interrogation of the demographic data of the participants included information on age, gender, educational attainment and occupation. In addition, the participants were asked about which Internet-enabled devices they currently use for online-banking and what authentication method they use for it. To this, answers were specified with the possibility of multiple answers. Additionally for conducting Experiment 2, we used three different potential assaults on the virtual database environment by means of three developed add-ons (developed by our federated partners). The add-ons based on Social Engineering included a written request for referral back to committee, which should not to be complied to, an additional, but unlawful interrogation of the mobile phone number after logging into the account, and a change in the recipient data in the background of the ongoing transaction. The last manipulation could only be recognized by participants through verifying the inserted transaction data (IBAN[2] and transfer amount) either on the TAN generator or in the resulting SMS. Last, for documentation of statements gained through the method of thinking aloud we designed three templates for each of the three blocks (i.e. per add-on). It was also noted, whether the fraudulent assault was recognized as such, whether the transfer data have been re-examined before entering the TAN and whether doubts about the legitimacy of the requests came up.

2.2   Procedures and Tasks

At the beginning of the computer-based experiment the background of the study was disclosed to the participants. They were pointed to the recording of monitor movement (Mouse Movement and keyboard entry) as well as image and sound and then asked to sign a written consent form. Then the participants were seated at the PC workstation and familiarized with the virtual database environment (Declaration of login and transaction methods).

For Experiment 1 two different transfers were to make (Fig. 1). Therefore, the sequence of the transaction methods was randomized. After the subjects had become familiar with the surroundings, the first transfer was launched by means of an exercise sheet including the short reason for referral, transaction information and step-by-step manual of the current used transaction method. Upon completion of this the participants

---

[2] IBAN = International Bank Account Number.

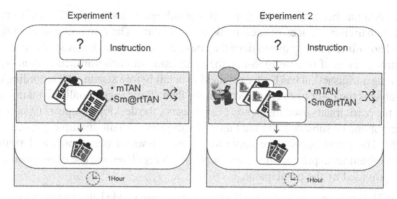

Fig. 1. Procedures of both experiments. Investigation Objective I: acceptance and suitability for use of the procedure. Investigation Objective II: survey of performance and visibility of safety-critical situations (i.e. add-ons)

were asked to complete a questionnaire for user acceptance, usability and suitability about using the transaction method in each case at an adjacent laptop. Thereafter, the second transfer was carried out with the other transaction method and requested afterwards. At the end of the experiment, the participants were asked to provide information on their own affinity for technology and on their demography. Prior to the adoption compensation for participating was given to the participants. This procedure was quite similar for Experiment 2, except as there were three transfers to make instead of two. To bring in experience, which problems occur in individual steps during the transaction, the subjects were instructed to express their ideas loudly through the method of thinking aloud. Additionally, we used three add-ons to mock a fraudulent assault. The allocation of the transaction process happened again randomized and balanced across all three tasks, but at least had each method applied for a task. The distribution of the three add-ons also happened in randomized order. After completion of the transfer, the subjects were asked to fill up the questionnaires about users` acceptance, usability and serviceability regarding the method used, but only once per procedure. This means, that one of the three blocks was completed without the three questionnaires. At the end of the experiment, the subjects were asked to provide information to their own affinity for technology and for their demography. Terminatory, it was open to the volunteers to provide information on expectations and possible assistance regarding the general online-banking process through a paper-based questionnaire. Both experiments lasted for about one hour.

3 Results of Both Experiments

3.1 Experiment 1

Participants. With the help of the volunteers portal of the Institute of Psychology and Ergonomics of the Technical University Berlin 12 women and 13 men aged 24 to 65 years ($M = 43.81, SD = 14.83$) were acquired for the first part of the user study. Voluntary participation has been remunerated at € 10 per subject. On average, 22 volunteers use the online banking services of their bank about 8 years. The remaining three subjects reported no online banking usage since they have excessively high privacy concerns and a too strong sense of insecurity. Since the application of each transaction method and performing a transaction has been explained in detail before starting the recordings, the three subjects have not been excluded from the data. To engage in online banking operations, the participants used the laptop (12 subjects), the desktop computer (9 subjects), the smartphone (7 subjects) and the tablet (4 sub-jects). Again, multiple answers were possible. The participants were naive to the experimental hypotheses and signed a written consent form prior to the experiment, which regulated the use of personal information provided by the participants.

Results. The analysis of technology affinity questionnaire yielded an average value of 1.76 within a five-point scale of "1 = Strongly agree" to "5 = Strongly disagree" that was used in all subsequent questionnaires, except for Question 7 in the questionaire for acceptance, which ranged from 1 to 3. From this we conclude, that the participants can be described as more enthusiastic about technology and are representativ for a comparative study in the technical field. For assesing the user acceptance the following seven questions were used. Thereby, statistically significant differences in transaction procedures arised with regard to the acceptance of effort for the operation, which goes hand in hand with the use of this procedure (t (24) = 4.201, p < .000), the thinking that the procedure increases ones own independence (t (24) = 3.375, p < .01), the acceptance of the wherewithal for using the procedure like indexed lists or additional technology (t (24) = 2.520, p < .05) and the perception that the execution of the transaction using the given transaction procedure was easy for the participants (t (24) = 1.809, p < .000). The mTAN process thereby experiences a greater agreement regarding the expenditure, the independence, the use of additional resources and the ease of the through-guidance of a transaction. Rating the appealing of the transaction processes captured only a marginally significant difference (t (24) = 2.021, p = .055) between the two transaction process. This suggests that participants respond only marginally better to the mTAN process. The perceived confidentiality against attacks by third arties associated with own data was answered with medium consent for both transaction procedures (Sm@rtTAN = 2:52 mTAN = 2.64, t (24) = −0.514, p = .612). This could indicate, that the participants are unclear about the confidentiality of their data to third parties with respect to both transaction procedures. The operation duration of a transaction by means of respective transaction process presented no significant difference between the two methods. Both transaction processes were found to be appropriate in their duration. In summary, the procedure was rated positive for mTAN rather than for Sm@ rtTAN process. Supplementary, viewing the user-friendliness of the transaction processes, the two transaction procedures differ not significantly in ease of use nor in intention, but they differ significantly in terms of the perceived usefulness (t (24) = 1.718, p < .05). Therefore, both methods awarded a perceived ease of use and the use of the method was considered. However, the perceived utility for the mTAN method seems to be more pronounced. The serviceability of the chosen transaction processes produced significant values within the given test categories. Regarding the task appropriateness (t (24) = 4.974, p < .000), the system`s ability for self description (t (24) = 2.959, p < .01), the system`s support for learning to use it (t (24) = 3.413, p < .01) and the controllability (t (24) = 4.487, p < .000) the two transaction procedures differ significantly within the five-point scale, which militates in favor for a better perceived usability of the mTAN process.

3.2   Experiment 2

Participants. Again 15 women and 10 men aged 19 to 71 years (M = 27.56, SD = 9.14.68) were advertised for the second part of the user study with the help of the volunteers portal of the Institute of Psychology and Ergonomics of the Technical University of Berlin. Voluntary participation has been remunerated again with € 10 per participants. On average, all participants used about 7 years the online banking services of their bank. To engage in online banking operations, the participants used the laptop (23 subjects), the desktop computer (13 subjects), the smartphone (9 subjects) and the tablet (4 subjects). Again, multiple answers were possible. The participants were naive to the experimental hypotheses.

Results
Questionaires. The calculation of the control variable of the technology affinity questionnaire yielded an average value of 1.94 within the five-point scale. We conclude that participants can be described as more enthusiastic about technology and are also representativ for a comparative study in the technical field. Evaluating the users`acceptance, the mTAN process experiences a greater agreement regarding the expenditure (t (24) = 11.431, p < .000), the independence (t (24) = 7.856, p < .000), the use of additional funds (t (24) = 9.632, p < .000) and perceived facility of transaction execution (t (24) = 9.667, p < .000). In addition, it can be concluded, that the mTAN process responses better to participants than the Sm@rtTAN process. However, the perceived confidentiality with data was significantly better for the Sm@rtTAN process (mTAN = 2.72; Sm@rtTAN = 2.16; t (24) = −3.055, p < .005). This might indicate, that participants feel safer regarding the confidentiality of their data when using the Sm@ rtTAN process. In summary, however, the process of transaction was rated better for using the mTAN method rather than for using the Sm@rtTAN process. Viewing the usability of the transaction process, the two transaction methods differ significantly in the three categories usefulness (t (24) = −7.544, p < .000), ease of use (t (24) = −6.313, p < .000) and intention (t (24) = −6.656, p < .000). From this rating it can be concluded that the participants perceive the mTAN process as a more user-friendly procedure. A similar conclusion can be derived from analyzings the items of the questionnaire on serviceability. Except for the rating category conformity of expectation all remaining categories differ significantly between the two transaction processes The task appropriateness (t (24) = −7.927, p < .000), the system`s ability for self description (t (24) = −2.489, p < .020), the system`s support for learning to use it (t (24) = −5.458, p < .000), the controllability (t (24) = −6.556, p < .000) and the tolerance for faults (t (24) = −2.866, p < .009) the two transaction procedures differ significantly within the five-point scale. Based on the average values, a more positive perception of the suitability for using the mTAN method can be assumed.

Performance and the Method of Thinking Aloud. First, we show the results for Add-on 1-Call for Refferal Back to Committee. In this fraud scenario 44 % of the participants did not realize, that it was a scam and 88 % of participants did not question the legitimacy of the request. 53 % of the participants did not verify the IBAN from the data in the TAN generator or in the SMS. Likewise, 47 % of the displayed amount was not additionally checked. However, since 67 % of the participants ignored the reffferal initially - partly by overreading, partly by the thought of carrying out the task - only 12 % of the participats returned misleadingly the unclaimed money to the fraudulant account. When analyzing the results of thinking aloud reasons like real appearance of the banking website, actually transfered credit on virtual account and plausibility of the refferal were stated. In addition, some participants reportet, that a sense of pressure built by encouraging and reporting account lockout (Social Engineering) led to their referral back to committee. Upon appearance of the request of Add-on 2 (request to indicate the mobile phone number) seven participants stopped the login process due to safety concerns. Further evaluation of the performance of this fraud scenario showed, that 68 % of the participants entered the mobile phone number without hesitation to complete the login process. Only 44 % of the participants expressed doubts about the legitimacy of this query. Stated reasons therefore were a lack of concern about the dissemination of the mobile phone number and a rather greater sense of security with an additional request. In addition, some participants would enter the mobile phone number due to an existing time constraint without thinking about it. In 50 % of cases, the IBAN has not been checked with the information in the TAN generator nor in the SMS. Moreover, only 39 % of the participants stated also to check the amount. Analysing the fraud scenario of Add-on 3 (change of transaction data in the background) we could identify, that 71 % of the participants did not recognize the fraud attempt. 65 % of the participants did not verify the IBAN within the TAN generator or in the SMS and 70 % of the participants did not reconcile the amount. In this scenario, we could detect through the method of thinking aloud, that the participants mostly check the IBAN and the amount in the appropriate input box on the banking website, but then rely on "the technology and the bank itself" regarding further data tranfer. One participant caused furthermore a great concern by his statement. After recognizing a fraudlent attempt he would indeed sign off immediately, but then log in again and also enter the transfer data again. Should the error occur again, he then would rely on the device used. The evaluation of the statements on expectations and possible assistance regarding the online banking showed, that there is a great desire for faster and more easily help in case of fraud and for more information about possible fraud scenarios. When handling the Sm@rtTAN generator, the participants wanted a better view of the charging status of the transaction data transfer. The participants stated, that the previous continuous bar display would not show this status clearly, which is why some participants interrupted the transmission themselves. A building up bar display would therefore constitute the transfer progress better. In addition, a feedback optimization for handling the generator could be displayed on the monitor. This statement was mainly related to the tilt angle of the Sm@rtTAN unit on the monitor. This indicator could be further supported by an audio feedback of the device itself, in which the device could play a sound in case of successful or aborted transfer of data. The participants noted moreover, that if the transfer was canceled, it was not easy to see on the monitor since the generator had to be held in front of the display window. Here, the participants would prefer better displaying on the monitor (for example, a status indicator or an indication on top of the beam with the flicker code). Using the process of manual TAN generation, it was also noted, that the IBAN should be easily recognizable and depicted in chunks. Recently, the participants wanted a better haptic feedback for using the keys of the generator. The soft keys were indeed found to be pleasant, but the feedback was sensed as lacking when pressing the button.

Limitations. In connection with the review of the transaction process, however, testing in a laboratory environment must be considered. In this it remains questionable for us on the one hand, to which extent the participants were able to put themselves into the situation of a real transfer from their own online-banking account and therefore if they acted as they would do in their actual account. It is not clear, whether the study situation influenced the actions of the participants, so we wonder if a more task-oriented character or a more security based character prevailed during the transfer tasks. On the other hand, the requirement to learn thre usage of a new device might have distortde the situational awareness of the participants or have deviated them from a safe course of action. Since in this study the transfer by means of the TAN generator unfortunately often did not work immediately, which may also concern a home user, attention could have been so drawn to the device and its function, that after a successful transmission the verification of the data could have been fallen of to a kind of "tunnel vision" through facilitating or the peak of the stress level. Thereby, the longed for, rapid completion of the transaction could have been desired and that could be the reason why the transaction data were no longer verified. The disruption of the smooth transition by using the Sm@rtTAN process could therefore have led the deteriorated rating compared to Experiment 1 of the Sm@rtTAN process.

4   Conclusion and Future Ongoing

In both conditions, the task of the participants was to carry out a transfer using one of the transaction techniques mTAN or Sm@rtTAN in a virtual banking environment. In both study sections a questionnaire on usability, acceptability and serviceability of the transaction techniques has been completed following the transfer. Additionaly, Experiment 2 dealt with the expression of the participants` individual thoughts using the method of thinking aloud. While the first part of this study was exclusively dedicated to the usability of the selected transaction methods, the second part included three attacks on a virtual banking environment, which were imitated by specially programmed add-ons. When documenting the statements and the transfer implementation increasing attention has therefore been paid to the detection of attack scenarios to encounter primal conclusions about safety awareness and behavior of the participants. It was also noted if the subjects disclosed personal information, such as a mobile phone number, when requested and if they checked their own transaction data (IBAN and amount of money) that was available in connection with the transfer. In summary, the results of both parts of the study evidence that users do know little about some of the fraudulent assaults and they often lack in screening for attack- and safety features and rechecking the transaction data. We conclude that customers should be supported with more information regarding a safe online banking use in order to ensure a more sensitive handling. Farther, the usability and the stated acceptance of the two transaction techniques differ to a great extent. In both studies the Sm@rtTAN process was evaluated worse than the mTAN process. However, this can also be partly attributed to an improper function of the Sm@rtTAN device. The process of conveying the transaction data from the website to the TAN displaying medium often demanded too much attention and thereby createed a high level of stress, so that users may have forgotten to check the transaction data. Since this could cause immense financial damage in real banking transaction, a higher functionality of the device has to be created. This could be achieved for example by a re-design of the device in the desired direction (see Experiment 2/Section Additional Statements). Deepening this approach a follow-up study will investigate this results by questioning experts on usability and design. Thereby, possible graphical changes in the banking website are to be worked out in terms of an enhanced secure proper application. These suggestions can be discussed in a focus group discussion then to involve the users at an early stage in the development process. In addition, in order to embed the user as a security resource conducive to the transfer sequence the focus must be placed on the wide-ranging information of users. At this juncture, fraud cases should be explaned transparent and preventive protection measures for the home user should be defined in an understandable way. In order to draw the attention of users to the key parameters of an online transaction a kind of "persuasive technology" should be used in a subsequent step. Also reflections on interactions between design alternatives and the formation of mental models of users as well as the adequacy of mental models will be interesting in this context. Further research should examine this idea, too.

Acknowledgments. We would like to thank the Federal Ministry of Education and Research (BMBF) for the financial steering of this research project within the federation project "Fraud protection for online banking" (BOB), as well as our federated partners for providing information and the test environment with the three prototypical online-banking fraud cases.

References

1. Bitcom. https://www.bitkom.org/Presse/Presseinformation/Online-Banking-ist-bequem-und-sicher.html
2. Fox, D.: Social engineering im online-banking und E-Commerce. Datenschutz und Datensicherheit **38**(5), 325–328 (2014)
3. Hadnagy, C.: Die Kunst des Human Hacking: Social Engineering-Deutsche Ausgabe. MITP-Verlags GmbH & Co. KG, Heidelberg (2012)
4. Bundeskriminalamt.: Bundeslagebild Cybercrime 2014. http://www.bka.de/DE/Publikationen/JahresberichteUndLagebilder/Cybercrime/cybercrime__node.html?__nnn=true
5. Bitcom. https://www.bitkom.org/Publikationen/2015/Leitfaden/Online-Banking/150105-OnlineBanking-Leitfaden.pdf
6. Schmuntzsch, U., Hartl, V.: Social Engineering beim Online-Banking – Nutzerstudie zur Identifizierbarkeit typischer Betrugsfälle. In: 11. Berliner Werkstatt Mensch-Maschine-Systeme – Tagungsband, Berlin, pp. 133–139 (2015)
7. Initiative D21. http://www.initiatived21.de/wp-content/uploads/2014/10/d21_fiducia_studie_onlinebanking_2014.pdf

8. Pousttchi, K., Selk, B., Turowski, K.: Akzeptanzkriterien für mobile Bezahlverfahren, pp. 51–68 (2002)
9. Claßen, K., Zur Psychologie von Technikakzeptanz im höheren Lebensalter: Die Rolle von Technikgenerationen, Dissertation, Psychologie an der Fakultät für Verhaltens- und Empirische Kulturwissenschaften der Ruprecht-Karls-Universität Heidelberg (2012)
10. Prümper, J., Anft, M.: Beurteilung von Software auf Grundlage der Internationalen Ergonomie-Norm ISO 9241/10 (1993). http://www.seikumu.de/de/dok/dok-echtbetrieb/Fragebogen-ISONORM-9241-110-S.pdf
11. Karrer, K., Glaser, C., Clemens, C., Bruder, C.: Technikaffinität erfassen – der Fragebogen, TA-EG. In: Lichtenstein, A., Stößel, C., Clemens, C. (eds.) Der Mensch im Mittelpunkt technischer Systeme. 8. Berliner Werkstatt Mensch-Maschine-Systeme, ZMMS Spektrum, Reihe 22, Nr. 29, pp. 196–201. VDI Verlag GmbH, Düsseldorf (2009)

Vibration Based Tangible Tokens for Intuitive Pairing Among Smart Devices

Donghan Park and Hyunseung Choo[✉]

Department of Electrical Engineering and Computer Science,
Sungkyunkwan University, Suwon, Korea
{silphid,choo}@skku.edu

Abstract. The usage of smart devices has significantly increased, and because of that the number of devices per person has been substantially increasing than a few years ago. In order to achieve the full potential of these devices, it is necessary to synchronize the data between them. However, paring and synchronization of these devices are difficult, which require a substantial amount of user experience. Recently, an interactive research, such as tangible user interface (TUI) has opened new avenues for more expressive and natural ways of user interaction with the system and devices. Based on TUI concepts, we proposed a novel method for pairing and synchronization among multiple devices using vibrating tangible objects. Our tangible tokens enable a new input modality for mobile application using vibration frequencies. Moreover, it also enhances the tactile feedback and user cognition. The pairing between the two devices is activated, when the devices sense and detect the vibration frequency of a token that was placed on their screens. For pairing, the devices use frequency information as authentication key. The proposed technique easily allows users to pair with the target device without knowing the target device information. In summary, the configuration of our proposed method also supports a range of novel interaction scenarios based on the physical object interface and its vibration frequencies. The physical feedback supports reliable and expressive tangible interactions with devices. Our experimental results advocate the purposefulness of our proposed method towards easy synchronization and demonstrate the feasibility of the proposed system.

Keywords: Device pairing · Identification · Multiple-device environment · Tangible user interface (TUI) · Mobile system · Sensing · Vibration

1 Introduction

Smart devices have an important role in our daily life, and from last decade, the rapid growth of these devices have achieved the essential part in our daily routines. Generally, it is very common for a single user to use multiple smart devices. However, it is very difficult for such user to synchronize data among these devices that increase the productivity and usability of these devices. Many companies involve different kind of protocols in these devices in order to enable data synchronization; among them, Bluetooth is one of the common solutions to handle this issue. This technology exists in many products, such as telephones, tablets, media players, robotics systems, handheld, and laptops.

© Springer International Publishing Switzerland 2016
T. Tryfonas (Ed.): HAS 2016, LNCS 9750, pp. 48–56, 2016.
DOI: 10.1007/978-3-319-39381-0_5

Another communication technology exists in near field communication (NFC), Quick Response (QR) Code, and techniques based on gesture recognition.

All these pairing techniques have several unique advantages. Commonly, these authentication and pairing procedures are very awkward for normal users, which effectively declines the user experience and practicality of the smart devices. For example, the users require searching the target device among the lengthy lists of devices when pairing takes place in one to many and many to many communication protocols [1]. Moreover, device identifiers in these lists are ambiguous for many users. Furthermore, to pair user phone with target device, user needs a mechanism to let user's phone know which nearby phone is the intended target. This involves bridging a "perception gap" in device pairing [2].

NFC offers an easy way for paring by simply requiring a close proximity between the devices to be paired. However, in the NFC, the pairing is less transparent and man-in-the-middle attacks cannot be prevented which is one of the main limitations of the NFC. Few approaches require additional hardware, which make the overall design bulky. In these approaches, there are chances of errors when the user behaves naturally. Some methodologies require that the target device must be in sight of the user, and the pairing is affected if there are any obstacles between the user and the target device. Moreover, when other people surround a user, it makes the pairing difficult.

There are several file sharing and data synchronization applications, which have received much praise and acceptance because of the simplicity of pairing; however, most of them are still inconvenient to use and lack the tangible benefits of physical interaction. Therefore, we have presented a new method of authentication and pairing smart devices based on physical and tangible tokens. By utilizing physical tokens, our proposed method is easy to adapt and intuitive because it only requires a simple touch with a tangible token to initiate the pairing between the two devices. Figure 1 shows a conceptual diagram of the proposed method. A token (that has its own unique ID) is activated using a button. To initiate a pairing between two devices, a tangible token has been placed on the surface of a smart device due to which it starts vibrating. By detecting this vibration pattern, the system is capable to determine the token ID. Then, by placing the same token on a second device, a connection through WiFi is established between these two devices, which share the same token ID. The proposed tangible system is composed

Fig. 1. Pairing between devices using the tangible tokens of the same frequency.

of unique tokens that are placed on smart device. The smart device identified these tokens based on vibration frequency. We used this technique for the initialization of the pairing session between multiple devices.

The rest of the paper is organized as follows. Section 2 presented detailed discussion on related works. The proposed prototype and its implementation are presented in Sect. 3. Section 4 describes the experimental setup for the proposed system. The experimental results and discussion are presented in Sect. 5. Finally, the paper is concluded with some future directions in Sect. 6.

2   Related Work

Utilizing the communication protocols such as Bluetooth and NFC, the applications provide easy and intuitive solutions for data sharing and synchronization. Bump and S-beam are the best examples of such applications that enable the smartphone users to transfer contact information, photos, and files between devices. To initiate a transfer in bump, two people physically knock their phones together. Similarly, S-Beam application requires the smart phones to touch each other back to back in order to initiate the pairing and data transfer. There are also many camera-based solutions for household device selection. QR Code is the case for integrated cameras that can be used to read visual codes. PresiShare [3] presented new interaction technique that leverages the affordances of QR codes to accelerate device pairing and content sharing.

Gesture recognition has been widely studied which provides a device pairing. Point&Connect [2] identified the target devices by the user physically pointing the target. The system captured the user's gesture, understood the target selection intention, and completed the device pairing. Moreover, this research suggested to further minimize this perception gap with a new intention-based device pairing paradigm. The system captured the intention of device selection via a simple pointing action. Similarly, Toss-it [4] allowed a user to identify targets and sent information to device in intuitive manner by utilizing their mobility when users perform a "toss" or "swing" actions in the intended direction, which were by the user in the real world. Air-Link [5] and DopLink [6] described air gesture recognition-based method, which detected the direction of movements using Doppler effects. Further, it allowed users to share files between multiple devices using in-air gestures by waving the hand from one device to another. In addition, users can easily exchange information such as photos between multiple devices.

Several existing approaches have been developed that have traditional input modality. TUI attempts to bring physical controls back into the reality. This combination of touch and TUI brought user applicability, feedback, and intuitive recognition [11]. Chan et al. in [7] presented Capstone, which used tangible blocks that allowed the underlying capacitive touchscreen to identify blocks and to sense how they arranged in 3D. The presented tangibles are designed to provide additional functionality to tangible-enhanced applications such as tangible board games or applications with tangible controls. Kratz et al. in [8] created artificial touch points using tangible object for creation of a multitude of physical controls. Their technique allowed the creation of a multitude of physical controls for capacitive touch screens. Ranging, for instance, getting rotary knobs or sliders from simple styli. Bianchi et al. in [9] presented tangible interfaces based on the magnetic sensing. This technology enabled various interfaces with mobile devices by exploring the design space of embedding magnets in tangible tokens. This technology has challenges in sensing the magnetic fields to create range of physical prototypes of interactive objects.

3 Prototype

3.1 Hardware Design

In this section, we have presented a hardware design, which is used to control the vibration frequency for identifying a single object. This prototype of a tangible token consists of a small functional Arduino (Gemma), coin shape linear vibration motor, battery, and button (as shown in Fig. 2a). The resultant shape of the proposed prototype is 37 × 37 mm cylindricality shape that is 3D Printed (as shown in Fig. 2c). The Gemma is located inside the 3D shape, which is a microcontroller board based on the ATtiny85. It has three digital input/output pins, micro USB connection, and JST connector for a 3.7 V battery. Moreover, we have placed a vibration motor that has 2-3.6 V operating range in the bottom. 3.7 V 280 mAh polymer lithium ion battery is used to keep the device small. To facilitate the detection of the touch input on screen, we positioned the vibration motor and touch material in the bottom side (as shown in Fig. 2b). It enables to detect the touch input in a precise manner. A 3.7 V battery is placed over the vibration motor that is attached to Gemma. Gemma enables the user to manipulate the vibration frequency by pressing the button on the top. The proposed prototype is designed to distinguish three different frequencies (2 Hz, 4 Hz and 6 Hz), and when the user presses the button, then each frequency has been activated accordingly.

Fig. 2. Prototype (Vibration Token). (a) Circuit board and Actuator, (b-c) Case and Dimensions

3.2 Software Design

We have developed an application that easily enables two devices to pair using tangible tokens based on touch interface and vibration frequencies. The proposed application consists of three modules such as touch manager, sensing the vibration analysis manager, and pairing manager. When the application is running, a vibrating tangible token with a certain frequency is placed on the screen. The smart device detects the token using the device touch event features, which are usually provided by the operating system. Using the touch event as a trigger, the smart device retrieves the raw data from the device accelerometers for a predetermined period (e.g. one sec). The vibration frequency of the token is detected using the raw data that was retrieved from the accelerometers in the mobile device. The changes in vibration frequency are also embedded in the raw data. We respective apply high pass and low pass filters on raw data in order to reduce the noise, and then convert the signal from its original form to a representative frequency form by using the fast Fourier transform (FFT) algorithm. After the filtering and conversion, current frequency of the object is determined. When touch event happens again, it automatically begins to collect the data for the next interval.

After determining the token's vibration frequency, pairing manager is initiated to establish a connection with the other device with the same token frequency. The proposed application uses the open sound control (OSC) protocol to broadcast the data to other devices [10]. Based on OSC protocol, each broadcast packet contains the tokens ID (vibration Hz) and devices' ID. When the other device receives the packet, it checks the devices' ID for the device identification and then checks the token ID to match with its own devices' token ID. We used OSC protocol because it does not require pre-authentication like other network protocols (Bluetooth, Wi-Fi Direct etc.). As the OSC protocol is weak on security and has some flaws, but we simply used OSC protocol to test the connectivity and send/receive function in the proposed prototype. Figure 3 shows the matching process of token ID for the pairing. Figure 3a shows initialization of single device using one token ID (Freq 2), Fig. 3b shows two devices initialized with same token ID (Freq 2), and hence, successfully paired. Figure 3c shows the case where devices are initialized with two different token IDs (Freq 2 and 6, respectively) that however, fail to make a pair because of different token IDs.

Fig. 3. Application. (a) Frequency detection on a device through token, (b) same frequencies enabling the devices to pair, (c) different frequencies preventing the devices to pair.

4   Experimental Setup

4.1   Procedure

For a thorough validation and testing, we have conducted some experiments in order to understand the basic usability characteristics and accuracy of the proposed prototype. We recruited three undergraduate and seven graduate students (total ten people, three female and seven male) and all are right handed. The age range for all the participants are between 21 and 36 years (whose average is 26.1 with standard deviation is 4.04). At the beginning, a brief introduction about the proposed approach is delivered to the participants, and all of them are required to provide their personal information. In introduction, we described and demonstrated three different vibration frequencies, tokens' interface, and sensing progress. Based on the instructions, the participants operate vibration token and conduct a pairing with each one of the vibration frequencies between 2–3 min, which was the process of the training.

For the testing (as shown in Fig. 4a), we have placed 4 devices on the table and all were connected to the same Wi-Fi network. The front three devices already set with different token vibration frequencies. In front of those devices, we put the paper showing the vibration frequency designated to a particular device. We separated the experiments in two tasks. We put one device in front of a participant, which can be either a Nexus or Galaxy S6. In the first task, all the participants perform the pairing set 6 times using the Nexus 5. Each set is organized into three trials; therefore, a participant in one task performs 18 pairing trials. After a short break time, in the second round, all the participants repeat the same process using the Galaxy S6. We randomly provided each pairing trial frequency to the user. Finally, all the participants filled a questionnaire and provided their feedback in a short interview. Each participant took approximately 20 min to complete all the tasks (such as brief introduction, training, testing, and short interview).

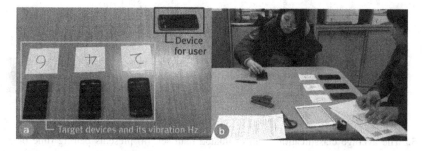

Fig. 4. (a) shows that three target devices are located with its vibration and a device is located in front of the user. (b) displayed that participant performs the trials in the task.

4.2 User Studies

The performance of the proposed approach has been evaluated in order to determine the usability and effectiveness of the proposed pairing method, and observes the intuitiveness of the user. For this purpose, we have conducted some experiments for the analysis of the time taken by each participant while performing each trial and its error ratio. In addition, we measure the users' recognition of different vibration frequencies. More specifically, we wanted to determine the tokens' interface that effectively used in pairing method. We examine the recognition accuracy of vibration interface in the pairing process.

For this experiment, we recorded both the classified results and the actual command that was given to the participants. To do so, we recorded the software/human error and pairing times. The software error is counted when the vibration sensing is not correct.

When user recognition of vibration is wrong or click the button by mistake, a human error is counted. The pairing time is defined as a period, which begins with certain frequency that is being told to the participant, and ends with the completion of device pairing. We processed the outcome of the approach by conducting a related process on user feedback, which focused on identifying the subset of tasks and activities presented in the scenarios that users reported to be important, interesting, and useful. The total number of trials analyzed was 360 (10 users × 2 tasks × 3 vibration frequencies × 6 sets).

5 Result and Discussion

Our experiments tested the users' recognition of the vibration frequency and usability of the token interface. Figure 5a presents that average pairing time of each trial for a particular frequency when the pairing is successful. Figure 5b shows the percentage of the system error and Fig. 5c is about the percentage of the human error. As mentioned earlier, system error occurs when a token is on proper vibration frequency, but application fails to detect it properly. By human error, we meant that when the user activates the touch event with wrong vibration frequency.

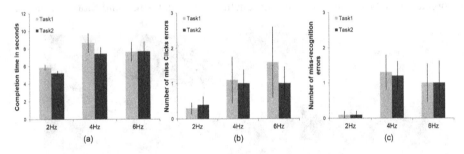

Fig. 5. The average classification from evaluated data set. (a) presents pairing time of each vibration frequencies (i.e., 2, 4, 6 Hz), (b) shows system error of configuration of frequency; while (c) describes the average user error.

Task 1 took average time 7.3 s with standard deviation (SD) 2.8. One-way ANOVA revealed no differences across frequency patterns. The 2 Hz pattern is the faster one having average time 5.8 s with SD = 0.9 followed by the 6 Hz pattern (7.6 s with SD = 3.3), and the 4 Hz pattern (8.6 s with SD = 3.2). Figure 5b shows the systems miss-classification; while Fig. 5c shows the number of human-made errors (miss-clicks).

Task 2 took average time 6.7 s with SD = 2.5 for completion, and one-way ANOVA revealed differences across patterns (F (27, 2) = 3.45, p < 0.05) with having again the 2 Hz pattern faster 5.2 s with SD = 0.8 followed by the 4 Hz pattern (7.4 s with SD = 2.2), and the 6 Hz pattern (7.7 s with SD = 3.3). It can be seen from Fig. 5c that errors were not statistically different.

These experimental results indicate that the 2 Hz pattern was the most usable, I.e., it is the fastest one that has least error. The 4 Hz and 6 Hz patterns led to very similar results and no difference among the two were found. However, based on the observation the users found that the 6 Hz pattern is easier than of the 4 Hz pattern. This is because, the users had to place the vibrating token on the screen after selecting the correct pattern using the button placed on the token. Overall users found that the 2 Hz and 6 Hz pattern are easier to recognize than of the 4 Hz one.

During the experiments, we found that the proposed prototype had some limitations; for example, it was difficult for users to change between the frequencies using the toggle button on the top. Nevertheless, the overall users' performance with the prototype suggests that this type of interface was easy to understand and use and that pairing by using physical objects can potentially lead to faster and more intuitive interactions than the GUI interfaces. Nevertheless, the results are encouraging and this suggests that the proposed approach is more robust in dynamic environments.

6 Conclusion and Future Work

In this paper, we proposed a novel method for pairing multiple devices using the physical objects. The proposed technique uses different vibration frequencies to identify and differentiate between different users. The experimental results and user studies suggest that the proposed methodology can be feasible in any environment. Moreover, the combination of tangible token and pairing method contributes to expand the interaction that addresses the perception gap problem by exploring how the sensing capabilities can be leveraged to create the tangible interfaces. In the proposed system, we used the physical token that provides vibration frequencies. Smart device can detect specific vibration frequency when a token is on the surface of it by the developed sensing algorithm and the embedded sensor. This information is used in the matching process of token ID for the pairing. This procedure makes the pairing steps easy, i.e., the users do not need to memorize the device name and ID. Additionally, the proposed system reduces the process of authentication and target selection. We improved the pairing method, which allows user to interact more flexibly with tangible objects.

In the future, we will perform more experiments with diverse evaluation criteria. In addition, we will explore procedures for manual calibration and mechanisms to limit the influence of the environment. Moreover, we will plan to develop a prototype, which will be much smaller and manageable to use by improving button interface and system. It will detect a wide range of frequencies more precisely and will test the user recognition that will enable to show the true potential of our proposed method.

Acknowledgments. This work was supported by Priority Research Centers Program through NRF funded by MEST (2010-0020210) and MSIP under G-ITRC program (IITP-2015-R6812-15-0001) supervised by IITP. The authors specially thank to Prof. Andrea Bianchi, Dept. of Industrial Design at KAIST, for his useful advice and comments.

References

1. Wong, F.-L., Stajano, F., Clulow, J.: Repairing the bluetooth pairing protocol. In: Christianson, B., Crispo, B., Malcolm, J.A., Roe, M. (eds.) Security Protocols 2005. LNCS, vol. 4631, pp. 31–45. Springer, Heidelberg (2007)

2. Peng, C., et al.: Point&Connect: intention-based device pairing for mobile phone users. In: Proceedings of the 7th International Conference on Mobile Systems, Applications, and Services, pp. 137–150. ACM (2009)
3. Geel, M., Huguenin, D., Norrie, M.C.: PresiShare: opportunistic sharing and presentation of content using public displays and QR codes. In: Proceedings of the 2nd ACM International Symposium on Pervasive Displays, pp. 103–108. ACM (2013)
4. Yatani, K., et al: Toss-it: intuitive information transfer techniques for mobile devices. In: CHI 2005 Extended Abstracts on Human Factors in Computing Systems, pp. 1881–1884. ACM (2005)
5. Chen, K.-Y., et al:. AirLink: sharing files between multiple devices using in-air gestures. In: Proceedings of the 2014 ACM International Joint Conference on Pervasive and Ubiquitous Computing, pp. 565–569. ACM (2014)
6. Aumi, M.T.I., et al.: DopLink: using the doppler effect for multi-device interaction. In: Proceedings of the 2013 ACM International Joint Conference on Pervasive and Ubiquitous Computing, pp. 583–586. ACM (2013)
7. Chan, L., Müller, S., Roudaut, A., Baudisch, P.: CapStones and ZebraWidgets. In: CHI 2012, pp. 2189–2192 (2012)
8. Kratz, S., Westermann, T., Rohs, M., Essl, G.: CapWidgets: tangible widgets versus multi-touch controls on mobile devices. In: CHI Ext. Abstracts 2011, pp. 1351–1356 (2011)
9. Bianchi, A., Oakley, I.: Designing tangible magnetic appcessories. In: Proceedings of the 7th International Conference on Tangible, Embedded and Embodied Interaction, pp. 255–258. ACM (2013)
10. Schlegel, A.: Open Sound Control(OSC) protocol. http://www.sojamo.de/libraries/oscP5/. Accessed 23 Feb 2016
11. Yu, N.-H., et al.: TUIC: enabling tangible interaction on capacitive multi-touch displays. In: Proceedings of the SIGCHI Conference on Human Factors in Computing Systems, pp. 2995–3004. ACM (2011)

Anonymous Authentication with a Bi-directional Identity Federation in the Cloud

Fatema Rashid[(⊠)] and Ali Miri

Department of Computer Science, Ryerson University, Toronto, Canada
{fatema.rashid,Ali.Miri}@ryerson.ca

Abstract. Cloud technology offers a completely new set of benefits and savings in terms of computational, storage, bandwidth and transmission costs to its users. In the cloud architecture, user space may be shared across various resources, leading to possible data exposure, and making mapping of users and their privileges a challenging job. Moreover the user has to keep track of many passwords and tokens for different applications. In many setting, anonymity of users accessing some or all services provides in this architecture also need to be guaranteed. In this paper, we propose a bi-directional federated identity management scheme that allows for anonymous authentication of users. Our proposed scheme is applicable to any combination of horizontal and vertical federations, across multiple cloud layers.

Keywords: Federated identity · Anonymous identification · Abstraction layers · Vertical identity federation · Horizontal identity federation

1 Introduction

Cloud computing has indeed revolutionized the concept of computing by promising users unlimited availability and accessibility of resources with convenience. The on-demand concept of cloud computing is at the core of this paradigm. Cloud computing allows users to access or use the services offered by the cloud on the go without actually owning the services through virtualization, web services, encryption, utility computing and the Internet [11]. A key security challenge in such environments is access control and authentication of users by semi-trusted cloud providers. Earlier models of application-centric access control, where each application keeps track of its collection of users and managing those users, are not suitable for a cloud-based architecture [7]. In the cloud architecture, user space may be shared across resources and applications, making mapping of users and their privileges a challenging job. Moreover the user has to keep track of many passwords and tokens for different applications. Federated Identity Management (FIM) deals with the establishment of trust relationships between various security domains by sharing information used for user authentication in order to reduce management complexity and security risks [2]. FIMs involve three main types of entities or players: the user, the Identity Provider (IdP) and the Service

© Springer International Publishing Switzerland 2016
T. Tryfonas (Ed.): HAS 2016, LNCS 9750, pp. 57–64, 2016.
DOI: 10.1007/978-3-319-39381-0_6

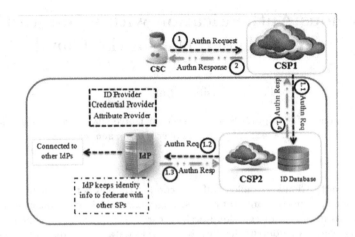

Fig. 1. Federated identity management

Provider (SP). IdPs are responsible for issuing and managing user identities and issuing credentials. SPs are entities that provide services to users according to their identities (see Fig. 1 [5]).

FIM also helps to simplify end-user authentication procedures by employing mechanisms such as single sign on (SSO) [2]. FIM solutions have been used in various applications, such as web resources allocations [7], web services [3], and grid computing [6].

Cloud computing generally operates on three levels of abstraction, namely Infrastructure as a Service (IaaS), Platform as a Service (PaaS), and Software as Service (SaaS). The IaaS layer includes the use of virtual machines to provide on-demand services to end users. The PaaS layer is a category of cloud computing services that provides a platform that allows users to develop, run, and manage their applications [8]. SaaS layer typically deals with software is licensed on a subscription basis, and is centrally hosted [8]. One should note that there are also sublayer services in the cloud with high utilization and usefulness such as Database as a Service (DaaS) or IDentity as a Servie (IDaaS). Since a typical cloud deployment has a layered structure made of IaaS, PaaS and SaaS, the services provided at these levels should be accessible to users in a secure, but seamless manner. Generally, higher levels of abstraction (layers) in a cloud utilize functionalities provided by lower levels. However, current federated identity solutions are limited to a single level only (e.g. IaaS or SaaS). Therefore if a SaaS provider needs to transfer the credentials of a user to lower layers, he has to implement his own solution, since the lower layers (IaaS and PaaS) are ignorant of any users signed in at the upper level. If the cloud is incorporating multiple IaaS, PaaSs or SaaSs providers interacting with each other, then the problem becomes more complex. FIM solutions over the cloud can hence be broken down into *vertical* and *horizontal identity federations*. Horizontal identity federation is a concept that enables the sharing of resources a Cloud Service Providers (CSP) at a particular service delivery layer such as IaaS, PaaS or SaaS, whereas in vertical identity federation, identities are shared vertically, from SaaS layer to PaaS to IaaS layers or throughout the layers of different cloud architectures [11]. Our proposed identification algorithm in this paper works with any combination of horizontal or vertical identity federations.

Keeping anonymity of users' identities and their activities also poses another challenge. Security has always been listed as of the key hurdles in acceptance of cloud computing as a viable technology, given the loss of physical control users can exercise over their data, applications, platforms or infrastructure resources. Cloud computing therefore requires an entity/user-centric model, where every entity's request for any service is bundled with the entity's identity and entitlement information [1]. The loss of control over users' data implies that in most cases users have to rely on the cloud access rules and policy for protection of their privacy. However, users typically have accept and are subject to different access policies for different CSPs. On-demand architectural set up will also enables CSPs to outsource users resource requirements to third parties, for which users may not have the same trust relationship. Or, for which CSPs will wish to procure requested services to their users through these third parties, while not allowing these parties to learn true user identities.

We therefore propose a merger of anonymous identification requirement with that of federated identity in order to attain the advantages offered by both. The anonymous identification component enables a user to prove his/her identity, without actually disclosing any identity credentials. Our integration of this anonymous identification component with a federated identity is done in such a fashion to make the cloud architecture secure throughout all the layers. Federated identity is integrated from SaaS to IaaS layers. The PaaS layer is used to hide the implementation details from the IaaS layer. SaaS users can access SaaS applications without any interference from the Identity Provider. The integrated identity architecture is based on the concepts presented in [1,10], but is tailored to fit in our scheme of anonymous identification. To the best of our knowledge, our work is the first proposed approach to integrate a bi-directional identity federation with anonymous authentication, which a provide a fine grain access control, while enabling cloud users to utilize cloud services within a federation.

The rest of the paper is organized as follows: Sect. 2 discusses some related work. Section 3 provides the details of the proposed scheme and conclusions are presented in Sect. 4.

2 Related Work

Federated identity with vertical and horizontal dimensions was discussed in [10]. In this work, authors present an approach in which the identities of the users are federated in both horizontal and vertical directions, with the help of a third party IdP. The users can use services from different clouds within the federation at all the three levels, namely IaaS, PaaS and SaaS. In their architecture, they introduced a module called *interceptor*, which could be used for authentication purpose by different users. Another module called *dispatcher* is used to keep a log of users in order to classify them for commercial purposes. This scheme does not take into consideration the need for anonymous identification issue and allows for different configuration setup of the interceptor used for user authentication purposes. In [1], authors introduced the concept of anonymous authentication to prevent misuse of customers' personal information by the cloud. Their anonymous authentication is based on two protocols, which we have explained in the following sections. However, their solution considers the cloud to be single entity, and does not provide any support for the typical layered structure of the cloud and horizontal and vertical federated identity managements.

Our proposed scheme build on these earlier work by combining the anonymous identification and the FIM concepts, which is further expanded to support both vertical and horizontal federated identities.

3   Proposed Scheme

As discussed in the earlier section, our aim is to integrate identity federation with anonymous authentication, in order to enable the users to have a complete control over the decision of with and how much information should be shared among different clouds under one federation. There are a number of benefits to such combination, which produces a comprehensive and secure federated identity environment for cloud users. These benefits include ability to provide Single Sign On (SSO) options. It also supports provisioning of identities within an organization addresses and the provisioning and deprovisioning of several types of user accounts, enabling service providers to reduce the cost of managing user attributes, passwords and login credentials by using trusted identity providers and provision of scalability [2]. Our scheme ensures anonymous authentication which makes it possible to prove a claim or assertion for authentication without disclosing any identifiable data. Within a cloud computing environment, this feature becomes even more useful for ensuring security, when using semi-trusted CSPs for different services. That is, If the users does not want to share their identity information with a specific CSP but would like to use their services, they can authenticate themselves anonymously on these semi-trusted clouds through an Identity Provider (IdP).

The proposed scheme has the advantage of being able to support vertical and horizontal identity federation, as well as anonymous identification. The overall architecture and flow of data of the proposed scheme is represented in Fig. 2.

3.1   Anonymous Identification

To achieve anonymous identification, we use the Fiat and Shamir identification scheme [4]. This scheme has been used in cloud settings for anonymous identification in [1,9], but these schemes did not consider the abstraction levels of the

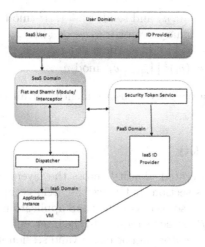

Fig. 2. Architecture of the proposed scheme

cloud. We regard cloud as a layered structure of SaaS, PaaS and IaaS layers, and thus propose to provide vertical and horizontal identity federation. The scheme has two protocols: issuing identity to an entity, and verifying identity of an entity [4]. Firstly the IdP selects a public integer n and a pseudo random function f, where f associates arbitrary strings to elements in the range $[0, n)$. Integer n is the product of two secret prime numbers p and q, where the values of p and q are only known to IdP.

Protocol 1(Issuing Identities by an IdP to a User). IdP formulates a string I, which contains all the relevant information about the user e.g. validity date etc. The IdP then performs the following steps [4]:

- Compute values $v_j = f(I, j)$ for identity information at indices j.
- Pick k distinct values of j for which v_j is a quadratic residue mod n, and compute the smallest square root s_j of v_j^{-1}.
- Issue an identity, which contains I, k s_j values and the selected k indices (For simplicity, one can use the first k indices $j = 1, 2, \cdots, k$).

Protocol 2: Verifying the Identity of the Entity. Fiat and Shamir verification [4] is based on the user A proving the possession of the k s_j values interactively, without revealing their values, or equivalently the bounded identity assigned to the user and his/her general information I by IdP. The main steps of the procedure can be repeated t times, where t can be treated as a security threshold parameter.

- A sends I to CSP, and CSP computes $v_j = f(I, j)$ for $j = 1, \cdots, n$.
- The following steps can be repeated t times to ensure that probability of error is less than 2^{-kt}.

- A picks a random $r_i \in [0, n)$ and sends $x^i = (r_i)^2 \mod n$ to CSP.
- CSP sends a random binary vector $(e_{i1}, \cdots, e_{ik})$ to A.
- A sends to CSP: $y_i = r_i \prod_{e_{ij}=1} s_j \mod n$.
- CSP checks that $x_i = (y_i)^2 \prod_{e_{ij}=1} v_j \mod n$.

CSP will accept the validity of user's identity, if all the t comparison pass the test.

3.2   Federated Identity

The working of the federated identity across the layers of the cloud architecture is explained in this section. It follows the architecture proposed in [10]. In our architecture, a SaaS user accesses the SaaS application interface using a web client, and submits his/her access request to the interceptor, controlling access to the resource. If the interceptor cannot find a valid session for the access request, it asks the user to authenticate himself/herself using credentials provided by an IdP of his/her choice, and accepted by the SaaS provider. The user can use the Fiat and Shamir identification scheme to verify the user identity. The interceptor validates the proof of authentication and requests a new security token from a Security Token Service (STS). The STS and interceptor trust each other for all transactions, which is managed by PaaS. The STS ensures that the user is allowed in the IaaS domain as well. This is where the vertical identity federation is being implemented by allowing the valid users to navigate from SaaS to IaaS with a single valid identity. The STS issues a new token containing the IaaS users' Id and is signed by the STS private key. For the first interaction, the SaaS users get registered accounts on the IaaS identity. A new identification is created for the user based on his SaaS identification. The IaaS identity Provider centralized the account information for all IaaS users, and share this information with the operating systems and thus ensuring that there is no need for account creation on each virtual machine. The interceptor forwards the access request to the application endpoint with the token obtained from STS. SaaS application captures the request and verifies the security token. If it is signed by the STS, it is considered authenticated. The SaaS application uses the IaaS identification embedded in the request to execute the actions on the authenticated user's behalf. There is a trust relationship with the STS, which is maintained by the PaaS administrator. Since the IaaS now recognizes the IaaS user, the operations are performed successfully. The request is then transferred to the SaaS application instance on the specific virtual machine owned by the IaaS user. As we mentioned earlier, that horizontal and vertical federation of identities across the layers of the cloud architecture are the core of our proposed scheme. The IaaS provider stores the minimum and essential account data and user information for the cloud. This information is replicated on different IaaS providers running on different virtual machines [10]. This gives the availability of the application to the user, no matter on which VM, the instance of the application is running. This setup provides the horizontal federation of the identity across all the IaaSs being used, and can provide a single sign on option to users.

4   Conclusion

In this paper, we discussed and focused on some of the security concerns in cloud computing, and in particular issues with user identity and its management. The need of federated identity is highlighted along with its possible benefits, such as support for single sign on capabilities. We discussed the requirement of anonymous identification in the cloud architecture, and proposed a combination of anonymous identification and federated identity solution. We further extend this approach to include both vertical and horizontal federated identity support. Vertical federation of identity aspect of our solution allows a user to choose the identity provider of his/her own choice, where as horizontal federated identity aspects ensures the use of multiple services across a given layer, possibly provided by different CSPs are also supported. Our future plans include the implementation of the proposed concept in the real life cloud settings. We would like to test our anonymous authentication scheme in terms of scalability and security. The implemented scheme should accomodate a large number of users coming from very diverse, but federated clouds.

References

1. Angin, P., Bhargava, B., Ranchal, R., Singh, N., Linderman, M., Othmane, L.B., Lilien, L.: An entity-centric approach for privacy and identity management in cloud computing. In: 2010 29th IEEE Symposium on Reliable Distributed Systems, pp. 177–183. IEEE (2010)
2. Chadwick, D.W.: Federated identity management. In: Aldini, A., Barthe, G., Gorrieri, R. (eds.) Foundations of Security Analysis and Design V. LNCS, vol. 5705, pp. 96–120. Springer, Heidelberg (2009)
3. Nadalin, A.: Oasis: Web services federation language (ws-federation) version 1.2. http://docs.oasis-open.org/wsfed/federation/v1.2/wsfederation.html.   Accessed Jan 2016
4. Fiat, A., Shamir, A.: How to prove yourself: practical solutions to identification and signature problems. In: Odlyzko, A.M. (ed.) CRYPTO 1986. LNCS, vol. 263, pp. 186–194. Springer, Heidelberg (1987)
5. Habiba, U., Masood, R., Shibli, M.A., Niazi, M.A.: Cloud identity management security issues & solutions: a taxonomy. Complex Adapt. Syst. Model. 2(1), 1–37 (2014)
6. Mikkonen, H., Silander, M.: Federated identity management for grids. In: Proceedings of the International conference on Networking and Services (ICNS 2006), p. 69. IEEE (2006)
7. Morgan, R., Cantor, S., Carmody, S., Hoehn, W., Klingenstein, K.: Federated security: the shibboleth approach. Educause Q. 27(4), 12–17 (2004)
8. National Institute of Standards, Technology: Special Publication 800–146: Cloud Computing Synopsis and Recommendations. National Institute for Standards and Technology, Gaithersburg, May 2012. http://nvlpubs.nist.gov/nistpubs/Legacy/SP/nistspecialpublication800-146.pdf
9. Ranchal, R., Bhargava, B., Othmane, L.B., Lilien, L., Kim, A., Kang, M., Linderman, M.: Protection of identity information in cloud computing without trusted third party. In: Proceedings of the 29th IEEE Symposium on Reliable Distributed Systems, pp. 368–372. IEEE (2010)

10. Stihler, M., Santin, A.O., Marcon Jr., A.L., Fraga, J.D.S.: Integral federated identity management for cloud computing. In: Proceedings of the 5th International Conference on New Technologies, Mobility and Security (NTMS), pp. 1–5. IEEE (2012)
11. Thomas, M.V., Dhole, A., Chandrasekaran, K.: Single sign-on in cloud federation using cloudsim. Int. J. Comput. Netw. Inf. Secur. (IJCNIS) **7**(6), 50 (2015)

An Integration of Usable Security and User Authentication into the ISO 9241-210 and ISO/IEC 25010:2011

Paulo Realpe-Muñoz[1]([✉]), Cesar A. Collazos[1], Julio Hurtado[1],
Toni Granollers[2], and Jaime Velasco-Medina[3]

[1] IDIS Research Group, University of Cauca, Popayán, Cauca, Colombia
{prealpe,ccollazo,jhurtado}@unicauca.edu.co
[2] GRIHO Research Group, University of Lleida, Lleida, Spain
antoni.granollers@udl.cat
[3] Bionanoelectronics Research Group, University of Valle,
Cali, Valle del Cauca, Colombia
jaime.velasco@correounivalle.edu.co

Abstract. Currently, computer security is one of the most important tasks. However, although there are works on the interfaces design secure and usable, it is necessary to perform an investigation to integrate these two attributes in a more easy way. Security problems for computer systems include vulnerabilities because they are hard to use and have poor user interfaces due to security constraints. Nowadays, finding a good trade-off between security and usability is a challenge, mainly for user authentication services. This paper presents an integration between the ISO 9241-210 standard to find a development process and a tool for evaluating qualitative and quantitatively usable security and user authentication, taking into account some aspects, attributes and characteristics of the ISO/IEC 25010:2011 allowing that the design requirements and its heuristic evaluation are suitable for the system.

Keywords: Usable security · Authentication · Attributes · Principles · Standards · Guidelines

1 Introduction

Computer security is the area of computer science in charge of the confidentiality and integrity of the systems and data. Most current applications have incorporated security features and privacy. However, security is generally a secondary goal for most users because it is complex to use. As a result of the above, wrong decisions are taken according to security, and therefore, important information is at risk. Usable Security (USec) is the field that investigates these issues, focusing on the design of security and privacy features that are easy to use [1].

Most applications, such as, e-commerce or e-banking, need to know the identity of the users. Knowing users identity, these applications allow to provide

© Springer International Publishing Switzerland 2016
T. Tryfonas (Ed.): HAS 2016, LNCS 9750, pp. 65–76, 2016.
DOI: 10.1007/978-3-319-39381-0_7

permissions to access their data. This access can be provided by authentication methods which could verify the identity of users. Although security and usability are essential in the authentication process as well, the requirements for having an appropriate level of security for authentication while maintaining its usability, could generate conflict with each other.

In literature has been conducted some research on usable security and user authentication, although a large number of research works have been made for computer security [2]. This is because the integration of HCI methods with security information methods is not straightforward, due to security addresses very complex cases without benefiting the use of an application. Therefore, finding a good trade-off between security and usability is always a challenge.

We believe that one way to strike a balance between usability and security, could come integrating international standards widely recognized by the academic and business community such as ISO 9241-210 and ISO/IEC 25010:2011 into USec and user authentication.

The standard ISO 9241-210 [3] is a framework for human-centered design processes that integrates different design and development appropriate in a particular context, complementing existing design methodologies. The ISO/IEC 25010:2011 SQuaRE (Systems and Software Quality Requirements and Evaluation) (ISO/IEC 25010:2011) [4] is the standard that defines the system and software quality, which is highly focused on system's quality of use.

However, to the best of our knowledge, there is no a process, qualitative and quantitative, that describes how to develop and validate systems taking into account the design requirements and principles (also called heuristics) allowing a good trade-off between security and usability, that is, a user-centered design process for usable security and user authentication. In addition, there is no a relationship between the attributes and characteristics of the standard ISO/IEC 25010:2011 that the community can use to evaluate security and usability, assuring that the user achieves a suitable experience for a website/application.

This paper presents an integration between the standard ISO 9241-210 to find a development process and a tool for evaluating qualitative and quantitatively usable security and user authentication, taking into account some aspects, attributes and characteristics of the standard ISO/IEC 25010:2011 allowing that the design requirements and its heuristic evaluation are suitable for the system.

The main contributions of this paper are: (1) an exhaustive literature review in order to obtain principles or heuristics for systems that require security and usability, (2) a heuristic development and evaluation (quantitative and qualitative) for usable security and authentication methods according to the standard ISO 9241-210, (3) the first set of principles for USec and user authentication, taking into account some attributes and characteristics of the standard ISO 25010:2011 (which defines the software quality), and finally, (4) we propose a level of importance for each principle obtained above.

This paper is organized as follows: Sect. 2 discusses related works. Section 3 presents the human-centered design. Section 4 shows an integration between ISO 9241-210 standard and a heuristic development for USec and user authentication.

Section 5 presents the specification of USec and user authentication through quality attributes. Finally, Sect. 6 we make our conclusions and future work.

2 Related Works

Some works have suggested processes that enable to develop principles and guidelines for specific or general purposes. Yeratziotis et al. [1] present a framework within the context of online social networks that are particular to the health domain. This framework has three components: process to develop USec heuristics, heuristic evaluation and a validation process. Wilson [5] presents a process for creating useful and usable heuristics, mainly focusing the user-centered design.

Sim et al. [6] propose a design approach based on evidence for developing specific heuristics. Mujinga et al. [7] define a model for developing heuristics taking into account the security and usability for e-banking applications. This model has the disadvantage does not have a real validation by experts and users. Shneiderman et al. [8] present a set of guidelines to assist in the creation of web sites. These guidelines are particularly relevant to the design of information-oriented sites, but can be applied across the wide spectrum of web sites.

Vidal et al. [9] present an application that use the human-centered design approach for interactive systems following the process defined by the ISO 9241-210 standard. Fidas et al. [10] apply the user-centered design approach to CAPTCHA mechanisms take into account the ISO 9241-210 standard.

In 2011, ISO announced the new standard for software product quality ISO-IEC 25010:2011 [4]. SQuaRE is the term that refers to the standard that defines the system and software quality. The difference with existing standard is software security and is defined as a quality characteristic. With this product model, to evaluate security of practical system has being researched [11,12].

Zapata [13] presents the development of a consolidated model designed especially to cover the security and usability attributes of a software product. As a starting point, a new usability model on the basis of well-known quality standards and models is built. Finally, Realpe et al. [14] present a systematic review of usability principles, evaluation methods and development processes for security systems. Moreover, a research approach to integrate usability and security for user authentication systems is proposed.

3 Human-Centered Design

The purpose of user-centered design (UCD) is to develop applications with a high degree of usability. To achieve this, the user becomes the most important element in the application development process. User-centered design is based on the fundamental aim to best address the users' needs and tasks. This is the feature that lead to the design process. The needs and tasks of users must also be in line with what is stated in the requirements documents [15].

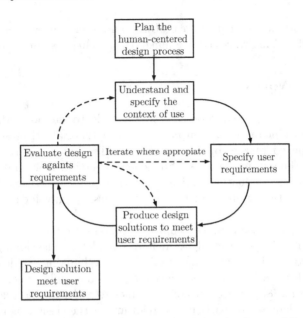

Fig. 1. Interdependence of the activities of Human-Centered Design [3]

The importance of interactive systems is reflected in the ISO 13407:1999 human-centered design for interactive systems processes, which is a guide for developing usable interactive systems incorporating the user-centered design. However, this standard was canceled and replaced by the ISO 9241-210. In this standard, the term user-centered design was replaced by human-centered design (HCD), because it addresses both stakeholders and users [9]. HCD is defined as follows: "Human-centred design is an approach to interactive systems development that aims to make systems usable and useful by focusing on the users, their needs and requirements, and by applying human factors/ergonomics, and usability knowledge and techniques" [3].

The standard ISO 9241-210:2010 provides a framework for human-centered design that integrates different design process and development appropriate in a particular context; complementing different design methodologies [9]. Figure 1 shows the activities and their interdependence defined by the standard [3].

Performing an interactive system implies that certain standards and procedures are followed by the development team. The general process defined by the standard ISO 9241-210 provides several iterations until to get all goals or requirements, they are indicated by the dotted lines [9].

4   Integration Between ISO 9241-210 and USec Design Process

According to the works presented in Sect. 2, a development model and heuristic evaluation to usable security and user authentication which could be used in a set wider of applications are proposed. In addition, using this model we developed the first principles set for USec and the main authentication methods (something the user knows, has and is) used by people currently. One of the important features of this model is its non-linearity: validation with experts and users can be performed independently because the results do not depend on the another one. The works presented in Sect. 2, include mainly qualitative evaluation. Our model (based on [1]) take into account quantitative and qualitative evaluation for USec and authentication methods. A complete representation of the integration between ISO 9241-210 and USec design process is presented in Fig. 2.

The process proposed is divided initially into three steps: (1) development of principles, (2) validation with experts and (3) validation with users. The first step allows to develop a set of principles for usable security and authentication methods according to literature. In the second step, the principles developed are evaluated by experts using a degree of importance. Finally, the third step, the principles must be applied in a specific context (website/application), the users perform tasks for a particular application provides us quantitative and qualitative data. The results are analyzed to improve the proposed principles.

According to the analysis of results in steps 2 and 3, the principles in step 1 could be modified or improved based on the recommendations and observations of the experts and users. At this point, the recommendations of the experts have priority due to they have knowledge and experience to determine whether the principles meet the necessary requirements. When the three steps have finished, a set of principles for usable security and user authentication is obtained. A complete representation of the process is presented in Fig. 2 b). A brief description of each step is presented as follows.

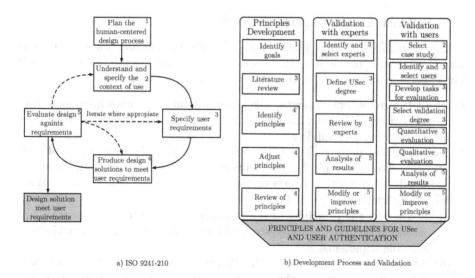

a) ISO 9241-210   b) Development Process and Validation

Fig. 2. Integration between ISO 9241-210 and development process

4.1 Principles Development (Step 1)

This step consists of 5 tasks for obtaining a set of principles preliminary.

1. **Identify Goals**: It is important to understand the purpose for developing principles or heuristics. Some goals could be: evaluate usability and security for a particular system, determine whether the system meets some quality standards, perform tasks and questionnaires to participants of the evaluation, among others.
2. **Literature Review**: A systematic literature review of principles of usability, security, privacy, user authentication, security usable and ISO / IEC standards is carried out. The study of literature is an essential requirement for knowing the requirements of the applications.
3. **Identify principles**: According to literature systematic review, the principles that might be part of the overall set (for USec and authentication methods) are identified. Each principle identified is formulated as a question, a brief explanation or examples to each question is carried out and the bibliographical sources are presented.
4. **Adjust principles**: According to the principles identified for USec and user authentication, they could be adapted to the corresponding quality attribute or characteristic (i.e. usability, security, accessibility, performance, reliability or operability). Other principles can be identified from some requirement presented in literature.
5. **Review of principles**: The review of the principles helps to place it in the appropriate attribute or characteristic. In addition, the wording is revised in order to modify or improve the question and explanation.

4.2 Validation with Experts (Step 2)

This step consists of four tasks, where experts on information security and human-computer interaction (HCI) review thoroughly the principles obtained. The experts give recommendations for improving the principles.

1. **Identify and select experts**: The experts should have knowledge and experience in areas of HCI and information security. This allows that the principles have credibility and validity.
2. **Define USec degree**: The USec degree represents the importance of each principle. To choose this degree of importance, a set of levels of importance is proposed, following the criteria of accessibility levels in W3C[1] (World Wide Web Consortium).
   (a) **S degree**: the principles of the S degree are **vital** to avoid security and usability breaches of the system and to assure that the user achieves a suitable experience.
   (b) **SS degree**: the principles of the SS degree are **important** to avoid security and usability breaches of the system and to assure that the user achieves a suitable experience.

---

[1] http://www.w3.org/TR/WAI-WEBCONTENT/.

(c) **SSS degree**: it is **advisable** to consider the principles of the SSS degree to avoid security and usability breaches of the system and to assure that the user achieves a suitable experience.

3. **Review by experts**: The experts evaluate the principles (according to the previous classification) using some kind of tool (e.g., MS Excel) and they evaluate the level of importance for each principle. In addition, they give general recommendations and for each principle.
4. **Analysis of results**: From the results, the analysis of results and conclusions are made.
5. **Modify or improve principles**: From the above analysis, the principles set may be modified or improved.

4.3 Validation with Users (Step 3)

This step consists of eight tasks where a group of users develop different activities, including the case study for validating.

1. **Select case study**: In this step, it is necessary to establish criteria (application domain, real scope, type of users, among others) in order to identify the website/application for validating security and usability. In this case, it is necessary to perform a procedure to determine the website/application for evaluating.
2. **Identify and select users**: Once the case study has been identified and selected, users are selected. There are no criteria for selecting the users. Preferably, one would approach potential users of the website/application.
3. **Develop tasks for evaluation**: The goals of the evaluation are described and the tasks that users make during their interaction with the website or application are developed.
4. **Select validation degree**: In this case, the degree of validation for users corresponds to a type previously established scale. Initially, a Likert scale is used.
5. **Quantitative evaluation**: Once users have been identified and the tasks have been developed, the case study is assessed quantitatively. For an authentication method, the evaluation quantitative could be authentication time, ease of learning, deep-processing and error probability. When finished, users complete a user satisfaction questionnaire.
6. **Qualitative evaluation**: Users (experts in HCI and security information) qualitatively assess the application using the principles of step 1 for USec and authentication methods. Finally, a questionnaire is developed in order to obtain recommendations.
7. **Analysis of results**: From the results, the analysis of results and conclusions are made.
8. **Modify or improve principles**: From the above analysis, the principles set may be modified or improved.

5   Specification of USec and User Authentication Through Quality Attributes

SQuaRE - ISO/IEC 25010:2011 [4] is a standard that defines the software quality system. However, there is no relationship between some attributes and characteristics of this standard and the principles of USec and authentication methods that the community can use for evaluating website and applications. To achieve this, some aspects of literature according to USec and authentication taking into account the ISO/IEC 25010:2011 should be considered.

From the systematic literature review, the works that might be part of the heuristic overall set (for USec and authentication methods) are: Ibrahim et al. [16], Nurse et al. [17], Katsabas et al. [18], Yeratziotis et al. [1], Mijinga et al. Mujinga2013, Bonastre et al. [19], Cranor et al. [20], Johnston et al. [21] among others. According to the above, the attributes and characteristics of the standard that could carry out this relation are usability, security, accessibility, reliability, operability and performance. Figure 3 is presented the relationship.

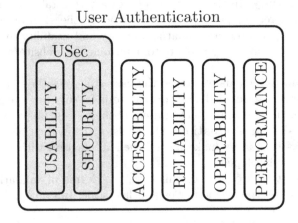

Fig. 3. Attributes for USec and user authentication

Some of these attributes have some characteristics which are included in the standard ISO/IEC 25010:2011. For security are included confidentiality, integrity, authenticity and non-repudiation. For performance are included time behaviour and minimal action. According to the systematic literature review and an exhaustive analysis, usability and security have the largest number of principles. Each principle found was analysed and located in the suitable place according to the process presented in Fig. 2. A total of 152 principles or heuristics which are distributed in specific attribute or characteristic is showed in Table 1. A brief description of each attribute or characteristic discussed above is presented as follows.

Table 1. Number of principles for each attribute

Attribute	Number of principles
Usability	75
Security	34
Accessibility	8
Performance	11
Operability	9
Reliability	15
TOTAL	**152**

1. **Usability**: based on Nielsen's 10 usability heuristics for user interface design [22], in addition, convey features are included [21]. Convey features inform the user of the available security features while the Nielsen's criterion of visibility allows the user to "see" if these features are active and being used.
2. **Security**: Our model of security according to ISO/IEC 25010:2011 have five important characteristics such as integrity, authenticity, confidentiality and non-repudiation and privacy.
3. **Operability**: It refers to the effort required to operate an authentication method.
4. **Accessibility**: Accessibility allows that everyone, regardless of cognitive, mobility and sensory skills, can use an authentication mechanism. This includes disabilities such as hearing, sight, mobility, learning and colour, which are pertinent in an authentication context. Accessibility also applies to levels of technical skills and literacy as well as the quality of the users equipment [23].
5. **Reliability**: Reliability indicates the ability to perform specific functions that allow carrying out a successful authentication. In this regard, it is also important to consider some aspects of security (integrity and confidentiality), maintenance and technical support.
6. **Performance**: For authentication methods, is taking into account two aspects [24]:
   (a) *Minimal action*: The capacity of the application to help users for achieving their tasks in a few steps.
   (b) *Time response*: It represents the time required to load the application, i.e., how fast the system responds according to the user's instructions.

As previously stated, the outcome from step 1 according to Fig. 2 is 6 attributes or characteristics and 152 principles for USec and authentication methods. Each attribute has its own set of principles that assist experts in applying the principle in practice. In Table 2 is presented an example of the principles of accessibility. In the first column, the heuristic is formulated as a question, in the second column is presented a short explanation or example of the principle and finally, the bibliographical sources of the principle are shown in the third column.

Table 2. Principles for accessibility

Principle	Comment	Source
Does the system allow to use graphical passwords to users with reading difficulties?	The images could help people to authenticate when they have reading difficulties (e.g., dyslexia)	[25]
In biometric authentication, is the system composed of standard devices?	Devices standard allow easy setting and use for users	[24]
In authentication using ownership factors, Does the server is integrated with software and hardware suitable?	Install software and hardware suitable, allow a better performance and usability for users in the authentication process	[23]
Does the system avoid using random keys in the step of registration or authentication?	Using random keys (e.g., One-Time Passwords) are difficult to use for users because it is not possible to memorize all passwords	[23]
In an authentication process, Does the system avoid extra effort?	The authentication process should be intuitive and effortless extra (e.g., cognitive or physical)	[23]
In an authentication system using inherence factors, Does the system can be configured for people with physical limitations?	People with physical limitations (e.g., dyspraxia), the system should be easily configured for these cases	[23]
Does the system provides users with alternatives to authenticate?	This could improve the availability and convenience of the system	[24]
Can the authentication method to be adapted for new and experienced users?	The authentication method should have settings options for new and experienced users	[23]

6   Conclusions and Future Work

Security is a problem area for user interface design. Consequently, developers require tools that can assist them to improve their designs in terms of usable security for websites/applications, for instance, user authentication. Security and privacy design issues can be reduced using the USec principles. This is an important contribution to the USec field.

We proposed an integration between the standard ISO 9241-210 to find a development process and a tool for evaluating qualitative and quantitatively usable security and user authentication, taking into account some aspects and attributes and characteristics of the standard ISO/IEC 25010:2011. Many users are not able to perceive the security issues correctly, generating a security threat due to misunderstanding and avoid tactics to protect the system.

Although there are different methods for evaluating the usability of security systems, these methods are not user-centered due to the lack of suitable principles. Future work will be oriented to analyze and review the heuristic set by experts in order to obtain a level of importance for each principle, in addition, examine the suggestions of the experts according to the principles set to be modified or improved.

Acknowledgement. Paulo Realpe-Muñoz thanks to Colciencias for the scholarship and to University of Lleida for the internship.

References

1. Yeratziotis, A., Greunen, D., Pottas, D.: A framework for evaluating usable security: the case of online health social networks. In: 6th International Symposium on Human Aspects of Information Security and Assurance (2012)
2. Payne, B., Edwards, W.: A Brief Introduction to Usable Security. IEEE Comput. Soc. **12**, 13–21 (2008)
3. International Standard ISO: ISO 9241–210 Ergonomics of Human-System Interaction - Part 210: Human-Centered Design for Interactive Systems. International Organization for Standardization ISO (2010)
4. International Standard ISO: ISO/IEC 25010–2011. Systems and software engineering - Systems and software Quality Requirements and Evaluation (SQuaRE) - System and software quality models. International Organization for Standardization ISO (2011)
5. Wilson, C.: Credible Checklists and Quality Questionnaires: A User-Centered Design Method, 1st edn. Morgan Kaufmann, San Francisco (2013)
6. Sim, G., Read, J.C., Cockton, G.: Evidence based design of heuristics for computer assisted assessment. In: Gross, T., Gulliksen, J., Kotzé, P., Oestreicher, L., Palanque, P., Prates, R.O., Winckler, M. (eds.) INTERACT 2009. LNCS, vol. 5726, pp. 204–216. Springer, Heidelberg (2009)
7. Mujinga, M., Eloff, M., Kroeze, J.: Towards a heuristic model for usable and secure online banking. In: 24th Australian Conference on Information Systems (ACIS), RMIT University, pp. 1–13 (2013)
8. Shneiderman, B., Leavitt, M.: Research-Based Web Design and Usability Guidelines. US Government Printing Office, Whashington D.C. (2006)
9. Vidal, D., Ibarra, J., Flores, B., Lopez, G.: Adoption of the Standard ISO 9241–21: 2010 on construction of interactive systems based in software. In: International Conference on Research and Innovation in Software Engineering. CANISOFT (2012)
10. Fidas, C., Hussmann, H., Belk, M., Samaras, G.: iHIP: towards a user centric individual human interaction proof framework. In: CHI Extended Abstracts, pp. 2235–2240. ACM (2015)
11. Haiyun, X., Heijmans, H., Visser, J.: A practical model for rating software security. In: 7th International Conference on Software Security and Reliability-Companion (SERE-C), pp. 231–232. IEEE (2013)
12. Colombo, R., Guerra, A., Balcao, A., Caruso, C.: Prioritization of software security intangible attributes. SIGSOFT Software Engineering Notes, pp. 1–7. ACM (2012)

13. Zapata, L.: Development of a Model for Security and Usability. Master Thesis. Universidad Politecnica de Madrid (2013)
14. Realpe, P., Collazos, C., Hurtado, J., Granollers, T.: Towards an integration of usability and security for user authentication. In: 16th International Conference on HCI, pp. 43:1–43:6 (2015)
15. Leventhal, L., Barnes, J.: Usability Engineering: Process, Products and Examples. Prentice Hall, Upper Saddle River (2007)
16. Ibrahim, T., Furnell, S., Papadaki, M., Clarke, N.: Assessing the usability of end-user security software. In: Katsikas, S., Lopez, J., Soriano, M. (eds.) Trust, Privacy and Security in Digital Business. LNCS, vol. 6264, pp. 177–189. Springer, Heidelberg (2010)
17. Nurse, J., Creese, S., Goldsmith, M., Lamberts, K.: Guidelines for usable cybersecurity: past and present. In: Third International Workshop on Cyberspace Safety and Security (CSS), pp. 21–26. IEEE (2011)
18. Katsabas, D., Furnell, S., Downland, P.: Using human computer interaction principles to promote usable security. In: 5th International Network Conference (2005)
19. Bonastre, L., Granollers, T.: A set of heuristics for user experience evaluation in e-commerce websites. In: 7th International Conference on Advances in Computer-Human Interactions, IARIA, pp. 27–34 (2014)
20. Cranor, L., Garfinkel, S.: Security and Usability: Designing Secure Systems that People can Use. O'Reilly Media, California (2005)
21. Johnston, J., Eloff, J., Labuschagne, L.: Security and human computer interfaces. Comput. Secur. **22**, 675–684 (2003)
22. Nielsen, J., Molich, R.: Heuristic evaluation of user interfaces. In: Proceedings of the SIGCHI Conference on Human Factors in Computing Systems, pp. 249–256. ACM (1990)
23. Renaud, K.: Quantifying the quality of web authentication mechanisms a usability. Perspect. J. Web Eng. **3**, 95–123 (2003)
24. Braz, C., Seffah, A., Poirier, P.: Designing usable, yet secure user authentication services: a user authentication protocol. In: 5th International Conference on Applied Human Factors and Ergonomics, vol. 20, AHFE, pp. 155–165 (2014)
25. Fritsch, L., Fuglerud, K., Solheim, I.: Towards inclusive identity management. Identity Inf. Soc. **3**, 515–538 (2010)

Secure Communication Protocol Between a Human and a Bank Server for Preventing Man-in-the-Browser Attacks

Takashi Tsuchiya[1], Masahiro Fujita[1], Kenta Takahashi[2],
Takehisa Kato[3], Fumihiko Magata[4], Yoshimi Teshigawara[5],
Ryoichi Sasaki[5], and Masakatsu Nishigaki[1(✉)]

[1] Shizuoka University, Hamamatsu, Japan
nisigaki@inf.shizuoka.ac.jp
[2] Hitachi, Ltd., Totsuka, Japan
[3] Toshiba Corporation Industrial ICT Solutions Company, Fuchu, Japan
[4] NTT Secure Platform Laboratories, Musashino, Japan
[5] Tokyo Denki University, Adachi, Japan

Abstract. Man-in-the-Browser (MITB) attacks are caused by malware that infects a web browser; hence, conventional secure communication channels between a machine (bank server) and a machine (web browser) such as SSL cannot prevent the attacks. In this paper, we propose an approach to preventing MITB attacks by constructing secure communication channels between a machine (bank server) and a human (end user). Our approach uses the user as a computational resource and requests the user to process an end side of the channel. Developing a challenge and response protocol that achieves the proposed channel, we conducted a safety evaluation of the protocol. The result shows that the protocol works safely under the assumption that the bank server can send a "challenge that malware in the browser cannot see" to the user. We also show that sending the challenge is feasible by applying CAPTCHA technology.

Keywords: Man-in-the-Browser attacks · Secure communication channel · CAPTCHA

1 Introduction

Recently, illegal money transfers via internet banking have been on the increase [1]. There are various types of illegal money transfers. In particular, Man-in-the-Browser (MITB) attacks have attracted attention. MITB attacks are caused by malware that infects a web browser. The browser is then capable of falsifying a user's web transactions and stealing the user's password. Many internet banking sites have prevented illegal money transfers by constructing a secure communication channel between a machine (bank server) and a machine (web browser) such as SSL [2, 3]. However, this secure communication cannot prevent MITB attacks. This is because the attacks are caused by malware that infects a web browser on the inside of the secure communication channel.

© Springer International Publishing Switzerland 2016
T. Tryfonas (Ed.): HAS 2016, LNCS 9750, pp. 77–88, 2016.
DOI: 10.1007/978-3-319-39381-0_8

To deal with MITB attacks, we propose an approach to preventing them by constructing a secure communication channel[1] between a machine (bank server) and a human (end user). We give an example of protocols to construct the channel, in particular, a challenge and response protocol using a "challenge that malware in the browser cannot see." It should be noted that, when constructing the channel, we cannot use well-known encryption techniques such as SSL. These cryptographic techniques are basically based on high *machine* computing power and therefore can be applied only to secure communication between a machine and *a machine*. In comparison, our protocol enables secure communication between a machine and *a human*. This is the main contribution in this paper. The organization of this paper is as follows. In Sect. 2, we give details on MITB attacks. We introduce our proposal in Sects. 3 and 4, and discuss it in Sect. 5. In Sect. 6, we describe related work. Finally, we present our conclusions in Sect. 7.

2   Internet Banking and MITB Attacks

2.1   Money Transfer Protocol

In this section, we describe a money transfer protocol used for internet banking. Here, for simplicity, we give a simple description.

Most banks use a money transfer protocol like shown in Fig. 1. The entities of the money transfer protocol are as follows.

- Bank server: The bank server is a server of a financial institution that provides the internet banking service. We assume that the bank server is safe, e.g., it is not possible to leak data and modify the processing in the server. The bank server is a machine; it therefore has a high computing power (and memory capacity) and does not have advanced cognitive abilities.
- User: The user is a customer who uses the internet banking service. When remitting his or her money to any account, he or she operates the PC in accordance with a money transfer protocol provided by the financial institution. We assume that the user perfectly operates the PC in accordance with the protocol. The user is a human and therefore has a low computing power (and memory capacity) and advanced cognitive abilities.
- PC: The PC is equipped with a keyboard and a display. It is connected to a bank server via the internet. A web browser is installed on the PC. The user uses the web browser to remit his or her money that is stored in the internet banking service. The PC (in fact, the browser) is a machine; it therefore has a high computing power (and memory capacity) and does not have advanced cognitive abilities.

Step 1.   The user inputs money transfer information X, e.g., account number, amount of money, to the PC.

Step 2.   The PC (web browser) sends the information to the bank server.

---

[1] In this paper, we define secure communication as preventing direct pecuniary damage caused by the falsification of malware.

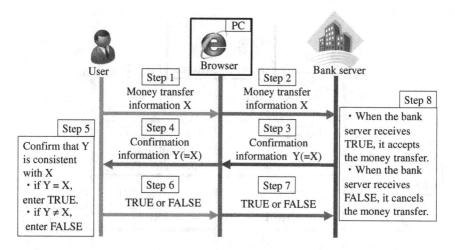

Fig. 1. Money transfer protocol

Step 3. To confirm the information, the bank server sends confirmation information Y to the PC. Typically, Y is consistent with X (Y = X).

Step 4. The PC receives Y and displays it to the user.

Step 5. The user confirms that Y is consistent with X and determines whether to perform the money transfer.

Step 6. When the user agrees with the remittance, the user inputs TRUE (the decision of money transfer) to the PC. When the user wants to cancel the remittance, the user inputs FALSE (the cancel of money transfer).

Step 7. The PC sends the TRUE or FALSE to the bank server.

Step 8. When the bank server receives TRUE, it accepts the money transfer. When the bank server receives FALSE, it cancels the money transfer.

2.2 MITB Attacks

MITB attacks can be classified into two types: information falsification and ID theft [4, 5]. As this paper is the first stage of the research, we focus only on the former type. In this type, malware in a PC (web browser) falsifies the transaction information. The procedure for this type of attack is shown in Fig. 2.

Step 1. The user inputs money transfer information X to the PC.

Step 2. The malware in the PC (web browser) alters X to X' and sends it to the bank server.

Step 3. The bank server sends confirmation information Y (= X') to the PC.

Step 4. The PC receives Y (=X'). The malware in the PC alters Y to Y' (=X) and displays it to the user.

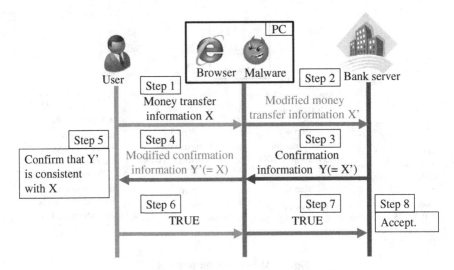

Fig. 2. Information falsification MITB attack

Step 5. The user reads Y' (=X) and confirms whether it is consistent with X. Since the malware alters Y (=X') to Y'(=X) in Step 4, the user accepts the money transfer.

Step 6. The user inputs TRUE (the decision of money transfer) to the PC.

Step 7. The PC sends TRUE to the bank server.

Step 8. The bank server receives TRUE and accepts the money transfer (X').

3 Secure Communication Protocol Between Human and Server

3.1 Concepts

We propose an approach to preventing the information falsification type of MITB attack shown in Fig. 2 by constructing a secure communication channel between a machine and a human. A secure communication channel between a machine (web browser) and a machine (bank server) cannot prevent MITB attacks. This is because the malware in the PC can take over the operation of the web browser. To fundamentally prevent the attacks, it is necessary to use a human as a computational resource and construct a secure communication channel between a machine (bank server) and a human (end user).

It should be noted that, however, humans have only low computing powers. We cannot use a well-known encryption technique such as SSL. Instead, a method that enables secure communication between a machine (who has a high computing power) and a user (who has a low computing power) is needed. We propose a challenge and response protocol using a "challenge that malware in the browser cannot see."

3.2   Proposed Protocol

Goal. With the information falsification type of attack, malware is able to falsify the information in Step 2 (money transfer information), Step 4 (confirmation information), and Step 7 (TRUE/FALSE) in Fig. 2. In this paper, we construct a secure communication protocol that prevents direct pecuniary damage to a user and bank caused by falsification in Steps 2, 4, and 7.

How to send a challenge that malware cannot see. Our protocol works under the assumption that a bank server is able to send the user a challenge that the malware in a browser cannot see. Let us consider that the server sends a set of data $\alpha_1 \sim \alpha_m$ through a certain type of channel to the user. The data is denoted as $\{\alpha_1, \alpha_2, \ldots, \alpha_m\}$. If the following requirements are met in the channel, the malware will not be able to see the challenge that is sent to the user through the channel.

(i).   The malware cannot obtain any data $\alpha_i (1 \leq i \leq m)$ from $\{\alpha_1, \alpha_2, \ldots, \alpha_m\}$.

(ii). Even if the malware knows a piece of data $\alpha_i (1 \leq i \leq m)$, the malware cannot find which portion of data $\{\alpha_1, \alpha_2, \ldots, \alpha_m\}$ stands for α_i.

(iii). The user (human) can obtain all data $\alpha_i (1 \leq i \leq m)$ from $\{\alpha_1, \alpha_2, \ldots, \alpha_m\}$.

It should be noted here that the malware also can use the channel to send the user a fake set of data $\beta_1, \beta_2, \ldots, \beta_n$. In other words, the malware can generate any fake data $\beta_1, \beta_2, \ldots, \beta_n$ from scratch. This means that if the malware knows the value of data $\{\alpha_1, \alpha_2, \ldots, \alpha_m\}$ in $\{\alpha_1, \alpha_2, \ldots, \alpha_m\}$, it is able to change some values among them (e.g., $\alpha_1 \to \beta_1$ and send $\{\beta_1, \alpha_2, \ldots, \alpha_m\}$ to the user. However, due to the definitions (i), the malware cannot carry out this falsification. It should be also noted that the malware is able to conduct replay attacks by capturing a genuine $\{\alpha_1, \alpha_2, \ldots, \alpha_m\}$ and resending it to the user. However, due to the definitions (ii), the malware cannot alter $\{\alpha_1, \alpha_2, \ldots, \alpha_m\}$.

Although there could be various approaches used to develop this sort of channel, in this paper, we will apply CAPTCHAs (Completely Automated Public Turing test to tell Computers and Humans Apart [6]) to implement it, as explained later in Sect. 4. We thus refer to the channel as a "CAPTCHA channel."

Procedure. The proposed protocol works as shown in Fig. 3. Note that $\{Y, R\}$ means that a pair of data Y and R is conveyed through the CAPTCHA channel, where R is a random number generated by the bank server.

Step 1.   The user enters money transfer information X to the PC.

Step 2.   The PC (web browser) sends X to the bank server.

Step 3.   To confirm X, the bank server sends confirmation information $\{Y, R\}$ to the PC. Here, Y is equal to X, and R is a random number generated by the bank server.

Step 4.   The PC receives $\{Y, R\}$ and displays it to the user. The user obtains Y and R from $\{Y, R\}$.

Step 5.   The user confirms that Y is consistent with X and decides whether to remit or cancel.

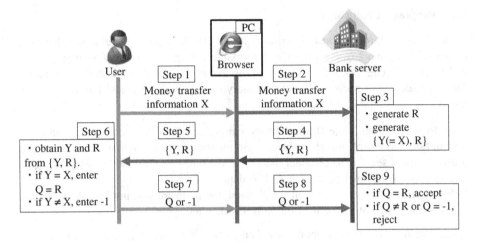

Fig. 3. Proposed protocol

Step 6.   When the user wants to remit, the user inputs Q (=R) to the PC. When the user wants to cancel the remittance, the user inputs −1 to the PC.

Step 7.   The PC sends Q or −1 to the bank server.

Step 8.   When the bank server receives Q that is consistent with R, it accepts the money transfer. When the bank server receives −1 or a value that is not consistent with R, it cancels the money transfer.

3.3 Safety Evaluation

To evaluate the safety of the proposed protocol (Fig. 3), we verified the effectiveness of the protocol under the situation where all combinations of falsifications have occurred.

Table 1 shows the results of the safety evaluation against all combinations of falsification. X, Y, R, and Q falsified in each step are denoted as X′, Y′, R′, and Q′, respectively. "No." is an index to distinguish the falsifications.

As shown in Table 1, falsifications No. 3, 4, 7, 9, 11–13, 15, 18, 21, 23, and 26–28 are 'impossible' owing to the definitions of the CAPTCHA channel in Sect. 3.2. (To be more precise, the malware cannot conduct falsifications highlighted in gray owing to the definition of the CAPTCHA channel in Sect. 3.2.) For example, for No. 3, to alter {Y(=X′), R} to {Y′(=X), R} in Step 5, the malware has to (1) modify {Y(=X′), R} to {Y′(=X), R} or (2) generate {Y′(=X), R} from scratch. Regarding (1), though the malware knows the value of X′, it cannot find the position of X′ from {Y(=X′), R} owing to definition (ii) of the CAPTCHA channel. Thus, the malware cannot modify {Y(=X′), R} to {Y′(=X), R}. Regarding (2), though the malware knows the value of X′, it cannot obtain the R from {Y(=X′), R} owing to definition (i) of the CAPTCHA

Table 1. Results of safety evaluation

No.	Step(s) in which falsification is conducted	Step 1	Step 2	Step 3	Step 4	Step 5	Step 6	Step 7	Step 8	Step 9	Possibility
1	Step 2	X	X'	{Y(=X'), R}	{Y(=X'), R}	{Y(=X'), R}	Y≠X	-1	-1	Reject	Possible
2		X	X'	{Y(=X'), R}	{Y(=X'), R}	{Y(=X'), R'}	Y≠X	-1	-1	Reject	Possible
3	Steps 2,5	X	X'	{Y(=X'), R}	{Y(=X'), R}	{Y'(=X), R}	Y'=X	Q=R	Q	Accept	Impossible
4		X	X'	{Y(=X'), R}	{Y(=X'), R}	{Y'(≠X), R}	Y'≠X	-1	-1	Reject	Impossible
5		X	X'	{Y(=X'), R}	{Y(=X'), R}	{Y'(=X), R'}	Y'=X	Q=R'	Q	Reject	Possible
6		X	X'	{Y(=X'), R}	{Y(=X'), R}	{Y'(≠X), R'}	Y'≠X	-1	-1	Reject	Possible
7	Steps 2,8	X	X'	{Y(=X'), R}	{Y(=X'), R}	{Y(=X'), R}	Y≠X	-1	Q'=R	Accept	Impossible
8		X	X'	{Y(=X'), R}	{Y(=X'), R}	{Y(=X'), R}	Y≠X	-1	Q'≠R	Reject	Possible
9		X	X'	{Y(=X'), R}	{Y(=X'), R}	{Y(=X'), R'}	Y≠X	-1	Q'=R	Accept	Impossible
10		X	X'	{Y(=X'), R}	{Y(=X'), R}	{Y(=X'), R'}	Y≠X	-1	Q'≠R	Reject	Possible
11		X	X'	{Y(=X'), R}	{Y(=X'), R}	{Y'(=X), R}	Y'=X	Q=R	-1	Reject	Impossible
12		X	X'	{Y(=X'), R}	{Y(=X'), R}	{Y'(=X), R}	Y'=X	Q=R	Q'≠R	Reject	Impossible
13		X	X'	{Y(=X'), R}	{Y(=X'), R}	{Y'(≠X), R}	Y'≠X	-1	Q'=R	Accept	Impossible
14	Steps 2,5,8	X	X'	{Y(=X'), R}	{Y(=X'), R}	{Y'(≠X), R}	Y'≠X	-1	Q'≠R	Reject	Possible
15		X	X'	{Y(=X'), R}	{Y(=X'), R}	{Y'(=X), R'}	Y'=X	Q=R'	Q'=R	Accept	Impossible
16		X	X'	{Y(=X'), R}	{Y(=X'), R}	{Y'(=X), R'}	Y'=X	Q=R'	Q'≠R	Reject	Possible
17		X	X'	{Y(=X'), R}	{Y(=X'), R}	{Y'(=X), R'}	Y'=X	Q=R'	-1	Reject	Possible
18		X	X'	{Y(=X'), R}	{Y(=X'), R}	{Y'(≠X), R'}	Y'≠X	-1	Q'=R	Accept	Impossible
19		X	X'	{Y(=X'), R}	{Y(=X'), R}	{Y'(≠X), R'}	Y'≠X	-1	Q'≠R	Reject	Possible
20		X	X	{Y(=X), R}	{Y(=X), R}	{Y(=X), R'}	Y=X	Q=R'	Q	Reject	Possible
21	Step 5	X	X	{Y(=X), R}	{Y(=X), R}	{Y'(≠X), R}	Y'≠X	-1	-1	Reject	Impossible
22		X	X	{Y(=X), R}	{Y(=X), R}	{Y'(≠X), R'}	Y'≠X	-1	-1	Reject	Possible
23		X	X	{Y(=X), R}	{Y(=X), R}	{Y(=X), R'}	Y=X	Q=R'	Q'=R	Accept	Impossible
24		X	X	{Y(=X), R}	{Y(=X), R}	{Y(=X), R'}	Y=X	Q=R'	Q'≠R	Reject	Possible
25		X	X	{Y(=X), R}	{Y(=X), R}	{Y(=X), R'}	Y=X	Q=R'	-1	Reject	Possible
26	Steps 5,8	X	X	{Y(=X), R}	{Y(=X), R}	{Y'(≠X), R}	Y'≠X	-1	Q'=R	Accept	Impossible
27		X	X	{Y(=X), R}	{Y(=X), R}	{Y'(≠X), R}	Y'≠X	-1	Q'≠R	Reject	Impossible
28		X	X	{Y(=X), R}	{Y(=X), R}	{Y'(≠X), R'}	Y'≠X	-1	Q'=R	Accept	Impossible
29		X	X	{Y(=X), R}	{Y(=X), R}	{Y'(≠X), R'}	Y'≠X	-1	Q'≠R	Reject	Possible
30	Step 8	X	X	{Y(=X), R}	{Y(=X), R}	{Y(=X), R}	Y=X	Q=R	Q'≠R	Reject	Possible
31		X	X	{Y(=X), R}	{Y(=X), R}	{Y(=X), R}	Y=X	Q=R	-1	Reject	Possible

channel. Thus, the malware cannot generate $\{Y'(=X), R\}$ from scratch. Similarly, the malware cannot do the other falsifications. As also shown in Table 1, falsifications No. 1, 2, 4–6, 8, 10–12, 14, 16, 17, 19–22, 24, 25, 27, and 29–31 are 'rejected' owing to the condition $Q \neq R$ or $Q = -1$ in Step 9.

As a result, all the possible illegal money transfers in Table 1 are 'rejected' or 'impossible'. Thus, the proposed protocol is safe against all combinations of falsification patterns. This means that the protocol realizes a secure communication channel between a machine and a human, so it enables MITB attacks shown in Fig. 2 to be prevented.

4   CAPTCHA Channel

4.1   How to Construct a CAPTCHA Channel

The proposed protocol is safe under the assumption that the CAPTCHA channel can be constructed. In this section, we explain a method for applying a CAPTCHA to develop the channel. A CAPTCHA is a Turing test to discriminate humans from machines [6] by using questions that a human can solve easily but a machine cannot.

A CAPTCHA used for the channel needs to meet definitions (i), (ii), and (iii) in Sect. 3.2. Hereafter, a CAPTCHA that meets the definitions and conveys a set of data $\{\alpha_1, \alpha_2, \ldots, \alpha_m\}$ as its answer is defined as $Cd(\alpha_1, \alpha_2, \ldots, \alpha_1)$. Using $Cd(\alpha_1, \alpha_2)$, the proposed protocol is described as in Fig. 4. So far, we have been able to send only one digit by using a CAPTCHA as will be explained later. The user needs to repeat our protocol for n times to send n digits of money transfer information.

To meet definition (i), $Cd(Y, R)$ must be a CAPTCHA that machines cannot solve. Many researchers reported that some CAPTCHAs can be solved by machines [7, 8]. Such CAPTCHAs cannot be used as the $Cd(Y, R)$. To meet definition (ii), $Cd(Y, R)$ must be a CAPTCHA where machines cannot find the position of Y and/or R from Cd (Y, R). Figure 5 is an example of a CAPTCHA which does not meet definition (ii) and hence the malware is able to falsify[2]. Such CAPTCHAs cannot be used as the $Cd(Y, R)$, either. To meet definition (iii), $Cd(Y, R)$ must be a CAPTCHA that is human readable. Basically, $Cd(Y, R)$ meets definition (iii) since the CAPTCHA is created with a question that humans can solve easily.

4.2   Example of CAPTCHAs that Meet the Definitions

There could be various CAPTCHAs that realize $Cd(Y, R)$. Figure 6 shows an example. The CAPTCHA is composed of upright objects, upside-down ones, and other objects. This CAPTCHA requests users to count the number of upright objects and the number of upside-down objects. The number of upright objects is Y, and the number of upside-down objects is R.

This CAPTCHA meets definitions (i), (ii), and (iii) as follows. Since malware does not have an ability to recognize whether an object is upright or upside-down [9], it cannot obtain Y and R from this CAPTCHA. Therefore, this CAPTCHA meets definitions (i) and (ii). In addition, understanding upright/upside-down objects and

---

[2] In the proposed protocol shown in Fig. 3, when the malware obtains X from the user in Step 1 and sends X' to the bank server in Step 2, the bank server sends Cd(Y(=X'), R) to the PC in Step 3. Suppose that Cd(X', R) is a CAPTCHA shown in Fig. 5, where X' is a position of an upright object and R is a position of an upside-down object. This CAPTCHA does not meet the definition (ii) and therefore the malware can find these positions in Cd(X', R). The malware knows the value of X entered by the user and X' sent by itself, and it can find the positions corresponding to X' and X in Cd (X', R). Then, the malware replaces the position of the X'-th object with the position of the X-th object in Cd(X', R). Consequently, Cd(X', R) becomes Cd(X, R). (Even though the malware is not capable of understanding which object is upright and/or upside-down, it can just replace these two objects with each other in Cd(X', R).) The malware sends it to the user in Step 5, and the transfer of illegal money is successful.

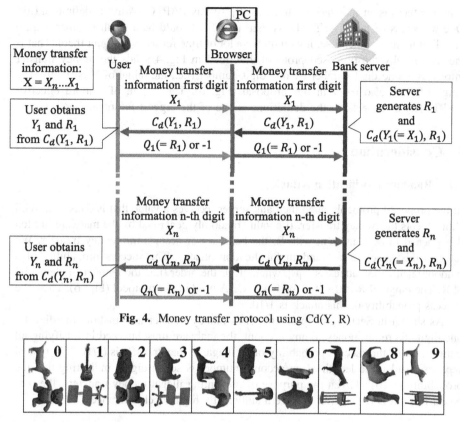

Fig. 4. Money transfer protocol using Cd(Y, R)

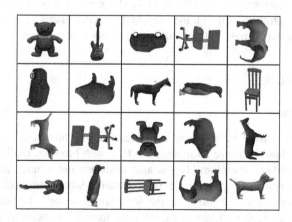

Fig. 5. Example of CAPTCHA that does not meet the definition (ii). Each position from the left object to the right one corresponds to values $0 \sim 9$. Among them, the position of upright object corresponds to Y, and the position of upside-down object corresponds to R (in this example, Y = 1 and R = 6)

Fig. 6. A CAPTCHA that meets the definition of a CAPTCHA channel. The number of upright objects is Y. The number of upside-down objects is R (in this case, Y = 6 and R = 4)

counting them is an easy task for humans [9], so this CAPTCHA meets definition (iii). One weakness of this CAPTCHA is that Y and R should be a small number, e.g., a one-digit number; otherwise, it would take a lot of time for users to count them. That is the reason why the proposed protocol described in Fig. 4 sends the money transfer information one digit number by one digit number (i.e., the range of Y is $0 \sim 9$). The range of R is also $0 \sim 9$ in our proposal (Fig. 6). The design of a more effective CAPTCHA that meets all the definitions is one of the biggest future studies.

5   Consideration

5.1   Random Falsification Attack

In the proposed protocol, when the bank server receives a value that is consistent with R, it accepts the money transfer. If a value randomly generated by the malware in Step 8 happened to be consistent with R, the bank server accepts the money transfer. We refer to this attack as a "random falsification attack". The success probability of a random falsification attack is $1/|R|$, where $|R|$ is the order (i.e., the number of elements) of R. The range of R is $0 \sim 9$ in the CAPTCHA used in our protocol (Fig. 6). Thus, the success probability of this attack is $1/10$.

As shown in Sect. 4, our protocol sends money transfer information one digit by one digit. To remit money to any account, the malware must succeed in falsifying all n digits. Thus, the success probability of an illegal money transfer is $(1/10)^n$. In typical Japanese banks, the length of an account number is seven digits, indicating that the probability $(1/10)^7$. Given the purpose of preventing illegal money transfers, the proposed method is considered to have a sufficiently high attack tolerance.

5.2   Usability

The user needs to repeat our protocol for n times to send n digits of money transfer information. The user has to solve the CAPTCHA n times. Compared with the conventional transfer protocol (Fig. 1), the proposed protocol places more of a burden on the user. We will experiment with evaluating usability in the future.

6   Related Work

6.1   Anti-malware

MITB attacks are caused by malware that infects a web browser. To prevent these attacks, the user should remove all malware in their web browser. Dedicated software, for example, PhishWall Premium [10], is able to detect and remove malware on the user's computer. However, given the current situation where subspecific malware is being created every day, the effect of the software is limited. In fact, it has been reported that it is difficult to detect Zeus, a typical malware to perform MITB attacks, by using security software due to a large number of subspecies [11]. Our proposed method is not to detect the malware, and thus prevents MITB attacks even if the web browser is infected by malware.

6.2   Transaction Signing

Transaction signing is a measure using secure hardware that is independent of the PC (hereinafter referred to as "token") to prevent MITB attacks [12, 13]. The procedure of transaction signing is as follows. The user generates a verification code based on the money transfer information by using a token. The user sends the money transfer information and the verification code together to the bank server. The bank server receives them and verifies the integrity of the money transfer information and the verification code.

Two methods of transaction signing have been reported. One method uses a token distributed by the bank [12]. With this method, it is necessary for users to always carry the token. Users may lose or not carry the token outdoors. In addition, the bank has to incur huge costs to distribute the tokens to all users. The other method is using a smart phone as a token [13]. With this method, the above problem cannot occur. However, given a situation where it has been reported that there is a large number of malicious apps, it is difficult to ensure that the smart phones are secure hardware anymore. Even if we prevent any infection at present, malware is expected to evolve in the future. This problem is similar to that of the anti-malware shown in Sect. 5.1.

As shown in Fig. 3, the proposed method can be implemented without any additional device to the conventional transfer protocol (Fig. 1). Therefore, a problem as described above cannot occur.

7   Conclusion

In this paper, we proposed an approach to preventing MITB attacks by constructing a secure communication channel between a machine (bank server) and a human (end user). Developing a challenge and response protocol that achieves the proposed channel, we conducted a safety evaluation of the protocol. The results showed that the protocol works safely under the assumption that a bank server can send a "challenge that malware in the browser cannot see" to the user. Sending the challenge is feasible by applying CAPTCHA technology. We will consider a CAPTCHA that is more suitable for the proposed protocol and perform usability experiments.

References

1. Online banking users suffer ¥1.4 billion in damage. http://www.japantimes.co.jp/news/2014/01/30/national/online-banking-users-suffer-1-4-billion-in-damage/#.VriNThiLS00
2. Bank of Taiwan. http://www.bot.com.tw/English/BankServices/ElectronicBankingServices/BOTSSLInternetBanking/Pages/default.aspx

3. Bank of America. https://www.bankofamerica.com/onlinebanking/online-banking-security-faqs.go

4. Man-in-the-Browser (MitB). https://www.trusteer.com/en/glossary/man-in-the-browser-mitb

5. Man In The Browser attacks scare banking world. http://securityaffairs.co/wordpress/17538/cyber-crime/man-browser-attacks-scare-banking.html

6. The Official CAPTCHA Site. http://www.captcha.net

7. Yan, J., Ahmad, A.S.E.: Breaking visual CAPTCHAs with naïve pattern recognition algorithms. In: 2007 Computer Security Applications Conference, pp. 279–291 (2007)

8. Golle, P.: Machine learning attacks against the ASIRRA CAPTCHA. In: 2008 ACM CSS, pp. 535–542 (2008)

9. Ross, S.A., Alex Halderman, J., Finkelstein, A.: Sketcha: A captcha based on line drawings of 3D models. In: Proceedings of the 19th International Conference on World Wide Web, pp. 821–830 (2010)

10. PhishWall. http://www.securebrain.co.jp/eng/web/phishwall.php

11. Symantec White Paper - Banking Trojans. https://www4.symantec.com/mktginfo/whitepaper/user_authentication/21195180_WP_GA_BankingTrojansImpactandDefendAgainstTrojanFraud_062611.pdf

12. SafeNet eToken 3500. http://www.pronew.com.tw/download/doc/eToken3500_PB_(EN)_web.pdf

13. Saisudheer, A.: M. TECH: smart phone as software token for generating digital signature code for signing in online banking transaction. IJCES 3(12), 1–4 (2013)

Security, Privacy
and Human Bevahiour

Proposed Privacy Patterns for Privacy Preserving Healthcare Systems in Accord with Nova Scotia's Personal Health Information Act

Maha Aljohani[1(✉)], Kirstie Hawkey[1], and James Blustein[1,2]

[1] Faculty of Computer Science, Dalhousie University, Halifax, Canada
mh578194@dal.ca, {hawkey,jamie}@cs.dal.ca
[2] School of Information Management, Dalhousie University, Halifax, Canada

Abstract. We propose privacy design patterns in the context of healthcare systems. These patterns are designed to support the Privacy-By-Design concept through the software lifecycle, focusing on the early design phase and mitigating privacy risks. As a departure point, we used Personal Health Information Act (PHIA) in Nova Scotia to derive the following five proposed privacy patterns: 1-request an access 2-request a correction 3-request not to disclose Personal Health Information 4-being notified if the PHI is lost, stolen or subject to unauthorized access 5-request a review. The patterns provide a guide to designers and developers in designing privacy-preserving systems in healthcare.

Keywords: Privacy patterns · Personal Health Information Act (PHIA) · Privacy-by-Design · Privacy Enhancing Technologies (PETs) · Personal information · ISO 29100 · Privacy-by-Policy

1 Introduction

In 2013, Nova Scotia's Personal Health Information Act (PHIA) came into effect to cover additional rules on top of the Personal Information Protection and Electronic Documents Act (PIPEDA) [1].

Laws and regulations alone do not prevent individuals from giving personal information nor prevent anyone from gaining access to someone else's personal information without permission. Privacy patterns are privacy design guidelines that can be used early in design lifecycles. The concept of Privacy-By-Design (PbD) is essential because it integrates concern for privacy from the first design steps and maintains such care throughout the design lifecycle [2]. Therefore, design privacy patterns are proposed to protect personal information by design and default. Proposing privacy patterns is motivated by the need to bridge the gap between laws and application. At the same time, another motivation is to maintain levels of privacy as hard copies are transferred into digital artefacts requires PbD.

Our overall objective is to provide Information Technology (IT) designers and developers a solid framework of privacy patterns that covers the privacy rights according to Personal Health Information Act (PHIA). A secondary goal is to validate the proposed

© Springer International Publishing Switzerland 2016
T. Tryfonas (Ed.): HAS 2016, LNCS 9750, pp. 91–102, 2016.
DOI: 10.1007/978-3-319-39381-0_9

patterns by comparing them to the principles of ISO29100 Privacy Framework and to identify the properties that are guaranteed when the system design follows the patterns. The proposed patterns will be used as an input to the prototype of a privacy portal to Electronic Health Records (EHRs) as future work.

2 Background and Related Work

In human-computer interaction, privacy is defined as the right of individuals to have control over the personal data shared online [3, 4]. Researchers have been studying privacy from different perspectives including privacy-preserving technologies, organizational approaches to serve the ultimate goal, which manages and protects personal information [5]. Privacy engineering can be defined as the effort made to design models, tools, methodologies and technologies embedded in system designs where they guarantee privacy protection depending on applicable laws [6]. The Freedom of Information and Protection of Privacy Act (1990) defines personal information as any recorded information that defines an individual when is disclosed [7].

2.1   Privacy-by-Design and Privacy Enhancing Technologies (PETs)

The International Privacy Commissioners and Data Protection Authorities, Ontario, Canada approved the Privacy-By-Design concept in October 2010 as an "essential component of fundamental privacy protection" [2, 8]. To support the concept of PbD, the proposed privacy patterns should help designers and developers to integrate privacy from the design phase and throughout the development cycle.

Borking [11] defined a PET as a "system of ICT [Information and Communication Technology] measures protecting informational privacy by eliminating or minimizing personal data thereby preventing unnecessary or unwanted processing of personal data, without the loss of the functionality of the information system." The European Commission adopted the same definition in 2007.

New privacy enhancing technologies are introduced to protect the privacy of users and at the same time allow them to share and communicate electronically, e.g. using the Internet. Examples of PETs are: (1) anonymizers[1] (which remove all personal information to preserve users' privacy thus providing users with the ability to browse the Internet without their identity being disclosed [12]); (2) Crowds (which aggregate users into diverse groups to hide personal information [13]). (3) Platform for Privacy Preferences (P3P) (which was designed in a way that helps users understand how their personal information is used by websites; it compares a website privacy policy and a user's privacy policy [14]). Other examples of PETs are 'cut-and-choose' techniques [15], 'onion routing' [16], and Privacy Incorporated Software Agent (PISA)[2].

---

[1] https://www.anonymizer.com.
[2] http://www.tno.nl/instit/fel/pisa.

2.2 Privacy Patterns

PETs are not the same as privacy patterns. PETs solve only one specific privacy problem in already implemented software such as TOR, that applies Onion Routing protocol, which uses many routers to encrypt the requests and process it in many layers, while privacy patterns are considered to be design frameworks and guidelines that can be used in similar contexts [9, 27]. Privacy patterns are structured to state a problem and propose solutions followed by known uses and related or similar patterns. Examples of already existing patterns are described in the sections that follow:

2.2.1 Informed Consent

Informed Consent for Web-Based Transaction Pattern was developed by Romanosky et al. [10]. When collecting personal information, websites often employ so-called cookies. Users are concerned that their personal information would be collected and used without their consent or not want to share their personal information. The problem rests on how designers can have a balance between the reasons for using the PHI and the users' concerns about how their PHI is used. To solve the problem, the web designer has to provide the user with the following elements: disclosure, agreement, comprehension, voluntariness, competence, and minimal distraction.

The pattern has been used in many well-known websites, such as Yahoo!, Google and ehealthinsurance.com during the filling of the registration form. Similar patterns include: informed consent [17, 18], need-to-know [18] and obtaining explicit consent pattern by Porekar et al. [19].

2.2.2 Minimization

A masked online traffic pattern by Romanosky et al. [10] focuses on solving the problem of minimizing the amount of personal information shared over a public network. The pattern uses the following techniques:

- Anonymity Techniques–to help the user to communicate but still be unidentified. Two types of systems can be used: Anonymizing systems, which help users to be completely anonymized to parties, and pseudonymous systems, which help users to not be identified as individuals
- Blocked Requests-to use software tools that block cookies and web bugs that are used to track users

The pattern is used by PET applications to insure anonymity such as Anonymizer (www.anonymizer.com) and Privoxy (www.privoxy.com). Related pattern is minimal Information Asymmetry by Romanosky et al. [10].

2.2.3 Access Data

Porekar et al. [19] designed the Access Control to Sensitive Data Based on Purpose to solve the problem of allowing individuals to be informed of the purpose of collecting information. The user should have the ability to decide which aspect or piece of information a third party should be allowed to have access to. The pattern applies the *Need-to-know*[3] mechanism to limit the amount of sensitive information transmitted to third parties. The pattern provides access to only what the user give permission to be accessed. P3P is well-known use of the pattern [14].

2.2.4   Feedback

Ambient notice by [21] solves the problem when the users' location information is used as a repeated model dialog with or without the users' permission. How can users get notice about every time a service is pulling location information? An ambient notice that appears instantly when location information is retrieved.is considered to be the solution. The notice should provide an opportunity for interaction in terms of permissions. Known uses of the pattern is the location-based service icons used in Mac OS/X where is it shown as a compass arrow that appears in the taskbar every time a software program is used identify the user's location.

Other patterns include outsourcing and non-repudiation by [18], data abstraction by [20] privacy dashboards, private link by [21], and instant user interface for information about personal identification information by [20].

3   Methodology Model

Nova Scotia's Personal Health Information Act (PHIA) was used as a departure point. This is to minimize the gap between the provincial laws and to modalize the laws as there is a gap between laws and technology. We believe this is going to provide more practical and easier understanding of privacy requirements in the very early design stages at a higher level of abstraction.

The process of deriving the proposed privacy patterns relied on both the currently available patterns and the investigation of the legal framework of PHIA to cover individuals' rights. Then, the proposed patterns were analyzed against the principles of ISO29100 Privacy Framework and to be used as design guidelines in the prototype of a privacy web-based EHRs portal.

We believe that the proposed patterns cover all aspects of the PHIA and provide a useful guide that should be implemented by any healthcare privacy-preserving system in Nova Scotia even before the design phase and throughout the design lifecycle. The rights according to PHIA are as follows: request an access, request a correction, request not to disclose Personal Health Information (PHI), being notified if the PHI is lost, stolen or subject to unauthorized access, request a review of company's decision for access or correction and make a complaint if the custodian did not follow the rules of PHIA. The design of the privacy patterns was implemented in the following sequence; designing one privacy pattern for each right; designing privacy patterns for rights that do not have matching or somehow matching patterns; discussing each pattern by explaining the context, problem, proposed solution, and related patterns.

---

[3] Provide users with feedback on collected information [18].

The template we followed in forming the proposed privacy patterns was derived from the Pattern-Oriented Software Architecture (POSA2) outline as a simplified version, which was developed by Bushman et al. [25]. In the following patterns, the term individual refers to the person whose personal health information is the subject of interest, and the term user refers to the professionals who gain access to that information.

4 Results and Discussion

Five privacy patterns are proposed to cover the individuals' rights based on PHIA. Keywords used in the description include: *Custodians:* Health care professionals, Eastern Health, Western Health, Central Health and Labrador-Grenfell Health, Provincial government departments when engaged in health care activities, the Public Health Laboratory, the Newfoundland and Labrador Centre for Health Information, and the Workplace Health and Safety Compensation Commission [22] *Data Subject:* Individuals, *Data Controller/Processor:* Organizations, their agents or both, *Data holder:* Organizations or a third party. The proposed patterns are as following:

4.1 Request an Access

The right assures individuals that they can view or receive a copy of their personal health information and some fees might be applied depending on the organization [1]. The Proposed Privacy Pattern is shown in Fig. 1.

Context: Personal Health Information, according to PHIA, offers individuals the access to information about them that is held by health sector organizations and providers.

Problem: Individuals want to use private healthcare systems that help them access their personal health information. Every individual has the right to have a level of control over the information by gaining access to the information and perform some tasks such as receiving or downloading a copy. Individuals have the right of access to the privacy policy of the organization or the third party that hosts the information.

Factors: Data Subject (DS) and Data Controller (DC).

Solution: To design an efficient privacy pattern, we need to provide transparency where DS can access the PHI. PHI is stored within organizations or on external servers. Users will be able to access the PHI and before that, they need to agree on what is saved on these servers according to their rights provided by the PHIA. As soon as they request access to the information, they need to deal with the consent once and another time after viewing the information to confirm that the information is up-to-date and/or correct. Viewing or delivering a copy of PHI should be limited to what the organization can view or deliver to DS based on the time the data was collected.

Agreement: The user must obtain consent in three situations: for access to the individual's sensitive information (PHI) regardless of where the information is stored; when the individual is being asked to agree to the initial or updated privacy policy of third parties who may host the information; and individuals have to agree on the information stored once individuals gain access. The individual whose PHI is the subject of the requests for consent has the right to opt-out at any time without any consequences.

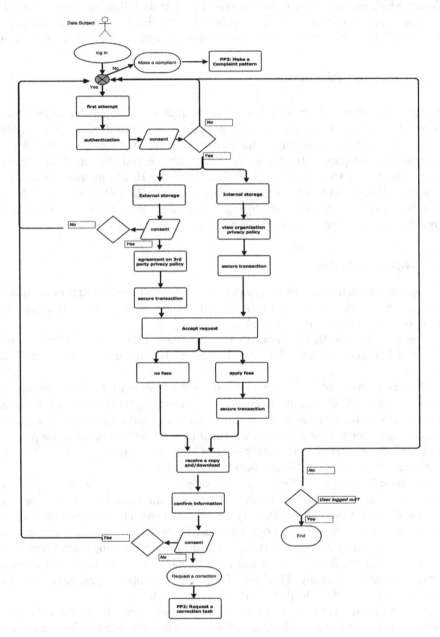

Fig. 1. Request an access proposed privacy pattern

Access Control: the user has to clarify the purpose of accessing the information and security measures have to be applied to download the copy, or they can view the document online (i.e., security patterns). Such controls should allow individuals to have a level of control over the information stored about them.

Feedback: the feedback feature should be applied in every pattern to inform and notify individuals of the ongoing changes either in privacy policies or the changes on the PHI.

Consequences: The proposed pattern applies Need-to-know and Informed Consent to complete the request. We are assuming that the authentication technique is reliable from the security requirements aspect.

Related Patterns: Access control to sensitive data based on purpose by [19] privacy pattern matches the right in one aspect in which the individual has the right to have a level of control over the collected information by providing access to the information. The privacy pattern known as Instant User Interface Pattern by [20] was designed to allow individuals to understand reasons for collecting the information by providing feedback and access to the information collected.

4.2   Request a Correction

Individuals have the right to ask to correct their health information. According to PHIA, the request should be formally written. If a company rejects the request, the individual has the right to file and submit a complaint to the review officer. It is important to transform the hard copies practices into digital forms to serve the ultimate goal of performing privacy patterns that can be considered as guidelines for designing health private system. It is considered as a subtask or follow-up task after requesting access to the PHI. The proposed Privacy Pattern is shown in Fig. 2.

Context: PHIA provides individuals the ability to request corrections if the information they gained access to are not up to date or not correct.

Problem: Individuals have the right to be able to correct the PHI they have on the system.

Solution: The request should be processed through many steps. The individual is asked to confirm a consent form that the entered information is correct. Health providers should review the information before approving it and saving it in the database.

Agreement: Individuals have to sign a consent regarding the changes they will make over the stored information. The changes include correcting the currently existing information or adding more information. The consent will save the individuals' rights and record who made the changes and when.

Review the Changes: It is the healthcare organization's responsibility to review the changes, confirm them and notify the individual's of the result of the review.

Feedback: the feedback feature should be applied in every pattern to inform and notify individuals of the ongoing changes on their PHI.

Consequences: The proposed pattern applies feedback, access control, and informed consent to be able to complete the request.

Related Patterns: Consent to access sensitive data by [19].

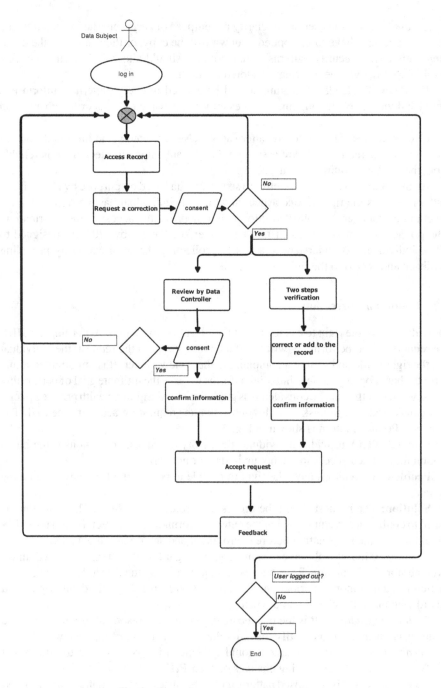

Fig. 2. Request a correction privacy pattern

4.3   Request not to Disclose Personal Health Information (PHI)

Individuals have the rights to request a record of activities in the form of a list of health agents or providers who accessed the online records and minimized access to the information. Therefore, the individual has the right to access, have a list of who accesses the information, and perform a task to limit individuals who can access the information and/ or request not to disclose. The proposed Privacy Pattern as shown in Fig. 3.

Context: The individual under this right is able to gain access to a list of activities carried out on the information (have a list of who accessed the information) and be able to request not to disclose information (choose from the list). The individual agrees on sharing the information with some health agents and organizations but wants to limit the access to a well-identified list of agents.

Problem: The individual wants to balance between what is shared and who can gain access. The second use of information shared between organizations without consent concerns individuals.

Solution: The privacy pattern protects individuals' health information by reducing the agents/organization that can access the PHI. This limits the PHI shared over organizations.

Access Control: DS requests a record of activities that have been done on the PHI regarding the list of agents who accessed the information. The DC retrieves the information either from a third party, which should be gained from an earlier agreement or from the organization server. The DS has the ability to; agree on the list or; limit the list by choosing from the list (blocking some), and request not to disclose at all to any of them.

Authentication: The system applies two-steps identity clarification technique to lock out unauthorized access and/or modification as a security measures we assume that they are applied in the system or through security patterns[4].

Consent: Individuals has to sign a consent form on the responsibilities associated with the task (not to disclose). The DC has to confirm changes and provide feedback. *Feedback:* the feedback feature should be applied in every pattern to inform and notify individuals of the ongoing changes on the new settings.

Consequences: The privacy pattern applies consent and feedback. It is part of the access pattern as the individual has to request access to be able to make the changes provided by this pattern.

Related Patterns: Masked online traffic pattern by [10] allows users to control what information to reveal and minimize the amount of personal health information shared.

Suggestion added to the proposed privacy pattern: Individuals would be able to choose the information that they decide they would like to reveal and mask the rest by providing levels of disclosure. The data abstraction pattern [20] allows individuals to control whom to reveal the information and provide feedback on who has access to the information. Individuals would be able to choose from a list of agents/health providers and control or decide who can access what. Private link pattern [21] works in limiting who can see the personal health information. Instant user Interface by [20] allows individuals to opt in or opt out.

---

[4] Security patterns and measures are out of the scope of this phase of the project.

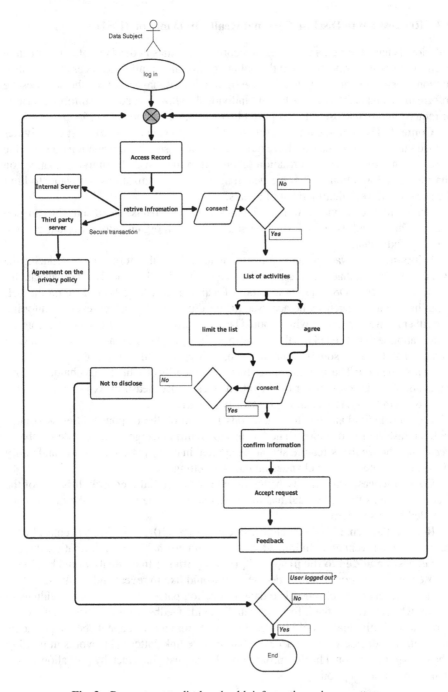

Fig. 3. Request not to disclose health information privacy pattern

The patterns *Being Notified* and *Request a Review* along with the detailed diagrams are in the full tech report [26].

5 Conclusion and Future Work

Six privacy patterns are proposed to cover the individuals' rights. We evaluated the proposed privacy patterns according to ISO29100. We believe that the principles can be mapped to our patterns.

Because the there is a lack of methods to validate privacy patterns and the lack of extensive work on privacy patterns, we will evaluate the proposed privacy patterns according to ISO29100 and the Process Oriented Strategies. To validate our privacy patterns, we compare each pattern to the ISO 29100 privacy framework [24] The ISO 29100 privacy Framework principles include consent and choice, purpose legitimacy and specification, collection limitation, data minimization, use, retention and disclosure limitation, accuracy and quality, openness, transparency and notice, individual participation and access, accountability, information security, privacy compliance.

For further research, these patterns along with design guidelines for the electronic health records portals are going to be used to create the portal's prototype as a second step of the project. The prototype will be tested for its usability and health customers' 'patients' behavior toward the implementation of rights and the level of acceptance.

We have used PHIA as a departure point and focused on the individuals' rights for this stage of the project. The proposed privacy patterns cover these rights and support the Privacy-by-Design concept by providing these privacy design guidelines from the first step of the system lifestyle.

Acknowledgments. This research was supported and funded by the Saudi Cultural Bureau in Ottawa-Saudi Royal Embassy.

References

1. Government Nova Scotia. Personal Health Information Act (2013). http://novascotia.ca/dhw/phia/public.asp
2. Cavoukian, A.: Privacy by design: leadership, methods, and results. In: European Data Protection: Coming of Age, pp. 175–202. Springer, Netherlands (2013)
3. National Research Council: Who goes there? Authentication through the lens of privacy. National Academies Press, Washington, D.C. (2003)
4. OECD: OECD guidelines on the protection of privacy and transborder flows of personal data (1980). http://www.oecd.org/home/
5. Brodie, C., Karat, C.M., Karat, J., Feng, J.: Usable security and privacy: a case study of developing privacy management tools. In: Proceedings of the 2005 Symposium on Usable Privacy and Security, pp. 35–43. ACM, July 2005
6. Guarda, P., Zannone, N.: Towards the development of privacy-aware systems. Inf. Softw. Technol. **51**(2), 337–350 (2009)
7. Office of the Information & privacy commissioner in Nova Scotia (2015). http://foipop.ns.ca
8. http://privacybydesign.ca

9. Chung, E.S., Hong, J.I., Lin, J., Prabaker, M.K., Landay, J.A., Liu, A.L.: Development and evaluation of emerging design patterns for ubiquitous computing. In: Proceedings of the 5th Conference on Designing Interactive Systems: Processes, Practices, Methods, and Techniques, pp. 233–242. ACM, August 2004

10. Romanosky, S., Acquisti, A., Hong, J., Cranor, L.F., Friedman, B.: Privacy patterns for online interactions. In: Proceedings of the 2006 Conference on Pattern Languages Of Programs, p. 12. ACM, October 2006

11. Borking, J.: Deridentity-protector. Datenschutz und Datensicherheit **20**(11), 654–658 (1996)

12. Seničar, V., Jerman-Blažič, B., Klobučar, T.: Privacy-enhancing technologies—approaches and development. Comput. Stan. Interfaces **25**(2), 147–158 (2003)

13. Damiani, M.L.: Privacy enhancing techniques for the protection of mobility patterns in LBS: research issues and trends. In: European Data Protection: Coming of Age, pp. 223–239. Springer Netherlands (2013)

14. W3C, Platform for Privacy Preferences, P3P 1.0 (2002). http://www.w3.org/P3P/

15. Chaum, D., Fiat, A., Naor, M.: Untraceable electronic cash. In: Goldwasser, S. (ed.) CRYPTO 1988. LNCS, vol. 403, pp. 319–327. Springer, Heidelberg (1990)

16. Communication COM (2007) 228: from the Commission to the European Parliament and the Council. On Promoting Data Protection by Privacy Enhancing Technologies (PETs) (2007)

17. Fischer-Hübnner, S., Köffel, C., Pettersson, J.-S., Wolkerstorfer, P., Graf, C., Holtz, L.E., König, U., Hedbom, H., Kellermann, B.: Prime Life (2010). http://primelife.ercim.eu/images/stories/deliverables/d4.1.3-hci_pattern_collection_v2-public.pdf

18. Compagna, L., El Khoury, P., Krausová, A., Massacci, F., Zannone, N.: How to integrate legal requirements into a requirements engineering methodology for the development of security and privacy patterns. Artif. Intell. Law **17**(1), 1–30 (2009)

19. Porekar, J., Jerman-Blazic, A., Klobucar, T.: Towards organizational privacy patterns. In: 2008 Second International Conference on the Digital Society, pp. 15–19. IEEE, February 2008

20. Bier, C., Krempel, E.: Common privacy patterns in video surveillance and smart energy. In: 2012 7th International Conference on Computing and Convergence Technology (ICCCT), pp. 610–615. IEEE, December 2012

21. Privacypatterns.org, accessed 2015. http://privacypatterns.org/patterns/

22. Department of Health and Community Services (2015). http://www.health.gov.nl.ca/health/phia/

23. Personal Health Information Act, Department of Health and Community Services (2014). http://assembly.nl.ca/Legislation/sr/statutes/p07-01.htm

24. ISO/IEC 29100. Information technology–Security techniques–Privacy framework. Technical report, ISO JTC 1/SC 27

25. Buschmann, F., Meunier, R., Rohnert, H., Sommerlad, P., Stal, M.: Pattern-Oriented Software Architecture. John Wiley, Chichester (1996)

26. The tech report is named CS-2016-01 and available at: https://www.cs.dal.ca/research/techreports/cs-2016-01

27. Dingledine, R., Mathewson, N., Syverson, P.: Tor: the second-generation onion router. In: Proceedings of the 13th USENIX Security Symposium (2004)

Information Security Application Design: Understanding Your Users

Ranjan Bhattarai[✉], Ger Joyce, and Saurabh Dutta

Rapid7, 100 Summer Street, Boston, MA 02110, USA
{rbhattarai,gjoyce,sdutta}@rapid7.com

Abstract. The basis of Human-Centered Design is the understanding of users' goals and needs. One way to empathize with users is to create Personas. Yet, traditional methods of creating Personas are time-consuming. In this work, members of the Rapid7 User Experience team illustrate how they have quickly created Personas using the Proto-Persona method. The method, which encapsulates a collective set of beliefs that an organization has about their users, enabled our organization to capture stories of 80 characters. Refining these during the process, resulted in 16 Proto-Personas, which were visualized within a Persona Ecosystem. This Ecosystem, and the Personas within, has allowed Rapid7 to design the right Information Security applications for the right users at the right time.

Keywords: Personas · Proto-Persona · Agile · User research

1 Introduction

Understanding users' goals and needs is the basis of Human-Centered Design [1]. Yet, many application design decisions are made without this understanding [2, 3]. The need for empathy led to the development of Personas [4], which are fictitious representations of users [5]. There are many advantages offered by Personas, including the effective communication about users and their needs [6], as well as their ability to guide decision making [7].

Personas, while fictitious, are generally created from upfront research. However, one of relatively recent challenges to design teams is that Agile software development processes are much faster than older software development approaches. Therefore, researchers and designers have less time for user-centered activities [8, 9], including the comprehensive research needed to create rich Personas. The contribution of this work is to unveil the process implemented at Rapid7, an Information Security application provider, which was modelled on the Proto-Persona approach pioneered by Gothelf and Seiden [10].

2 Related Work

Since their introduction in the late 1990's, Personas have been a topic of debate among Human-Computer Interaction (HCI) researchers and practitioners. Cooper [4], like many others, has argued that Personas are necessary, as many organizations' products are not empathetic to users' needs and goals [11, 12]. This lack of empathy often results

© Springer International Publishing Switzerland 2016
T. Tryfonas (Ed.): HAS 2016, LNCS 9750, pp. 103–113, 2016.
DOI: 10.1007/978-3-319-39381-0_10

in frustrated customers and even failed businesses. Consequently, many researchers have come to the defense of Personas. For instance, researchers have argued that Personas can help pinpoint the actual types of users of a product [13], as well as ensuring that the right problems are being addressed [14]. The Personas can then be shared within the organization [15], which allows for the user to be brought to the forefront, resulting in designs built specifically for the right type of user [16, 17]. With these arguments in favor of Personas, many organizations have begun to utilize the method within their design process [18].

However, not all HCI researchers and practitioners are enthusiastic about Personas. When Pruitt & Adlin, [19] state that Personas have an element of fiction, other researchers argue that this is a reason why many HCI researchers and practitioners cannot relate Personas to real people [20]. This became an issue for Blomquist & Arvola [21] when they found that the participants in a study were uncomfortable using Personas. Yet, while Personas can have an element of fiction, they need to be grounded in research, otherwise they will not be effective. Unfortunately, being grounded in research does not always transpire [22, 23], and this can cause distrust of Personas among HCI researchers and practitioners [24].

Further concerns regarding Personas have been raised by Nielsen [20], who argues that there is no typical understanding of Personas, subsequently each organization and HCI team essentially creates and uses Personas their way with no standards in place. For example, while a common understanding of Personas is that they help with design [7], researchers have found that Personas might not be used for design at all, and instead can simply be used for communication [25]. Even with Personas, designers continue to express their own desires and subjective views, occasionally rarely referring to Personas, which defeats the purpose of creating the Personas in the first place [26]. Yet, despite these concerns Personas remain a popular method of Human-Centered Design [15].

One of the primary gaps in our knowledge regarding Personas revolves around much of the Literature focusing on traditional Persona development. For instance, Mulder & Yaar [27] concentrate on time-consuming upfront quantitative and qualitative user research that eventually lead to Personas. Thus, the development of Personas within fast-paced Agile environments, as advocated by Ambler [28] and Leffingwell [29], such as Ad-hoc Personas and Proto-Personas, is currently under-represented within the Literature. Until this research has been completed, we are left to wonder if accurate, useful Personas can be developed quickly, and still be useful for design teams to build the right product, at the right time, for the right user.

3 Alternatives to Traditional Approaches

Alternative approaches to Persona creation, such as Proto-Personas [10, 30] and Ad-Hoc Personas [31], were proposed to enable organizations to quickly take steps towards understanding users. While not a replacement to the research-driven Persona creation, these methods can still be effective and can be a catalyst for an organization to adopt a customer centric point of view.

Norman [31] conveyed that while Ad-Hoc Personas "…are created quickly, …do not use real data, and…are employed without much background information and attention to detail.", they were still useful in generating empathy and enabling a user or a customer point of view.

Gothelf [30] proposed the Proto-Persona method, which can encapsulate a collective set of beliefs that an organization has about their users. These collective beliefs can then be validated. A significant difference between the Proto-Persona method and the traditional method driven by research data, is that the Proto-Persona method enables participation and contribution by a diverse group of stakeholders across the organization. Not only does this result in a strong cross-sectional contribution, but involvement in the creation process fosters early buy-in and support during persona rollout. Another benefit of this method is the rapid surfacing of differing and conflicting beliefs about the customer/user. These differences are successively discussed, probed, and resolved. Similarly, this method also illuminates areas of strong agreement. The overall output of this method is a set of Proto-Persona that reflect a reasoned set of hypothesis that can be validated against the real world data. This remainder of this work focuses on the use of the Proto-Persona method within Rapid7.

4   Proto-Persona Method

The development of Proto-Personas is at its core a moderated working session. The session produces a host of artifacts that capture the individual and the group's beliefs about users. After the working session, one or more HCI practitioners digitize and synthesize the materials, and present them back to the group to ensure continued alignment.

4.1   Before the Session

It is critical to ensure that a diverse group of individuals representing a wide cross-section of the organization are selected for this kind of session. The most important requirement, other than time commitment, is the fact that participants interact with the organization's customers in some form. However, potential participants must be screened. The danger of simply inviting eager individuals is that a substantial amount of opinion-based data might be collected. While this will occur regardless of the screening process, this should be minimized by inviting individuals who currently or in the past have had direct contact with customers.

4.2   During the Session

The moderator kicks off the session with a short presentation that covers the purpose of the session, the various sections, the amount of time the team is expected to spend on each session, and the expected output at the end of the session. The moderator also introduces the team to each of the various sections of the session at a high level with examples of output associated to each section from other sessions. Additionally, the moderator ensures all of the cross-functional teams represented in the session are called out to emphasize one of the core purposes of the session– namely, cross-functional collaboration and alignment to better understand and serve the organization's users. Finally, before commencing the session, the moderator pauses for, and answers, any questions participants might have.

Gothelf [30] suggests two 3-hr working sessions, ideally one session a week, and conducted within two consecutive weeks. Our team found it logistically difficult follow this model as many participants were not co-located, and needed to travel to attend the session. Instead, we opted for one, slightly longer working session (about five hours with breaks), during which we were able to achieve all our goals.

We also conducted three separate rounds of Proto-Persona sessions at three different locations that develop three different product lines. We fully understood that participants in each location would be focused on their product lines, but we wanted to capture the widest variety of perspectives and beliefs within our organization. After analysis of all of the characters from the sessions, we began to see recurring themes and that the personas behaviors, beliefs, needs and goals transcended product lines.

The Proto-Persona session has 3 parts: Character Development, Meet the Cast, and Character Refinement. From our experience running these sessions, a break before Character Refinement is needed and appreciated by participants (Fig. 1).

Fig. 1. A cross functional team working through Character Development part of the session. We conducted three separate sessions across our offices to accommodate wider participation.

Part 1: Character Development. During the Character Development section of the Proto-Persona process, all participants write down their beliefs about customers or product users. A character development worksheet is critical for this process (see Fig. 2). The moderator shows a sample completed worksheet, and distributes blank worksheets to all participants. The moderator then asks the participants to reflect back on one or more interactions with customers and/or users, and to write down their understanding of the customer/user's needs, beliefs, behaviors, and goals. The moderator also clarifies that participants can create as many characters as they wish.

The worksheet is a letter-sized piece of paper divided into quadrants. In the top left quadrant, **Biography and Picture**, participants list a set of salient customer/user characteristics. In the bottom left quadrant, **Demographics**, participants fill in more details about the character that shed. In the top right quadrant, **Behaviors and Beliefs**, participants showcase what the character believes in and what he/she does. Finally, in the

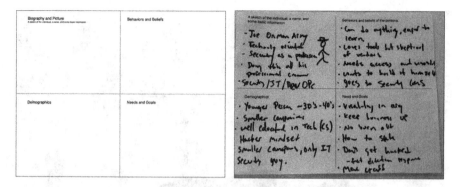

Fig. 2. A side by side view of the Persona Worksheet before and after it was filled in by participants.

bottom right quadrant, **Needs and Goals**, participants list what the character wants to ultimately achieve.

In all sessions, we have found that exhibiting a completed worksheet help participants understand how to populate their worksheets. We have also had to remind our participants to go beyond product specific enhancements and postulate the reasons behind such enhancements.

Part 2: Meet the Cast. Meet the Cast is the part of the process where participants introduce their characters to the rest of the group. This is a particularly exciting time in the session, as this is most likely the first time participants have written or spoken about the user or customer in this way. Before commencing this part of the session, the moderator reminds participants to introduce the character(s) they have developed similar to how they might introduce a friend at a party. The focus on storytelling enables participants to move away from worrying about the beauty of the artifact, such as the legibility of their handwriting, focusing instead on the story of the character they are introducing. The moderator requests that participants stand in front of the wall labeled "Meet the Cast" as they introduce their character(s). Once a participant is finished introducing their character(s), the participant affixes their completed worksheet(s) on the wall. As this process unfolds, the entire wall is covered by various characters and their stories.

During Meet the Cast we observed that, regardless of their functional background within the organization, all participants generated multiple characters, and were visibly excited to share the stories of each character. As participants told their stories, many within the group verbally agreed with the points made– which were the first signs of alignment. The storytelling also helped humanize, and began to generate empathy for, the characters. (Fig. 3)

Part 3: Character Refinement. Character Refinement is the most challenging step in the Proto-Persona process. Character Refinement demands strong focus from both the moderator as well as all participants. Allowing participants to take a break before this step enables enhanced focus during this final part of the process. During the Character Refinement phase, the group identifies similar characters, merging each into one

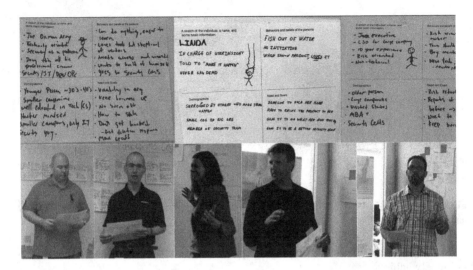

Fig. 3. A snapshot of a Meet the Cast presentation and a sample of its accompanying artifacts

character, thus effectively reducing the overall data. At the request of participants, the moderator will group similar characters by either physically moving the worksheets into a group, or by using a colored post-it note to indicate similarities. Should disagreements arise within the group during the Character Refinement phase, dialogue is encouraged within the group to resolve differences. Initial focus on easy-to-solve disagreements enables constant forward movement while avoiding larger disputes. The end goal is to get to a manageable number of characters, with a view to start considering each Proto-Persona's attributes. With attributes defined and measured, further opportunities arise for Character Refinement.

To that end, the next step involves identifying what those key attributes might be, and to plot those on an abstract scale. Based on the character stories, a few key attributes will naturally emerge. Should this not be the case, the moderator can kick start this process, by using demographic information, such as years of experience or technological fluency, and asking the group to consider if these attributes are significant for the business. In one of our sessions, the group felt that the number of years of experience did not domain expertise. Therefore, the group amended this attribute appropriately. In another session, the group thought that the personality of the character, introverted/extroverted, was a significant attribute to consider. Having defined each attribute, the group measured each on an attribute scale from 0 to 5. Once again, disagreements were resolved through dialogue.

It is important to clarify with the participants that the attribute scale and the numbers plotted are not absolute values. The attribute scale establishes a relative degree of sophistication and enables comparison between two Proto-Personas on a same attribute. In all our sessions a 0 was synonymous with none and a 5 was the ultimate sophistication on that attribute. Often, we found that participants had a difficult time agreeing on a specific number along the attribute scale. As discussions unfolded, participants proposed a range for a particular attribute (see Fig. 4). Participants considered a single digit to be overly simplistic, resulting in an incorrect reflection of the diverse user population the group was attempting to serve. For example, we used a range, 3 to 5, instead of a specific number to capture a security knowledge of an executive proto-persona.

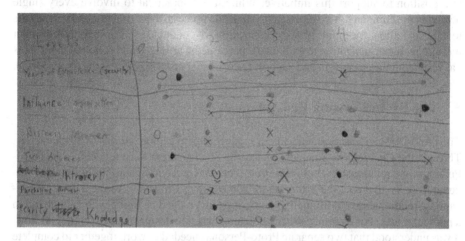

Fig. 4. The moderator plotted the metrics along an abstract scale. Each participant choose a color and a symbol like an "x" or "o" or a "dot" to represent the character they were plotting against. One can also see how the need for range was expressed by connecting lines between symbols.

A key point to remember is that both the attributes and the attribute scale are hypotheses, and are subject to change based on field research. The focus during this part of the session should be on narrowing down of the characters and continued alignment among the participants.

4.3 After the Session

While the Proto-Persona session can be exciting, and at times challenging, participants walk away with a sense of accomplishment, as well as with a shared point of view about the types of customers or users that exist. For the moderator and the HCI practitioners present, the next step is to rapidly digitize, analyze, and synthesize learnings. Having a follow-up shorter session within one week with the original participants enables the presentation of the digitized Proto-Personas. This, in turn, enables final agreement, ensures momentum, and continued focus on the overall Proto-Persona initiative. While it is not necessary for participants to meet in person during the follow-up session, it is important that all Proto-Persona artifacts be available in digital format for further discussions.

4.4 Follow Up Sessions

One should fully anticipate changes and not fall into the trap of finalizing Proto-Personas, or converting them as Personas without research from the field. After the Proto-Persona session and additional analysis, key characters will emerge as important to the organization. These characters are the ones that should be vetted with the original participants in a follow-up session to ensure that the team agrees on the synthesis.

Another area of follow-up are key executives and stakeholders who ultimately are in a position to support this initiative. While it is impractical to involve every single person in the company, it is important to share the process, the artifacts and the synthesis to date, and allow for input. In our organization we conducted multiple rounds of input throughout the organization to explain the process, the artifacts, and solicited input. This has resulted in larger buy-in and support from a wider cross-section of the organization.

5   The Proto-Persona Ecosystem

The Proto-Persona sessions enabled our organization to capture stories of 80 characters. Through the Character Refinement phase, the 80 characters were reduced to 16 Proto-Personas. As relationships between Proto-Personas were not clear, an Ecosystem was developed. To that end, the Proto-Persona Ecosystem allowed us to see a basic organizational relationship. Additionally, the Ecosystem enabled us to see who is involved in a particular task. For example, when our team wished to design an easy setup workflow, it was understood that two separate Proto-Personas needed to work together to complete the task. This was not a question of whether one Proto-Persona was primary and the other secondary, rather, it was the understanding that the workflow needed to account for both Proto-Personas. The ability to expose this level of interconnection between Proto-Personas via the Ecosystem helped us demonstrate the need to really understand the users involved in many of the complex workflows.

Fig. 5. Example of a Persona Ecosystem used to demonstrate the organizational hierarchy. In many companies some of these roles outlined are performed by one individual, while some organizations have multiple individuals performing one role.

The Proto-Persona Ecosystem is not part of the Proto-Persona method. The authors arrived at this communication tool as we saw a need an opportunity to provide more clarity around the hierarchy and the interconnectedness between Proto-Personas in a single view. The ecosystem also allowed us to capture the prevailing hypothesis of how inter-dependent our customers are within their organization's functional groups. (Fig. 5)

6 Conclusion

This paper summarized the Proto-Persona methodology, and how the method can enable organizations to jump start the process of better understanding their customers and users. Specifically, Proto-Persona sessions align internal points of view to arrive at a set of testable hypotheses about a customer or a user. These hypotheses can then be further validated, adjusted, and refined based on field data. The paper also introduced the Proto-Persona Ecosystem that visually demonstrates a Proto-Persona's organizational hierarchy and inter-dependence with others.

Another aspect of the Proto-Persona method is inclusiveness. Unlike the traditional methodology, where much of the process, data, and analysis stay within the purview of a small group of researchers, Proto-Persona methodology enables participation from a cross-functional team from the beginning. This fosters an early buy-in, confidence in the process, and a sense of collective ownership of the output. These factors are beneficial when Personas are rolled out to larger audiences within the organization.

While this paper focused primarily on the methodology, further validation, socialization, and use of Personas during product and service decisions is the ultimate goal. Validation is a continuous process and as new attributes are discovered, these need to be captured, analyzed, and applied to the appropriate persona.

Socialization of Personas within the organization is another challenging, yet critical step that requires a careful rollout strategy. In our experience, this requires numerous rounds of education, evangelization, and feedback sessions at various levels. We recommend starting with the Proto-Persona session participants, as these individuals are well positioned to provide additional context to the team and can also become a point of contact when questions arise.

As product teams embark on their daily work, it is essential that as a part of the rollout strategy, a wide variety of artifacts such as Persona posters, cards, and slides are generated and made visible across office locations, and electronic copies be shared as widely as possible. Ultimately, Personas are tools, and regardless of the method used to generate them, their goal is to enable organizations and teams to make product and service decisions from a customer or user point of view.

References

1. Kim, J.W.: Human computer interaction. Ahn graph (2012)
2. Dahl, D.W., Chattopadhyay, A., Gorn, G.J.: The use of visual imagery in new product design. J. Mark. Res. **36**(1), 18–28 (1999)
3. Wiegers, K., Beatty, J.: Software Requirements. Pearson Education, New York (2013)

4. Cooper, A.: The Inmates Are Running the Asylum: Why High Tech Products Drive Us Crazy and How to Restore the Sanity. Macmillan, London (1999)

5. Adlin, T., Pruitt, J.: The Essential Persona Lifecycle: Your Guide to Building and Using Personas: Your Guide to Building and Using Personas. Morgan Kaufmann, Burlington (2010)

6. Ma, J., LeRouge, C.: Introducing user profiles and personas into information systems development. In: Proceedings of the Americas Conference on Information Systems, AIS (2007)

7. Long, F.: Real or imaginary? the effectiveness of using personas in product design. In: Proceedings of the Irish Ergonomics Society Annual Conference, pp. 1–10. Irish Ergonomics Society (2009)

8. Haikara, J.: Usability in agile software development: extending the interaction design process with personas approach. In: Concas, G., Damiani, E., Scotto, M., Succi, G. (eds.) XP 2007. LNCS, vol. 4536, pp. 153–156. Springer, Heidelberg (2007)

9. Humayoun, S.R., Dubinsky, Y., Catarci, T.: User evaluation support through development environment for agile software teams. In: Smart Organizations and Smart Artifacts, pp. 183–191 (2014)

10. Gothelf, J., Seiden, J.: Lean UX: Applying Lean Principles to Improve User Experience. O'Reilly Media Inc., Sebastopol (2013)

11. Gulliksen, J., Goransson, B., Boivie, I., Blomkvist, S., Persson, J., Cajander, A.: Key principles for user-centered systems design. Behav. Inf. Technol. **22**(6), 397–409 (2003)

12. Schaffer, E.: Institutionalization of usability. Pearson Education, Boston (2004)

13. Hourihan, M.: Taking the "you" out of user: my experience using personas. Boxes and Arrows (2004). http://www.boxesandarrows.com/archives/taking_the_you_out_of_user_my_experience_using_personas.php. Accessed 21 Jan 2016

14. Negru, S., Buraga S.: Towards a conceptual model for describing the personas methodology. In: Proceedings of the ICCP 2012. IEEE (2012)

15. Junior, P.T.A., Filgueiras, L.V.L.: User modeling with personas. In: Proceedings of the 2005 Latin American Conference on Human-Computer Interaction, pp. 277–282, ACM (2005)

16. Goodwin, K.: Perfecting your personas. Cooper Interact. Des. (2004). http://www.cooper.com/newsletters/2001_07/perfecting_your_personas.htm. Accessed 1 Feb 2016

17. Miaskiewicz, T., Kozar, K.A.: Personas and user-centered design: how can personas benefit product design processes? Des. Stud. **32**(5), 417–430 (2011)

18. Manning, H., Temkin, B., Belanger, N.: The power of design personas. Forrester Res. (2003). http://www.forrester.com/ER/Research/Report/0,1338,33033,00.html. Accessed 14 Jan 2016

19. Pruitt, J., Adlin, T.: The persona lifecycle: keeping people in mind throughout product design. Morgan Kaufmann, Burlington (2010)

20. Nielsen, L.: Personas - User Focused Design. Springer Science & Business Media, London (2012)

21. Blomquist, Å., Arvola, M.: Personas in action: ethnography in an interaction design team. In: Proceedings of the Second Nordic Conference on Human-Computer Interaction, pp. 197–200. ACM (2002)

22. McQuaid, H.L., Goel, A., McManus, M.: When you can't talk to customers: using storyboards and narratives to elicit empathy for users. In: Proceedings of the 2003 International Conference on Designing Pleasurable Products and Interfaces, pp. 120–125. ACM (2003)

23. Chang, Y., Lim, Y., Stolterman, E.: Personas: From Theory to Practices. Proceedings of the Building Bridges, pp. 439–442. ACM, (2008)

24. Chapman, C.N., Milham, R.P.: The persona's new clothes: methodological and practical arguments against a popular method. In: Proceedings of the Human Factors and Ergonomics Society, HFES, pp. 634–636 (2006)

25. Matthews, T., Judge, T., Whittaker, S.: How do designers and user experience professionals actually perceive and use personas? In: Proceedings of the SIGCHI Conference on Human Factors in Computing Systems, pp. 1219–1228. ACM (2012)

26. Friess, E.: The sword of data: does human-centered design fulfill its rhetorical responsibility? Des. Issues **26**(3), 40–50 (2010)

27. Mulder, S., Yaar, Z.: The User is Always Right: A Practical Guide to Creating and Using Personas for the Web. New Riders, San Francisco (2006)

28. Ambler, S.: Tailoring usability into agile software development projects. In: Law, E., Hvannberg, E., Cockton, G. (eds.) Maturing Usability Quality in Software, Interaction and Value, pp. 75–95. Springer, Heidelberg (2008)

29. Leffingwell, D.: Agile Software Requirements: Lean Requirements Practices for Teams, Programs, and the Enterprise. Addison-Wesley Professional, Boston (2010)

30. Gothelf, J.: Using proto-personas for executive alignment. UX Mag. **821** (2012). https://uxmag.com/articles/using-proto-personas-for-executive-alignment. Accessed 21, Feb 2016

31. Norman, D.: Ad-Hoc Personas and Empathetic Focus (2004). http://www.jnd.org/dn.mss/personas_empath.html. Accessed 27 Feb 2016

Responsibility Modelling and Its Application Trust Management

Andrew Blyth[✉]

Information Security Research Group (ISRG), Faculty of Computing,
Engineering and Science, University of South Wales-Pontypridd,
RCT, Pontypridd CF37 1DL, UK
andrew.blyth@southwales.ac.uk

Abstract. A narrative of trust can be constructed via an explicative dialog that views trust as both a technical and social construct. From a technical viewpoint trust can be measured in-terms of reliability and dependability, while from a socio standpoint trust can be viewed as (a) the Need to trust, trust based on Identification, trust based on Competence and finally trust based on Evidence. In this paper we will develop a socio-technical model of trust that utilises the concepts of responsibilities and roles so as to link the technical and social aspects of trust into a single inductive logical framework. A role can be viewed from a structural and functional perspective allowing us to express the concepts of behaviour and within a socio-technical system and to logically reason about. We will further develop a logic graphical model of responsibility using both causal and consequential modal operators. From this model we will explore the relationship between the elements of a tasks execution and the actions communication associated with a task and hence a responsibility. We will use this logical model to show how a argument of consistency can be constructed and from that a measure of trust within a socio-technical construct derived.

1 Introduction

Socio-Technical systems (STS) in organisational development is an approach to complex organisational work design that recognises the interaction between people and technology in workplaces [3,5]. By socio-technical systems we mean people (individuals, groups, roles and organisations), physical equipment (buildings, surroundings, etc.), hardware and software, laws and regulations that accompany the organisations (eg. laws for the protection of privacy), data (what data are kept, in which formats, who has access to them, where they are kept) and procedures (official and unofficial processes, data flows, relationships, in general anything that describes how things work, or better should work in an organisation) [4].

The target is to construct a framework that will allow us to reason about the level of trust as a stateful model on a socio - technical systems level so as to better capture the dynamics of a cybernetic organisation and its state of affairs. It is in the cybernetic organisations nature that we can find the arguments for the need

© Springer International Publishing Switzerland 2016
T. Tryfonas (Ed.): HAS 2016, LNCS 9750, pp. 114–127, 2016.
DOI: 10.1007/978-3-319-39381-0_11

of a more social approach, as they are biological as much as they are artificial. Within the context of responsibility modelling and Socio-Technical systems we can define trust as follows:

Trust is a particular assessment of an agent or group of agents will fulfil a responsibility.

The socio - technical systems (STS) have as a main target to blend both the technical and the social systems in an organisation [9,10]. That is considered necessary as both aspects are of equal importance but independently, optimal arrangements for both might not be applicable and trade offs are required [3]. We will use stateful models to express the status quo of an organisation, i.e. the current state of the systems, personnel and processes at each discrete moment before and after an event has occurred. This is going to give us a better perspective of the dependencies, responsibilities and finally reliabilities that run through the entire hierarchical chain of an organisation. Thus it will allow us to be able to run different threat scenarios and detect the potential vulnerabilities in a corporate network through forward and backward chaining and thus to identify when trust is compromised.

2   Bakground

Socio - technical systems are focusing on the groups as working units of interaction that are capable of either linear cause - effect relationships, or non - linear ones more complex and unpredictable [3]. They are adaptable to the constantly changing environment and the complexity that lies in the heart of most organisations. The concept of tasks, their owners, their meaningfulness and the entire responsibility modelling as well as the dependencies are also a big part of this theory. In this study we treat people and systems as actors of certain tasks over a state of affairs. They are agents that comply with the same rules and norms, when it comes to the way they operate and interact with other agents for the accomplishment of a state of affairs. By agents we mean individuals, groups of people or systems that hold roles and thus responsibilities for the execution or maintenance of certain tasks with certain objectives.

Along with the socio - technical systems approach we will use Role Theory on the agents as each one of them in an organisation fulfils some roles in association with certain states of affairs [11]. Role Theory emphasises the fact that roles are basically sets of rights and responsibilities, expectations, behaviours or expected behaviours and norms. Peoples behaviour in organisations is bounded by specific context subject to both social and legal compliance, depending on their position in the hierarchy. The objective of this is to be able to assist the performance of Responsibility Modelling on the socio - technical systems [2], to analyse their internal structure, the responsibility flows and the dependabilities. This will provide us with the necessary information and structure upon which we can apply scenarios that simulate behaviours deviating from the expected (e.g. attack scenarios), along with logical rules that best describe the organisation at hand, its expected behaviour and targets and that will allow us to locate vulnerabilities in the supply chain and express cause and effect, in case anything changes to the environment beyond expectation.

Different types of threats and countermeasures, different exposures, the variety of information and the heterogeneous data make it hard to manage risk. Thus, it is clear that, given the level of complexity of Information Systems Security (ISS) risk management, simple linear models as proposed in most of the existing approaches will not be able to capture such complexities. [4]. For this reason, we suggest the socio - technical systems approach combined with Role Theory and eventually Responsibility and Interaction Modelling, as we think it works much better than linear models and is far more capable of mapping down the complex relationships that more realistically represent organisations of any size. It is the nature of the information they provide that makes them appropriate for impact assessment and vulnerability analysis.

3   Expressing and Modelling Responsibilities

Responsibility modelling is the analysis and design technique of the responsibilities within an organisation with the purpose of exploring the internal structure and the dependabilities in the socio - technical system [2]. It is one way of exploring the relationships amongst personnel, technical infrastructure, resources and business processes. What is interesting is that the risk associated with any deviation from the expected behaviour can be explored. In the event of an unanticipated change, a before and after analysis can determine what effect the event had on the socio - technical system. In this situation, applying vulnerability analysis will help illustrate the systems strengths and weaknesses and reveal the associated risks.

According to dictionary definitions, responsibility has two meanings:

- The state of having a duty to deal with a certain state of affairs.
- The state of being accountable or to blame for a certain state of affairs.

The first case has a causal connotation meaning the agent has the responsibility for doing something - making an event happen. The second case has a connotation of blame between the actual action and the results of it but does not necessarily imply causality for the agent held accountable. For example, the parents are held responsible for the actions of their children. As a result, two types of responsibilities can be distinguished, a causal responsibility and a consequential responsibility [2]. For instance, each member of a crew of a ship or a plane is causally responsible for the performance of certain tasks but the captain or the pilot is always consequently responsible for the state of the ship or plane. Within the context of a responsibility we can explore the following:

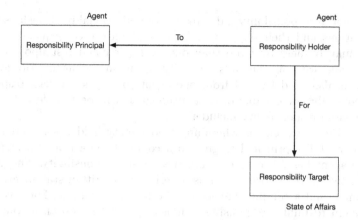

Fig. 1. A responsibility model

- Role assignment: All roles must be executed by am agent and that agent must have had the role assigned to it.
- Role Authorisation: An agent must be authorised by another agent to take on a specific role.
- Rights and Mode Authorisation: A agent can only engage in the usage of an right/mode on the context of a role that they are authorised to execute.

Responsibility is associated with agents, resources and tasks as defined in the Ontology for a Socio-Technical Systems Model (See Fig. 2), and it is defined as the duty from one agent (the responsible) to another (the authority or principal) for the accomplishment of a state of affairs, whether this is the execution, maintenance or avoidance of certain tasks, subject to conformance with the organisational culture (Fig. 2). Thus the characteristics of a responsibility consist of: who is responsible to whom, for what state of affairs, which are the obligations of the responsibility holder in order to fulfil his responsibility and what type of responsibility it is [2]. There are two type of agents that can exist within a socio-technical system: (a) a human and (b) a computer system.

- Causal responsibility lies effectively between one agent and a state of affairs, while the consequential responsibility is a three way relationship between two agents and a state of affairs. In this case the agent who holds the responsibility can be held accountable, culpable or liable to the authority agent as seen in Fig. 2. Apparently, the most important part of the diagram for the consequential responsibility is the relationship between two agents as the most important question to be answered is who is responsible to whom and in what respect?. On the other hand, for the causal responsibility the most important part is the relationship between the agent and the task as the most important question to be answered is who is responsible for this action?. Causal responsibility is a dynamic behavioural relationship between an agent and a state of affairs.

- Consequential responsibility indicates the organisational relationships with in organisations and their objectives. Due to its nature consequential responsibility may be held by more than one agent, it could rest upon an entire organisation, whereas the causal usually lies upon one agent. However, the latter can also be delegated from one agent to another, causal responsibility is normally not capable of that although it can be transferred. Type of consequential responsibility include:
  - *Accountability.* This is where an responsibility holder is required by the responsibility principal to give an account of the actions through which the agent has failed to discharged a causal responsibility. This account can take various forms such as a verbal or a written statement. Both a human and a computer agent can be held accountable. For a computer system to fulfil a responsibility it is required to keep an account of its actions.
  - *Liability.* This is where an responsibility holder is required the responsibility principal to be liable for some form of recompense with regard to the failure to causal responsibility. The liability typically take the form of some resource, such as money, that is given to the responsibility agent that the failure of the responsibility holder has impacted upon. Both a human and a computer agent can be held liability. However for a computer system to fulfil a liability it is required to have an understanding of the resources that are at stake and the implications of the loss of these resources so that informed actions can be taken. A key distinction between a human and a computer is that a computer can only be held liable for informed actions, where as a human can only be held liable for both informed and uninformed actions.
  - *Culpability.* This is where an responsibility holder is required by the responsibility principal to be culpable of the actions through which the agent has failed to discharged a causal responsibility. Culpability typically take the form of blameworthiness and results in the withdrawal of some right from the responsibility holder. Typical forms of culpability resulted in the imprisonment of the responsibility holder. A computer system can not be held culpable and punish as a computer system has no social, moral and ethical framework within which to understand culpability.

The key distinctions between a causal responsibility and a consequential are:

- Within causal responsibility only a single agent can hold a responsibility, where within consequential responsibility multiple agents can hold a responsibility.
- Within causal responsibility the responsibility target is a state of affairs representing a up-set of the state of affairs. Where as with consequential responsibility the responsibility target is the definition of a role relationship between two agents.

4   Sematics of an STS Model

In order to reason about a socio—technical system (STS) model we need to be able to express the semantics of the model such that a variety of modal action logic operators can be utilised. To express the semantics of a socio—technical model we make use of a Kripke Frame, [13, 14] $\langle W, R \rangle$, where W is a non-empty set defining a set of possible worlds or state of affairs, and R is a binary relation on W such that $R \subseteq W \times W$. The relation R is formed from the interactions that a role holder performs in moving an organisation from one possible world w_1 to the next w_2. Elements in W are called worlds and R is known as the accessibility relation.

A Kripke Frame utilises a possible world semantic model to express reasoning constructs. From a socio—technical system we can say that elements of W can include:

- Responsibility Types and Responsibilities.
- Agents, Roles and Resources.
- Access Rights.

A Kripke Model/Structure is a triple $\langle W, R, \Vdash \rangle$ where $\langle W, R \rangle$ is a Kripke Frame and $\Vdash$ is a relation between nodes and formulas, and is called the labelling function, such that:

$$w \Vdash \neg A \text{ if and only if } w \nVdash A$$
$$w \Vdash A \to B \text{ if and only if } w \nVdash A$$
$$\text{or } w \Vdash B$$
$$w \Vdash \Box A \text{ if and only if } u \Vdash A \text{ for all}$$
$$u \text{ suchthat } wRu \tag{1}$$

From a definitional perspective we can read $w \Vdash A$ as meaning *"w satisfies A"*, *"A is satisfied in w"*, or *"w forces A"*. The relation is called the *satisfaction relation, evaluation*, or *forcing relation*. The satisfaction relation is uniquely determined by its value on propositional variables. We can view the satisfaction relation as a binary trust operator. A formula A is *valid* for:

$$A \text{ model} \langle W, R, \Vdash \rangle, w \Vdash A \text{ for all } w \in W$$
$$A \text{ frame } \langle W, R \rangle, \text{ if it is valid in } \langle W, R, \Vdash \rangle$$
$$\text{for all posisble } \Vdash$$
$$A \text{ class } C \text{ of frames, if it is valid in every}$$
$$\text{member of } C \tag{2}$$

We can construct a model of an STS as a possible world denoted W_{STS} using atoms such as responsibility, roles, etc., and defining a set of relation R_{STS}, over the elements in the possible W_{STS}, such that a Kripke Frame is defined as follows: $M_{STS} = \langle W_{STS}, R_{STS} \rangle$. Via the application of Kripke Frame semantics we will be able to construct a set of formula through which we can reason about the security requirements and explore the security impact of threat scenarios against an STS and thus allows us to express trust requirements and patterns of behaviour that conform to trust.

5   Role Definition

At its simplest level the concept of a role is used to define behaviour in terms of a set of rights, duties, expectations, norms and behaviours that a person has to face and fulfil [1]. In expanding this concept with the a model of a socio technical system we may say that [1]:

- A role defines the division of labour and takes the form of a series of interactions between two roles. A role always stands in a relationship with another role and it is through this relationship that interactions flow.
- A role is both a descriptive and a normative concept that can be used to represent many different organisational realities from the structured to the unstructured.
- A role is to be treated as the basic building blocks that make it possible to move between organisational requirements and the requirements of individual agents. (e.g. from the organisation's role in a project to the way these responsibilities devolve to the roles of members of the project team).
- A role defines norms of behaviour and thereby system requirements. Roles include "appropriate" and "permitted" forms of behaviour, guided by organisational norms, which are commonly known and hence determine expectations and requirements.
- A role defines the relationships between role holders and the behaviour they expect of one another, which in turn defines many environmental requirements.

When modelling a socio-technical system we distinguish between different types of roles relationships, such as: master–slave, supervisor–subordinate, peer–peer and supplier–customer.

A role is only meaningful when it stands in relationship to another role. A role functions to define the tasks/interactions that an agent must execute in collaboration with other agents in order to fulfil a responsibility. A role must be performed by an agent and an agent can only fulfil a consequential responsibility through the execution of one, or more, roles. For a role to be meaning it must stand in relationship tot another role. Hence our concept of role allows us to distinguish the following:

- Agencies and agents with associated responsibilities to other agencies and agents.
- Tasks that interact through the utilisation of resources and are structured into actions and operations.

A formal type model for role– relationships enables us to represent and analyse the relations between functional and structural concepts and to express the way in which they operate in real organisations. An agent fulfils a responsibility via the performance of a set of roles in a logical sequence or pattern.

6 The RAR Model

A key requirement for the development of a impact assessment system is the ability to express taxonomic and ontological structures that represent an enterprise view of a cybernetic socio-technical model of an organisation. Such structures are depicted in Fig. 2. The socio-technical cybernetic enterprise model shown in Fig. 1 presents a basic taxonomy and ontology of roles, acts and resources. Roles are viewed as primary manipulators of the state or structure of the system, and a act is the only object that can create, modify or destroy other objects. Acts are the operations that change the state of the system, and they are performed by roles.

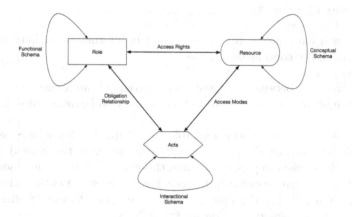

Fig. 2. A responsibility model

All actions must induce state changes in the system that is visible. The resources can be of two types: physical or logical, where physical resources are tangible objects such as servers, and logical resources include information, time etc. When modelling organisations at the enterprise level, resources act either as tokens of responsibility signifying that an agent has a binding responsibility upon it, or as objects for which some agency is responsible. An important type of logical resource is data. When data are passed from one action to another interactions occur, the data being the bearer of those interactions.

The basic component of our model takes the form of an entity-relation schema defining three sorts of entities: roles, acts, and resources. It defines a set of relations between these entity types. The basic entities are of three types:

- Roles:
  - Roles are the used to define the nature/type of behaviour used to fulfil a responsibility.
- Actions:
  - An act is to be distinguished from the doer of the actions. Thus an act is a functional answer to a what question, and takes a verbal form.
- Resources:
  - Resources are answers to with, or by-means-of-what questions. When modelling business process a resource is known as a data object [8].

Between these three types of basic entities there are six kinds of relations:

- Act-Act
  - Acts interact with each other. Such interactions are usually mediated by the exchange of resources, though direct interactions, such as interrupts, can also occur.
- Act-Resource
  - The relation between an activity and a resource is an access mode, such as reads or writes (for information resources) or provides or consumes (for commodity resources).
- Resource-Resource
  - The relation between resources is what in information technology terms is called, the conceptual schema.
- Role-Resource
  - The relation between an agent and a resource is an access right, such as the right: to-create, to-destroy, to-allocate, to-take-ownership-of.
- Role-Act
  - The set of acts with which an role constitutes the behaviour associated with that role. By the role-act relationship we mean two related things: a capability exists to perform act and this capability by virtue of some legal instrument can be enforced by recourse to something outside the system (e.g. judicial). For example, we can make some elementary distinctions between the role-act relationships as follows:
    - The Observer of an act knows that it is taking place.
    - The Owner of an act has the ability to destroy it; (the owner of an act may differ from the creator of an act, since ownership can be transferred).
    - The Customer of an act has the ability to change its specification.
    - The Performer of the act is the role responsible for executing the act and performing the interactions.
- Role-Role
  - The set of roles with which an role has some relation constitute the structural role of that agent and relates to the responsibilities and obligations that bind agents together in webs that form organisational structures.

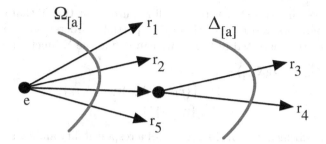

Fig. 3. Responsibility and roles

An agent fulfils a responsibility via the performance of a set of roles in a logical sequence or pattern [12]. We can define a set of Boolean functions that define the order within which a set of roles are executed. For example, within a hospital, a doctor agent cannot deliver a treatment to the patient until the doctor has diagnosed the patient's illness.

The role operator $\Omega_{[a]}(r_1, r_2, .., ., r_n) \rightarrow \{\top, \bot\}$ says that the agent a performs the ordered set of roles and/or role operators $r_1, r_2, .., ., ., r_{n-1}, r_n$ in a linear sequence. The role r_{n-1} must be complete before the role r_n can be performed, and the role r_1 is the initial role in the sequence. The role r_{n-1} may be said to be functionally dependant on the role r_n.

The role operator $\Delta_{[a]}(r_1, r_2, .., ., r_n) \rightarrow \{\top, \bot\}$ says that the agent a performs the ordered set of roles and/or role operators $r_1, r_2, .., ., ., r_{n-1}, r_n$ in parallel. The role r_{n-1} is performed at the same time as the role r_n and there is no functional dependancy between the roles r_{n-1} and r_n. From a temporal perspective within this function, roles can start and terminate at different points in time, but for the function to be true all roles must be successfully performed.

An agent a fulfils a responsibility e by performing a set of role operators $\{o_1, o_2, ..., o_n\}$ in a structured order, denoted by the operator $\nabla_{[e]}$. Within Kripke Semantics we can express when a responsibility e is fulfilled as for a Kripke Frame M and a state of affairs w: $M, w \Vdash \nabla_{[e]} \rightarrow \{o_1, o_2, ..., o_n\}$. We can identify the agent responsible for performing a role operator via the function ψ, such that

$$\psi(\Delta_{[a]}(...)) \rightarrow a \text{ and } \psi(\Omega_{[a]}(...)) \rightarrow a \tag{3}$$

We can identify the roles and role-operators that an agent performs via the function ψ^{-1}, such that

$$\psi^{-1}(\Delta_{[a]}(o_1, o_2, ..., o_n)) \rightarrow \{o_1, o_2, ..., o_n\}$$
$$\psi^{-1}(\Omega_{[a]}(o_1, o_2, ..., o_n)) \rightarrow \{o_1, o_2, ..., o_n\} \tag{4}$$

Within Fig. 3 we can say that the responsibility e is fulfilled via the pattern that conforms to the sequential execution by agent a of the roles r_1, r_2 and r_5 and the parallel execution, by the agent a, of the roles r_3, and r_4. By combining our role functions we can assert the following with reference to Fig. 3.

$$\nabla_{[e]} \rightarrow \{\Omega_{[a]}\{r_1, r_2, \Delta_{[a]}\{r_3, r_4\}, r_5\}\} \tag{5}$$

When processing this structure we will require a function Σ that extracts all of the role operators and returns them as a partially ordered set. For example, using the pattern illustrated in Fig. 3, we can define the Σ function as follows:

$$\Sigma(\nabla_{[e]}) \rightarrow \{$$
$$\Omega_{[a]}\{\{r_1, r_2, \Delta_{[a]}\{r_3, r_4\}, r_5\}, \tag{6}$$
$$\Delta_{[a]}\{r_3, r_4\}\}\}$$

A role is performed within the context of a responsibility and by an agent. We can define an agent's permission to perform a role as consisting of the following as defined in Fig. 2:

- The Authority to perform the role.
- The Capability to perform the role.
- The Access Rights to perform the role.

7   Functional Schema

We can decompose the behaviour of a role into a set of linguistic constructs and interactions, called speech acts, that the role holder executes. This behavioural specification forms the definition of the function that the agent is required to execute to fulfil a responsibility, and when modelling business a process role relationship is known as a swim lane [8]. With the model of a socio-technical system we can model behaviour as a set of interactions where each interaction is a directed graph of a set of speech acts. The execution of these sets of interactions allows us to validate the hypothesis the a set of roles meet a trust requirement.

A speech act is a basic unit of communication being a spoken or written utterance that results in meaning being assigned to a linguistic expression [6,7]. Speech acts always involve at least two agent roles: speaker and hearer (though these can on occasion be the same individual). Speech acts form larger wholes called conversations, which exhibit systematic regularities that can be studied and analysed.

An example of a conversation is to authenticate someone; it consists of a number of speech acts such as requesting a token of identification, confirming its authenticity with an authority, and finally accepting the individual as genuine (or not). Speech acts are modelled as taking place over the obligation interface link between structural roles. There are several types of speech acts, of which the four main categories are propositional acts, illocutionary acts, perlocutionary acts and instrumental acts.

- A propositional act is a statement which can be evaluated to be true or false, such as "It is Christmas Day today" or "There'll always be an England". Propositional acts can be evaluated to be true or false (though it may not be easy to determine which, as in the second of our examples). We do not say anything more about how the evaluation is performed, nor about the theory of truth we are assuming. Propositional acts can meaningfully be uttered by people or machines.

- An illocutionary act, or illocution, is always performed when a person utters certain expressions with an intention for example, "I promise to write the letter" or "I refuse to pay the bill". When the intention has been recognised by the hearer(s), the illocutionary act has been successful, and we say its meaning has been understood. Questions of the truth of an illocution do not arise; rather, the act creates a commitment that in a moral sense binds the future behaviour of the parties and pledges them to certain activities or expectations. Illocutionary acts can be expressed through mechanical means as well as vocal means. They are, however, always an expression of human concern or intention.
- A perlocutionary act, or perlocution, is an act that produces effects on the feelings, attitudes or behaviour of the hearer(s), for example to get someone to write a letter on request. Again, truth of a perlocutionary act is not an issue; success is, and occurs when the perlocutionary act has its desired effect. When modelling business process an perlocutionary act can be viewed as an event [8].
- Instrumental acts not only facilitate the examination and formalisation of when, where and by whom a task is performed, they also aid the elucidation and identification of what resources are required and manipulated by the agent entity performing the act. An instrumental act can be decomposed down into small instrumental acts. An example of an instrumental act, is when the electrician agent fixes an appliance for the homeowner person agent. In performing this act the agent is not only discharging his responsibility but also consuming a resource. When modelling business process an instrumental act can be viewed as an activity [8].

8   A State of Affairs

A state of affairs within the context of Kripke semantics is defined as part of a Kripke Frame $\langle W_{STS}, R_{STS} \rangle$, such that a possible world w is defined as $w \in W_{STS}$. The nodes and relations that can exist with a possible world and a state of affairs, as follows:

- A Responsibility type defines the nature of the responsibility in terms of consequential or causal constructs. Let R_t be the set of responsibility types that exist in a socio—echnical system.
- A Role is a norm/patterns of behaviour within the context of a responsibility. Let R_o be the set of roles in a socio—echnical system.
- A Resource relates to the source or supply from which we can derive benefit, and hence we can say that the resource is consumed in the context of a task. Let R_c be the set of resources in a socio—echnical system.
- An Access Right is the ability to perform basic actions on a resources such as: *read, write, create, amend, take—wnership—f give—wnership—o* and *destroy*.
- A responsibility is the modal operator $\Box$ expressing the relationship from one agent (the responsible) to another (the authority or principal) for the accomplishment of a state of affairs. Let A_{resp} be the set of responsibilities in a socio—echnical system

- A responsibility operator ∇ defines the sequence/patterns of role operators required to be performed by an agent to fulfil a responsibility.
- The role operators $\Omega_{[a]}$ and $\Delta_{[a]}$ define the sequencing order for the performance of a set of roles.

Now that we have defined the state of affairs S_t as part of a Kripke Frame $\langle W_{STS}, R_{STS} \rangle$ and hence a possible world $w \in W_{STS}$, such that $S_t \subseteq w$, we can define a security requirement as the $\Vdash$ operator. The goal in asserting a set of requirements is to identify where a contradiction or omission is present in the model. For example, an agent cannot be responsible for α and $\neg\alpha$ at the same time within a Kripke Semantic Model. Such a thing would be viewed as a contradiction.

9 Summary and Conclusions

In this paper we have sought to demonstrate how the application of a formal approach to the modelling of a socio—echnical system can be used to model trust. We have achieved this by the development of a set of logical operators relating to what a responsibility is and how it is fulfilled via the performance of a set of roles. In particular the application of hard— and soft—contradiction within a Kripke Model can be seen as a powerful tool allowing us to express and validate trust operators.

References

1. Biddle, B.J., Thomas, E.J.: Role Theory. Wiley, New York (1966)
2. Dewsbury, G., Dobson, J.: Responsibility & Dependable Systems. Springer, London (2007)
3. Fox, W.M.: Socio-technical system principles and guidelines: past and present. J. Appl. Behav. Sci. **31**(1), 91–105 (1995)
4. Sun, L.: An information systems security risk assessment model under Dempster-Shafer theory of belief functions. J. Manag. Inf. Syst. **22**(4), 109–142 (2006)
5. Cooper, R., Foster, M.: Socio-techical systems. Am. Psychol. **26**, 467–474 (1971)
6. Searle, J.R.: Speech Acts: An Essay in the Philosophy. Cambridge University Press, Cambridge (1984)
7. Thomson, J.J.: Acts and Other Events. Contemporary Philosophy Series. Cornell University Press, Ithaca (1977)
8. Sherry, K.J.: BPMN Pocket Reference: A Practical Guide To The International Business Process Model And Notation Standard BPMN Version 2.0. CreateSpace Independent Publishing Platform, Seattle (2012)
9. Baxter, G., Sommerville, I.: Socio-technical systems: from design methods to systems engineering. Interact. Comput. **23**(1), 4–17 (2011)
10. Baxter, G.: Socio-technical systems. In: LSCITS Socio-Technical Systems Engineering Handbook. University of St Andrews (2011)

11. van Dam, K.H., Nikloic, I., Lukszo, Z. (eds.): Agent-Based Modelling of Socio-Technical Systems, 1st edn. Springer, Netherlands (2013)
12. Charitoudi, K., Blyth, A.: A socio-technical approach to cyber risk management and impact assessment. J. Inf. Secur. 4(1), 33–41 (2013)
13. Goldblatt, R.: A Kripke-Joyal semantics for noncommuntative logic in quantales. In: Advances in Modal Logic, vol. 6 (2006)
14. Stirling, C.: Modal And Temporal Properties of Processes. Springer, New York (2001)

Security by Compliance? A Study of Insider Threat Implications for Nigerian Banks

Tesleem Fagade[✉] and Theo Tryfonas

Cryptography Group, University of Bristol, Bristol, UK
{tesleem.fagade,theo.tryfonas}@bristol.ac.uk

Abstract. This work explores the behavioural dimension of compliance to information security standards. We review past literature, building on different models of human behaviour, based on relevant theories like deterrence theory and the theory of planned behaviour. We conduct a survey of IT professionals, managers and employees of selected banks from Nigeria as part of a sector case study focussed in this region. Our findings suggest that security by compliance as a campaign to secure information assets in the Nigerian financial institution is a farfetched approach. In addition to standards, banking regulators should promote holistic change of security culture across the sector. Based on an established model of Information Security Governance Framework, we propose how information security may be embedded into organisation security culture in that context.

Keywords: Information security · Compliance · Insider threats · Standards · Information security culture

1 Introduction

Information security management policies are often difficult to be successfully implemented because significant issues of diffused liability and incentives are not appropriately distributed. Information systems exploitation is not always a consequence of technical or policy failure, but often due to the lack of balanced incentives between the designers and users of such systems [1]. Despite managements' efforts to protect organization data, problems of identity theft, database breaches and stolen passwords continue to be major challenges faced by corporate organizations and government agencies [2]. Today, one of the biggest challenges faced by organisations is system misuse by insiders, whose actions are deeply rooted on non-compliance to regulatory standards. It has been established that the weakest link in information security defence is the human element [3, 4], implying that of the most considerable threats comes from insiders. Lack of compliance by employees to information security policies is claimed to be responsible for more than half of information systems security breaches [5]. It is often difficult for organisations to balance the psychological, incentive and communication need of employees due to the complex nature of human behaviour. If all end-users are rational, cyber security will be a straight game between defenders and attackers of information assets. However, insider actions that are not necessarily

© Springer International Publishing Switzerland 2016
T. Tryfonas (Ed.): HAS 2016, LNCS 9750, pp. 128–139, 2016.
DOI: 10.1007/978-3-319-39381-0_12

malicious but inconsistent with policy and difficult to explain (e.g. clicking on links in phishing emails) place attackers at significant advantage against system defenders and wider risk exposure to organisation security.

The ISO/IEC27001 is an international standard for best practices in Information Security Management Systems (ISMS), which outline comprehensive requirements for safeguarding organisations information assets. It defines baseline requirements and controls for the assessment of ISMS, under the principle of confidentiality, integrity and availability [6]. Standards guidelines did not necessarily address how to capture the thought process of system adversaries; there seem to be more concerted effort on the implementation of physical, policy and technical measures to mitigate anticipatory threats. Some of the previous research on this subject [7] identified that the size and need of organisations vary when it comes to protecting IT infrastructure, and that different organisations require different security treatments. Hence, the one-cap-fits-all approach of Standards undermine the effectiveness of security by compliance.

1.1 'Compliant Security'

It is quite possible to meet compliance requirements and still be insecure within the context of information security. Organisations can easily implement all of the baseline security requirements in Standards to become compliant, yet not secure. For instance, compliance requirement of the National Institute of Standards and Technology (NIST) suggests that data should be encrypted at FIPS 140 level. If a full disk encryption is carried out but the encryption key is stored on the same disk, compliance requirements may have been addressed while still insecure. A secure and compliant approach would be full disk encryption and independent key management.

Business executives often focus on the cost of implementing compliance programs and once achieved, they operate under the assumption that compliance equates security. In practice, control baseline may be enough for business executives and regulators, but it is insufficient in providing holistic security protection. Security auditors and management may combine efforts to develop useable security policies but employee compliance to policies cannot be guaranteed. In a publicly reported 2014 cyber heist [9, 10], a Nigerian bank lost £23.5m through an insider operating with rogue third party contractors. Incidentally, the bank has been certified ISO27001 compliant, in line with the regulatory requirement of Central Bank of Nigeria (CBN). The CBN is Nigerian apex bank responsible monitoring, reforming and regulating the activities of banks and other financial institutions in Nigeria [8]. This goes to show that organisations can implement the toughest security policies, but performance is largely down to users. Cyber criminals would rather target authorized users who already sits within an organisation, than having a crack at multiple layers of outside facing firewalls.

While compliance processes are aimed at hardening organisations security defence, sometimes, how standards are interpreted can actually contribute to a porous security postures. If employees consider guidelines difficult to interpret or irrelevant to a business unit, it can easily give ground to non-compliance by way of accidental or deliberate introduction of threats to the environment [11]. Cases of security breaches due to negligence, intent and lack of understanding of policy requirements continue to make rounds despite the certification status attained by other Nigerian banks. Some employees continue to ignore security guidelines, while some find the extra steps introduced to complete tasks as interfering with job productivity. It has been suggested that users often fail to adhere to policy requirements because it is burdensome and there is no rational justification to comply from users' economic perspective; especially if the benefit is largely speculative, or the consequence is of little or no harm to the users [12]. There is a thin line between security and productivity [13], some employees often felt compelled to opt for productivity at the expense of security and compliance, when additional steps are required to complete a task. In a survey of more than 500 professionals, over 60 % admitted to using personal accounts to store and disseminate sensitive organisation data [14], because they felt that consumer options are more intuitive and easier to use than approved technology that sits within policy guidelines. Policy is an important aspect of security but it is only as effective as the technology and people backing it.

In this paper we explore the behavioural dimension of compliance to information security. Building on different models of human behavior, including deterrence theory and the theory of planned behavior (Sect. 2), we conduct a survey of IT professionals, managers and employees of selected banks from Nigeria as part of a sector case study focussed on the region (Sect. 3). In light of our results and discussion (Sects. 4 and 5) and based on an established model of Information Security Governance Framework (Sect. 5), we propose how information security may be embedded into organisation security culture in that context (Sect. 6).

2 Relevant Work

Security standards and written policies assume perfect rationale of users of information assets. Humans are not programmable machines, and often behave in manners that are completely out of the norm [15]. There are many studies on why it is challenging to enforce compliance in humans. Starting with technical security, [16, 17] pointed out why it is difficult to audit human behaviour in the same way technical auditing tools work. Irrational behaviour borders on frustration, anger or despair propelled by lack of job satisfaction, vendetta, financial and personal problems [18]. However, when organisations conduct security audits, it is the technical side that is often mostly addressed. Log files may capture and report unauthorized insider activities but the behaviour and motive is not necessarily captured. Therefore technical security audits verify consequences of behaviour but not the actual behaviour itself.

Organisations often apply deterrence measures to enforce policy compliance but studies [19, 20] based on deterrent theory suggested that employees' motivation differs across organisations, therefore, deterrent measures that work with one organisation may not necessarily fit into another. Deterrence implies rational behavior and even standards like ISO/IEC27001, COBIT and NIST draw on the principle of General Deterrence Theory [18], where rational users of information assets are expected to fit within a certain frame of reference. Unfortunately; that is not always the case. Deterrent actions, through reward or punishment has been shown to fail in organisations. Again, contrary to perfect rational assumption, punishing employees for accidental misuse or negligence may yield negative consequences. Besides, it is impractical, time consuming and expensive to monitor employees continuously in order to enforce or deter certain behaviours. Without a grounded insight into the understanding of employees' motivation, deterrent measures as a means to address insider threat may not necessarily work.

Other works that explored the theory of planned behaviour [21, 22] suggested that training and awareness are the most significant factors that influence human behaviour and attitude towards information security. It was argued that attitude, perceived expectation and subjective norm are the incentive components of behavioural intention. Hence, change in employee attitude that is in line with corporate expectations can be addressed with information security awareness campaigns. Although, some organisations put concerted effort into training with the hope of addressing security awareness gaps, but it is clear that training is not sufficient to ensure compliance and training is not the same as security culture [4]. What then can be done to ensure compliant behaviour? Can change be unforced? How can compliance be integrated into organisation security culture? This is the open space that our work tries to address in our specific context.

3   Research Method

Survey methodology can be used to study employees' opinion, attitude and behavioural patterns within the context of information security [23]. We carried out a survey of four banks in Nigeria to gain the understanding of how security awareness and employee behaviour impacts on policy compliance. The survey is designed to capture how compliance-certified financial institutions implement policies and how employees respond to situations within the context of information security. The banks selected for this survey have all obtained ISO27000 certifications, in line with the directives of CBN. In view of the banks' reluctance to share vulnerability information, results are anonymously obtained for this work.

The survey was conducted online and it followed a methodology as described in [23, 24]. Questions are divided into 3 parts; security culture statements, knowledge and awareness statements and demography. Security culture statement assesses the behavioural pattern of employees that could undermine effective implementation of policies. Knowledge and awareness statement assesse the understanding of security policy requirements, while the demography question captures survey representatives for segmentation analysis. The recruitment strategy for this work is based on random selection from a presumably representative group of bank employee.

The survey questions follow a Likert scale response model (strongly agree, agree, uncertain, disagree and strongly disagree), except question 1, which is on survey demography. Survey tool chosen for this work is Google Forms, an online survey application that allows real time response, collation and analysis of data. The survey was conducted over 2 weeks and respondents were invited to take part in through email communication, after obtaining initial clearance from the CISO. Table 1 shows extracted sample of questions contained in the online survey.

Table 1. Extracts from the online information security survey

	Demography					
1	What is your job level/department in your organization?	Executive/ senior level manager	IT department	Operations	HR & Administration	Others: Please specify
		Strongly agree	Agree	Uncertain	Disagree	Strongly disagree
	Security culture statements					
2	Information Security interferes with job productivity.	O	O	O	O	O
3	You can share your password with other people if you trust them.	O	O	O	O	O
4	It is safe to open any email attachment if it is not in the spam/junk box.	O	O	O	O	O
	Knowledge/awareness statements					
9	Your organisation has information security policy and you know where to locate a copy.	O	O	O	O	O
10	Your organisation has provided security awareness and training to all employees.	O	O	O	O	O
11	You know how to identify and report suspicious/actual security breaches.	O	O	O	O	O
12	Information is permanently lost when files on hard drives are erased or formatted.	O	O	O	O	O

4   Results and Analysis

The demography of respondents is shown in Fig. 1. 15.8 % represents the executive/ senior manager level, 12.3 % from the IT department, 14 % from HR and administration, 40.4 % from Operations and 17.5 % represents other categories. Job functions of other categories include marketing, accountancy, risk management, sales and predictive analysis. Our data is analyzed by assigning a range values from 1 to 5 for each survey question categorized under the security culture statements and the knowledge/awareness statements. Such that, if a statements is true from security standpoint, 5 corresponds to 'strongly agree' and 1 corresponds to 'strongly disagree'. We then analyzed respondents by demography based on collective points. The maximum score per respondent is 55 points, which implies good security behaviour and compliance, while lower scores down to the minimum of 11 points lean towards poor security posture and non-compliance. Results from the security culture statement and knowledge/awareness statements is shown in Fig. 2.

As a summary, more than 50 % of respondents view security measures as inconvenient add-on but necessary in getting some jobs done. Organisations need to ensure that security steps are viewed and implemented as part of job requirements. It is interesting to see that 12.1 % strongly disagree and 9.1 % disagree that their organisations has information security policy and they know where to locate a copy. Users who are not aware of organisation information security policy or know where to locate a copy pose a significant risk. It could be that such users simply forget that security policy exists or find policy statements hard to understand. When asked if respondents know how to report actual (or suspicious) security incidents, 22.6 % of respondents have no idea on how to do that. When users cannot identify a potential security threat or who to contact when there is a breach/compromise, such users may continue to expose information assets to threat by making further use of compromised devices. A significant number or respondents constituting 28 % are misinformed on how to dispose of sensitive electronic information. They assumed that data is permanently lost when deleted or when hard drives are formatted, this can pose a significant risk to an organisation. Forensic solutions that can erase end-of-life classified data need to be integrated in asset disposal policy.

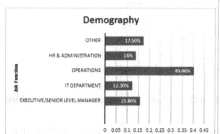

Fig. 1. Demography of respondents   **Fig. 2.** Information security compliance results

The survey findings indicate that there is a high sense of security awareness but secure practice and behaviour is low, which can have a significant impact on compliance. Although, not surprising, there seem to be higher evidence of compliance by employees in the IT department more than any other respondents. Considering that this survey is administered on employees from compliant certified financial institutions, it supports our understanding that security by mere compliance is a wishful approach to information security issues in Nigerian banking institutions.

5 Information Security Cultural Framework

Organizational culture has been described as the shared values, behaviour, attitude and practices that sustain connections among people, processes and policies. It is suggested that the management and governance of security is most effective when it is integrated into the culture of organisational behaviour and actions [25]. Habitual behaviour propagates, and it often require concerted efforts to break the norm. If organisations want to project the habit of secure behaviour, perhaps a long term goal that is in line with the direction of an organizational security culture is a better approach [4], rather than focusing on quick certification status, then assuming that all technical and human processes are secured. Organizational security culture is defined as the assumptions, attitudes and perceptions that are accepted and encouraged with the aim of protecting information assets, so that attributes and custom of information security begins to emerge as the way things are done in an organisation [26]. Thus a strong information security culture is vital for managing organisational information assets. A number of studies recognized the need for creating security culture [17, 27–29] where employees have the attitude, skill and knowledge to support

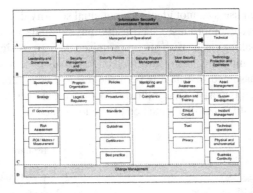

Fig. 3. Information Security Governance Framework (adopted from [31])

information security objectives. However, steps on how to embed security into the culture of an organisations are not addressed [30].

We will use a model of information security governance framework adopted from [31], in an attempt to show how information security culture can influence a change in organisation security postures. Although, the adopted framework did not specifically elaborate on how security practices can be embedded in organisation culture, but it provided a single point of reference and comprehensive structure upon which organisations can cultivate an acceptable level of information security culture. The frame work shown in Fig. 3 provided a starting point for the governance of information security. It explains how guidelines and control implementations can identify and address the technical, procedural and human components of information risks.

The information security governance framework is derived from the integration of four different information security frameworks; ISO/IEC27001, PROTECT, Capability Maturity Model and Information Security Architecture (ISA) [31]. Key categories of the framework that is most relevant to this work are discussed below:

1. Leadership and governance
This category comprises of executive level sponsor of policies and strategies for addressing the threats of information security. This category also covers the compilation and measurement of control effectiveness, in ensuring that organisation long term security goals are met.

2. Security management and organisations
This category addresses organisations legal and regulatory requirements for information security, for instance, it is now a regulatory requirement for all Nigerian banks to be ISO27001 certified. Also, the National Information Technology Development Agency (NITDA) guidelines on data protection draft (2013), requires that all federal agencies and private organisations that owns, use or deploy information systems within Nigeria is covered by the guidelines [32]. Organisation information security design, composition and reporting structure is also addressed in this category.

3. Security policies
Security policies must be implemented through effective process and compliance while taking into account other components like legal and ethical considerations.

Security policies are the overall organisation intention and direction as expressed by the management [33]. Policies provide specific guideline for employee behaviour and procedures when interacting with information systems. Example may include point-specific policy statement covering internet acceptable use.

4. Security program management

This category involves auditing and compliance monitoring of both technical and human elements of security programs. It must be ensured that policies, processes, procedures and controls are managed through continuous monitory, for timely response to security breaches. Employee behaviour monitoring could include internet usage and technology monitoring could be network traffic monitoring.

5. User security management

User security awareness, ethical conduct and trust are all addressed in this category. Ethical conduct is a vital component of security culture, it must be developed and communicated as part of a corporate code of conduct. For instance, organisation ethics may include unauthorized data alteration or disclosure. Security awareness program needs to be promoted and maintained throughout the organisation and the management need to find ways to integrate the element of mutual trust between all stakeholders.

6. Technology protection and management

This involves physical and technical protection measures around information assets. As part of the implementation of the security governance framework, it must be ensured that appropriate technology controls are included in asset management, technical operations, physical environments and business continuity. Continuous monitoring of technical controls is also important in order to keep pace with rapid technology changes.

6 Embedding Security in Organisational Culture

An organisation's compliance status does not necessarily present desired changed behaviour of employees. However, given objective situations, it is unlikely that employees would be tempted to break the law, if compliance is ingrained into organisation cultural and daily routine [34]. Embedding security into organisation culture must adopt a top-bottom approach, starting with management buy-in and then gradually including everyone in the organisation. It has been shown that top management buy-in and support has enormous impact on policy enforcement and organisational culture [35]. Management top hierarchy are responsible for imposing measures which can have great influence on employee attitude, behaviour and motivation; hence, there has to be a demonstration of commitment by the management before there can be any success of integrating security in organisation culture.

Using data security as an example, some organisations understand the need for data protection but may not know how to prioritize that for all employees. Since most organisations are covered by national or international data protection acts; this should be the starting point for embedding data security into organisation culture. Management top hierarchy should be able to understand and communicate their organizations' legal/regulatory obligations under data protection laws. Data protection should then be included in organisation information security policy, which may further include policy subsets like regular data backups and unauthorized use of portable devices on corporate computers. Policy subsets should show clear guidelines and best practices for ensuring data confidentiality, integrity and availability at all times. Through user awareness and ethical code of conduct programs, employees should become sensitized about organization's position on data protection. It should be communicated why data is vital for business continuity, how data loss may impact on business and what measures can be taken to ensure data security. Most importantly, data security should become the responsibility of all employees and not only dedicated to a small unit of staff.

Technical solutions that complement a data protection policy can then be introduced as part of security plan. Although, employees often see security steps as inconvenient add-ons that impact on productivity; technical solutions can be introduced gradually, while focusing initially on components that constitute everyday security issues. Policy subset that safeguards data loss may require that employees must regularly backup data, but compliance can be enforced if data backup becomes part of job functions. Technical solutions that can be leveraged as part of data security strategy may simply be a system, which forces or reminds employee to do a data backup every day. Perhaps, if all employees that interact with information systems cannot logoff after a day's work without completing backups to the central server, this function will become embedded in the organisation security culture where data backups become part of job requirement, rather than inconvenient security measure. Other policy subsets can then be applied to support compliance, for instance, disabling the USB ports on all organisation computers to control unauthorized copying of confidential information. Also, implementing a system that compel users to change passwords at intervals may ensure compliance and reduce threats posed by employees that are susceptible to social engineering.

Through these measures, employees will become involved in the process of security whereby **security requirements are incorporated within operational system architecture.** As employees learn to comply with the requirements of a policy, and observed behavioural change starts to emerge to the point where secure behaviour becomes second nature, a change in organizational culture which is also security driven will become evident. Thereafter, management can begin to gently introduce other policy requirements in stages until the entire policy becomes embedded in the organizational culture. Through continuous assessment, the effectiveness of each security component embedded in the organisation culture can be measured over a given period of time. Security metrics may be based on how many times an organisation has recorded incidents of data loss since data backup has become part of job requirements. Employees will ultimately identify those changes as part of corporate culture and may not require extra motivation, reward or punishment to perform those functions. There are additional benefits of improved reputation and efficiency for organisations that have sound security practices integrated in its culture, ultimately becoming compliant and secured.

7 Conclusion

We believe that in addition to compliance, organisations need to cultivate information security culture because compliance is not the same as security. In addition, there is no guarantee that employees will comply with policy requirements. Human factors continue to represent the gap between processes and technology, and there is no difference between malicious intent, negligence or external attacks in terms of diminishing IT functions. There is insufficient understanding of the risks posed by users of information assets, therefore, management are mostly focused on achieving compliance status without necessarily understanding that compliance is just a part of information security.

The strongest influence on organisation culture begins with the position of leadership. Leadership acceptance and active participation in holistic cultural change, is a key aspect of information security. Executive level security representation and a change in management behaviour, will reflect on employees' behaviour too. Information security channel of communication should be clearly defined and all employees need to be part of security. Often, organisations have dedicated IT units that enforce the implementation of information security policies, rather than promoting a sense of shared responsibility where security is a required function for everyone. Once the overall mind-set of an organisation begins to change, a culture where security is pivotal will begin to emerge and compliance will inevitable become an integral part of organizational culture. If policy compliance becomes natural to employees, it will be much easier for new employees to emulate acceptable behaviour through observation. It is unlikely that information security culture can be covered by a single framework or few technical solutions. Future research may consider how to integrate other frameworks with the one adopted for this work and also suggest how human-centric technical solutions can be integrated into organisation security culture. This model hasn't been tested in other security domains, but it has been subjected to critique from industry experts with good feedback on its feasibility. As part of future work, there will be a robust comparative empirical model to test the validity of observations made through this work.

References

1. Ross, A.: Security Engineering: A Guide to Building Dependable Security Systems, 2nd edn. Wiley, New York (2008)
2. Corriss, L.: Information security governance: integrating security into the organizational culture. In: Proceedings of the 2010 Workshop on Governance of Technology, Information and Policies, Austin, Texas, USA, pp. 35–41. ACM (2010)
3. Aurigemma, S., Panko, R.: A composite framework for behavioral compliance with information security policies. In: Proceedings of the 2012 45th Hawaii International Conference on System Sciences, pp. 3248–3257. IEEE Computer Society (2012)
4. Renaud, K., Goucher, W.: The curious incidence of security breaches by knowledgeable employees and the pivotal role a of security culture. In: Tryfonas, T., Askoxylakis, I. (eds.) HAS 2014. LNCS, vol. 8533, pp. 361–372. Springer, Heidelberg (2014)
5. Siponen, M., Vance, A.: Neutralization: new insights into the problem of employee systems security policy violations. MIS Q. **34**(3), 487–502 (2010)
6. ISO/IEC 27001:2013 Information technology - Security techniques - Specification for an Information Security Management System. The British Standard Institute 2014
7. Karjalainen, M., Siponen, M.T., Puhakainen, P., Sarker, S.: One size does not fit all: different cultures require different information systems security interventions. In: PACIS, p. 98 (2013)
8. Central Bank of Nigeria (2015). http://www.cenbank.org/. Accessed 04 Dec 2015

9. Chima, O.: How Bank Insiders Connive with Fraudsters. This Day Live (2015). http://www.thisdaylive.com/articles/how-bank-insiders-connive-with-fraudsters/204219/. Accessed 03 Dec 2015

10. Morgan, L.: Nigerian bank IT worker on the run after £23.5m cyber heist, IT Governance Blog (2014). http://www.itgovernance.co.uk/blog/nigerian-bank-it-worker-on-the-run-after-23-5m-cyber-heist/. Accessed 18 Dec 2015

11. Da Veiga, A., Eloff, J.H.P.: A framework and assessment instrument for information security culture. Comput. Secur. 29(2), 196–207 (2010)

12. Herley, C.: So long, and no thanks for the externalities: the rational rejection of security advice by users. In: Proceedings of the 2009 Workshop on New Security Paradigms Workshop. Oxford, United Kingdom, pp. 133–144. ACM (2009)

13. Albrechtsen, E.: A qualitative study of users' view on information security. Comput. Secur. 26(4), 276–289 (2007)

14. GlobalSCAPE. Protecting Digitalized Assets in Healthcare. Whitepaper (2013). http://dynamic.globalscape.com/files/whitepaper_healthcare.pdf. Accessed 18 Dec 2015

15. Alavi, R., Islam, S., Mouratidis, H.: A conceptual framework to analyze human factors of information security management system (ISMS) in organizations. In: Tryfonas, T., Askoxylakis, I. (eds.) HAS 2014. LNCS, vol. 8533, pp. 297–305. Springer, Heidelberg (2014)

16. Wall, J.D., Iyer, L. Salam A.F., Siponen, M.: Conceptualizing Employee Compliance and Non-compliance in Information Security Research: A Review and Research Agenda. Dewald Roode Information Security Workshop, Niagara Falls, New York (2013)

17. Vroom, C., von Solms, R.: Towards information security behavioural compliance. Comput. Secur. 23(3), 191–198 (2004)

18. Theoharidou, M., Kokolakis, S., Karyda, M., Kiountouzis, E.: The insider threat to Information Systems and the effectiveness of ISO17799. Comput. Secur. 24(6), 472–484 (2005)

19. Park, S., et al.: Towards understanding deterrence: information security managers' perspective. In: Kim, K.J., Ahn, S.J. (eds.) Proceedings of the International Conference on IT Convergence and Security 2011, vol. 120, pp. 21–37. Springer, Netherlands (2011)

20. D'Arcy, J., Herath, T.: A review and analysis of deterrence theory in the IS security literature: making sense of the disparate findings. Eur. J. Inf. Syst. 20(6), 643–658 (2011)

21. Waly, N., Tassabehji, R., Kamala, M.: Measures for improving information security management in organisations: the impact of training and awareness programmes. In: Proceedings of the UK Academy for Information Systems Conference, Oxford, Paper, vol. 8 (2012)

22. Gundu, T., Flowerday, S.V.: Ignorance to awareness: Towards an information security awareness process. SAIEE Africa Res. J. 104(2), 69–79 (2013)

23. Da Veiga, A., Martins, N., Eloff, J.H.P.: Information security culture - validation of an assessment instrument. South. Afr. Bus. Rev. 11(1), 147–166 (2007)

24. Deloitte. Insight into the Information Security Maturity of Organisations, with a Focus on Cyber Security. Central Asia Information Security Survey Result (2014). https://www2.deloitte.com/content/dam/Deloitte/kz/Documents/risk/KZ_Deloitte_Information_Security_Survey_2014_EN.pdf. Accessed 16 Dec 2015

25. Department of Homeland Security. Build Security In. Governance and Management (2015). https://buildsecurityin.us-cert.gov/articles/best-practices/governance-and-management. Accessed 08 Jan 2016

26. Martins, A., Elofe, J.: Information security culture. In: Ghonaimy, M.A., El-Hadidi, M.T., Aslan, H.K. (eds.) Security in the Information Society: Visions and Perspectives, pp. 203–214. Springer US, MA (2002)

27. Sherif, E., Furnell, S., Clarke, N.: An identification of variables influencing the establishment of information security culture. In: Tryfonas, T., Askoxylakis, I. (eds.) HAS 2015. LNCS, vol. 9190, pp. 436–448. Springer, Heidelberg (2015)

28. Furnell, S., Clarke, N.: Organizational security culture: Embedding security awareness, education, and training. In: Proceedings of the IFIP TC11 WG, vol. 11, pp. 67–74 (2005)

29. Ruighaver, A.B., Maynard, S.B., Chang, S.: Organizational security culture: Extending the end-user perspective. Comput. Secur. **26**(1), 56–62 (2007)

30. Lim, J.S., Ahmad, A., Chang, S., Maynard, S.: Embedding information security culture emerging concerns and challenges. In: PACIS 2010 Proceedings. Paper 43 (2010)

31. Veiga, A.D., Eloff, J.H.P.: An information security governance framework. Inf. Syst. Manage. **24**(4), 361–372 (2007)

32. NITDA. National Information Technology Development Agency: Guidelines on Data Protection (2013). http://www.nitda.gov.ng/wp-content/uploads/Guidelines-on-Data-Protection-Final-Draft-3.5.pdf. Accessed 08 Jan 2016

33. Merete Hagen, J., Albrechtsen, E., Hovden, J.: Implementation and effectiveness of organizational information security measures. Inf. Manage. Comput. Secur. **16**(4), 377–397 (2008)

34. Jackson, J., Bradford, B., Hough, M., Myhill, A., Quinton, P., Tyler, T.R.: Why do people comply with the law? Legitimacy and the influence of legal institutions. Br. J. Criminol. **52**(6), 1051–1071 (2012)

35. Knapp, K.J., et al.: Information security: management's effect on culture and policy. Inf. Manage. Comput. Secur. **14**(1), 24–36 (2006)

Current Trend of End-Users' Behaviors Towards Security Mechanisms

Yasser M. Hausawi[✉]

Department of Information Technology,
Institute of Public Administration, Jeddah, Saudi Arabia
hawsawiy@ipa.edu.sa

Abstract. End user's Security-related behaviors are key factors on success or failure of information security mechanisms' application. Such security mechanisms are being rapidly modified sophisticatedly. Consequently, end-users' behaviors are being changed, newly developed, and/or innovated as a result of the modifications of the mechanisms. Therefore, tracing the change of the end-user's security related behaviors is an essential activity that should get continual attention from the security professionals. Unfortunately, behavioral studies on information security are out of most security professionals' scope, despite the common believe that end-users must be involved in security mechanisms' development. This article focuses on tracking the current trend of both positive and negative behaviors of end-users who are not security experts. The tracking process is based on semi-structured interviews with security experts who deal with end users on daily bases.

Keywords: Security · Usability · Human computer interaction · HCI · HCI-SEC · Security-related behaviors · Security enhancement approaches

1 Introduction

Among security community, there has been a wide spread conceptual thought that end-users are the enemies of security mechanisms. Therefore, a considerable amount of studies have been conducted to figure out if such a hypothesis is true. There are many famous research studies such as [1,7,12] have been conducted to investigate whether end- users are the enemies of security or not. As a result of the studies, it became clear that end-users are divided into two groups, legitimate end-users and adversaries [3], and it became even clear that the legitimate end-users are not the enemies, while the adversaries are the real enemies of security mechanisms. However, despite the fact that the legitimate end-users are not the enemies, they also behave in ways that can affect security mechanisms both positively and negatively citemayron2013secure. Having two different possible behaviors, it is important to distinguish between the behaviors that can be considered as positive and those that can be considered as negative. In the cases that the users perform negative behaviors during their interaction with security mechanisms, there is a set of important concerns raised. These concerns are:

© Springer International Publishing Switzerland 2016
T. Tryfonas (Ed.): HAS 2016, LNCS 9750, pp. 140–151, 2016.
DOI: 10.1007/978-3-319-39381-0_13

- Whether legitimate end-users, who behave negatively against security, be considered as enemies or not;
- Whether we should differentiate between the legitimate users themselves and their behaviors or not;
- The best security approaches to be followed in order to promote the positive behaviors of the legitimate end-users, and limit their negative behaviors.

To clear up all of the above concerns, a series of consecutive studies should be conducted such as the work of Stanton et al. in [8,10]. It is important to be aware of the fact that during the last decade, there has been rapid change in the development of user-security interaction. Sequentially, end-user behavior toward security is being changed frequently as well. Therefore, there is a continual need to frequently investigate end users' behaviors and to not rely on the previously studied behaviors of users toward security.

To begin this research, an initial exploratory study has been conducted to investigate the current state of end-users behaviors when interacting with security mechanisms. Human-computer interaction Behavioral researchers in [2,4,6] recommended interviews and focus groups as the best initial exploration research methods used to help in better identifying problems. Therefore, the previously mentioned research methods are the best ways to identify legitimate endusers' positive and negative behaviors towards security mechanisms.

This study focuses on identifying the current state of legitimate end-users' behaviors and the best approaches to deal with such behaviors. To this end, a set of interviews have been conducted to survey security experts' experiences and interactions with end-users and digital security.

The reminder of this article is structured as follows: Sect. 2 presents the related work on investigating end-users' behaviors towards security mechanisms.

2 Related Work

According to Stanton et al., successful application of security mechanisms relies on the behaviors of end users who interact with such mechanisms [8]. While Security professionals and administrators are responsible for creating, developing, and configuring practical security mechanisms, end-users are responsible for practicing and appropriately using the mechanisms [5]. Accordingly, Whitten and Tygar stated that security mechanisms can only be a as effective as should be if they are used correctly [12].

Unfortunately, the research work on security-related behavior is very limited despite its importance on making security mechamesms applicable [11]. However, Stanton et al., conducted an interview study that involved 110 participants (managers, IT professionals, and regular employees), the result of their study was a collection of 94 security related behavior list that nine of which were then used in a following survey study. Among those selected behaviors, sharing and writing credentials were among the common negative security related behaviors [9]. In addition, Stanton et al. transformed 91 out of the collected 94 security-related behaviors into a more manageable six-element taxonomy [10].

3 Methodology

3.1 Interview Design

The semi-structured strategy is used to design the interview. The reason for using the semi-structured strategy is to get the benefits of both using a rigid script of well-defined, ordered questions to control the flow and consistency of the interview, and keeping the interview opened up for both depth and breadth topic exploration [4]. To give the interviewee the freedom of answering questions, five of the questions (62 %) are open-ended, two are unstructured-closed questions, and one is a structured-closed question. Among the five open-ended questions, two of them are followed with the two unstructured- closed questions. The structured-closed question is followed by another related open-ended question. The flow of the questions is structured based on the five following major topics: security compromising, negative behaviors, positive behaviors, security enhancement approaches, and open topics of mind. Table 1 shows the questions, their topics, and their types.

3.2 Participants

Thirty-one expert from the U.S and Saudi Arabia (23 males and 8 females) participated in the study; all are security experts and have experience with end users. Their work experience is between 8 and 30 years, with an average experience of 19 years. Their daily interaction with end-users ranges from 1 to 7 h, with an average 4 h.

3.3 Tools

Rigid scripts were used by the interviewers to keep the interview consistent and controlled. The scripts consist of an introduction part and set of questions in an organized and well-defined order. Moreover, the scripts were provided with noting areas for each question. At the top of the scripts, there is a field to record the code the interviewee. It is worthwhile to state that the interviewers read from the scripts, while the interviewees had no scripts to reference, rather, the questions were read one by one to them by the interviewers. Figure 1 depicts the script. The interviews were voice recorded in order to make sure that all the important information is not missed and also to double check the hand-written recorded data after the end of each interview. Microsoft Excel 2013 was used to store and analyze the collected data.

3.4 Analysis and Evaluation

Because of the nature of the exploratory semi-structured interviews and having a lot of open-ended questions, the collected data are grouped, categorized, organized, and then displayed. The open-ended and the unstructured-closed questions are analyzed based on the following steps:

Table 1. Interview's questions

No.	Question	Topic	Type
1	Please tell us your favorite story on how an end user or end users compromised security. Please use as much detail as you like	Compromising Security	Open-ended
2	What are some other behaviors that you have encountered that users make that negatively affect security?	Negative Behavior	Open-ended
3	Which of these activities, in your opinion, has the most impact on security, and which one the least?	Negative Behavior	Unstructured-closed
4	On the other hand, could you please tell us about some things that users do that in your experience, improves security?	Positive Behavior	Open-ended
5	Which of these activities, in your opinion, has the most impact on security, and which one the least ?	Positive Behavior	Unstructured-closed
6	Of the following four approaches, which one do you think is most effective for enhancing security? a. Enforcing security policies, b. Training users, c. Motivating users, d. Rewarding users	Security Approaches	Structured-closed
7	Is there another approach that you think is effective?	Security Approaches	Open-ended
8	Is there anything else that you would like to add?	Open Topic	Open-ended

1. Counting the number of behaviors cited in each question.
2. Ordering (descending) the behaviors for each question.
3. Rating the behaviors for each question.
4. Display the results of the rating.

The structured-closed question is analyzed based on the following steps:

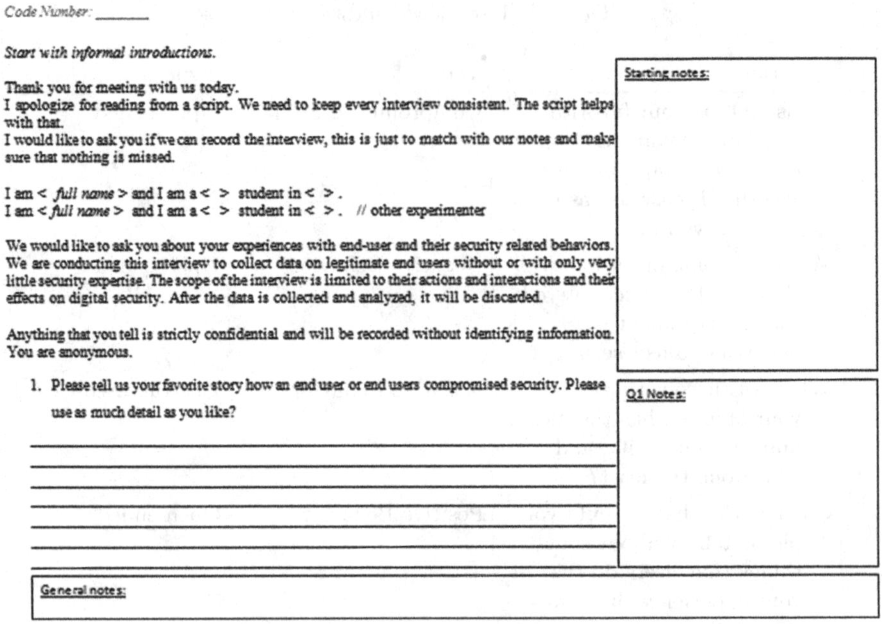

Code Number: _____

Start with informal introductions.

Thank you for meeting with us today.
I apologize for reading from a script. We need to keep every interview consistent. The script helps with that.
I would like to ask you if we can record the interview, this is just to match with our notes and make sure that nothing is missed.

I am < *full name* > and I am a < > student in < > .
I am < *full name* > and I am a < > student in < > . // other experimenter

We would like to ask you about your experiences with end-user and their security related behaviors. We are conducting this interview to collect data on legitimate end users without or with only very little security expertise. The scope of the interview is limited to their actions and interactions and their effects on digital security. After the data is collected and analyzed, it will be discarded.

Anything that you tell is strictly confidential and will be recorded without identifying information. You are anonymous.

1. Please tell us your favorite story how an end user or end users compromised security. Please use as much detail as you like?

Starting notes:

Q1 Notes:

General notes:

Fig. 1. A snapshot of the Interview's Script

1. Creating four groups of rankings as the following:
   (a) First choice (4 points).
   (b) Second choice (3 points).
   (c) Third choice (2 points).
   (d) Fourth choice (1 point).
2. Putting each approach in one of the four based on each interviewee ranking. Where represents an approach.
3. Counting the number of occurrence for each approach in each group.
4. Multiplying the total count of each approach of each group by that groups' point.
5. Summating approach's results from each group.
6. Listing the four approaches along with their results.
7. Ordering the approaches.
8. Rating the approaches.
9. Displaying the results of the rating.

4   Interview Results

The results of the interview study are presented based on the five major topics that are: security compromising, negative behaviors, positive behaviors, security enhancement approaches, and open topics of mind.

4.1   Security Compromising Stories

Sharing Credentials: There are many different security-compromising stories all share one common incident that is sharing credentials. The following are summarized descriptions of the stories:

- A project team having one credential to share accessing the same resources.
- Faculty staff members give their credentials to IT support staff member when fixing their banners. The IT support staff member writes the credential on a paper and access to the faculty staff's banner and look at students' grades.
- Single sign-on credential sharing.

Over Trusting: There are two types of over trusting in digital security, one is over trusting people by not protecting self's security related stuff protected (such as credentials and devices), another is over trusting technology by not investigating whatever software brings up (such as pop-ups and default configurations and installations). Another form of over trusting technology is when users believe that devices are self-secured properly. The following are summarized descriptions of the stories:

- Clicking OK without reading the contents of the messages.
- Grandfather clicks OK on fake security popups coming through emails from trusted people.
- Storing sensitive data in USBs.

Lack of Knowledge and Awareness: Sometimes important security decisions alert end-users in the form of a pop-up, the pop-up asks the user if they would like to accept or reject security actions that the end-user lacks knowledge and awareness of. As a result, end-users prefer not choose any. The following are summarized descriptions of the story:

- End users try to get rid of the pop-ups in a safest way by cancelling the pop-up or closing it. The reason for that is because end users don't know the right answer.

Other Stories: There are some security compromising stories narrated by the interviewees such as:

- A web administrator wrote his credentials on his screen. The students got the credentials and changed the site contents.
- Compromising an official public website to perform a security homework assignment.
- A project team having one credential to share accessing the same resources.

Table 2. Negative behaviors

No.	End-users' negative behaviors
1	Sharing credentials
2	Over trusting people
3	Writing credentials down
4	Clicking OK without reading
5	Not logging off
6	Downloading programs
7	Not having security software
8	Allowing auto remembering of credentials via browsers
9	Bypassing security
10	Keystrokes
11	Lack of awareness of importance of security
12	Not applying least privileges
13	Not checking default configurations
14	Not locking screens
15	Not updating security software
16	Reusing credentials
17	Sending stuff to wrong resource
18	Setting easily security questions
19	Signing on from unsecure networks
20	Turning software programs off without turning them on again
21	Using jump drives

4.2   End-Users' Negative Behaviors

A total of 21 different negative behaviors were collected. Table 2 lists the collected behaviors, and Fig. 2 shows the percentage that each behavior got.

Among the 21 negative behaviors, 6 negative behaviors were chosen by the experts to be the most behaviors that negatively impact security (Sharing credentials, Over trusting people, Clicking OK without reading, Not having security software, Turning software programs off without turning them on again, and Lack of awareness of importance of security), where sharing credentials behavior got the highest attention.

On the other hand, among the 21 negative behaviors, 5 negative behaviors were chosen by the experts to be the least negatively impacting behaviors (Sharing credentials, Downloading programs, Keystrokes, Not locking screens, and Writing credentials down), while sharing credentials behavior got the highest attention. It is worthwhile to mention that one answer was missed, because the interviewer forgot to ask the interviewee about the least negative impact behavior.

End-Users' Negative Behaviors

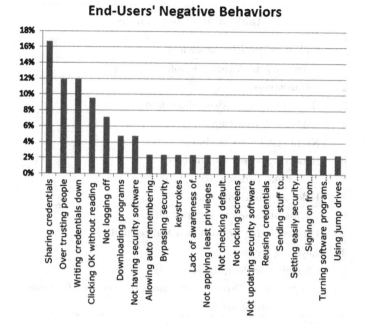

Fig. 2. Negative behaviors' percentage

4.3   End-Users' Positive Behaviors

A total of 15 different positive behaviors were collected. Table 3 lists the collected behaviors, and Fig. 3 shows the percentage that each behavior got.

Among the 15 positive behaviors, 5 behaviors were chosen by the security experts to be the behaviors that most positively impacts security (Complying with security policy, Keeping software updated, Layering security, Paying attention to security alerts, and Self-awareness), where self-security awareness behavior got the highest attention.

Among the 21 positive behaviors, 4 behaviors were chosen by the security experts to be the behaviors that positively impact security the least, whereas protecting personal security stuff behavior got the highest attention. It is worthwhile to mention that 3 answers were missed, because the interviewers forgot to ask the interviewees about the least positive impact behavior.

4.4   Security Enhancement Approaches

The topic of security enhancement approaches is designed in a different structure than other security topics. It is more controlled despite the fact that it is an open area of study. The reason for this type of design is to get the best of the currently available approaches first, then with a follow up question the interviewee is given a chance to add approaches not yet listed or to propose new approaches.

Table 3. Positive behaviors

No.	End-users' positive behaviors
1	Complying with security policy
2	Self-awareness
3	Having unique credential per system
4	Asking before acting
5	Keeping software updated
6	Reporting to security officers
7	Protecting personal security stuff
8	Deleting unknown emails
9	Paying attention to security alerts
10	Differentiating between self and technology
11	Layering security
12	Changing credentials frequently
13	Not trying to discover new things that are not for tasks
14	curiosity about security
15	Education

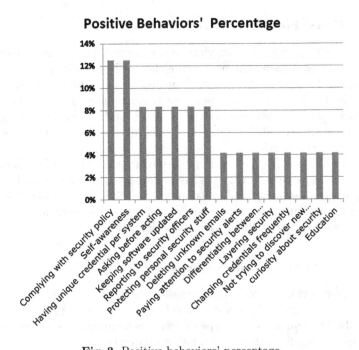

Fig. 3. Positive behaviors' percentage

Among the 4 listed approaches (Training users, Motivating users, Enforcing security policies, and Rewarding users), training users was the most recommended by the interviewees (34 %), second, motivating users (29 %), then enforcing security policies (26 %), and the least recommended approach is rewarding users (11 %). Figure 4 illustrates the ratings.

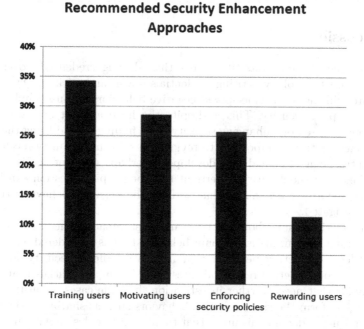

Fig. 4. Security enhancement approaches percentage

In addition, the interviewees added a set of approaches as the following:

- Assessing security
- Promoting users self-awareness
- Restricting security
- Punishing users
- Turning technology off
- Educating users
- Designing simpler user interfaces
- Designing informative security systems
- Hiring IT staff with security experience

4.5 Open Topics

The interviewees talked about very important issues related to end users' behaviors that usually are not considered when security mechanisms are designed and developed. The issues are listed as the following:

- Security policies must be usable.
- Improving user decision-making by having better design.
- People have to address their level of security.
- Security designers must understand the users' needs.
- Balancing quality attributes is a very important issue.
- Security officers should be nice with legitimate end-users, as they are not security enemies.

5   Discussion

Looking at the above results, it is clear that sharing credentials, over trusting people and technology, writing credentials down, and clicking OK without reading are still the most wide-spread negative behaviors end-users exhibit that negatively impact security. This is despite the huge amount of research and development focused on enhancing security. This finding should bring the attention to a fact that: it is important to review the way that security mechanisms are currently being designed and developed. Perhaps some of the issues that are mentioned by the security experts at the open topics question can help in redesigning security mechanisms that address the negative behaviors that are yet to be mitigated.

One interesting result about the most and least impacting negative behaviors is that: sharing credentials is the only behavior that is considered as both the most and least impacting behavior that negatively affects security simultaneously. Such a contradicting result indicates that sharing credentials is an important behavior that needs further investigation. In some cases, security experts, themselves, perform the same negative behaviors such as sharing credentials or writing credentials down! This infers that there might be design flaws in security mechanisms' designing methodologies.

6   Conclusion and Future Work

This initial exploratory interview was conducted to collect data on legitimate end-users with or without very little security knowledge from security experts' viewpoints. A total of 21 negative, and 15 positive security-related behaviors had been collected and analyzed. Four well-known security enhancement approaches had been investigated and ranked to find the best among them. Moreover, nine other proposed enhancement security approaches have been proposed and need to be investigated in further research. A set of six design principles had been gathered from the security experts that may help in enhancing security mechanisms design, most of which are user-centered. Future step is to get the end-users' viewpoints about the causes for performing both of the negative and positive behaviors when interacting with security mechanisms. Then the results are interrelated and analyzed with the results of this interview to create a solid foundation for new design methods for security mechanisms. When this is finished an experimental study will be conducted to evaluate the new security methods.

Acknowledgment. The author would like to thank the Institute of Public Administration (IPA) in Saudi Arabia and Florida Institute of Technology in the U.S. for their support of this work.

References

1. Adams, A., Sasse, M.A.: Users are not the enemy. Commun. ACM **42**(12), 40–46 (1999)
2. Converse, J.M., Presser, S.: Survey Questions: Handcrafting the Standardized Questionnaire, vol. 63. Sage, Thousand Oaks (1986)
3. Hausawi, Y.M.: Towards a usable-security engineering framework for enhancing software development (2015)
4. Lazar, J., Feng, J.H., Hochheiser, H.: Research Methods in Human-Computer Interaction. Wiley, New York (2010)
5. Ng, B.-Y., Kankanhalli, A., Xu, Y.C.: Studying users' computer security behavior: A health belief perspective. Decis. Support Syst. **46**(4), 815–825 (2009)
6. Ritter, F.E., Kim, J.W., Morgan, J.H., Carlson, R.A.: Running Behavioral Studies with Human Participants: A Practical Guide. Sage Publications, Thousand Oaks (2012)
7. Sasse, M.A., Brostoff, S., Weirich, D.: Transforming the weakest link a human/computer interaction approach to usable and effective security. BT Technol. J. **19**(3), 122–131 (2001)
8. Stanton, J.M., Mastrangelo, P.R., Stam, K.R., Jolton, J.: Behavioral information security: Two end user survey studies of motivation and security practices
9. Stanton, J.M., Stam, K.R., Guzman, I., Caldera, C.: Examining the linkage between organizational commitment and information security. In: IEEE International Conference on Systems Man and Cybernetics, vol. 3, pp. 2501–2506 (2003)
10. Stanton, J.M., Stam, K.R., Mastrangelo, P., Jolton, J.: Analysis of end user security behaviors. Comput. Secur. **24**(2), 124–133 (2005)
11. Stephanou, A.: The impact of information security awareness training on information security behaviour. Ph.D. Thesis (2009)
12. Whitten, A., Tygar, J.D.: Why johnny can't encrypt: A usability evaluation of pgp 5.0. In: USENIX Security, 1999 (1999)

Share to Protect

Quantitative Study on Privacy Issues in V2X-Technology

Teresa Schmidt[✉], Ralf Philipsen, and Martina Ziefle

Human-Computer Interaction Center,
RWTH Aachen University, Aachen, Germany
{schmidt,philipsen,ziefle}@comm.rwth-aachen.de

Abstract. Currently, V2X-technology is a highly prominent research topic. The numerous advantages, possible applications and development opportunities of this intelligent technology connection into everywhere traffic situations encourage research associations worldwide to work together. Main goals are the reduction of traffic accidents, optimization and increase of energy efficiency and formation of a dense information network. However, without the acceptance of the technology from the users' side, the needed data and information may not be provided. In order to understand the users' attitude towards privacy and data security, the present study focuses the willingness to share data depending on different traffic situations. Using an empirical research approach, it can be stated, that users tend to be more willing to share (different types of) data to reduce the probability of a severe event. Although the necessity is transported, a general rejection of transferring (any kind of) data could be detected.

Keywords: V2X-technology · V2X-communication · Privacy · User acceptance data · Security

1 Research Perspective and State of the Art

The steadily growing motorized individual traffic in metropolitan areas and the urban environment is a significant part of the quality of life enhancing mobility today. With reports on more than 300,000 traffic accidents each year (in Germany), which involve personal injuries or mortality, it is still a dangerous and unsafe part of life. In these accidents, human error is still the most common cause [1]. Technology can be used to reduce traffic accidents, which can be confirmed by the decreasing number of automobile crashes during the implementation of driver supporting systems [2, 3]. This highlights the clear potential of improvement in the economic and ecological balance of road traffic through the implementation of novel technologies. A promising approach addressing the safety and economical problems is the use of innovative transport technology.

By networking traffic participants among themselves and with their environment (Vehicle-to-X), the transport may become not only safer, but more efficient, more environmental friendly and more comfortable. In this sense, driver assistance systems

© Springer International Publishing Switzerland 2016
T. Tryfonas (Ed.): HAS 2016, LNCS 9750, pp. 152–163, 2016.
DOI: 10.1007/978-3-319-39381-0_14

(e.g. adaptive cruise control), which work with information exchange through on-board sensors, have already been established. Vehicle-to-X-technology (V2X), is based on the exchange of transport-related real-time data. Given the extent of the obligatory data collection in the context of successful and effective V2X-communication, critical aspects arise on protecting the privacy of their users [4]. The many possibilities of surveillance and mass data collection are negative contrasts to personal (motion) freedom. However, the success of V2X-applications can only be secured if users are willing to disclose information about themselves. To launch V2X-technology into actual traffic scenarios, it is of utmost importance, that users are willing to share different types of data [5].

By sharing real-time data, the outcomes expect to relieve the driver warning and assistance systems, optimize the intelligent, centralized traffic management, and gain reductions in emissions through more efficient driving [6–9]. Further, connecting all traffic participants prospects an improvement of energy efficiency [10] as well as a reduction of fatalities [11].

Leading goals of the V2X-technology are therefore dependent on traffic participants to share different types of information about themselves with the infrastructure, the vehicle and other traffic participants. For this reason, the involvement of the potential user is indispensable in the system design. According to this claim, this present study analyses user acceptance patterns for privacy and data security aspects of V2X-communication in different traffic situations. With focus on the question if the severity of the situation determinants the willingness to share (personal) data.

Former studies showed, that a refusal of providing the information increases the more personal an information gets on the one hand [12] and on the other hand especially in comfort and infotainment centered contexts.

Overall, the results illustrate a skeptical attitude on behalf of potential users. This leads to the current research question, if an increasing severity of a traffic situation may shift the rejection of transferring data towards an approval.

2   Question Addressed and Methodological Approach

To explore, whether the severity of a traffic situation determinants the willingness to share (personal) data, this research follows a scenario based approach. First, we carried out potential user focus groups to identify traffic situations in which the use of V2X-technology seemed possible and helpful to the participant. Further, we conducted an online survey. To be able to communicate the vision of V2X-communication, we introduced three of the beforehand identified traffic situations with an illustration and informative text. Each scenario represents a situation with distinct characteristics (see Sect. 2.3). The described situation proceeds without damage due to the use of V2X-technology. The following research design was pursued (Fig. 1):

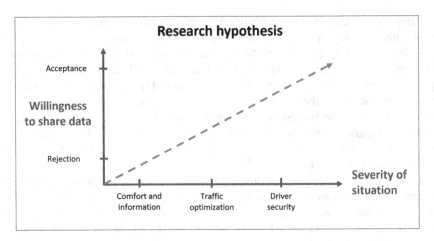

Fig. 1. Research hypothesis: the willingness to share data will increase when the traffic situation becomes more severe.

2.1 Questionnaire Design

The online survey comprises the following elements:

Demographical data of the user was questioned in the first part of the survey. Followed by a question about the driver's licence(s), the experience as driver of a vehicle due to a previous or current job (parcel service, truck driver, emergency service etc.) was queried as well as the frequency of vehicle usage. Further, the technical self-efficiency was measured [13], the individual confidence in one's capability to use technical devices. Closing this part, the participants should indicate their individual driving behaviour with a set of 11 items (6-point Likert scale, 5 = full agreement) regarding risks in traffic.

The next section introduced the traffic situations, which let participants envision the use of V2X-technology on different levels. A closer description follows (see Sect. 2.2).

The following section comprised privacy and data security. With a set of seven items (6-point Likert scale, 5 = full agreement), the type of (possibly shared) data was questioned. Here, we divided the data types as follows:

- Current motion data (e.g. position)
- Intention to move (e.g. planned route in navigation system)
- Information of past trips (e.g. average speed, preferred routes)
- Type of road user (e.g. bus, pedestrian)
- Vehicle specifications (e.g. safety equipment)
- Demographic data of driver (e.g. age, gender)
- Physiological data of driver (e.g. reaction rate, emotional state)
- Other personal data of driver (e.g. driving experience)

Further, the storage duration (capture and process, short term, long term) of the data and possible recipients (local road users, local road infrastructure, central servers of traffic management and public authorities, central servers of companies) were identified.

2.2   Scenarios

The following traffic situations were introduced to demonstrate different possibilities of interaction between the vehicle, the driver, the infrastructure and other traffic participants.

Driver (and Vehicle) Security. Participants had to envision to be the driver of a car, which drives on a highway towards the end of a traffic jam. However, the end of the traffic jam is hidden behind a curve, but as all cars are equipped with V2X-technology, the information about the jam arrives in the participant's car early enough to start a slow down. The severity of the situation is classified high (see Fig. 3).

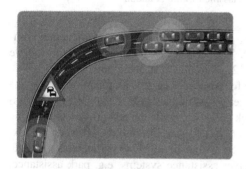 

Fig. 2. Medium severity classified traffic situation.   **Fig. 3.** High severity classified traffic situation.

Optimization of Traffic. Again, out of the perspective of the driver, the second scenario described a situation in which the participants are driving on a multilane way. With the right lane ending, their car need to rearrange to another line with the zipper method. To improve or maintain the traffic flow, the communicating vehicles use V2X-technology, which also allows a reduced fuel consumption. The severity of the situation is classified as medium (see Fig. 2).

Comfort and Information. The participants had to envision to drive through an unknown city. The smart vehicle is able to actively give them information about touristic spots, shopping malls or cultural events. Using V2X-technology, the car communicates with the infrastructure or city itself and displays all possibilities onscreen in the car. Information about opening hours or entry fees, e.g. of a nearby museum can also be displayed. The severity of the situation is classified low (see Fig. 4).

2.3   Sample

In total 169 people participated in this study. Their age ranged from 17 to 68 years with an average age of 32.18 years (SD = 12.63). 50.3 % (n = 85) participants were male, 49.7 % (n = 84) female. The most-often stated educational attainment was a university degree (43.2 %, n = 73), followed by the graduation from high school (41.4 %,

Fig. 4. Low severity classified traffic situation.

n = 70) and vocational trainings (8.9 %, n = 15). The remaining participants completed secondary school (6.5 %, n = 11). The technical self-efficiency in the sample was rather high with M = 3.68 (SD = 1.12, scale min = 0, scale max = 5).

All participants hold a driving license for passenger cars. With regard to the private vehicle use the following frequencies arise: 59 participants (35.1 %) used their car(s) on a daily base, 46 used it 1-3 times a week (27.4 %), while the rest drove less than one time a week. Furthermore, 29 participants (17.2 %) were professional drivers, i.e. taxi or bus drivers, courier drivers or truck drivers. Almost half of the participants (47.3 %, n = 80) had previous experience with driver assistance systems, e.g. park assistance, distance control or lane assistants. The average willingness to take risks in road transport was rather low (M = 1.70, SD = 0.81, scale min = 0, scale max = 5).

3   Results

The presentation of the results is structured as follows: First, the willingness to share different types of data in the scenarios studied will be presented. Second, the consent to the capturing, processing and storing of data by various possible users will be described.

3.1   Willingness to Share Data

The willingness to share data varied to a great extend depending on the type of data and the purpose of use (see Fig. 5). Significant main effects of data types were found in all scenarios (*Security*: $F(7,162) = 81.844$, $p < .001$, *Optimization*: $F(7,162) = 68.594$, $p < .001$, *Comfort*: $F(7,160) = 27.747$, $p < .001$). However, the effect sizes decrease from the security-related scenario to the optimization-related and finally the comfort-related scenario.

Besides the effects of data type scenario-based effects could be observed. Pairwise comparisons of the scenarios revealed that the willingness to share a certain type of data differs significantly depending on the purpose of use. For most of the data types the following rule was observed: The higher the severity of the usage context the more likely participants were willing to share information (p < .05 for all pairwise comparisons). Exceptions were found regarding the current motion data, information about the intention to move and the demographic data of the driver: First, the participants did not distinguish between the security- and optimization-related scenario regarding their willingness to exchange data about their current motion (pairwise comparison n.s.). Second, highest approval rates regarding sharing information about the intention to move and the driver's demography were found in the scenario related to comfort improvements.

Statistical analyzes with gender, age, technical-self-efficiency or risk taking in road transport as between subject factors in the repeated measurement design revealed no significant effects on the differences between the scenarios regarding the willingness to share data.

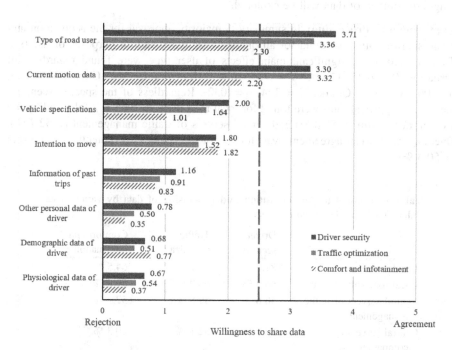

Fig. 5. Average willingness to share various types of data differentiated by the purpose of use

Overall, a willingness to share data could only be shown for two types of data in two specific scenarios. Only information about what type of road user the participant is, e.g. pedestrian, bicyclist, or car, (*Security*: M = 3.71, SD = 1.64; *Optimization*: M = 3.36, SD = 1.91) and current motion data (*Security*: M = 3.30, SD = 1.68; *Optimization*: M = 3.32, SD = 1.72) achieved positive approval ratings (M > 2.5) regarding the data exchange for the purpose of security or optimization. Regarding comfort-based scenarios a neutral to slight rejecting position could be shown for the same types of data.

Regardless of the scenario, the transmission of all remaining types of data was rejected averagely, e.g. information of future (*Intention to move*, M_{max} = 1.82, SD = 1.95) or past movement (*Information about past trips*, M_{max} = 1.16, SD = 1.60). The lowest openness was found regarding personal data. There was a strict rejection to share demographic or physiological data, as well as other personal data of the driver (M < 1.0 for all scenarios).

3.2   Data Users

Beside the types of data, the information's possible users and usage was analyzed and will be presented in the following section. To begin with, the possible users who should be allowed to capture and process data will be described. Afterward, the short- and long-term storage of data will be explored.

Capturing and Processing: In summary, a majority approval for the acquisition and processing of data was found for all queried user types and all purposes of use (see Table 1). However, significant main effects of user type were found regarding all scenarios (*Security*: Cramer-V = .235, p < .001, *Optimization*: Cramer-V = .205, p < .001, *Comfort*: Cramer-V = .114, p = .032). Regardless of the specific scenario, the highest approval rates were found for local road users (> 64.5 %), followed by the local infrastructure (> 59.8 %) and central servers of traffic management (> 52.7 %). Overall, the lowest agreement was found for companies as potential data users (> 50.3 %).

Table 1. Consent to the **acquisition and processing** of data by various users differentiated by the purpose of use.

	Driver security	Traffic optimization	Comfort and information
Local road users	81.7 %	78.7 %	64.5 %
Local road infrastructure	68.6 %	66.9 %	59.8 %
Central servers of traffic management	58.6 %	59.8 %	52.7 %
Central servers of companies	52.1 %	52.1 %	50.3 %

In addition, main effects of the scenario type were identified that have to be considered in relation to the potential users: There was a clear and significant distinction between the security- and optimization-related scenarios on the one hand and the comfort-related on the other hand for local road users and infrastructure as well as for servers of traffic management (p < .05 for all pairwise comparisons between *Security* and *Comfort* or *Optimization* and *Comfort*). Basically, the approval rates were significantly lower in the comfort-based scenario regarding the aforementioned user groups. In contrast, the presented scenario had no significant effect on the approval rates for companies as potential user that captures and processes data.

Short-term Storage: In addition to the plain acquisition and processing of data, the short-term storage of information up to one week was explored. As indicated in Table 2, the local road users are no longer the preferred data handlers in terms of retention. In fact, the participants expressed higher approval to local road infrastructure and central servers of traffic management as potential storage locations regardless of the presented scenario. Again, companies got the lowest agreement rates. Regardless of the differences between the individual users, short-term storage of data was refused by a majority of the participants for all potential users and purposes of use (max approval rate: 24.3 %).

Table 2. Consent to the **short-term storage** of data by various users differentiated by the purpose of use.

	Driver security	Traffic optimization	Comfort and information
Local road users	15.4 %	15.4 %	10.1 %
Local road infrastructure	24.3 %	20.7 %	14.2 %
Central servers of traffic management	24.3 %	18.3 %	10.7 %
Central servers of companies	11.8 %	10.7 %	8.3 %

Again, main effects of user type and presented scenario could be identified. Pairwise comparisons revealed the already known distinction between the security- and optimization-related scenarios on the one hand and the comfort-related on the other hand for all user groups but companies. Their approval ratings were again independent from the given scenario.

Long-term Storage: Last, the long-term storage in terms of a permanent storage with undefined retention time was analyzed. As shown by Table 3, the overall agreement rates were rather low (< 10 %) for all users and scenarios, whereby a clear rejection of this storage period could be identified.

Table 3. Consent to the **permanent storage** of data by various users differentiated by the purpose of use.

	Driver security	Traffic optimization	Comfort and information
Local road users	1.8 %	2.4 %	3.0 %
Local road infrastructure	5.3 %	5.3 %	3.6 %
Central servers of traffic management	7.1 %	5.9 %	5.3 %
Central servers of companies	5.3 %	4.7 %	5.3 %

Clear preferences in terms of preferred data handlers did not emerge in any of the described scenarios. Accordingly, there were no significant main effects of the scenario type and the potential user group.

In accordance with the willingness to share different types of data, the scenario-related effects were not influenced by the researched user factors.

4 Discussion and Outlook

This research was directed to privacy issues and acceptance patterns in V2X-technology out of a socio-psychological perspective. With an increasing research attention worldwide, the idea of integrating smart vehicles, able to communicate not only with their infrastructure, but also with other (and weak) traffic participants, raises new research directions and ambitions [14, 15]. It is strived for a higher energy efficiency, saving time through traffic [16, 17] and a more secure mobility behavior [18], but also questions about public perception, privacy and technical acceptance rise steadily [19–21].

Therefore, an understanding of perceived data security and the participants' willingness to share data is an inevitable necessity for future V2X-research. Based on different traffic scenarios, this quantitative research approach focused on the question, whether the willingness to share data increases with the severity of the traffic situation. Taking (potential future) users into account and looking at three different traffic events, the results show, that the more severe a situation is perceived, the more willingness to share data can be detected. Although, it seems rather logical to decrease the possibility of a fatal event for "a small price", the trade-off of providing information to ensure the higher safety level is still questionable for the user, which is displayed in the results.

By giving the user the opportunity to offer or decline eight different data types, it became evident, that all data types differ significantly in their likeliness to be shared (in all scenarios and overall).

Although it should be mentioned, that the effect of differentiating likeliness to share data in terms of the data type decreases, the less severe a situation gets. Or in other words: if a situation is not hazardous, there are no perceived differences of data types, but a full rejection.

Overall, a strong rejection to share data is prominent. Only the data types "current motion data" and "type of road user" are agreed upon in all traffic situations. A very strong rejection was given to "physiological data, demographical data and other personal information". From a communicational point of view, user mostly agree on transferred data which relate to a current status (current motion data, type of road user, vehicle specifications). The agreement decreases slightly, when it comes to data, which relate to future information (intention to move). Even less approval was given to data, which maintained information about what happen in the past (information about past trips) and an absolute rejection could be identified to personal data (as mentioned beforehand).

Further, the results show that participants despite the overall rejection show a tendency to be more willing to share personal data in a situation, which increases comfort and provides information compared to increasing safety or optimize traffic.

Possible reasons could be the understanding, that an information about the "intention to move" may be important to generate better information (and/or offers) from the system towards the user. A perceived importance to gather more information about a target location. Also, "demographic data" could be perceived as important for infotainment scenarios, in order of suitable suggestions (e.g. special entry fees for a museum for elderly).

In addition to the willingness to share different types of data, potential users and storage periods of the information have been explored. It became clear that the usage context's severity effects the agreement to share data with certain user groups. In particular, participants made a significant distinction between security- and optimization-related scenarios on the one side and purposes of use that only aim to increase comfort on the other side. Interestingly, this distinction was not made for companies as potential data distributors, which were not accepted to capture, process or store data by a majority of the sample at all, which hints at a general lack of confidence in commercial exploitation of user information. A similar unambiguous rejection was found regarding the long-term storage of data. Here, even the main effects of the scenario and the user group found for data capturing and short-term storage were covered.

Consequently, the results lead to implications for the development of V2X-technologies: Data exchange in transport cannot be generalized. User's clearly distinguish between the types of information, the potential receivers and the purposes of use. However, currently a predominantly negative attitude towards sharing data can be identified. Hence, the question arises, what advantages need to be provided, so that the user agrees on the transfer of data and communication. A step forward would be to identify the accepted trade-offs out of a users' perspective. Not only the user requirements of the so-called early adopter are necessary, but also insights of opponents of this technology should be taken into account in order to integrate a holistic users' perspective into the early stages of the design circle of new technology, specifically V2X-technology.

Therefore, our next research step will focus on the identification of trade-offs between perceived advantages and drawbacks. Using a conjoint analysis method, which offers the combination of a statistical estimation algorithm and a measurement model. Here, we focus on the future communication and acceptance of V2X-technology in order to include potential users (as active part) and possible opponents (as passive part) in today's research. To enhance the acceptance of V2X-technologies, it is important to integrate users in the future development. In that way current barriers can be dismantled, because only then can a holistic launch of V2X-communication succeed and gain the full potential of this technology. In order to gain more protection, we need to share information. Share to protect.

Acknowledgements. We would like to thank the anonymous reviewers for their constructive comments on an earlier version of this manuscript. Also, we owe gratitude to the research group on mobility at RWTH Aachen University, which works in the Center for European Research on Mobility (CERM) supported by the Excellence Initiative of German State and Federal Government. Many thanks go also to Juliana Brell and Iana Gorokhova for their valuable research input.

References

1. Statistisches Bundesamt: Verkehrsunfälle [traffic accidents] – Fachserie 8 Reihe 7 (2014). https://www.destatis.de/DE/Publikationen/Thematisch/TransportVerkehr/Verkehrsunfaelle/VerkehrsunfaelleM.html. Accessed 2 Feb 2016
2. Farmer, C.M.: Effect of electronic stability control on automobile crash risk. Traffic Inj. Prev. **5**(4), 317–325 (2004)
3. Breuer, J.J., Faulhaber, A., Frank, P., Gleissner, S.: Real world safety benefits of brake assistance systems. In: 20th International Technical Conference on the Enhanced Safety of Vehicles (ESV) (2007)
4. Zimmer, M.: Surveillance, privacy and the ethics of vehicle safety communication technologies. Ethics Inf. Technol. **7**(4), 201–210 (2005)
5. Othmane, L.B., Weffers, H., Mohamad, M.M., Wolf, M.: A survey of security and privacy in connected vehicles. In: Benhaddou, D., Al-Fuqaha, A. (eds.) Wireless Sensor and Mobile Ad-Hoc Networks, pp. 217–247. Springer, New York (2015)
6. Le, L., Festag, A., Baldessari, R., Zhang, W.: V2X communication and intersection safety. In: Meyer, G., Valldorf, J., Gessner, W. (eds.) Advanced Microsystems for Automotive Applications. VDI-Buch, pp. 97–107. Springer, Berlin, Heidelberg (2009)
7. Katsaros, K., Kernchen, R., Dianati, M., Rieck, D., Zinoviou, C.: Application of vehicular communications for improving the efficiency of traffic in urban areas. Wirel. Commun. Mob. Comput. **11**(12), 1657–1667 (2011)
8. Gajananan, K., Sontisirikit, S., Zhang, J., Miska, M., Chung, E., Guha, S., Prendinger, H.: A cooperative its study on green light optimisation using an integrated traffic, driving, and communication simulator. In: 36th Australasian Transport Research Forum (ATRF), Brisbane, Queensland, Australia (2013)
9. Iglesias, I., Isasi, L., Larburu, M., Martin, A., Peña, A.: Networked clean vehicles, how the environment information will improve fuel efficiency and CO2 emissions. SAE Int. J. Fuels Lubricants **2**(1), 167–171 (2009)
10. Themann, P., Kotte, J., Raudszus, D., Eckstein, L.: Discrete dynamic optimization in automated driving systems to improve energy efficiency in cooperative networks. In: Proceedings of IEEE Intelligent Vehicles Symposium, Dearborn, Michigan, USA, pp. 370–375 (2014)
11. Volvo (a): Volvo Cars and POC to demonstrate life-saving wearable cycling tech concept at International CES 2015. https://www.media.volvocars.com/us/enus/media/pressreleases/155565/volvo-cars-and-poc-to-demonstratelife-saving-wearable-cycling-tech-concept-at-international-ces-2015. Accessed 22 Jan 2016
12. Schmidt, T., Philipsen, R., Ziefle, M.: Safety first? V2X – percived benefits, barriers and trade-offs of automated driving. In: Full Paper Submitted to the International Conference on Vehicle Technology and Intelligent Transport Systems, Vehits 2015 (2015)
13. Beier, G.: Kontrollüberzeugungen im Umgang mit Technik [Locus of control when interacting with technology]. Rep. Psychol. **24**(9), 684–693 (1999)
14. Volvo (b): Volvo Car Group's first self-driving Autopilot cars test on public roads around Gothenburg. https://www.media.volvocars.com/global/en-gb/media/pressreleases/145619/volvo-car-groups-first-self-driving-autopilot-cars-test-on-public-roads-around-gothenburg. Accessed 22 Jan 2016
15. Google Inc.: Google Self-Driving Car Project. https://plus.google.com/+GoogleSelfDrivingCars. Accessed 28 Jan 2016
16. Van Driel, C.J.G.: Driver support in congestion: an assessment of user needs and impacts on driver and traffic flow (2007)

17. simTD - Sichere Intelligente Mobilität Testfeld Deutschland. http://www.simtd.de/index. dhtml/object.media/deDE/8127/CS/-/backup_publications/Projektergebnisse/simTD-TP5-Abschlussbericht_Teil_B-2_Nutzerakzeptanz_V10.pdf. Accessed 2 Feb 2016
18. Lefevre, S., Petit, J., Bajcsy, R., Laugier, C., Kargl, F.: Impact of v2x privacy strategies on intersection collision avoidance systems. In: IEEE Vehicular Networking Conference, Bosten, United States (2013)
19. Harvey, C., Stanton, N.A.: Usability evaluation for in-vehicle systems. CRC Press, Boca Raton (2013)
20. Zhou, T.: The impact of privacy concern on user adoption of location-based services. Ind. Manage. Data Syst. 111(2), 212–226 (2011)
21. Acquisti, H.A., Brandimarte, L., Loewenstein, G.: Privacy and human behavior in the age of information. Science 347(6221), 509–514 (2015)

The Impact of Security Cues on User Perceived Security in e-Commerce

Samuel N. Smith$^{(\boxtimes)}$, Fiona Fui-Hoon Nah, and Maggie X. Cheng

Missouri University of Science and Technology, Rolla, MO, USA
{snsww4,nahf,chengm}@mst.edu

Abstract. Users are expected to assess the level of security of e-commerce websites before conducting online transactions. In this research, we examine user assessment of security of e-commerce web pages based on cues presented on the web pages. A pilot study was conducted in which each subject assessed six e-commerce web pages with varying cues (i.e., HTTP vs. HTTPS, fraudulent vs. authentic URL, padlocks beside fields), and the findings are reported.

Keywords: Security cues · e-commerce · Cybersecurity · Information security

1 Introduction

For more than a decade, the information security research community has cited users as the "weakest link in the security chain" [1, p. 122]. In other words, a highly advanced security system—which typically consists of firewalls, email encryption, etc.—may not be effective at protecting an organization due to unintended behaviors of its users. For example, a robust email encryption software may not benefit an organization if users misuse or fail to use the encryption methods [2]. Hence, it is important to study and understand human factors in information security. Despite continuing research effort in cybersecurity, organizational information security continues to be negatively affected by human factors. In an IBM report titled "2014 Cyber Security Intelligence Index" [3], it was found that of the 109 security incidents IBM investigated for their clients throughout 2013, more than 95 % were found to "recognize 'human error' as a contributing factor" [p. 3]. Hence, we still have a long way to go in understanding and addressing human factors that lead to undesirable user behavior in information security.

In this paper, we are interested in examining user perceptions of security cues in e-commerce. We refer to security cues as elements of a web page interface that are intended to signal information security. For example, an HTTPS (Hypertext Transfer Protocol Secure) connection is indicated in a web browser window and signals to the user that the web page is using a connection which has been verified by a security protocol, typically SSL (Secure Sockets Layers). Although an HTTPS connection is a reliable way of determining web page security, other security cues also exist. For example, some interfaces, such as log-in screens, include images of padlocks within or near submission fields which are used for entering sensitive information (see Fig. 1).

However, the concern with a number of security cues in e-commerce is that they can be fabricated by a website designer and used for malicious purposes, such as

© Springer International Publishing Switzerland 2016
T. Tryfonas (Ed.): HAS 2016, LNCS 9750, pp. 164–173, 2016.
DOI: 10.1007/978-3-319-39381-0_15

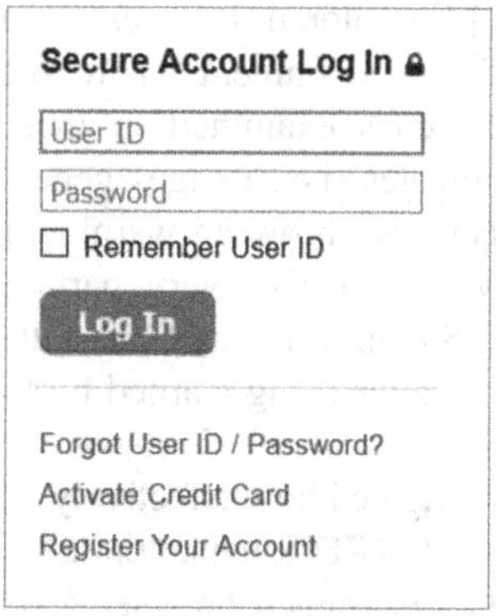

Secure Account Log In 🔒

User ID

Password

☐ Remember User ID

Log In

Forgot User ID / Password?

Activate Credit Card

Register Your Account

Fig. 1. Padlock displayed near login fields

signaling a false sense of security to lure a user into providing sensitive information, including information associated with a credit card number. Therefore, these cues become questionable or unreliable in certain contexts, such as phishing (i.e., the practice of directing users to fraudulent websites). When a security cue is indeed unreliable or fabricated, we refer to it as a security miscue. Given that information security is essential when conducting e-commerce, it is crucial to gain an understanding of how users assess and respond to various security cues (or miscues) in e-commerce. Hence, our research question is:

"How do users assess and respond to security cues in e-commerce?"

We explored this research question by conducting a pilot study in which subjects evaluated online checkout screens that contained variations in terms of security cues and miscues to determine changes in users' perceptions of e-commerce security. The cues we examined consist of: (1) an HTTP vs. HTTPS connection, (2) an authentic vs. fraudulent URL (Uniform Resource Locator), and (3) padlocks vs. no padlocks displayed next to credit card information input fields.

2 Literature Review

We conducted a review of the literature on related work. Studies show that users are more concerned about the content of a web page (e.g., logos) than the security indicators on a web page [4, 5]. Hence, users become susceptible to fraudulent websites, i.e., phishing websites, whose content appears to be authentic. Previous research has examined the components of phishing and how to prevent users from falling victim to an attack. Dhamija et al. [6] took an experimentation approach by asking subjects to evaluate the security of different websites to determine how accurately the subjects could identify phishing attempts. A large number of phishing websites were undetected by the subjects, due to a lack of knowledge of the workings of computer systems and their associated security systems and indicators [6].

Similarly, Schechter et al. [7] explored the question of whether users would enter their passwords in an e-banking environment where security cues had been added, manipulated, or removed. The cues examined in their research comprise HTTPS indicators, site-authentication images (i.e., images generated by a website to authenticate its security and identity), and browser warning pages found within Internet Explorer 7. The results show that nearly every participant entered their password despite the removal of an HTTPS connection and site-authentication images. More than half entered their password even after being warned by the browser that the web page may not be secure.

Herzberg and Jbara [8] investigated how effectively users could identify fraudulent websites which varied in terms of HTTPS indicators and browser security certificates. In one phase of the testing, they examined browser security add-ons which could be customized by the user to fit their preferences. Their results show that the use of customizable security add-ons led to significantly higher user detection rates of fraudulent websites [8].

3 Methodology

To assess the impact of security cues on user perceived security in e-commerce, a pilot study was designed in which users rate their perceived sense of security, trustworthiness, and safety when viewing e-commerce web pages that contain various security cues and miscues. An e-commerce environment was utilized in the study because it is an online scenario where information security is crucial. The online checkout screen of a popular office supply store, Staples, was slightly modified to provide six different variations for subjects to evaluate in a within-subject experiment.

The original checkout screen did not display fields for payment and billing information until the user had entered their complete shipping information. We wanted to display still images of checkout screens to the user and determine how they perceive the security, trustworthiness, and safety of the web page. Therefore, we modified the original checkout screen to display all relevant input fields that a user would typically encounter when purchasing an item online (see Fig. 2). We also slightly modified the text in the tab near the top of the screen to display "Staples Checkout" since we felt it was more appropriate for the context. In addition, we changed the wording of the shaded checkout header above the input fields to "Shipping and Payment Info" to reflect the displayed input fields.

We manipulated three security cues: connection type (HTTP or HTTPS), the URL (fraudulent or authentic), and whether or not padlocks were displayed next to the credit card information input fields (i.e., these padlocks are miscues or invalid security cues). Although generating all combinations of these three cues would result in 8 variations of the checkout screen ($2 \times 2 \times 2$), we discarded two of them: (1) secure connection (HTTPS) with a fraudulent URL and no padlocks displayed next to input fields, and (2) secure connection (HTTPS) with a fraudulent URL with padlocks displayed next to input fields. We used the insecure connection (HTTP) scenario to assess the effect of a fraudulent vs. authentic URL. Thus, we used a total of 6 variations of the checkout screen (see Table 1). The security cues used in the study are shown in Figs. 3, 4, 5, 6 and 7.

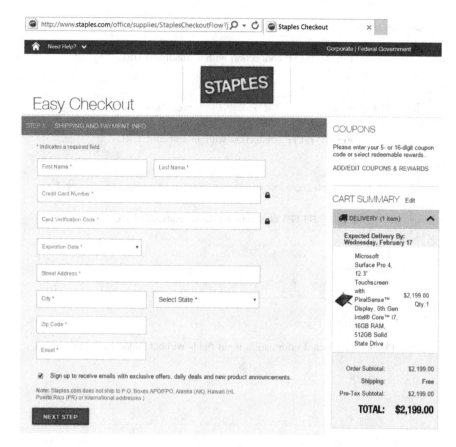

Fig. 2. A checkout screen for the pilot study

Table 1. Checkout screen variations.

1	Unsecure connection (HTTP), phishing URL, no padlocks displayed next to credit card input fields
2	Unsecure connection (HTTP), phishing URL, with padlocks displayed next to credit card input fields
3	Unsecure connection (HTTP), authentic URL, no padlocks displayed next to credit card input fields
4	Unsecure connection (HTTP), authentic URL, with padlocks displayed next to credit card input fields
5	Secure connection (HTTPS), authentic URL, no padlocks displayed next to credit card input fields
6	Secure connection (HTTPS), authentic URL, with padlocks displayed next to credit card input fields

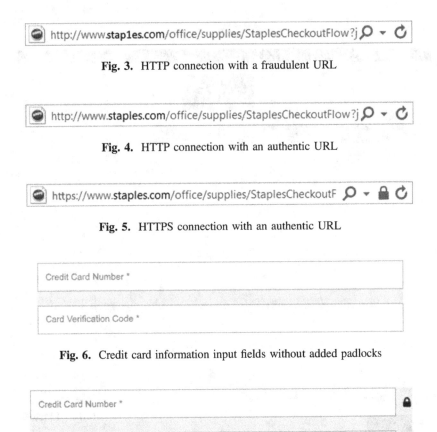

Fig. 3. HTTP connection with a fraudulent URL

Fig. 4. HTTP connection with an authentic URL

Fig. 5. HTTPS connection with an authentic URL

Fig. 6. Credit card information input fields without added padlocks

Fig. 7. Credit card information input fields with added padlocks outside the fields (miscues)

After examining each checkout screen, the participant was given a set of questions (see Table 2) to answer using a 7-point Likert scale (i.e., 1 = strongly disagree to 7 = strongly agree) to assess the following variables:

1. **Intended Purchase Behavior:** The likelihood that the user would carry out the transaction.
2. **Trust:** The degree to which the user perceives the web page to be trustworthy.
3. **Security:** The degree to which the user perceives the web page to be secure.
4. **Safety:** The degree to which the user perceives the web page to be safe.

After all six checkout screens had been evaluated, the participant was asked to provide demographic information and any open-ended comments or feedback.

Table 2. Measurement of variables.

Variable	Items
Intended Purchase Behavior	1. I would perform the transaction on this web page
	2. I would carry out the transaction on this web page
	3. I would complete the transaction on this web page
Trust	1. I would enter my personal information into the web page
	2. I trust the web page
	3. I believe that the web page is trustworthy
Security and Safety	1. The web page appears to be (secure/safe)
	2. The web page gives me a sense of (security/safety)
	3. I believe that the web page is (secure/safe)

4 Data Collection

Fourteen undergraduate and graduate students were recruited from a Midwestern university to participate in the pilot study. Their ages ranged from 18-34. Of the fourteen subjects, seven were female and seven were male. Upon arrival, each participant was provided with an informational document on the experiment. They were given a scenario in which they had to imagine that they were about to begin a new career and were shopping online to purchase a new laptop. They were told that they would be shown six checkout screens for the laptop and that they would be given a questionnaire after each screen to determine whether or not they would proceed with the online purchase. All subjects viewed the checkout screens in the order listed in Table 1.

5 Findings

In this study, we assessed the effects of (i) HTTP vs. HTTPS connection; (ii) an authentic vs. fraudulent URL; (iii) padlocks vs. no padlocks displayed next to credit card information input fields. We averaged the item responses for the same variable in each condition and used paired t-tests to compare them across different conditions.

To assess the effects of HTTP vs. HTTPS connection, we carried out paired t-tests to compare user responses of:

- Screenshots 4 and 6 (HTTP vs. HTTPS with padlocks displayed next to credit card information input fields)
- Screenshots 3 and 5 (HTTP vs. HTTPS with no padlock displayed next to credit card information input fields)

Table 3 shows the descriptive statistics and paired t-test results for comparisons of screenshots 4 and 6 (HTTP vs. HTTPS with padlocks), whereas Table 4 shows the descriptive statistics and paired t-test results for comparisons of screenshots 3 and 5 (HTTP vs. HTTPS with no padlock).

The results show that when padlocks were displayed next to the credit card fields, subjects perceived the HTTPS connection to offer an increased level of security and

Table 3. Descriptive statistics and paired t-tests for screenshot 4 vs. 6 (HTTP vs. HTTPS with padlocks).

Variable	Mean	Standard deviation	p-value (1-tailed)
Behavior (screen 4)	4.98	1.61	0.07
Behavior (screen 6)	5.50	1.37	(p > 0.05)
Trust (screen 4)	4.93	1.55	0.05
Trust (screen 6)	5.48	1.33	(marginal)
Security (screen 4)	4.76	1.53	0.03*
Security (screen 6)	5.43	1.31	(p < 0.05)
Safety (screen 4)	4.90	1.58	0.03*
Safety (screen 6)	5.55	1.34	(p < 0.05)

* $p < 0.05$

Table 4. Descriptive statistics and paired t-tests for screenshot 3 vs. 5 (HTTP vs. HTTPS with no padlock).

Variable	Mean	Standard deviation	p-value (1-tailed)
Behavior (screen 3)	4.50	1.87	0.15
Behavior (screen 5)	5.14	1.51	(p > 0.05)
Trust (screen 3)	4.38	1.83	0.14
Trust (screen 5)	5.07	1.48	(p > 0.05)
Security (screen 3)	4.29	1.87	0.13
Security (screen 5)	5.00	1.47	(p > 0.05)
Safety (screen 3)	4.38	1.84	0.12
Safety (screen 5)	5.12	1.50	(p > 0.05)

sense of safety than the HTTP connection (see Table 3). As presented in Table 3, the difference in trust perceptions is marginal and the difference in behavior is not significant. When there were no padlocks displayed next to the credit card fields, subjects did not perceive any difference between the HTTPS connection and the HTTP connection (see Table 4). These results are interesting in that the presence of padlocks next to the credit card fields (i.e., miscues or invalid security cues) sensitized subjects to perceive HTTPS to be safer and more secure than HTTP, but when no padlock was present, subjects did not perceive any difference between HTTPS and HTTP.

To assess the effects of an authentic URL (i.e., staples.com) vs. a fraudulent URL (i.e., staples.com), we conducted paired t-tests to compare user responses of:

- Screenshots 2 and 4 (a fraudulent URL vs. an authentic URL with padlocks displayed next to credit card information input fields)
- Screenshots 1 and 3 (a fraudulent URL vs. an authentic URL with no padlock displayed next to credit card information input fields)

Table 5 shows the descriptive statistics and paired t-test results for comparisons of screenshots 2 and 4 (fraudulent vs. authentic URL with padlocks), whereas Table 6 shows the descriptive statistics and paired t-test results for comparisons of screenshots 1 and 3 (fraudulent vs. authentic URL with no padlock).

Table 5. Descriptive statistics and paired t-tests for screenshot 2 vs. 4 (fraudulent vs. authentic URL with padlocks).

Variable	Mean	Standard deviation	p-value (1-tailed)
Behavior (screen 2)	4.10	2.06	0.03*
Behavior (screen 4)	4.98	1.61	(p < 0.05)
Trust (screen 2)	4.02	1.98	0.03*
Trust (screen 4)	4.93	1.55	(p < 0.05)
Security (screen 2)	3.74	1.87	0.02*
Security (screen 4)	4.76	1.53	(p < 0.05)
Safety (screen 2)	3.98	2.00	0.02*
Safety (screen 4)	4.90	1.58	(p < 0.05)

* p < 0.05

Table 6. Descriptive statistics and paired t-tests for screenshot 1 vs. 3 (fraudulent vs. authentic URL with no padlock).

Variable	Mean	Standard deviation	p-value (1-tailed)
Behavior (screen 1)	4.83	1.62	0.27
Behavior (screen 3)	4.50	1.87	(p > 0.05)
Trust (screen 1)	4.60	1.75	0.36
Trust (screen 3)	4.38	1.85	(p > 0.05)
Security (screen 1)	4.29	1.67	0.50
Security (screen 3)	4.29	1.87	(p > 0.05)
Safety (screen 1)	4.56	1.86	0.39
Safety (screen 3)	4.38	1.84	(p > 0.05)

The results show that when padlocks were displayed next to the credit card fields, subjects were able to distinguish between the fraudulent vs. authentic URL in all aspects assessed, i.e., e-commerce purchase behavior (i.e., transact or not), trust, security and sense of safety (see Table 5). When there were no padlocks displayed next to the credit card fields, subjects did not perceive any difference between the fraudulent and authentic URL (see Table 6). These results are interesting in that the presence of padlocks next to the credit card fields (i.e., miscues or invalid security cues) sensitized subjects to become more cautious in identifying fraudulent vs. authentic URLs to avoid phishing whereas subjects did not perceive the security of fraudulent vs. authentic URLs differently when there was no padlock.

To assess the effects of padlocks vs. no padlocks displayed next to credit card information input fields, we conducted paired t-tests to compare user responses of:

- Screenshots 5 and 6 (padlocks vs. no padlocks with HTTPS connection)
- Screenshots 3 and 4 (padlocks vs. no padlocks with HTTP connection)

Table 7 shows the descriptive statistics and paired t-test results for comparisons of screenshots 5 and 6 (padlocks vs. no padlocks with HTTPS connection) whereas Table 8 shows the descriptive statistics and paired t-test results for comparisons of screenshots 3 and 4 (padlocks vs. no padlocks with HTTP connection).

Table 7. Descriptive statistics and paired t-tests for screenshot 5 vs. 6 (padlocks vs. no padlocks with HTTPS).

Variable	Mean	Standard deviation	p-value (1-tailed)
Behavior (screen 5)	5.14	1.51	0.14
Behavior (screen 6)	5.50	1.37	(p > 0.05)
Trust (screen 5)	4.07	1.48	0.10
Trust (screen 6)	5.48	1.33	(p > 0.05)
Security (screen 5)	5.00	1.47	0.08
Security (screen 6)	5.43	1.31	(p > 0.05)
Safety (screen 5)	5.12	1.50	0.08
Safety (screen 6)	5.55	1.34	(p > 0.05)

Table 8. Descriptive statistics and paired t-tests for screenshot 3 vs. 4 (padlocks vs. no padlocks with HTTP).

Variable	Mean	Standard deviation	p-value (1-tailed)
Behavior (screen 3)	4.83	1.87	0.10
Behavior (screen 4)	4.50	1.61	(p > 0.05)
Trust (screen 3)	4.60	1.85	0.06
Trust (screen 4)	4.38	1.55	(p > 0.05)
Security (screen 3)	4.29	1.87	0.07
Security (screen 4)	4.29	1.53	(p > 0.05)
Safety (screen 3)	4.56	1.84	0.08
Safety (screen 4)	4.38	1.58	(p > 0.05)

Subjects did not perceive any difference between having padlocks and not having any padlock next to the credit card fields, regardless of whether the URL indicated HTTPS or HTTP connection. The results are consistent with actual security because padlocks next to the credit card fields do not change or enhance actual security.

Overall, our findings suggest that displaying padlocks next to the credit card fields sensitized subjects to look for other security cues in assessing security. Even though the display of padlocks by themselves did not change users' perceived sense of security, they changed users' sensitivity to security cues.

6   Discussion and Conclusions

Our findings are interesting in that user perceptions of the security of a connection (HTTP vs. HTTPS) and the detection of fraudulent vs. authentic e-commerce websites are moderated by fabricated padlocks displayed next to input fields. We did not expect such findings. Padlocks displayed in the body of a web page do not affect the security of that web page; they are simply images that any web designer can place into a web page. However, they primed our subjects to look for important security cues (i.e., HTTP vs. HTTPS and authenticity of the URL). Even though these padlocks do not increase security, they help to sensitize subjects to important security cues. However, four of the fourteen subjects specifically mentioned that the padlocks next to the credit card fields increased their sense of security. As one participant noted, "The locks next to some fields make it seem like it goes further to protect your security." The perceptions that these padlocks have created for these subjects could pose a serious problem since padlocks in the body of the web page are unreliable security cues, i.e., miscues, that can be easily fabricated for malicious purposes. Also, three out of fourteen subjects mentioned that they use online website reviews when deciding whether or not a web page is secure. It would be intriguing to further examine the degree to which users trust online website reviews when evaluating the security of a web page.

There are several limitations in this pilot study. Since we used a fixed order of screenshots in the study, there could be an ordering effect. As subjects progressed through the screenshots and noticed differences between them, they may have learned to become more proficient in assessing the security of web pages based on these cues. For example, it is possible that the increases in the degrees to which subjects perceived the web pages to be trustworthy, secure, and safe were the results of exposure bias to the checkout screens. Since we only had a small sample size in this pilot study, it was not feasible to include variations in the order of checkout screens to entirely rule out the possibility of ordering effects. This pilot study was carried out to explore user perceptions of basic security cues, and to help us refine the experimental procedures for the full-scale study. In our full-scale study, we will address the above issues by counterbalancing the order of screenshots and using a sample size that provides good statistical power.

Acknowledgements. This research is supported by National Science Foundation grant CNS/1537538 and the Laboratory for Information Technology at Missouri University of Science and Technology.

References

1. Sasse, M., Brostoff, S., Weirich, D.: Transforming the 'weakest link'—a human/computer interaction approach to usable and effective security. BT Technol. J. **19**(3), 122–131 (2001)
2. Whitten, A., Tygar, J.D.: Why Johnny can't encrypt: a usability evaluation of PGP 5.0. In: Proceedings of the 8th USENIX Security Symposium, pp. 169–184 (1999)
3. IBM Corporation: IBM Security Services 2014 Cyber Security Intelligence Index, pp. 1–12. IBM Global Technology Services, Somers, NY (2014)
4. Kauer, M., Pfeiffer, T., Volkamer, M., Theuerling, H., Bruder, R.: It is not about the design—it is about the content! making warnings more efficient by communicating risks appropriately. In: Proceedings of the 6th Annual Conference of the Department of Security and of the Society for Computer Science, pp. 187–198 (2012)
5. Darwish, A., Bataineh, E.: Eye tracking analysis of browser security indicators. In: International Conference on Computer Systems and Industrial Informatics, pp. 1–6 (2012)
6. Dhamija, R., Tygar, J.D., Hearst, M.: Why phishing works. In: Conference on Human Factors in Computing Systems, pp. 581–590 (2006)
7. Schechter, S., Dhamija R., Ozment, A., Fischer, I.: The emperor's new security indicators. In: IEEE Symposium on Security and Privacy, pp. 51–65 (2007)
8. Herzberg, A., Jbara, A.: Security and identification indicators for browsers against spoofing and phishing attacks. ACM Trans. Internet Technol. **8**(4), 1–36 (2008). Article 16

Mass Surveillance in Cyberspace and the Lost Art of Keeping a Secret

Policy Lessons for Government After the Snowden Leaks

Theo Tryfonas[1]([⊠]), Michael Carter[2], Tom Crick[3], and Panagiotis Andriotis[4]

[1] Crypto Group, University of Bristol, Bristol, UK
theo.tryfonas@bristol.ac.uk
[2] Surveillance Studies Centre, Queen's University, Kingston, Canada
michael.carter@queensu.ca
[3] Department of Computing, Cardiff Metropolitan University, Cardiff, UK
tcrick@cardiffmet.ac.uk
[4] The Information Security Group, University College London, London, UK
p.andriotis@ucl.ac.uk

Abstract. Global security concerns, acts of terrorism and organised crime activity have motivated nation states to delve into implementing measures of mass surveillance in cyberspace, the breadth of which was partly revealed by the whistleblower Edward Snowden. But are modern nation states fighting a battle in the wrong space? Is mass surveillance of cyberspace effective and are the conventional metaphors of technology control appropriate for it? Can algorithms detect, classify and decide effectively on what constitutes suspicious activity? We argue that as cyberspace is a construct that has only recently been viewed strategically, let alone indoctrinated (the UKs cyber-security strategy is only four years old), the societal impact of such bulk measures is yet much unclear – as are the assumptions about the fitness of state organisations that are charged with their oversight and the potential for unintended consequences. Recent experiences highlight the role of multiple forms of intelligence inputs, especially human- and community-based, and the need for application of such intrusive measures in a targeted manner. We believe that intrusive measures, where necessary, must be used decoupled from the seductive promises of advanced technology and ought to go hand-in-hand with means that strengthen the affected communities to identify, report and battle extremism and organised crime, in ways that safeguard the fundamental principles of our contemporary democratic Western states.

Keywords: Surveillance · Cyberspace · Public trust

This work has been supported in part by the European Commission through project NIFTy (ISEC 2012 Action Grants HOME/2012/ISEC/INT/4000003892). The ideas discussed appeared first as a talk at the Digital Citizenship and Surveillance Society conference in Cardiff in June 2015. They were subsequently refined into this paper partly via serendipitous encounters enabled by the social medium of Twitter.

T. Tryfonas (Ed.): HAS 2016, LNCS 9750, pp. 174–185, 2016.
DOI: 10.1007/978-3-319-39381-0_16

1   Introduction

In the fall of 2014, UN Special Rapporteur Ben Emmerson submitted his report
on practices of mass surveillance by state actors and the threat that this approach to intelligence gathering poses to universal civil and political rights [1].
Emmerson called for open and transparent discussion between government and
citizens to inform and determine an appropriate balance between public security
and personal privacy. The Special Rapporteur pointed out that what is techno-
logically possible is not necessarily desirable or responsible. This is an argument
that surveillance scholars such as Kirstie Ball have been making for several years
now [2]. However, traction for this debate was limited until June 2013 when files
leaked by NSA whistleblower Edward Snowden were published in the Guardian
by journalist Glenn Greenwald [3].

Two years after the initial release of Snowden files, surveillance legislation
remains highly contested in Canada, the US and the UK. Perhaps most notably
is the sunsetting of section 215 of The Patriot Act and subsequent passing of
the USA FREEDOM Act[1] in the United States in early June 2015 [4]. Days
later the Senate of Canada passed controversial anti-terrorism Bill C-51[2], which
would amend a number of other acts, as well as enact the Security of Canada
Information Sharing Act, receiving sustained public opposition from big business, journalists, law professors, activists and the privacy commissioner [14]. A
week prior to these developments the latest rendition of the so called 'snooper's
charter' in the UK was announced in the 2015 Queen's Speech. Former deputy
Prime Minister Nick Clegg publicly opposed the legislation, currently known as
the Investigatory Powers Bill[3], arguing it threatens the privacy rights of citizens.
Its details are not fully fledged yet at the time of writing, but it is expected to
be a contentious bill and Prime Minister David Cameron has at various points
pointed towards banning the use of strong encryption – albeit there would be
fierce opposition to legislation against it.

These measures are indicative of state attempts to curb terrorism threats
by enabling the development of surveillance capabilities that are of bulk collection nature, rather than targeted to specific individuals. Proponents of these
argue that the proliferation of high technology, including anonymity, cryptography and secure communication tools, enables organised crime and terrorists,
extremists etc. to communicate safely and go undetected. On the other hand
privacy activists advocate the fundamental need for safe spaces to develop one's
ideas, the human right to privacy and an individual's need to protect themselves
from abusive regimes. There is thus a significant research – and national security
– focus on analysing and profiling digital and online behaviour [5,6].

Cyber security is thus emerging as one of the most challenging aspects of
the information age for policymakers, technologists and scholars of international

---

[1] https://www.congress.gov/bill/113th-congress/house-bill/3361.
[2] http://www.parl.gc.ca/HousePublications/Publication.aspx?
     DocId=6932136\&Col=1\&File=4.
[3] https://wiki.openrightsgroup.org/wiki/Investigatory_Powers_Bill.

relations. It has implications for national security, the economy, human rights, civil liberties and international legal frameworks. Although politicians have been aware of the threats of cyber insecurity since the early years of Internet technology, anxiety about the difficulties in resolving or addressing them has increased rather than abated [7,8,12]. In response, governments have begun to develop robust (and wide-reaching) national cyber security strategies [9–11] to outline the way in which they intend to address cyber insecurity. However, in many states where critical infrastructure such as utilities, financial systems and transport have been privatised, these policies are heavily reliant upon what is referred to as the 'public-private partnership' as a key mechanism through which to mitigate the threat. In the UK and US, the public-private partnership has repeatedly been referred to as the 'cornerstone' or 'hub' of cyber security strategy [13], which further raises questions regarding mass surveillance and data retention, particularly who has access to private citizens' data.

In this paper we develop an argument about the place of mass cyberspace surveillance in society. We believe that deployment of intrusive systems on line, where necessary, should be of clear and transparent purpose to the public and accompanied by measures that empower the affected communities to tackle the root causes of concern, e.g. radicalisation, hate speech etc. Drawing on analogies from other surveillance systems we develop the idea of co-creation, in the civic innovation sense of the term, arguing that otherwise Western states risk developing non-transparent and unaccountable structures of power that undermine the fundamental values of their civilisation.

The rest of the paper is organised as follows: Sect. 2 provides some further background to the issue of mass surveillance of cyberspace with an emphasis in the Anglo-Saxon West and discusses aspects of the Snowden leaks; Sect. 3 develops some fundamental ideas and draws on analogies from other domains to explore the difficulties and challenges involved; Sect. 4 introduces our ideas and policy recommendations for a system-of-systems approach and co-creation of intrusive technologies; and finally we conclude with an overview Sect. 5.

2   Background

The debate on mass surveillance, which is comprised of several threads, has engaged a range of social groups including politicians, law makers, journalists, academics, tech firms, activists, artists and the general public. The term mass surveillance is used to distinguish the bulk collection of data from targeted surveillance, which typically involves a 'person of interest'. Central to this aspect of the debate is the legal warrant, which is traditionally issued upon satisfaction of a certain level of suspicion. In the case of Canada, for example, Bill C-13, which was passed in the fall of 2014, significantly lowered the level of suspicion required to justify the collection of personal data. Bill C-13 also addressed the distinction between data and meta data, which is a hotly debated topic in surveillance legislation. In particular, Bill C-13 reduces the limitations on collecting meta data under the guise that it is not intrusive. Advocates of expanded surveillance powers for the state have attempted to mollify concerns by arguing that meta data does not threaten the political or civil rights of citizens because it is data about communication and not the content of communication. This argument has been routinely problematized by opponents who point out that metadata can reveal religious beliefs, political leanings and intimate relationships. Moreover, meta data is used by state actors to kill people, as was famously announced by former NSA and CIA director Michael Hayden [15].

As legislation governing surveillance practices in Western society continues to evolve, a related debate is emerging. In early June, UN Special Rapporteur David Kaye submitted his report on the right to freedom of opinion and expression [16]. Kaye argued that encryption and anonymity in digital communications is fundamental for the preservation of privacy and the protection of opinion and belief. The Special Rapporteur framed encrypted communication as a tool for citizens to protect their human rights from infringement by government agencies. Moreover, he called for the mobilization of state resources to ensure all individuals using digital communication can do so with encryption. Just prior to the release of the report, Nico Sell, co-founder of leading encrypted messaging app Wickr[4], launched a non-profit organization with this goal in mind.

However, less popular apps like Wickr and more mainstream social networking services like WhatsApp and Snapchat are being targeted by governments. In January 2015, UK Prime Minister David Cameron publicly announced his intention to ban communications that are not accessible by government agencies. Cameron asked for and quickly received support for this position from President Obama. The movement to ban encryption points towards the criminalization of private communication, which would threaten a variety of political, civil and human rights. Moreover, security experts have noted that weakening communication by demanding back door access will increase vulnerabilities and by extension could compromise national security. In May 2015, over 140 technology firms, including Apple, Google and Symantec, sent an open letter[5] to President Obama urging him not to push for government access to encrypted communication. In the meantime, apps that offer individuals encrypted communication are proliferating as concern for privacy in mainstream society climbs.

The Snowden leaks revealed a wide portfolio of projects and initiatives both from the NSA in the US, CSIS in Canada and GCHQ in the UK. These range from specific data collection projects such as Optic Nerve, aimed at Yahoo! webcam traffic (Fig. 1), to influencing the development of cryptographic standards to contain vulnerabilities, so they can be penetrated easier [17]. In this varied context the Anderson report [18] that was released recently as a comprehensive review of the UK's capabilities and practice prior to revamping the existing legislation, emphasised a number of issues, amongst the most important - and contested - of which, was the suggestion for judicial rather than ministerial oversight.

---

[4] https://www.wickr.com/.
[5] https://www.washingtonpost.com/world/national-security/
tech-giants-urge-obama-to-resist-backdoors-into-encrypted-communications/
2015/05/18/11781b4a-fd69-11e4-833c-a2de05b6b2a4_story.html.

SECRET STRAP1

Reference: B/7199BA/5001/5/114
Date: December 2008
Copy no:
Issued by: B18, CCHQ

27. Unfortunately, there are issues with undesirable images within the data. It would appear that a surprising number of people use webcam conversations to show intimate parts of their body to the other person. Also, the fact that the Yahoo software allows more than one person to view a webcam stream without necessarily sending a reciprocal stream means that it appears sometimes to be used for broadcasting pornography.

28. A survey was conducted, taking a single image from each of 323 user ids. 23 (7.1%) of these images contained undesirable nudity. From this we can infer that the true proportion of undesirable images in Yahoo webcam is 7.1% ± 3.7% with confidence 95%.

OPTIC NERVE – Yahoo Webcam display and target discovery

Summary
A report on the development of OPTIC NERVE - a web interface to display Yahoo Webcam images sampled from unselected intercept and a system for proportionate target discovery

Fig. 1. Yahoo! webcam traffic monitoring report snapshots from Snowden's cache.

Politicians have already started countering the suggestion by claiming that despite the wide and varied nature of operations, ministers can have more topical information than judges and make decisions quicker, as opposed to going through the overheads of a judiciary procedure. However, due to the wide reach of operations it is questionable how much in depth understanding can law makers develop in the short amounts of time to decide in the absence of a transparent and well defined process. Another interesting point raised after the leaks is about the level of access and trust vested to a third-party, private contractor by security services, which may be indicative of the lack of resourcing of the relevant agencies – and adding to the need for sufficient oversight.

3   Developing Public Understanding of Surveillance in the Context of Cyberspace

3.1   Deconstructing State Imagery of Cyber Surveillance

Politicians use many metaphors and analogies to promote the idea of cyberspace surveillance among the public. David Cameron, the UK Prime Minister, talked in early 2015 about the need for the state to be able to eavesdrop digital communications over the Internet, just as it can happen over the telephony network. Drawing on analogies between the more familiar phone technology and the public's understanding of a legitimate wire-tapping process, he tried to construct an image of accepted mass surveillance.

Another frequently used analogy is the case of the closed-circuit television (CCTV) surveillance systems. This is a familiar, and very tangible, system which in the UK at least enjoys large amounts of public tolerance and even approval [19], even at the face of lack of real evidence of its effectiveness [20]. We will get back to this a bit later, discussing the experience of institutionalisation of CCTV as a means of surveillance, particularly in the UK where it is widely deployed across the country.

Security services in turn have played a role in constructing further the popular image of surveillance in cyberspace. Firstly, they persist in disassociating bulk collection from mass surveillance and differentiating between metadata and content. This is an attempt to legitimise operations based by necessity on a wide scan surface dictated by the complex, interconnected nature of the Internet. In his valedictory speech at the Cabinet War Room on 21 Oct 2014, Sir Iain Lobban, previous head of GCHQ, having just assured that, of the huge volumes of information trafficked on-line, GCHQ were able to capture, store and process only a tiny amount, he went on to say:

"We access the internet at scale so as to dissect it with surgical precision. Practically, it is now impossible to operate successfully in any other way. You can't pick and choose the components of a global interception system that you like (catching terrorists and paedophiles), and those you don't (incidental collection of data at scale): it's one integrated system." [21]

This reinforces the view of cyberspace surveillance as a wide surface scanning process (a Panopticon, as envisaged by Bentham in Fig. 2) followed by a clinical application of targeted algorithmics that would be able to pave the way for the more targeted content analysis by real people. The focus on metadata, bulk collection and automated processing before reasonable suspicion has been raised for a human to intervene, constructs an argument about this practice not constituting surveillance, in the sense of its warranted and targeted application.

Whether the Panopticon metaphor matches the underlying security requirements is a significant question. This is because a metaphor is a conceptual construct able to shape action, as demonstrated by several scholars, including e.g. Tsoukas [22]. Very soon after the attacks of 9/11, Lackoff argued that inappropriately framing the reaction as a 'war on terror' would produce unintended consequences [23]. Other research shows how secure systems implementation is shaped by the dominant security metaphors in use within organisations [24].

The Panopticon metaphor imposes the surveillance burden upon everyone, whether they are watched or not. This usually creates fundamental mistrust among many quarters of society towards government and the security services. But even viewed as bulk collection, it implies a huge sifting load for them. The report excerpts of Fig. 1 demonstrate how the signal to noise ratio increases with bulk collection. The OPTIC NERVE programme was riddled with footage of genitals and posed significant challenges to intelligence officers as of how to handle the situation.

But the 'clinical' perception of the algorithmic component is problematic as well. Just as errors in human judgement may lead to tragic outcomes such as the shooting of Brazilian citizen Charles de Menezes in London by police in the aftermath of the 7/7 attacks, similarly algorithms may equally fail (the headline of Fig. 3 is indicative of such a failure). In fact the absence of human judgement may cause this aspect to be perceived as even more untrustworthy.

Another implicit assumption to legitimise this view is that this activity is organised under a framework of strong oversight. Particularly for the Anglo-Saxon world and especially for the UK, in the light of the strong leadership of

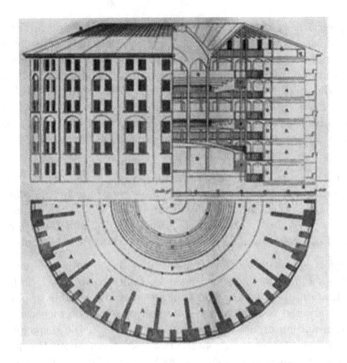

Fig. 2. Part of Jeremy Bentham's designs for a Panopticon prison.

prominent politicians such as Winston Churchill, Margaret Thatcher and Tony Blair, this assurance is almost taken for granted. However, history suggests that in the absence of oversight, socio-political circumstances may provide opportunity for exploitation of such structures. The experience of the rise of the Nazi party in the Weimar Republic is in line with this observation. Finally, we often also forget that the Internet is in reality a young technological development that it is yet much unexplored in terms of national security and military doctrine and use; for example, the UK's Cyber Security Strategy is less than five years old [10].

3.2 Personal Attitudes and the Personal Data Dimension

An interesting dimension of surveillance in cyberspace comes from the personal attitudes of the general public towards intrusive technology and its take up. Most recent disruptive innovations such as social networking platforms and wearable technologies are in fact privacy-intrusive by design. Computational paradigms that are based on the Cloud utilise lightweight computational intelligence of embedded systems and devices and harness the power of on-line servers to process large amounts of personal data. This 'commoditization' of personal data happens on the trade off of personal service provision (e.g. wayfinding) in return for targeted advertising or aggregated consumer behaviour insight development that is then cashed in by the service provider, e.g. the GoogleAds model [25].

2 August 2013, 18 46

Americans googling 'pressure cookers' end up being questioned by security forces

Photo: EPA

Married couple from Suffolk County, New York, was unpleasantly surprised by discovering six men from a joint terrorism task force at their house who came to check if they were terrorists. The raid was caused by "suspicious" web search of "pressure cookers" and "backpacks".

It seems that "pressure cookers" internet inquiries attract close attention of the US security

Fig. 3. Failures of algorithmic determination after the Boston bombings.

Despite the fact that providers of services such as Google and Facebook usually operate in multi-jurisdictions, which make difficult a coherent legislative approach and leave a lot of issues with respect to protection of personal data, there is a huge take up of their services. It seems that the personal value realised for each user, combined with the unclear implications/risks to the individual from their use have contributed largely to this. This is despite general concerns of legislators for their operation, as in the case of Belgium that investigated Facebook tracking of users, even when not logged in [26]. Also despite journalists and researchers have flagged how both in terms of practicalities such as extended data retention periods (e.g. [27]), but also how theoretically can be shown that providers tend to maximise their payoffs when they misuse personal data [28].

We argue that one of the side effects of this is the casualisation of attitudes towards privacy rights. There is a creeping indifference that could develop to passive acceptance through repeated interaction and use of such technologies – in a way that Giddens describes as routinisation in his theory of structuration [29]. However, familiarity with people giving up personal data in return for real value should not necessarily be viewed negatively in the context of cyber surveillance. We will argue in the following section that such relationship can be at the centre of the creation of new surveillance systems, built upon consensus where intelligence is necessary and there is clear understanding of its value to all stakeholders.

4   Co-creating Viable Surveillance Systems

We referred earlier to CCTV as an example of a surveillance technology that has been relatively successful, from a technology acceptance and use point of view. That is particularly apparent in the UK, where it is estimated that there are over 4 million cameras in operation, although police investigations suggest that this may be an over-estimation [30]. It is interesting to note that CCTV overall is really a collection of ad hoc installations of security cameras that offer access to footage of varying quality. These include public spaces monitoring as well as private surveillance systems for both corporate and personal property.

In reality CCTV is a system-of-systems that has emerged out of societal consent and adds some value (mostly evidential) to the law enforcement process. It is not standardised in terms of technical configurations or modes of operation, but of course its use is regulated, as personal data protection legislation applies. Notices of CCTV enforcement are for example mandatory to be displayed at the physical spaces that are monitored. Operators are also obliged to obfuscate streams that may be intrusive of personal space that could be accidentally included in the footage, e.g. certain frames that capture nearby windows. In Canada individuals may also be blocked out if they are in the frame and not directly relevant to an investigation. And in order to build public confidence, several operation centres in cities, such as traffic controllers, would include in their governance structures some involvement of members of the public, or elected local councillors.

Regardless of the heated debate about the effectiveness of CCTV against crime [19,20], its proliferation and acceptance in some societies is notable. This is certainly the case in the UK, where CCTV rose to public prominence largely in the 80's. Part of its take up may be due to the campaign against football hooliganism as well as ground safety fears after the tragedy of Hillsborough. Some researchers also suggest that they became instruments of enforcing an image of a tough stance against crime by political parties, especially New Labour [31].

The simplicity of purpose of a video surveillance system and the ability to relate its operation to a societal challenge (in this case football violence and public safety in grounds) established the technology in the collective social mind as something intrusive, yet necessary. This facilitated take up across public spaces of local councils (e.g. car parks), motorways, even on board means of transport, as well as in private businesses and buildings. Market forces and accessibility to the technology enabled everyone that may have had interest in it to install and operate such systems, creating space for the general public to serve as co-creators of the overall CCTV system-of-systems.

Translating this into the cyber domain, there is a need for related technology to be viewed as an enabler, as opposed to being demonised and fundamentally mistrusted. Greater transparency of Internet surveillance programmes and sufficient oversight structures would assure the public of the role of technology. Further education and public understanding of surveillance would help. This is not incompatible with the secrecy that security services claim must surround their operations; in fact they ought to assume that adversaries are suspicious of their practices. The Panopticon metaphor needs to be revisited as until now it has blurred the realisation of the need to intervene earlier in the radicalisation lifecycle to debunk their propaganda messages and the appeal of radicalism to young and vulnerable members of society. There is a need for more human-centric intelligence, open source and targeted operations, as opposed to passive monitoring and algorithmic determination implied by the current paradigm. We believe that if the purpose is clear and the community is able to see the value to them, they will even tolerate the trade off of personal data in return for confronting effectively this threat, as suggested even by the commercial experiences discussed earlier.

5 Conclusions

In light of global security challenges that include radicalisation and terrorism, but also increasing use of high technology by organised transnational crime, it is tempting for national states and their security services to develop mass surveillance programmes. The seductive promise of technological capability however, may not be a solution that is as relevant as human centric intelligence, as both wide surface scanning and artificial intelligence face their challenges as we have argued. And in any case this kind of capability is retrospective and missing the crucial stage of early intervention at the root cause of phenomena such as radicalisation of young persons to jihadist ideologies.

Creating powerful capabilities with insufficient oversight increases the potential for abuse of power and risks the loss of confidence and support from the wider public. This is exactly one of the aims of dissident groups and so we believe that organised states should refrain from developing surveillance capabilities in absentia of their key stakeholders, particularly the wider public. It is only with public trust that these may be successfully deployed. It is also essential that the paradigm of their development is one of a system-of-systems, i.e. viewed as an integral part of the wider state capability for countering terrorism and other organised crime. The whole picture ought to include early intervention to counter and debunk the appealing propaganda of terror groups and also to enable affected communities to report to, and cooperate with, the relevant authorities in confidence.

It is tempting for security services to explore every avenue of technology to counter such a severe threat. But the resulting programmes ought to respect fundamental rights of Western democracies, operate under strict due diligence and be accepted by the public, much like the example of CCTV in Britain. For, if the state in the process creates inadvertently the Matrix, it ought to be aware that the next historic revolution may come exactly from within it.

References

1. Emerson, B.: Annual report of the Special Rapporteur to the Human Rights Council, March 2014
2. Ball, C.: Organization, surveillance and the body: towards a politics of resistance. In: Lyon, D. (ed.) Theorising Surveillance: The Panopticon and beyond, pp. 296–317. Willan Publishing, Collumpton (2006)
3. Greenwald, G.: No Place to Hide: Edward Snowden, the NSA and the Surveillance State, Hamish Hamilton, 2014
4. Kelly, E.: Senate approves USA Freedom Act, USA Today, 2 June 2015
5. Gosling, S.: Snoop: What Your Stuff Says About You. Profile Books, London (2009)
6. Oatley, G., Crick, T.: Changing faces: identifying complex behavioural profiles. In: Tryfonas, T., Askoxylakis, I. (eds.) HAS 2014. LNCS, vol. 8533, pp. 282–293. Springer, Heidelberg (2014)
7. Obama, B.: Remarks by the President On Securing Our Nation's Cyber Infrastructure, May 2009. http://www.whitehouse.gov/the_press_office/Remarks-by-the-President-on-Securing-Our-Nations-Cyber-Infrastructure/
8. Department for Business, Innovation & Skills: 2014 Information Security Breaches Survey. UK Government (2014)
9. Bush, G.W.: The National Strategy to Secure Cyberspace. The White House, February 2003
10. Cabinet Office: Cyber Security Strategy. UK Government, November 2011
11. Cabinet Office: National Cyber Security Strategy 2014: progress and forward plans. UK Government, December 2014
12. Cabinet Office: Keeping the UK safe in cyber space. UK Government, December 2014
13. Carr, M., Crick, T.: The Problem of the P3: Public-Private Partnerships in National Cyber Security Strategies. In: Proceedings of 1st International Conference on Cyber Security for Sustainable Society (2015)
14. House of Commons of Canada: Bill C-51, first reading, 30 January 2015
15. Ferran, L.: Ex-NSA Chief: We Kill People Based on Metadata, abcNEWS, 12 May 2014
16. Kaye, D.: Report on encryption, anonymity, and the human rights framework, first report to the Human Rights Council, Office for the High Commissioner for Human Rights (2015)
17. Hales, T.: The NSA back door to NIST. Not. AMS **61**(2), 191–192 (2014)
18. Anderson, D.: A Question of Trust - Report of the Investigatory Powers Review, Independent Reviewer of Terrorism Legislation, 11 June 2015
19. Ditton, J.: Crime and the city. Br. J. Criminol. **40**(4), 692–709 (2000)
20. Woodhouse, J.: CCTV and its effectiveness in tackling crime, House of Commons Library Standard Note SN/HA/5624 (2010)
21. Lobban, I.: Sir Iain Lobban's valedictory speech as delivered, GCHQ website (2014)
22. Tsoukas, H.: The missing link: a transformational view of metaphors in organizational science. Acad. Manag. Rev. **16**(3), 566–585 (1991)
23. Lackoff, G.: Metaphors of terror. In: Return to The Days After, essays written in the aftermath of September 11, 2001. University of Chicago Press (2011)
24. Tryfonas, T.: On Security metaphors and how they shape the emerging practice of secure information systems development. J. Inf. Syst. Secur. **3**(3), 21–50 (2007)
25. Google Inc. http://www.google.com/ads/

26. Interdisciplinary Centre for Law and ICT/Centre for Intellectual Property Rights (ICRI/CIR), KU Leuven: From social media service to advertising network: A critical analysis of Facebooks Revised Policies and Terms, DRAFT 31 v1.2, March 2015

27. Kravets, D.: Which Telecoms store your data the longest?.secret memo tells all. Wired Magazine (2011). http://www.wired.com/2011/09/cellular-customer-data/ Accessed 28 September 2011

28. Anastasopoulou, K., Tryfonas, T., Kokolakis, S.: Strategic interaction analysis of privacy-sensitive end-users of cloud-based mobile Apps. In: Marinos, L., Askoxy- lakis, I. (eds.) HAS 2013. LNCS, vol. 8030, pp. 209–216. Springer, Heidelberg (2013)

29. Giddens, A.: The Constitution of Society: Outline of the Theory of Structuration. Polity Press, Cambridge (1984)

30. Gerrard, G., Parkins, G., Cunningham, I., Jones, W., Douglas, S.: National CCTV Strategy. Home Office, London (2007)

31. McCahill, M., Norris, C.: CCTV in Britain Urbaneye. Working Paper no. 3. Centre for technology and Society, Technical University of Berlin (2002)

Optional Data Disclosure and the Online Privacy Paradox: A UK Perspective

Meredydd Williams[(⊠)] and Jason R.C. Nurse

Department of Computer Science, University of Oxford, Oxford, UK
meredydd.williams@cs.ox.ac.uk

Abstract. Opinion polls suggest that the public value their privacy, with majorities calling for greater control of their data. However, individuals continue to use online services which place their personal information at risk, comprising a Privacy Paradox. Previous work has analysed this phenomenon through after-the-fact comparisons, but not studied disclosure behaviour during questioning. We physically surveyed UK cities to study how the British public regard privacy and how perceptions differ between demographic groups. Through analysis of optional data disclosure, we empirically examined whether those who claim to value their privacy act privately with their own data. We found that both opinions and self-reported actions have little effect on disclosure, with over 99 % of individuals revealing private data needlessly. We show that not only do individuals act contrary to their opinions, they disclose information needlessly even whilst describing themselves as private. We believe our findings encourage further analysis of data disclosure, as a means of studying genuine privacy behaviour.

Keywords: Online privacy · Privacy paradox · User study · Disclosure

1 Introduction

Privacy principles have been present throughout human history, with the Ancient Greek philosopher Socrates drawing distinctions between the "outer" and "inner" self [19]. Warren and Brandeis' *Right to be Let Alone* [33] placed privacy within the Western democratic consciousness, and across much of the world it is clearly established as both a legal and a human right [29]. However, whilst ephemeral utterances were once lost in the ether, now all our electronic communications are logged, stored and used for later processing. With today's spontaneous conversations persisting decades into the future, privacy is at a crossroads.

Previous studies have suggested individuals care about their privacy. The Pew Research Center [28] found that 86 % of surveyed US citizens reported taking steps to remain private online, whilst 88 % in a UK poll claimed to value their privacy [32]. Despite these self-reported surveys, many examples speak to the contrary. Another Pew poll found that 74 % of US respondents used location-based services on their smartphones, allowing their movements to be tracked in

© Springer International Publishing Switzerland 2016
T. Tryfonas (Ed.): HAS 2016, LNCS 9750, pp. 186–197, 2016.
DOI: 10.1007/978-3-319-39381-0_17

real-time [35]. Employees are dismissed due to embarrassing online disclosures [21], burglars survey social networking sites to select their targets, and the use of various technologies leads to an increasing number of privacy risks [5,24]. Later research [7] found that individuals valued their online browsing history at only €7, the price of a fast-food meal. We are presented with the "Privacy Paradox" [3], where individuals claim to value privacy but do little to actively protect it.

The novelty of this paper is to examine the paradox empirically, comparing what individuals claim about their privacy actions with their data disclosure behaviour. Previous research [23] has taken a two-phase approach, judging participants' actions to be less private than their reported intentions. Other work [17] questioned individuals on their privacy perceptions, before finding they unwisely judged user interfaces. However, these privacy evaluations were distinct from initial questioning, with little research empirically assessing behaviour during replies. Culnan [12] discovered many demographic factors might influence privacy concern, including age, wealth and education level. However, the majority of previous work has been conducted in the US, with British privacy perceptions rarely considered. In contrast, our research studied how the UK public perceive privacy, how privately do they act, and which privacy-protective technologies do they use. Through this, we examined how different demographic groups view privacy, and whether those who claim to value their privacy act privately with their own data.

In achieving these goals, we first surveyed existing work on the Privacy Paradox. Conventionally, interpretations are split into two groups: opinion-oriented and behaviour-oriented [2]. The former considers the disparity due to a lack of user education, whilst the latter judges individuals to exchange privacy for convenience. Whereas Acquisti [1] justified user actions through the behavioural economic theory of bounded rationality, Jensen et al. [17] attributed the disparity to individuals' misjudging their own abilities. Next, we built on the position paper by Williams [34] by conducting a physical survey across several cities in the UK. We analysed our collected data on three levels: firstly, to study how the British public view privacy; secondly, to investigate how different demographic groups regard the topic; and thirdly, to examine whether those who claim to value privacy act privately with their own data.

The remainder of our paper is structured as follows. Section 2 reviews the literature concerning privacy definitions, demographic studies and the Privacy Paradox. Section 3 then describes our research questions, the methodology of our physical survey, and how we designed against response biases. Section 4 continues by presenting our survey results, performing data analyses, and discussing our findings. Finally, we conclude the paper in Sect. 5 and consider possibilities for further work.

2   Literature Review

Before we discuss privacy in greater detail, we should produce a clear definition. Clarke [10] found distinctions between information privacy, media privacy,
interception privacy, and bodily privacy, with Burgoon [6] also regarding an
informational privacy component important. For the purposes of our work, any
reference to privacy concerns information privacy, i.e. "*the interest an individual
has in controlling, or at least significantly influencing, the handling of data about
themselves*" [10]. This is due to the fact we are studying data distribution rather
than more societal interactions.

Previous research has compared demographic groups based on their privacy
opinions. Whilst Han and Maclaurin [15] found online privacy concern generally
increased with age, other work considered whether younger people might be better at protecting themselves due to their greater knowledge of modern technology
[4]. Sheehan [30] found women to be more concerned than men, although other
studies [8] have shown that male users tend to falsify their personal data more
frequently. As previously mentioned, Culnan [12] discovered several demographic
factors which might influence concern for privacy, including age, wealth and education level. All this previous research was undertaken in the US, whilst our work
studies whether demographic factors have an influence in the UK. Furthermore,
whilst polls are generally undertaken online, reducing participation from certain
demographic groups [13], our survey was conducted in an accessible manner on
public streets.

The Privacy Paradox has been analysed in a variety of contexts. Barnes [3]
studied the teenage use of social networking sites, finding that whilst teens freely
disclose their personal information, they still express outrage when their privacy
is invaded. Norberg *et al.* [23] questioned participants on their willingness to disclose data, before requesting the same information several weeks later through
market researchers. They discovered that regardless of the type of information,
the disclosure level was far greater than what respondents had initially claimed.
Motiwalla *et al.* [22] used an auction scenario to analyse disclosure behaviours,
finding stated concerns to be a poor predictor of future actions. Although these
studies illuminate the Privacy Paradox, analyses are performed after-the-fact and
therefore other variables, such as changes in context [20], could have an effect.
Acquisti [1] considered bounded rationality, finding that users might focus on
short-term gratification, without considering the long-term privacy risks. Syverson [31] rejected that individuals act irrationally, claiming they weigh costs
against benefits in a sensible manner, with this echoed by findings of a January 2016 US poll [27]. Although economic analyses are enlightening, we decided
to investigate the matter empirically to compare opinions with actions. In his
comprehensive 2015 literature review, Kokolakis [18] urged future research to
make use of data rather than relying on self-reported claims. We combined these
approaches, comparing reported opinions with empirical disclosure behaviour.

3   Research Methodology

We explored three main research questions (RQ) through our survey on the Privacy Paradox. These are as follows:

1. How do the UK public regard online privacy, and which privacy-protective technologies do they use?
2. How do demographic groups in the UK differ from each other in their perceptions of privacy?
3. Do those who claim to value their privacy act privately when given the option to disclose sensitive demographic data?

We undertook a physical survey of the UK's general adult population, choosing London, Birmingham, Cardiff and Oxford for study due to their varied locations and differing population sizes (8.6M, 1M, 350K, and 154K, respectively). We began preparing the survey several months before the study, both through acquiring university ethical approval and to allow for an iterative design process. We also received explicit authorisation from the various city councils to conduct our research. The demographic queries, survey questions and options for reply were updated frequently before the form was finalised. We then undertook a pilot study for one day in Oxford to ensure that the questionnaire was appropriate for our research. The final survey was undertaken in August 2015, with participants asked how they value privacy, how they view their own level of privacy-consciousness, and which tools they use to protect themselves.

We divided the questionnaire into five sections: Required Demographics, Optional Demographics, Opinions, Actions, and Informed Consent. The Required Demographics included gender and age range and were used to study how different sections of UK society regard online privacy. The Optional Demographics allowed empirical analysis of data disclosure and comprised of marital status, employer and Twitter handle. Participants could either choose to answer these questions or select "Prefer Not To Say", with only the presence or absence of this data taken into consideration. The Opinion section asked participants to rate their agreement with privacy statements (for example, "privacy is of importance to me") on a five-point Likert scale from "Strongly Agree" to "Strongly Disagree". We requested these opinions before individuals reported their actions, as a means of reducing priming effects and social desirability bias [14]. The final opinion asked participants to self-evaluate their own level of privacy, and this was compared with their reported actions and disclosure behaviour.

In the Actions section, participants were questioned on their online habits (for example, "how often do you share your location on social networking sites?"), with a six-point Likert scale ranging from "Always" to "Never" with "Unsure" and "N/A" included. We chose this frequency scale both to reduce the risk of acquiescence bias [9], where participants just agree with the researcher, and to reflect that individuals might protect information differently in different contexts. Both the Opinion and Action questions were designed to be neutral to also reduce this acquiescence risk. The Informed Consent section notified participants of study purpose and redressal procedures, important matters for performing ethical research. We used a chocolate bar reward to incentivise participation, and whilst some individuals might complete the questionnaire just for personal gain, we found most respondents were interested in providing their opinion.

Several risks exist from surveying the general public in a self-reporting manner, and we remained cognisant of possible response biases. Non-response bias [16] could have been encountered if those opposed to disclosing data therefore avoided our survey. Whilst this was considered, we assured participants that their data would be stored securely and that the survey had passed ethical approval procedures. Social desirability bias could influence participants to exaggerate their privacy concern, and therefore we used the amount of disclosed data as a proxy for privacy behaviour. Some respondents might provide further information for completeness or in reaction to demand characteristics [25]. Furthermore, privacy behaviour is contextualised [20] and individuals might disclose more data knowing that the survey is for academic purposes and conducted through the University of Oxford. However, participants were instructed that these fields were not mandatory and the "Prefer Not To Say" options offered a simple alternative. Respondents might claim to be using privacy-protective technologies falsely, either due to misconceptions or to appear privacy-conscious. Jensen *et al.* [17] found that individuals often claimed to understand a technology, but then were unable to answer simple questions about it. To reduce this risk, we included the fictitious *PrivBrowse* product, in the technique of Presser *et al.* [26], so participants who state they use this tool could be highlighted. Whilst false data is often discounted from datasets, we study PrivBrowse responses to evaluate respondents' perceptions of privacy-protective technologies.

4   Results and Discussion

4.1   Participants

We collected a total of 112 physical responses from across the UK, with 94 % of the participants identifying themselves as UK residents. Our gender ratio was reasonably balanced, 57 % female and 43 % male, and at least 9 % of participants came from each age bracket. More than 10 % also came from each education level other than PhD, suggesting a varied cross-section of the British public. Our survey greatly benefits from being physically-conducted, as online polls can reduce participation from certain demographic groups [13]. 71 % reported to use computers as part of their job, highlighting how ubiquitous technology has become in the UK.

4.2   Analytical Techniques

We first used Cronbach's alpha (α) to measure our scale reliability, with coefficients in excess of 0.7 considered to represent internal consistency. Fortunately, our $\alpha = 0.81$ and therefore fulfilled this requirement.

We utilised a number of techniques to study correlation and differentiate between datasets. We used Spearman's Rank Correlation Coefficient (ρ) to measure two-variable linear correlation from 1 for total positive correlation to 0 for no correlation to -1 for total negative correlation. This technique is used for ordinal data, which we receive from ranking our Likert scale responses numerically. We studied the p-value to assess the probability the result is due to chance, with a $p < 0.05$ representing statistical significance.

To determine whether two datasets were significantly different from each other, we used the Mann-Whitney-Wilcoxon test for our ordinal opinion data and the two-tailed Student's t-test otherwise. We again required $p < 0.05$ to indicate differences were probabilistically not due to chance.

In investigating our research questions (RQ), we studied five variables: the mean amount of *data disclosed* (0–3), the mean *privacy opinions* (1–5), the mean *online privacy opinions* (1–5), the mean privacy *self-evaluations* (1–5), and the mean self-reported *action scores* (1–4). This *action score* ranged from most to least private, with "Unsure" and "N/A" answers deemed to represent a neutral response. In each case, the lower the value of the variable, the more 'private' a participant was considered to be. For the remainder of the paper, we use $\bar{x}$ to denote mean values, ρ for correlation coefficients and include p-values when differences are statistically significant.

4.3   RQ1: Privacy Opinions and Protective Technologies

In answering our first research question, we analysed respondents' opinions and actions. We found participants overwhelmingly claim to be concerned about their privacy. 92 % reported they found privacy important to them, 69 % strongly agreeing with the statement compared to 2 % in disagreement. Similarly, 93 % agreed *online* privacy was important, with less than 3 % disagreeing with the statement. Participants were more reserved over self-evaluations of their own privacy, but 81 % still agreed that they acted privately. We now compare these opinions with reported actions to investigate the Privacy Paradox.

Whilst the complete list of action results are shown below in Table 1, we focus on privacy-protective technology use, looking to address our first research question. Not even half of the respondents claimed to clean their web browser history frequently, which is worrying considering less than 2 % were unsure of their answer. With the retention of browsing histories and cookies potentially enabling online tracking, this could place a large number of individuals at risk. 42 % of participants had not used protective browser plug-ins, despite the popularity of ad-blocking software. Data encryption is applied rarely, with only 6 % of respondents always performing the task. This comes in contrast to the 66 % who admitted to never encrypting at all. Less than 5 % of participants claimed to use Tor[1] frequently, with 75 % having never used the software. Anecdotally, one respondent reported that the technology was used by criminals, and this stigma might explain its lack of common usage. Despite efforts to increase PGP[2]

---

[1] https://www.torproject.org/.

[2] https://www.gnupg.org/.

Table 1. Self-reported action frequencies (%)

Action	Always	Often	Rarely	Never	Unsure	N/A
How often do you clean your Internet browser's history?	15.2	31.3	25.9	23.2	1.8	2.7
How often do you use Internet browser plug-ins/ extensions to protect your privacy?	15.2	21.4	12.5	42.9	5.4	2.7
How often do you encrypt data on your computer?	6.3	8.9	15.2	66.1	0.9	2.7
How often do you store unencrypted data within a cloud provider such as Dropbox?	17.9	16.1	13.4	44.5	1.8	5.4
How often do you share public posts on social networking sites such as Facebook?	17.9	18.8	17.0	25.9	0.9	19.6
How often do you share your location on social networking sites?	3.6	10.7	29.5	36.6	0	19.6
How often do you use Tor for your web browsing?	1.8	2.7	7.1	75.9	7.1	5.4
How often do you use PrivBrowse for your web browsing?	0	6.3	1.8	82.1	5.4	4.4
How often do you use encryption tools for your emails?	7.1	8.9	4.5	72.3	3.6	3.6
How often do you read the terms and conditions on websites you use?	14.3	18.8	22.3	40.2	1.8	2.7
How often do you check permissions before installing smartphone apps?	19.6	11.6	15.2	30.4	0.9	22.3

usability, still 72 % of individuals have never encrypted their emails. Only 7 % claimed to use email encryption consistently, and assuming our sample is somewhat representative, this suggests that the vast majority of UK public email is open to eavesdropping.

Despite the overwhelming concern claimed for privacy, with 92 % agreeing with its importance, individuals do not take actions to protect themselves. We found little correlation between *privacy opinions* and *action scores* (correlation coefficient $\rho = 0.02$), reflecting that just because a participant claims to value privacy, it does not mean they act privately. *Online privacy opinions* also had little correlation with *action scores* ($\rho = -0.03$), suggesting the existence of the Privacy Paradox. Interestingly, we found no correlation between *self-evaluations* and *action scores* ($\rho = 0.06$), which could indicate poor privacy self-awareness. Potential reasons for these disparities include a lack of privacy awareness, the inconvenience of using protective tools, or simply because individuals might not associate certain actions with acting privately.

Remarkably, 8 % of participants claimed to have used the PrivBrowse tool, despite it being fictitious. We found these individuals cared less about both privacy and online privacy than average but evaluated themselves similarly private. The group might have responded in this manner through a simple misconception or due to social desirability bias.

4.4   RQ2: Demographic Comparisons

For our second research question, we investigated whether younger adults care less about privacy, or are better able to protect themselves. We also studied how different genders regard the topic, and whether those better educated in privacy matters act more privately.

Whilst several age groups significantly differed in *action scores*, these did not follow a clear pattern based on youth or age. Similarly, although we found several significant differences for *online privacy opinions* and *self-evaluations*, these did not follow a consistent trend. To investigate a direct distinction, we split respondents into 18–45 and 46 and above groups. Those less than 46 would have been born at least in 1970 and likely experienced the personal computer revolution of the 80 s onwards. Although not significantly, we found older individuals acted more privately, disclosed less information, and rated themselves as more private. In contrast, younger adults reported to care more about both privacy and online privacy. We went on to examine whether younger respondents used privacy-protective technologies more frequently, and this was found to be true. Although the *action scores* did not differ significantly, those under 46 years of age reported more frequent usage of all five technologies (browser history erasure, browser privacy plug-ins, data encryption, Tor and email encryption). This could dispel the myth that age correlates with privacy concern, as although older individuals acted more privately, those less than 46 use technologies more frequently to protect themselves.

We continued by studying whether gender, education or computer usage affected privacy perceptions. Regarding gender, we found women to be significantly more confident than men ($\bar{x} = 1.7$ vs $\bar{x} = 2.1$, $p = 0.01$) through their *self-evaluations*. Curiously, this did not translate into lower female *action scores*, with men faring better than women. This appears to support earlier work by Sheehan [30] which found that men are more likely to act to protect their privacy, represented by our male respondents also disclosing less data. Whilst significant differences were not seen through education level, those with Master's degrees acted most privately, disclosed the least information, and cared most about both privacy and online privacy. Those who used PCs during their employment had better *action scores*, disclosed less data, cared more about privacy, and evaluated themselves as more private, though these differences were not significant in our study.

To further analyse whether knowledge affects privacy perceptions, after our public survey was completed we surveyed an additional 25 cybersecurity researchers. 80 % of this sample were male, 80 % were under 36, and all were UK residents with at least a Bachelor's degree. We found the researchers' *action scores* were significantly more private than the general public ($\bar{x} = 2.4$ vs $\bar{x} = 2.7$, $p < 0.01$), and they revealed fewer optional demographics. Education clearly has an effect: those with Master's degrees acted most privately in the public sample, with cybersecurity researchers disclosing even less data. This might suggest that privacy awareness campaigns and training sessions would be beneficial in encouraging the public to act more privately.

4.5   RQ3: Data Disclosure Behaviour

In answering our third research question, we investigated how data disclosure behaviour correlates against privacy opinions, actions, and self-evaluations. All three optional demographic queries possessed a "Prefer Not to Say" option and privacy should be a salient thought when completing a survey on the topic.

In spite of this, 96% of participants willingly disclosed their marital status, suggesting that individuals do not treat these details privately. Whilst 12% of respondents revealed their Twitter handles, only 13% explicitly chose not to. The remaining individuals claimed to not possess an account, and whilst this might be an anti-disclosure tactic, if more respondents used Twitter then the disclosure rate would likely increase. Since the handle enables direct contact with the user, it is still concerning that over one in ten participants would needlessly reveal this information. 56% of respondents chose to reveal their employer, with this figure increasing to 84% when including the unemployed and retired. On modal average, 72% of respondents disclosed two items of data needlessly, with over 99% revealing at least one piece of optional information. Assuming our sample is somewhat representative, the UK public are very willing to disclose their personal data.

We finally studied the effect that opinions and self-evaluations have on data disclosure. We discovered that both *privacy opinions* (correlation coefficient $\rho = 0.06$) and *online privacy opinions* ($\rho = 0.15$) bore little correlation with the amount of *data disclosed*, with the latter comparison shown above in Fig. 1. The heatmap suggests that regardless of how much an individual might profess to value online privacy, they are just as likely to divulge optional demographic information. *Self-evaluations* ($\rho = 0.06$), were also found to have a minimal effect on disclosure behaviour, suggesting individuals reveal data regardless of their beliefs. Of greatest concern, reported *action scores* ($\rho = 0.05$) did not correlate with *data disclosed*, reflecting that even those who claim to act privately needlessly reveal their information. Here we illuminate another angle of the Privacy Paradox: not only do individuals report actions different to their opinions, they disclose information needlessly even whilst describing themselves as private.

5   Conclusions

In this paper, we investigated the UK public's perceptions of online privacy, their use of privacy-protective tools, and how different demographic groups regard the topic. We found that whilst the vast majority of participants claim to value

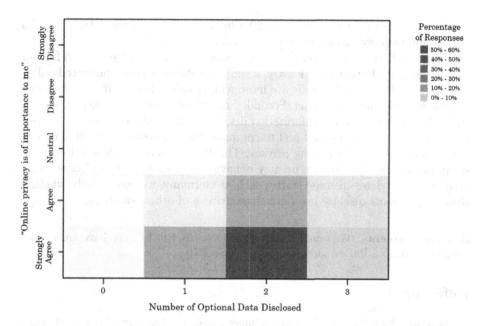

Fig. 1. Rating of online privacy importance as compared to disclosure behaviour

privacy, they do not act to keep their information safe. Although 93 % of respondents agreed with the importance of online privacy, fewer than half even cleaned their browser history regularly. This might be due to insufficient privacy education, apathy, or because respondents do not appreciate the risks they encounter in their use of online services [11,24]. We saw that younger adults do not necessarily care less about online privacy, in fact they use protective technologies more frequently than their older counterparts. Education also played a strong role: those with Master's degrees acted most privately in the public sample, with cybersecurity researchers disclosing even less data. Finally, we discovered that information disclosure does not correlate with privacy opinions or reported actions. With 96 % of respondents divulging their marital status and more than half disclosing their employer with little need, the British public appear very willing to reveal their personal information. In total, over 99 % of individuals disclosed at least one piece of data needlessly, with over one in ten revealing their Twitter handle. No correlation was found between participants' opinions and the actions they took, validating the existence of the Privacy Paradox. We develop the concept further to show that individuals disclose information needlessly even whilst describing themselves as private.

Whilst we hope our research will assist others in analysing data disclosure, we accept limitations to our work. Although our four selected cities provided variations in population size and location, we did not survey all areas of the UK. A more representative future work would cover cities in Scotland and Northern Ireland, canvas a larger number of sites, and include rural locations in addition to cities. Whilst we also do not consider 112 physically-surveyed respondents an insignificant sample, this figure could be increased through the future use of a mixed-mode survey including an online form.

With the Privacy Paradox receiving increased interest, there is much further work to conduct in this area. Firstly, a similar survey could be conducted online to examine whether individuals are more willing to disclose their data to a web form or to a physical researcher. Secondly, the effect of privacy salience could be studied against the level of information disclosure. We could conduct both a privacy survey and an unrelated poll to compare whether respondents disclose less data when actively considering privacy. Thirdly, we could conduct a European study to empirically compare privacy behaviour across different cultures. With privacy laws stricter in some states, such as Germany, we could study whether these respondents disclose less data than citizens of other countries.

Acknowledgments. We would wish to thank the UK EPSRC who have funded this research through a PhD studentship in Cyber Security.

References

1. Acquisti, A.: Privacy in electronic commerce and the economics of immediate gratification. In: Proceedings of the 5th ACM Conference on Electronic Commerce, pp. 21–29 (2004)
2. Baek, Y.: Solving the privacy paradox: a counter-argument experimental approach. Comput. Hum. Behav. **38**, 33–42 (2014)
3. Barnes, S.: A privacy paradox: social networking in the United States. First Monday **11**(9) (2006) http://firstmonday.org/ojs/index.php/fm/article/viewArticle/1394
4. Blank, G., Bolsover, G., Dubois, E.: A New Privacy Paradox. Technical report (2014)
5. Bloxham, A.: Most burglars using Facebook and Twitter to target victims, survey suggests (2011). http://www.telegraph.co.uk/technology/news/8789538/Most-burglars-using-Facebook-and-Twitter-to-target-victims-survey-suggests.html
6. Burgoon, J.K.: Privacy and Communication, vol. 6. Routledge, Abingdon (1982)
7. Carrascal, J., Riederer, C., Erramilli, V., Cherubini, M., de Oliveira, R.: Your browsing behavior for a big mac: economics of personal information online. In: Proceedings of the 22nd International Conference on World Wide Web, pp. 189–200 (2013)
8. Chen, K., Rea Jr., A.I.: Protecting personal information online: a survey of user privacy concerns and control techniques. J. Comput. Inf. Syst. **44**(4), 85–92 (2004)
9. Churchill Jr., G.: A paradigm for developing better measures of marketing constructs. J. Mark. Res. **16**(1), 64–73 (1979)
10. Clarke, R.: Introduction to dataveillance and information privacy, and definitions of terms. Technical report (1999)
11. Creese, S., Goldsmith, M., Nurse, J.R.C., Phillips, E.: A data-reachability model for elucidating privacy and security risks related to the use of online social networks. In: Proceedings of the 11th IEEE International Conference on Trust, Security and Privacy in Computing and Communications, pp. 1124–1131 (2012)
12. Culnan, M.: Consumer awareness of name removal procedures: implications for direct marketing. J. Direct Mark. **9**(2), 10–19 (1995)

13. Evans, J., Mathur, A.: The value of online surveys. Internet Res. **15**(2), 195–219 (2005)
14. Fisher, R.: Social desirability bias and the validity of indirect questioning. J. Consum. Res. **20**(2), 303–315 (1993)
15. Han, P., Maclaurin, A.: Do consumers really care about online privacy? Mark. Manag. **11**(1), 35–38 (2002)
16. Hansen, M., Hurwitz, W.: The problem of non-response in sample surveys. J. Am. Stat. Assoc. **41**(236), 517–529 (1946)
17. Jensen, C., Potts, C., Jensen, C.: Privacy practices of internet users: self-reports versus observed behavior. Int. J. Hum Comput Stud. **63**(1), 203–227 (2005)
18. Kokolakis, S.: Privacy attitudes and privacy behaviour: a review of current research on the privacy paradox phenomenon. Comput. Secur. (2015)
19. Konvitz, M.: Privacy and the law: a philosophical prelude. Law Contemp. Probl. **31**(2), 272–280 (1966)
20. Morando, F., Iemma, R., Raiteri, E.: Privacy evaluation: what empirical research on users' valuation of personal data tells us. Internet Policy Rev. **3**(2), 1–11 (2014)
21. Mosbergen, D.: Day-care employee fired for Facebook post saying she hates 'being around a lot of kids' (2015). http://www.huffingtonpost.com/2015/05/05/daycare-worker-fired-facebook-kaitlyn-walls_en_7210122.html
22. Motiwalla, L., Li, X., Liu, X.: Privacy paradox: does stated privacy concerns translate into the valuation of personal information?. In: Proceedings of the 18th Pacific Asia Conference on Information Systems (2014)
23. Norberg, P., Horne, D., Horne, D.: The privacy paradox: personal information disclosure intentions versus behaviors. J. Consum. Aff. **41**(1), 100–126 (2007)
24. Nurse, J.R.C.: Exploring the risks to identity security and privacy in cyberspace. XRDS Mag. **21**(3), 42–47 (2015)
25. Orne, M.: On the social psychology of the psychological experiment: with particular reference to demand characteristics and their implications. Am. Psychol. **17**(11), 776–783 (1962)
26. Presser, S., Couper, M., Lessler, J., Martin, E., Martin, J., Rothgeb, J., Singer, E.: Methods for testing and evaluating survey questions. Pub. Opin. Q. **68**(1), 109–130 (2004)
27. Rainie, L., Duggan, M.: Privacy and information sharing. Pew Research Center (2016)
28. Rainie, L., Kiesler, S., Kang, R., Madden, M., Duggan, M., Brown, S., Dabbish, L.: Anonymity, privacy, and security online. Pew Research Center (2013)
29. Robertson, A.: The United Nations covenant on civil and political rights and the European convention on human rights. Br. Yearb. Int. Law **43**, 21 (1968)
30. Sheehan, K.: An investigation of gender differences in on-line privacy concerns and resultant behaviors. J. Interact. Mark. **13**(4), 24–38 (1999)
31. Syverson, P.: The paradoxical value of privacy. In: Proceedings of the 2nd Annual Workshop on Economics and Information Security (2003)
32. TRUSTe: 2015 TRUSTe UK consumer confidence index. Technical report (2015). http://www.truste.com/resources/privacy-research/uk-consumer-confidence-index-2015/
33. Warren, S., Brandeis, L.: The right to privacy. Harvard Law Rev. **4**(5), 193–220 (1890)
34. Williams, M.: A study of society's perception of online privacy. In: Proceedings of the 1st Interdisciplinary Cyber Research Workshop, pp. 28–29 (2015)
35. Zickuhr, K.: Three-quarters of smartphone owners use location-based services. Pew Research Center (2012)

Security Technologies

Assessing the Feasibility of Adaptive Security Models for the Internet of Things

Waqas Aman[✉]

Norwegian Information Security Laboratory (NISLab),
Faculty of Computer Science and Media Technology,
Norwegian University of Science and Technology (NTNU), Gjøvik, Norway
waqas.aman@ntnu.no

Abstract. Internet of Things (IoT) is a heterogeneous and dynamic space as it connects a variety of sensing, mobile and other physical objects. Traditional security controls and mechanisms tend to enforce pre-defined and manual risk mitigation approaches that manage security in a particular context. They seem to be insufficient in IoT scenarios that have a diverse and evolving technology outlook and threat spectrum. Adaptive security can be a suitable candidate for IoT security as it can observe and respond to threats dynamically. However, it is challenging to identify how practical are the existing adaptive security solutions in IoT-driven ecosystem. In this paper, we present an evaluation framework that assesses the feasibility of adaptive security models in IoT settings. The framework evaluates a given model from an adaptive risk management perspective and assesses the extent to which it is aware of its ecosystem. Moreover, it captures the essential features of a given model, such as adaptation aptitude and architectural aspects. Therefore, the framework determines the security as well as the architectural capabilities of a model. We have evaluated various models and have identified major trends and gaps in their modeling approaches.

Keywords: Internet of things · Adaptive security · Feasibility · Risk management

1 Introduction

IoT aims to bring together various computing, sensing and communication objects having autonomous capabilities to offer more flexible services and innovative business models. However, frequent changes in the environment, its diverse and evolving technology outlook, and the presence of mobile objects make an IoT-based system a more complex and dynamic ecosystem. According to a survey made by Cisco, around 50 billion IoT enabling devices will be in circulation by 2020 [6]. From an information security perspective, connecting these devices together will also introduce new means and opportunities for the adversaries to target consumers, service providers, industrial and government assets. HP and OWASP in a recent study [1] revealed that 70 % of the devices in the IoT

© Springer International Publishing Switzerland 2016
T. Tryfonas (Ed.): HAS 2016, LNCS 9750, pp. 201–211, 2016.
DOI: 10.1007/978-3-319-39381-0_18

use unencrypted network service, 60 % have a vulnerable user interface, 90 % collect and communicate personal information, 80 % use passwords of insufficient length and complexity, and 70 % of the time an attacker can identify a user account using enumeration techniques. These statistics indicate that IoT security is a significant challenge and critical concern, and needs to be appropriately addressed.

Providing reliable and efficient security measures in IoT scenarios through traditional security controls may not be practical as they have a limited protection scope, and they enforce inflexible and manual threat mitigation strategies [5]. For instance, a network intrusion prevention system (IPS) only protects a particular operational unit only from network related threats. Its protection policy consists of predefined rules with only one objective, i.e. the asset (network) protection. It does not regard any user or QoS objectives in its protection strategies. Sometimes, these controls, such as an intrusion detection system (IDS), lack mitigation mechanism and support monitoring and analysis activities.

IoT-based environments are deemed as autonomous spaces and adaptation is considered a desirable and key attribute in related ecosystems [14]. Adaptive security can be a potential candidate to manage the security-related concerns in such a dynamic and heterogeneous space. Adaptive security continuously observes and analyzes security changes in the environment and responds dynamically to any potential risk [2]. However, IoT has a complex outlook. It is a multi-vendor space with devices having different design and communication stacks that are evolving rapidly to accommodate future technologies and to meet business needs. Because of the diversity and evolving elements, the threat landscape in IoT is much broader and dynamic than the traditional ICTs [5]. Therefore, it is challenging to identify a feasible adaptive security solution for related ecosystems.

To address this challenge, in this paper, we present a comparison framework to assess the feasibility of an adaptive security model for IoT-related spaces. It evaluates the extent to which a given model is complete from an automated risk management solution perspective, and reflects on to what extent context awareness is built into it. Such awareness is an essential factor in taking dynamic risk mitigation decisions as it reduces the probability of creating false alarms and assists in making optimal adaptation decisions. Furthermore, it also reveals the adaptation aptitude to realize what characteristics from those benchmarked by the IBM [7] for adaptive and autonomic systems are satisfied by an underlying model. We have also identified various architectural attributes, such as extensibility, scalability, testability, to address how well a model is suitable for a heterogeneous environment like the IoT.

Our comparative study of different adaptive security models reveals that some of the models focus only a particular security objective, e.g. authentication or confidentiality, and, therefore, have a limited protection scope. In an adaptation loop, i.e. monitoring, analysis and response, most of the proposal emphasized on the methods related to the analysis component and did not explain how the various components may interact to realize the whole adaptation loop.

In some of the models, ontology has been used as a runtime adaptation knowledge, which is an effective way to address relationships between objects in heterogeneous spaces, such as the IoT [19]. It is also realized that the majority of the evaluated models have only addresses security in a protection context. However, other elements, for instance, user and QoS preferences that may be negatively influenced by a security response, were disregarded.

The paper is organized as follows. In Sect. 2, we present our proposed framework and detail its attributes. Section 3 provides a brief introduction to the reviewed models. The feasibility of these models is assessed in Sect. 4 which also details the major trends and gaps in these models. Finally, the paper will be concluded in Sect. 5.

2   The Evaluation Framework

The proposed evaluation framework consists of three perspectives, i.e. risk management, adaptation aptitude, and architectural attributes. Risk management itself is a comprehensive process and can include business processes, like change management, which may require further time and resources and, thus, may not be realized in dynamic response mechanisms executed at runtime. However, here we refer to it as an adaptive risk management process where resources for risk mitigation decisions are available and can be utilized at runtime. We have generalized this process into three major operations, i.e. risk monitoring, analysis, and response, which can be found in all standard risk management frameworks, like the ISO 27005:2011 [12] or the NIST Risk Management Framework (RMF) [16]. Although may adaptation includes all the operations stated above, in this study we have also used the term adaptation as a risk mitigation or response context as this stage of risk management decides and take the necessary action against the risk faced. The following aspects are investigated in the adaptive risk management perspective:

(i) The modular completeness, i.e. which of the major risk operations are addressed in a given model?
(ii) What methods or techniques are utilized to perform these operations?, and
(iii) What type of context awareness is built into the model?

Context awareness is an essential attribute deemed in the IoT [17] and provides the necessary information to assess a risk faced [15]. It characterizes the who, what, where, when, and why of an entity, i.e., a person, place or an object, as defined in [3], and therefore, provide the ability to perform accurate risk analysis and take optimal risk mitigation (adaptation) decisions. In this study, we refer to the *context* as the fundamental requirements and knowledge, i.e. user requirements, situation-awareness, QoS preferences including resource requirements, and security objectives, required to assess a given situation to adapt optimally.

The adaptation aptitude evaluates the autonomous properties of a given model. These properties are emphasized by the IBM to be satisfied by an autonomic system [7]. They are referred to as *Self*-attributes and includes self-optimization, self-configuration, self-healing, and self-protection. As adaptive security solutions aim to mitigate threats dynamically at runtime, we recognize them as autonomous systems. Besides these properties, we have added the Change Scope attribute. This attribute will reflect the scope of change(s) that the adaptation system can monitor and react to in the IoT and can be triggered by users, things (device/app), or by the environment itself. The Self-properties are evaluated from a security viewpoint and are described (in security terms) as follow:

(i) *Self-Optimization:* The ability of a system to re-adjust or tune the parameter(s) of a security mechanism. For instance, changing encryption from DES-128 to DES-256 to meeting confidentiality needs.

(ii) *Self-Configuration:* The ability of a system to change security mechanisms at runtime, e.g. introducing CAPTCHA or a biometric modality to circumvent login misuse, or replacing a routing algorithm with another.

(iii) *Self-Healing:* The ability of a system to react to errors and disruptions

(iv) *Self-Protection:* The ability of the system to detect and respond to threats faced dynamically.

The underlying system to investigate these properties can be the operational environment, in this case, the IoT ecosystem, or the adaptive security system, i.e. the application(s) or computing systems(s) responsible for adaptation. We study the first three properties in the ecosystem context and the last one in the adaptive security system, context. The term security mechanism corresponds to a security method, algorithm or module built into a thing in the IoT ecosystem to achieve the Confidentiality-Integrity-Availability and other security-related objectives.

Moreover, the framework also stresses on the design features of a model. IoT being a diverse technology space has unique architectural needs. For example, it may not be practical to embed risk management activities in a sensory object because of the limited resource available [4]. Such activities may be distributed or transferred to external objects or systems having the required resources. Hence, it is important to understand the design attributes offer by an adaptive security model before it is adopted to deal with threats in the IoT. This framework assesses the follow design aspects:

(i) The extent to which a model is *extensible* to address technology diversity in the IoT; how *scalable* it is to accommodate the evolving future needs; whether it is/can be *supported* by test scenarios and implementation guideline for development and validation.

(ii) *Control:* It reflects the point of control where the adaptation logic is implemented. It can be internally at a thing level or external to a thing. External control can further be realized in a centralized or in a distributed manner.

3   Reviewed Models

The proposed framework is applied to five adaptive security models that aim to protect assets dynamically in the context of IoT and related concepts. A brief introduction of them is given as follows:

Game-based Adaptive Security (GbAS): Hamdi and Abie, in [11] have proposed a game-based security adaptation model for the IoT. Based on earlier proposals, they have suggested four models, i.e., energy, communication channels, memory, and intruder, to represent the context required for adaptation. Corresponding to the mentioned contexts, they have recommended a set of adaptive security policies based on probabilistic rules. Using these probabilities they have identified utility functions and have formulated a Markov game model for security adaptation. The model is suggested to be used in body area networks (BAN) in eHealth setup, and it describes how security and energy efficiency trade-off can be achieved in the BAN.

Requirements-driven Adaptive Security (RdAS): Salehie et al. [18] have suggested a requirements-driven approach towards security adaptation. Consisting of three models, i.e., threat, asset and security goals, the requirements model forms a basis for risk evaluation and adaptation. Based on Fuzzy Cognitive Maps (FCM) [13], the authors have suggested a casual network to assess the chances of a risk, identify potential countermeasures, and their utility in terms of efficiency. RdAS has mainly focused on how knowledge for risk analysis can be implemented and how it can provide input to adaptation activities.

Event-Driven Adaptive Security (EDAS): EDAS [4] provides a holistic solution towards security adaptation in the IoT. It aims to monitor thing-generated security-related events from the IoT assets. EDAS analyzes these continuous event logs using event correlation for any threat and corresponding risks and suggests a runtime ontology to adapt optimally to a risk faced. The authors have not provided any particular analysis methods however they claim that one can combine various event-based analysis techniques, such as probabilistic and statistical methods, to detect and predict a threat. The EDASs ontology consists of three contexts, i.e., user, security, and device/application (thing), that contains the necessary capabilities, service and user requirements, and countermeasures as the knowledge required to optimally reconfigure security during execution.

Ontology-based Security Adaptation (ObSA): Antii and Eila, in [10], have also suggested an ontology-based security adaptation for smart spaces. Their adaptation model uses security measures that are collected from the monitoring agents in the monitored environments. Although the authors have provided a risk equation upon which risk can be calculated, they have not discussed how threat can be identified in their model. Their risk equation is a product of the threat level and the asset value. They have mainly considered security objectives in their model and have not discussed any non-security influences, such as performance and usability, etc., that might be affected by an adaptation decision.

Context-Adaptive Security Framework (CASF): Dey et al. [8] have a developed a context-aware adaptive framework for mobile cloud computing scenarios. It is an adaptive authentication framework that works on the principle of cognitive learning. They have conceptualized CASF as a finite state machine (FSM) with four states. At each state, a pattern represented as a tuple, consisting of the information extracted from a user request and a stored profile, is analyzed for any intrusions. At a given time there can be four different patterns each assigned a set of probabilities. The analysis is performed by the state machines implemented in the cloud. The adaptive authentication is performed in an inflexible way as a request is either allowed or denied as it does not implement any other authentication mechanisms. The authentication itself is implemented in the authentication module that employs a Message Digest and Location-based Authentication (MDLA) [9]. The model also has an adaptive module that aims to dynamically adapt to a cloud infrastructure that has a maximum service uptime during disruptions. However, this component is not appropriately elaborated in detail to reason on how it supports self-healing as claimed.

4   Models Feasibility in the IoT

To evaluate the feasibility of the models for IoT, we present a comparison of the studied models in each domain of the proposed framework, as explained in the following sub-sections. Moreover, a discussion on each of them is provided to reflect on the practicality of the models in the IoT ecosystem and what trends and gaps do these models exhibit.

4.1   Adaptive Risk Management Aptitude

As can be seen in Table 1, most of the models tend to cover all the operations of adaptive risk management. However, only EDAS has detailed the methods necessary for each operation. It can also be concluded that there is a wide variety of methods to choose from when dealing with risk analysis and modeling. On the other hand, we have found that most of the models, such as RdAS, ObSA, GbSA, CASF, mainly emphasize the risk modeling and have disregarded how threats can be discovered in the ecosystem, which forms the basis of risk analysis. Threat identification is a challenging job in the IoT as its environment has a complex threat spectrum [5] due to the diverse technology presence. Moreover, GbAS, ObSA, and CASF have taken adaptation as an approach that only fulfills the security objectives, such as confidentiality. However, it is recognized that security always involves one or more trade-offs, like memory, processing power, accessibility, efficiency, etc., which must also be considered during adaptation decisions particularly in IoT ecosystems where resource restricted objects are the main drivers and humans are actively involved. Most of the models emphasize only a few of the objectives and therefore, lack to provide protection from an array of threats faced by the IoT.

Table 1. Risk management aptitude evaluation

Attribute		GbAS	RdAS	EDAS	ObSA	CASF
RM Operation Supported	Monitoring	No	No	Yes	Yes	Yes
	Analysis	Yes	Yes	Yes	Yes	Yes
	Adaptation	Yes	Yes	Yes	Yes	Yes
RM Methods	Monitoring	None	None	thing-generated events collection	Security measurements (no further info on what might they be)	User Request (no further info)
	Analysis	Energy: Relaxation Effect Channel Fading; Finite State Markov Chain (FSMC) Memory: Batch Markov Arrival Process (BMAP) Intrusion: Sceptible-Infective-Recovered with Maintenance model	Fuzzy Cognitive Mapping	Complex Event Processing	Security Ontology	Pattern matching using Cognitive learning and FSMs
	Adaptation	Game Theoretic		Runtime Ontology		
	User Requirements	No	Yes-usability only	Yes	No	No
Context Awareness	QoS Preferences	Communication, Memory, Battery	Performance only	Yes	No	Service Uptime
	Security Objectives	Authentication	CIA-Accountability	Any (depends on the type of interested events)	Conf. & Integrity	Authentication
	Situation Awareness	Transition matrix with current and previous state probabilities	Fuzzy casual network building	Event Correlation	Not defined	Cognitive Learning

Table 2. Adaptation aptitude evaluation

Attribute	GbAS	RdAS	EDAS	ObSA	CASF
Change Scope	Device/app	All	All	Device/app	User Activity
Self-Optimization	Yes	No	Yes	Yes	No
Self-Configuration	No	Yes	Yes	Yes	No
Self-Healing	Communication only	No	Yes	No	Yes
Self-Protection	Authentication only	No clear info	Yes	No	No

4.2   Adaptation Aptitude

Adaptive security aims to react to a security change in the system. This change can be triggered by its users, the environment or by the devices or apps in it, which needs to be monitored and analyzed. Our study reveals, as shown in Table 2, that GbAS, ObSA, and CASF are only interested in a particular change and, therefore, may not address the changes (and corresponding threats) that may be triggered by other components. Similarly, withstanding against the disruptions, i.e. self-healing, has not been addressed adequately or is absent entirely. Self-healing needs to model methodically as it may address accidental concerns, such as channel fading and any soft/hardware errors. Moreover, apart from EDAS, none of the studied models have clearly discussed the notion of self-protection to defend against the threats faced by analysis and decision-making system.

4.3   Design Attributes Comparison

Table 3 shows the design comparison of the studied models. As IoT is mainly driven by lightweight objects, any attempt to control adaptation internally or locally at a thing level would most likely fail because of the low power, computation and storage resources. For instance, GbAS attempts to execute the respective operations locally at a node level. However, as things in the IoT tend to grow in number, their interaction becomes inevitable. With scaling networks internal or local adaptation may not be feasible in the IoT, particularly for low-end objects, like the body sensors in GbAS scope. Scalability also depends on the number of request made and the type of information processed and stored. Therefore it wise to implement the analysis and decision-related components external to the thing as done in EDAS, RdAS, and CASF where appropriately resources can be allocated for respective operations.

Furthermore, the more components are loosely coupled, it is easier to test and modify the components. This is helpful in extending the network to accommodate new assets which might require new components. Such an attempt also increases reusability. However, the more we extend the monitoring scope or features and related components, efforts required to manage and maintain them also increases. Such efforts could be reduced by making the components, for example, the knowledge required for adaptation, to evolve autonomously.

Table 3. Design attributes comparison

Attribute	GbAS	RdAS	EDAS	ObSA	CASF
Extensible	No-Limited to sensor devices. Monitoring other "changes" may require new modeling	Yes-Requirement modeling is independent of asset in scope	Yes-independent of the type of device and have loose coupling among components	Yes-The ontology can be exteded to accommodate the "changes"	No-new modules will be added to address other Assets and changes
Scalable	No - Cannot adapt security when large quantity of packets arrive or when neighboring nodes increase	No detail info. Components interaction and the type of information process is not presented	Yes-Computations and storage are done externally on systems with appropriate resources	No detailed info. the type of information process is not presented	Yes-Cloud resources are used to address network growth
Control	Internally at node (thing) level	External to the asset. It can be realized centrally or in a distributed manner	External-Centralized and Distributed	The case study reflects that the adaptation is controlled internally in a monitored asset	External to an asset. In Cloud
Support	Easy to test the efficiency in simulated environments. No implementation guideline available to realize how components may interact	Easy to develop test scenarios for simulated environments. No implementation details provided for Monitoring and Adaptation components	Easy to test individual components as loosely coupled. Detailed implementation provided	As a component model it is easy to text individual component. However there is no implementation explanation given	It is simple to create profile and request patterns for testing. No implementation details provided

In the studied models, only CASF tends to evolve its knowledge by utilizing cognitive learning tools. Moreover, except for the EDAS, no other study provides enough information for the development or adoption of a potential model for the IoT security.

5   Conclusion

Adaptive security can be a useful tool to address the complex threat in a dynamic and evolving space like the IoT. There is a multitude of models that attempt to achieve adaptive security with different perspectives. This study provides an evaluation framework that intends to assess the capability and feasibility of such models in the context of IoT and aims to investigate their architectural, risk management, and adaptation aspects. As an example, we have evaluated a few related studies and have identified the various features they offer, the techniques they utilize and have highlighted their advantages and limitations. The framework, thus, provides a benchmark for the service providers to evaluate a given model for their respective IoT applications and provide an assessment tool for the research community to identify and investigate the various gaps they recognized in the current studies. Our comparative study reveals that most of the models monitor only a set of security changes which limit them from the exposure to a wide threat variety in the IoT. Apart from a few models, they lack to address all the risk management components to approach adaptation holistically and do not provide threat assessment details which provide a basis for risk management.

References

1. Owasp internet of things top 10 project. http://tinyurl.com/lg2sxgv. Accessed on 15 Mar 2016
2. Abie, H., Balasingham, I.: Risk-based adaptive security for smart IoT in eHealth. In: Proceedings of the 7th International Conference on Body Area Networks, pp. 269–275. ICST (Institute for Computer Sciences, Social-Informatics and Telecommunications Engineering) (2012)
3. Abowd, G.D., Mynatt, E.D.: Charting past, present, and future research in ubiquitous computing. ACM Trans. Comput. Hum. Interact. (TOCHI) **7**(1), 29–58 (2000)
4. Aman, W., Snekkenes, E.: EDAS: an evaluation prototype for autonomic event driven adaptive security in the internet of things. Future Internet **7**(3), 225–256 (2015)
5. Aman, W., Snekkenes, E.: Managing Security trade-offs in the internet of things using adaptive security. In: The 10th International Conference for Internet Technology and Secured Transactions (ICITST-2015), pp. 362–368, London, UK (2015)
6. CISCO: Internet of things. http://www.cisco.com/web/solutions/trends/iot/overview.html. Accessed on 5 Nov 2015
7. An architectural blueprint for autonomic computing. IBM Publication (2003)

8. Dey, S., Sampalli, S., Ye, Q.: A context-adaptive security framework for mobile cloud computing. In: 2015 11th International Conference on Mobile Ad-hoc and Sensor Networks (MSN), pp. 89–95. IEEE (2015)

9. Dey, S., Sampalli, S., Ye, Q.: A light-weight authentication scheme based on message digest and location for mobile cloud computing. In: 2014 IEEE International Performance Computing and Communications Conference (IPCCC), pp. 1–2. IEEE (2014)

10. Evesti, A., Ovaska, E.: Ontology-based security adaptation at run-time. In: 2010 4th IEEE International Conference on Self-Adaptive and Self-Organizing Systems (SASO), pp. 204–212. IEEE (2010)

11. Hamdi, M., Abie, H.: Game-based adaptive security in the internet of things for eHealth. In: 2014 IEEE International Conference on Communications (ICC), pp. 920–925. IEEE (2014)

12. ISO 27005: 2011: Information technology-Security techniques-Information security risk management, ISO (2011)

13. Kosko, B.: Fuzzy cognitive maps. Int. J. Man Mach. Stud. **24**(1), 65–75 (1986). http://www.sciencedirect.com/science/article/pii/S0020737386800402

14. Ma, H.D.: Internet of things: objectives and scientific challenges. J. Comput. Sci. Technol. **26**(6), 919–924 (2011)

15. MacDonald, N.: The future of information security is context aware and adaptive. Gartner RAS Core Research Note G 200385 (2010)

16. NIST: Risk management framework (RMF) overview, April 2014. http://csrc.nist.gov/groups/SMA/fisma/framework.html. Accessed on 15 Mar 2016

17. Perera, C., Zaslavsky, A., Christen, P., Georgakopoulos, D.: Context aware computing for the internet of things: a survey. IEEE Commun. Surv. Tutorials **16**(1), 414–454 (2013)

18. Salehie, M., Pasquale, L., Omoronyia, I., Ali, R., Nuseibeh, B.: Requirements-driven adaptive security: protecting variable assets at runtime. In: 2012 20th IEEE International Requirements Engineering Conference (RE), pp. 111–120. IEEE (2012)

19. Wang, W., De, S., Toenjes, R., Reetz, E., Moessner, K.: A comprehensive ontology for knowledge representation in the internet of things. In: 2012 IEEE 11th International Conference on Trust, Security and Privacy in Computing and Communications (TrustCom), pp. 1793–1798. IEEE (2012)

OpenStack Firewall as a Service Rule Analyser

Daniel Csubak[1(✉)] and Attila Kiss[1,2]

[1] Faculty of Informatics, Department of Information Systems,
Eotvos Lorand University, Budapest, Hungary
csuby@caesar.elte.hu, kiss@inf.elte.hu, kissa@ujs.sk
[2] Faculty of Economics, Department of Mathematics and Informatics,
J. Selye University, Komárno, Slovakia

Abstract. Cloud platforms are important and current topics of research interest and OpenStack is one of the most well known and most used of them. As more companies start to use it to create and manage their virtual machines, virtual subnets, and virtual networks, security and firewall usage gets more and more attention, since OpenStack has a Firewall as a Service (FWaaS) module which allows packet filtering on virtual routers that connect the subnets. When dealing with enormous firewall rulesets, one cannot find the possible error risks in it on the spot. Our prototype can help the administrator to better understand the rules, by getting data via OpenStack's API and run queries on it offline, without sending any packets. By using our tool, the administrator can get a human readable answer for questions similar to what type of packets can reach a particular network from another, which can help him to understand the rulesets, and to find holes, or loops in the firewall configuration, which can cause security leaks.

1 Introduction

Cloud platforms are important and current topics of research interest nowadays. Many companies started to use public, or private clouds because of the advantageous characteristics of cloud computing:

- Agility, meaning that it is easier to re-provision the infrastructure,
- Cost reduction, which depends on the activity,
- Location independence, meaning that the infrastructure is off-site, usually provided by a third party, and accessed through the Internet,
- Easier to maintain,
- Multitenancy, which enables sharing the resources and cost between multiple users,
- Reliability, by multiple redundant sites,
- Scalability.

As more companies start to use it to create and manage their virtual machines, and virtual networks, security and firewall usage gets more and more attention. Large virtual networks containing many virtual machines are not

T. Tryfonas (Ed.): HAS 2016, LNCS 9750, pp. 212–220, 2016.
DOI: 10.1007/978-3-319-39381-0_19

uncommon, and if more resources are needed, the structure can be more complicated. When huge amount of resources are managed, firewalls come into the picture for controlling packet flow, and for their configuration, rules, and rulesets are needed to achieve this. In the case of enormous networks, the understanding, and reconfiguring of the rulsets are a challenging task for the administrator, or maintainer of the firewalls. Furthermore, because of the complex structure, there can be holes, or loops in the rulesets, which can cause security leaks, and are not easy to find.

In Sect. 2 OpenStack, its main components, and its Firewall as a Service (FWaaS), which is packet filtering firewall, and uses the firewall rulesets are introduced. Section 3 summarizes our motivation for the creation of the firewall rule analyser tool, and in Sect. 4 we analyse related articles. Section 5 presents the used model, especially the router-subnet graph, and the method, we simulate the packet sending for discovering where the packets are allowed to travel in the network, and in Sect. 6 we discuss the questions of the implementation of the tool, and present some limitations of it in Subsection 6.1. We show our results in Sect. 7, and present our plans related the future of the tool in Sect. 8. In Sect. 9 we summarize our work.

2 OpenStack and FWaaS

OpenStack is an open source software to create and control private and public clouds. Their community grows every day, and many large company uses it. There are complete Operating System built for OpenStack by e.g. RedHat, or Canonical. OpenStack is now at version Liberty, and is developed further.

OpenStack is capable of creating, and managing virtual machines, and virtual subnets, organizing them into virtual networks. There are many components in OpenStack, each for different services. The most important are the following [5]

- OpenStack Compute (Nova), which is responsible for the creation, and management of virtual servers, and provisioning.
- Block Storage (Cinder) is providing persistent block storage for the running devices.
- Object Storage (Swift) stores, and retrieves unstructured data objects through HTTP based API.
- OpenStack Networking (Neutron) is an API driven, pluggable system, that scales well, and manages the networks. It is responsible for IP addresses of the machines, management of firewalls, load balancers, etc.
- Identity Service (Keystone), which is responsible for authentication of the users.
- OpenStack Image Service (Glance) manages the virtual machine images.
- OpenStack Telemetry Service (Ceilometer) is the monitoring component.
- Dashboard (Horizon) is a web-based portal, which is used to interact with OpenStack.

In our case, the most interesting part is networking. Virtual machines can be organized into virtual subnets, which can form virtual networks. Between networks routers act as gateways, connecting one to another. While routers are useful as gateways, on every one of them a single packet filtering firewall instance can be run. This service is called Firewall as a Service (FWaaS). Packet filtering firewalls operate mostly in the network layer [4], with some information from the transport layer. They investigate the protocol, source, and destination of every packet that crosses them, and make a decision whether the packet is allowed to pass, or is to be dropped. They are not stateful, and they do not look inside the packets for further investigation. Packet filtering firewalls use rules, in the form of

- protocol,
- action, meaning the packet filtering decision,
- source and destination IP address or subnet,
- source and destination port or port range.

From these parameters protocol and action must be specified, the others are optional, in which case the default value is any (meaning any IP address, or any port). Firewall rules are grouped into rulesets, in which the order of the rules is very important, since the most packet filters use the first matching rule method, when the rules are being evaluated. It means the first matching rule will be applied to the packet, while the rest will be ignored.

OpenStack can use various firewall software via drivers, and all of them can be managed by the same API or the dashboard. For this, OpenStack FWaaS have a generalized structure for firewall rules, rulesets, etc., from which the drivers generate configuration files for the different firewalls. The generalized information can be gathered from OpenStack via the Networking API.

3 Motivation

OpenStack Network API can be used to obtain generalized information about the network topology, and the firewall rulesets, regardless the implementation of the firewall functionality. This kind of study was not done before, and it offers a generic solution for many different firewalls, which have drivers in OpenStack.

In this case the users are system administrators, whose task is to maintain the network, and the firewall rulesets in it. When large number of virtual networks, and hosts are managed in OpenStack, many rules are needed in packet filtering, which are not easy to understand. The users are in need of tools, that help them in the interpretation of the topology and the rules, to identify security leaks in the network and find conflicts in the rulesets.

For administrators it is very important that firewall rule analysis should not bother the every day functionality. For this, offline analysis is performed, where no actual sending is needed, after the network topology, and the firewall rulesets are present, no additional traffic is generated in the network.

4   Related Work

In [1], Mayer et al. presented an offline firewall analyser prototype and a tool, Firewall Analyzer (FA). Their query engine accepts the description of the network topology in a subset of Firmato's MDL language [7], which later they automated to create. The network topology was modeled based on the gateway-zone graph concept. To understand the basics, consider the structure of the model. In this, the network is partitioned into zones, which are connected by gateways. Each gateway has an interface for each adjacent zone, and packets leaving the zones can be filtered by the gateways on the corresponding interface. The gateway-zone graph is a bi-partite graph $H = ((G \cup Z), I)$. The vertices consist of the set of gateways, and the set of zones, while the set of interfaces I forms the edges. The graph contains an edge from $g \in G$ to $z \in Z$, if g has an interface, for which z is an adjacent zone.

For understanding the firewall's ruleset they used the configuration file syntax of LMF, and in FA they added support for Check Point and Cisco firewalls. After understanding the network topology and the firewall's ruleset, they built a gateway-zone graph on which the queries can be performed. A flooding-like method was used for the discovering of the allowed paths offline. As the result of this process, large queries could be evaluated to see what kind of traffic is allowed to go from the source to the destination.

While their tool supports large queries, e.g. from any source to any destination using any service, it cannot support all the firewalls, furthermore, the building mechanism of the gateway-zone graph, with the manual parts in it can be tiresome. In contrast of these, OpenStack's firewall ruleset language is generalized, and started to be widely used by many vendors, who created drivers for their own software. In the case of the building of the model OpenStack's Network API offers a generalized output for the topology, too, so it is easy to be obtained.

Margrave, another firewall analysis tool is presented in [2]. It focuses on user-end scenarios, and decomposes Cisco IOS firewall's configuration into policies. Margrave maps both policies and queries into first-order logic formulas. To answer a query, its formula is conjoined with all references policy formulas, and then a solution is computed. Kodkod [8] is used to solve the first-order formulas using SAT solving.

In [3] a simple SQL-like query language, called the Structured Firewall Query Language (SFQL), for describing firewall queries is introduced. As the foundation of their query processing algorithms, the Firewall Query Theorem is presented, along with the decision diagram based query processing algorithm, and the Firewall Query Algebra.

5   Model

Our model is kind of similar to the one presented in [1]. We used OpenStack's terminology for the naming, to be convenient. A virtual network consists of several virtual subnets, from which virtual IP addresses can be allocated for the virtual machines. Virtual networks are connected via its virtual subnets by virtual routers. Each of these routers have numerous interfaces (ports), that are connected to one particular virtual subnet. Any virtual router can run one single packet filtering firewall instance, which has a ruleset called firewall policy. Rulesets are containing various number of firewall rules. Since OpenStack's FWaaS only support packet filtering now, these rules are in the form that has been presented above.

We built a gateway-subnet graph, which is as follows, $G = (V, E)$, where every vertex in V is exactly one subnet or a router, and there is an edge between two nodes, if they are connected. It is trivial from the construction of the graph, that edges only can exist between subnets and routers. Each router has a priority list of the rules of its firewall. When we simulate the packet sending process, we use a flooding-like method, with some preconceptions. If a packet reaches a router with a firewall on it, we apply the rules to the packet in the first matching rule way.

We constructed a router-subnet graph, which is as the following: $G = ((R \cup S), I)$, where R is the set of virtual routers, S is the set of virtual subnets. There is an edge between $r \in R$ and $s \in S$ if r has an interface, $i \in I$, which is connected to s. It is trivial from the construction of the graph, that edges only can exist between virtual subnets and virtual routers. Firewall policies are attached to the routers, which they belong. These policies form a priority list, since the rules are evaluated according to the first matching rule policy.

They can answer questions like can a packet sent from a source port of a given source host, a destination host's given port. To achieve this, we used a flooding method that works as the follows. The evaluation starts from the source, simulating the sending mechanism via each of its adjacent virtual routers. On the routers, the firewall policies are evaluated, whether the packet could pass, or not. If it passes, the adjacent subnet does exactly the same, except that it will not send back the packet. An individual process ends, when a packet is denied by a firewall, or reaches the destination host. The whole process ends, when every individual process ends (no more packet simulation runs). In the end, the paths, the points, where the packets are dropped, etc. can be identified. The flooding method has its trivial disadvantages, but it can discover all the possible paths, which can lead to the destination.

6   Implementation

We implemented our tool in python. The code base is easy to understand, and flexible, can be reused for the implementation of other representational structures, or sending methods.

We used the `python-neutronclient` package to connect to OpenStack's Networking API. Calls of the API were used to get the needed information out of OpenStack:

- `neutron.list_ports()` is used to get the interfaces (ports) from the Networking API. This includes the id of the subnet, an interface is connected to, and the id of the router, the interface belongs to.
- `neutron.list_subnets(subnet_id)` is used to get information about a subnet specified by `subnet_id`. This includes the IP address range of the subnet.
- `neutron.list_routers(device_id` is used to get data about the router specified by `device_id`.
- `neutron.list_firewalls()` returns the list of firewall instances including the id of the router it is run on, and the id of the policy of the firewall.
- `neutron.list_firewall_rules()` lists the firewall rules with the parameters that were introduced above and the id of the policy it belongs to.

The answers from the API come in JSON format, which is easily parsed by python into a dictionary-like format. After the API calls, no other data is needed from OpenStack.

The nodes of the router-subnet graph are implemented as different instances of classes in python. Each instance stores the ids of adjacent nodes, and these are used as pointers to that object. Furthermore, router instances store their firewall policy, on which the firewall decision is based.

The simulation of sending from a source IP address and port, to a destination IP address and port, by using a given protocol is goes as follows:

- The subnets belonging to the addresses are calculated.
- The source simulates sending on each of its ports.
- On the adjacent routers, the firewall decision is made.
  - If the packet can pass, the packet can reach the connected subnet, and the same process starts from there, except for that the subnet will not send back the packet on the port it arrived on.
  - If the packet is denied, the process ends on that path.

At the end, the different paths and firewall decisions are present.

6.1 Limitations

To keep the model simple, and make the implementation easy, we used some limitations, which later have to be updated.

The current implementation can only process cases with the query engine, where the **any** clause is not present. This means, any subnet, any port, and any protocol cannot be used in queries. This limits only the comfort of the functionality, since the any queries can be processed as separate queries.

7   Results

The main result of our work is the FWaaS rule analyser tool itself.

We tested our tool in a real OpenStack environment. We used devstack [6] to build the environment on one of our machines with 24 cores, 50 GB of RAM,

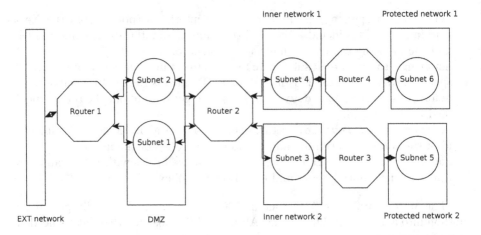

Fig. 1. An example topology with 6 virtual networks, and 4 virtual routers.

with Debian jessie. Devstack is a script to quickly create OpenStack environment with the most components in it for development purposes.

During our tests, we created several topologies with different attributes to see, if our tool is capable to process them. We started the tool from many different hosts to many others as destinations, and the results showed, that it is the planned, and implemented functionality works.

Since our infrastructure could not run many virtual networks, and hosts, we do not want to present irrelevant data about running times on small networks.

On Fig. 1 an example topology can be seen which is smaller, but similar to one of our test cases. In the example, on each virtual router a FWaaS is run, so we had to evaluate their rules, when a router was on the path. Take the following question: can a host from the external network (public) reach one, in Protected network 1 using TCP protocol, and port 22? To investigate this, after our tool have built the subnet-router graph the simulation of sending will start. From the EXT network the appropriate packet is sent by flooding, and Router 1 makes a firewall decision. Let's assume that the packet is allowed to pass, so it reaches Subnet 1, and Subnet 2. From there, the flooding continues. Assume that Router 4 will drop the packet, while Router 3 will let it pass. Because of the flooding method, this inconsistency will be seen, and the administrator can decide whether it is intentional to use different firewalling, or it is because of mistyped configuration.

8   Future Work

We have multiple plans for the future of our tool. It can be organized into three sections, firstly the work out of the limitations, second the test on enormous environment, and third the extension of functionality.

The first section is trivial, we want to work out the limitations of any type queries, so the tool can be more comfortable to use.

In the second section we plan to implement a simulator to mock OpenStack's Networking API, so we can simulate huge networks with many firewall rules, which is now limited by our physical resources. By this, performance testing will be possible, and we can compare the running time of the tool on different large networks.

The third section contains work to replace the flooding like discovering algorithm, which later can be used as a base for comparison for the new algorithms, that rely more on the structure of the network, or the firewall rulesets.

9 Summary

We studied OpenStack, as one of the most popular, and widely used cloud platforms nowadays. It can create and manage virtual machines, which can be organized into huge virtual networks, connected by virtual routers, which can run simple packet filtering firewall instances. In the case of enormous networks, it is a hard task for the system administrators to understand, and maintain the firewall rules. This is the point, where our tool come in the picture.

Our tool, written in python, uses OpenStack's Networking API to get the data about the virtual network topology, and the firewall rulesets, and runs offline queries on it. To support this, we build a router-subnet graph from the data of the topology, and apply the firewall rules on it in the given points. The tool can answer queries like from a source to a destination, can a given packet travel through the network, or not.

Our tool uses the generalized structures of OpenStack for the virtual networking topology, and the firewall rules, so in the view of the many supported firewall technology, it can be used on the products of many different vendors, who has drivers for their software in OpenStack. By using the tool, loops, misconfigured rules, and holes can be found easier in firewall configurations.

Acknowledgement. Authors thank Ericsson Ltd. for support via the ELTE CNL collaboration.

References

1. Mayer, A., Wool, A., Ziskind, E.: Offline firewall analysis. Int. J. Inf. Secur. **5**(3), 125–144 (2006)
2. Nelson, T., Barratt, C., Dougherty, D.J., Fisler, K., Krishnamurthi, S.: The margrave tool for firewall analysis. In: LISA (2010)
3. Liu, A.X., Gouda, M.G.: Firewall policy queries. IEEE Trans. Parallel Distrib. Syst. **20**(6), 766–777 (2009)
4. Stallings, W.: Handbook of Computer-Communications Standards; Vol 1: The Open Systems Interconnection (OSI) Model and OSI-Related Standards. Macmillan Publishing Co. Inc., New York (1987)

5. OpenStack Open Source Cloud Computing Software, 2 February 2016. https://www.openstack.org/software/
6. Devstack - an OpenStack Community Production, 19 January 2016. http://docs.openstack.org/developer/devstack/
7. Bartal, Y., Mayer, A., Nissim, K., Wool, A.: Firmato: a novel firewall management toolkit. ACM Trans. Comput. Syst. (TOCS) **22**(4), 381–420 (2004)
8. Torlak, E., Jackson, D.: Kodkod: a relational model finder. In: Grumberg, O., Huth, M. (eds.) TACAS 2007. LNCS, vol. 4424, pp. 632–647. Springer, Heidelberg (2007)

Interactive Discovery and Retrieval of Web Resources Containing Home Made Explosive Recipes

George Kalpakis[1(✉)], Theodora Tsikrika[1], Christos Iliou[1], Thodoris Mironidis[1],
Stefanos Vrochidis[1], Jonathan Middleton[2], Una Williamson[2],
and Ioannis Kompatsiaris[1]

[1] Information Technology Institute, CERTH, Thessaloniki, Greece
{kalpakis,theodora.tsikrika,iliouchristos,mironidis,
stefanos,ikom}@iti.gr
[2] Police Service Northern Ireland, Belfast, UK
{jonathan.middleton,una.williamson}@psni.pnn.police.uk

Abstract. This work investigates the effectiveness of a novel interactive search engine in the context of discovering and retrieving Web resources containing recipes for synthesizing Home Made Explosives (HMEs). The discovery of HME Web resources both on Surface and Dark Web is addressed as a domain-specific search problem; the architecture of the search engine is based on a hybrid infrastructure that combines two different approaches: (i) a Web crawler focused on the HME domain; (ii) the submission of HME domain-specific queries to general-purpose search engines. Both approaches are accompanied by a user-initiated post-processing classification for reducing the potential noise in the discovery results. The design of the application is built based on the distinctive nature of law enforcement agency user requirements, which dictate the interactive discovery and the accurate filtering of Web resources containing HME recipes. The experiments evaluating the effectiveness of our application demonstrate its satisfactory performance, which in turn indicates the significant potential of the adopted approaches on the HME domain.

Keywords: Interactive search engine · Homemade explosives · Dark web

1 Introduction

The large number of terrorist attacks that have taken place worldwide during the past 20 years has put increasing pressure to law enforcement agencies (LEAs), so as to uphold the rule of law by raising their awareness against terrorist groups to the highest level possible. The recent escalation of terrorist attacks clearly indicates that the war against terrorism should be fought with all the available means, including alternative solutions offered through the continuous advancement of technology. At the same time, the rapid growth of broadband technologies, along with the abundance of online resources for storing content, has resulted in the proliferation of the information being shared globally. This growth has facilitated the diffusion of knowledge in many different domains, nevertheless it has resulted in sharing information online that poses a threat to the society,

© Springer International Publishing Switzerland 2016
T. Tryfonas (Ed.): HAS 2016, LNCS 9750, pp. 221–233, 2016.
DOI: 10.1007/978-3-319-39381-0_20

such as material that can be used for supporting acts of terrorism, including information for the manufacture and use of homemade explosives (HMEs) which can be exploited for subversive use. The availability of such material on the Web provides the subversive with the ability to thoroughly study the process of synthesizing HMEs, using common household goods and easy to purchase items. Hence, it is vital for LEAs to exploit technologies that will enable them to cope with this threat by automatically identifying resources with HME information.

To meet this challenge, this work proposes a novel interactive search engine for the discovery and retrieval of Web resources including HME content, with particular focus on HME recipe information. Such information, present both on Surface and Dark Web, can be found on various types of Web resources, such as Web pages, forums, and social media posts. The proposed application enables the discovery of HME content through a user friendly interface. The interactive search engine is built based on the continuous need for LEAs to discover HME information on the Web and to filter the most significant resources by interacting with tools capable of accurately distinguishing the most relevant resources within the HME domain. It employs a hybrid model consisting of four major components that provide several advanced facilities: (i) a **Web Crawling** component focused on the HME domain (ii) a **Querying** component which submits HME domain-specific queries to general-purpose search engines, (iii) a **Post-Processing Classification** component which reduces the potential noise of the discovery results, and (iv) an **Interactive Graphical User Interface** which facilitates the user communication with the search engine's main components.

The main contribution of this work is the integration of domain-specific technologies in a novel interactive search engine for the discovery and retrieval of heterogeneous Web resources containing HME information, as well as the adaptation of domain-specific search technologies in the context of the HME domain. This interactive search engine has been developed in a user-driven manner in collaboration with and based on the requirements of LEA personnel, and provides access to HME crawling and querying tools via a unified Graphical User Interface tailored to facilitating the intelligence gathering process. Additionally, this application provides a combination of domain-specific tools applied both to Surface and Dark Web, where illegal and potentially harmful information is usually stored. To the best our knowledge, this is the first attempt to develop an interactive search engine designed to facilitate the discovery of HME information that combines search and crawling capabilities.

2   Use Cases and Requirements

This section discusses the end-user requirements of the proposed interactive search engine that are elicited based on appropriate use cases for HME discovery. The use cases have been provided by law enforcement and security agents in the context of HOMER project[1] who have offered guidance for a user-oriented development.

---

[1] http://www.homer-project.eu/.

Use Case 1. Search for HME-related Content in an Extremist Forum: LEAs need to detect user posts present in specific Web forums in Surface and Dark Web discussing the process of synthesizing an HME recipe, and providing feedback on how to use such a product in terrorist activities. For example, consider the case that a group of users, members of a forum identified for its extremist character, discuss their intention of manufacturing an HME for using it in an imminent terrorist attack.

Use Case 2. Search the Web for Information Related to an Explosive: LEAs need to constantly discover new sources with HME content and monitor the advancements in the manufacture of HMEs by submitting keyword-based queries enhanced with a mechanism for their automatic formulation or expansion. They, also, need to get results ranked by their relevance to the HME domain. Such information is usually being shared online and indexed by general-purpose search engines of Surface and/or Dark Web. For instance, consider the case there is intelligence that a specific substance not previously used is currently being considered for subversive use.

Both use cases reflect the challenge of developing an interactive search engine for supporting searches for HME content on Surface and Dark Web. Table 1 presents the core requirements of the interactive search engine as emerged by the two use cases.

Table 1. Interactive search engine requirements

Requirements	Description	Use Case
R1 – Traverse the Web looking for HME content	Search for Web resources via a classifier-guided crawler focused on the HME domain	UC1
R2 – Submit keyword-based automatically formulated queries for finding HME-related content	Search for HME Web resources by submitting automatically formulated queries to general-purpose search engines based on keywords applied to a set of domain-specific query patterns	UC2
R3 – Submit keyword-based automatically expanded queries	Search for HME Web resources by expanding keyword-based queries using a set of query expansion rules and submitting them to general-purpose search engines	UC2
R4 – Filter the returned results	Re-rank the return results by estimating their relevance to the HME-domain based on classification	UC2
R5 – Interactive User Interface	Provide an interactive Graphical User Interface for running, configuring and parameterizing the different modes of search provided	UC1, UC2
R6 – Perform searches for HMEs in Dark Web	Develop a tool supporting focused crawling in Dark Web anonymous networks, and query submitting in general-purpose search engines for Dark Web resources.	UC1, UC2

3   Related Work

This section first discusses the state-of-the-art approaches in the field of domain-specific search and then examines the major research efforts for discovering terrorist or extremist-related content on Web resources.

Domain-specific search can be considered as a well-established research area, since a considerable number of techniques have been developed to tackle this issue. The main methodologies used for the implementation of domain-specific search tools for the discovery of Web resources on a given topic can be divided into two categories: (i) methods based on focused Web crawling and (ii) methods based on the indexes and search infrastructures of existing general-purpose search engines. For the first category of methods, the state-of-the-art approaches [1] adopt classifier-guided crawling strategies based on supervised machine learning methods that rely on (i) the hyperlinks' local context, and/or (ii) global evidence associated with the entire parent page. For the second category of methods, existing general-purpose search engines (e.g., Google, Yahoo!, etc.) are employed and domain-specific queries generated semi-automatically or fully automatically are submitted to them. The queries generated semi-automatically are based on abstract query patterns that can then be instantiated into multiple query instances corresponding to sequences of domain-specific keywords and attributes [2]. More complex domain-oriented queries can be automatically generated by applying machine learning techniques in order to extract terms referred to as "keyword spices" [3, 4]. However none of these approaches have been applied and adapted in the context of the HME domain.

In the field of discovering terrorist-related information on the Web, a thorough research [5] has paved the way for the development tools that aim to collect and analyze Web content generated by international terrorist groups. To this end, the most comprehensive suite of text mining and Web mining tools for performing link and content, analysis has been developed in the context of the Dark Web project at the University of Arizona [6]. However, this project has addressed the whole breadth of terrorist and extremist content, rather than HME information, as done here. Furthermore, research efforts have been conducted for performing focused crawling in Dark Web forums moderated by extremist groups by using a human-assisted accessibility approach [7]. Moreover, another methodology, applied in a set of Jihad Web sites, has been proposed for collecting and analyzing Dark Web information for aiding the process of intelligence gathering [8]. Again, they deal with a wider scope of information, rather than only with HMEs. Additionally, a work related to HMEs presents a mechanism for automatically identifying the relevance of already discovered multimedia content (videos/images) to the HME domain based on concept detection [9]; however, this work deals with the identification of HME-related content in multimedia, rather than with the discovery and retrieval of such information from the Web. Furthermore, a relevant research effort presents a framework corresponding to a Knowledge Management Platform for managing the discovery, analysis and retrieval of HME-related content [10]; nevertheless, this work is mainly concerned with the general framework's architecture focusing on the HME knowledge management, rather than on the discovery of HME information from the Web. Contrary to the aforementioned papers, this work proposes a novel interactive search engine that focuses on HME information both on Surface and Dark Web, based on an innovative hybrid infrastructure, which consists not only of an interactive search mechanism, but also of a complementary online crawling tool, capable of traversing the Web on user demand. The search engine exploits domain-specific approaches and is being developed in a user-driven manner with the goal to fulfill the requirements of its end users.

4   HME Search Engine Architecture

This section provides a high level overview of the interactive search engine architecture for the discovery of Web resources with HMEs, which is designed based on the user requirements described earlier. As shown in Fig. 1, the underlying fundamental concept behind the adopted methodology in our application is the use of an interactive interface (R5) that provides access to different functionalities. The search engine enables the users (i.e. police and anti-terrorism/intelligence officers) to perform customized searches both on Surface and Dark Web (R6) for HME-related content by taking advantage of a hybrid model based both on focused crawlers (R1) and general-purpose search engines (R2, R3). The results of the discovery procedure go through a classification process on user demand for filtering out the potential noise (R4).

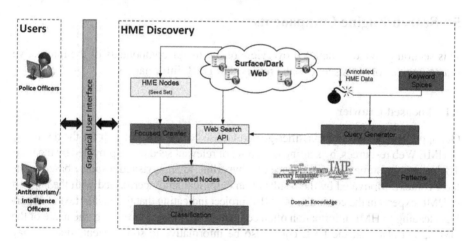

Fig. 1. Interactive search engine architecture

Our application's discovery and retrieval mechanism relies on a hybrid architecture, which combines into a joint workflow (i) a crawling facility where a Web crawler focused on the HME domain, starting from a predefined set of seed pages, performs selective traversal of Web resources by estimating their relevance to the HME domain based on supervised machine learning classifiers (R1), and (ii) a querying facility where HME domain-specific queries are submitted to general-purpose search engines; such queries are either formulated using query patterns in conjunction with domain knowledge (R2), or are expanded based on the methodology of "keyword spices" (i.e. domain-specific keywords generated with the aid of supervised machine learning techniques) (R3) [8]. These two methods are complementary, since the latter aims to exploit the large coverage of existing indexes containing Web resources already crawled in the very large scale by general-purpose search engines, as well as the search infrastructures they provide, while the former aims to address the inherent difficulties in the generation of effective domain-specific queries that would lead to the discovery of relevant Web resources, and also to go beyond what is already covered by existing indexes, by identifying new Web resources relevant to the HME domain that have not yet been indexed by a general-purpose search engine. Also, this hybrid infrastructure goes beyond exploring and discovering resources found typically on Surface Web. Both the crawling and the querying facility are capable of discovering HME resources on Dark Web (R6), whose nature facilitates the proliferation of information used for illegal and terrorist activities. Moreover, the use of focused crawling avoids dependencies on external services (i.e. existing search engines), thus ensuring the long-term viability of the application. Finally, post-processing filtering is performed on user demand based on a classification process (R4) for reducing the potential noise in the results obtained by both discovery approaches.

5   Search Engine Components

This section provides a detailed overview of the major components of the interactive search engine for the discovery and retrieval of HME information.

5.1   Focused Crawler

Our application employs a classifier-guided focused crawling approach for the discovery of HME Web resources, by starting from a set of relevant seed pages provided by the user. To this end, it estimates the relevance of a hyperlink to an unvisited resource based on its local context. Motivated by the results of an empirical study performed with the support of HME experts in the context of HOMER project indicating that the anchor text of hyperlinks leading to HME information often contains HME-related terms (e.g. the name of the HME), and also that the URL could also be informative to some extent, since it may contain relevant information (e.g. the name of the HME), we follow recent research [11] and represent the local context of each hyperlink using: (i) its anchor text, (ii) a text window of x characters (e.g. $x = 50$) surrounding the anchor text that does not overlap with the anchor text of adjacent links, and (iii) the terms extracted from the URL. Each sample is represented (after stopwords removal and stemming) using a tf.df term weighting scheme, where tf(t,d) is the frequency of term t in sample d, normalized by the maximum frequency of any t in that sample, and df(t) is the number of samples containing that term in the collection of samples. The classification of this local context is performed using a supervised machine learning approach based on Support Vector Machines (SVMs), given their demonstrated effectiveness in such applications [12]. The confidence score for each hyperlink is obtained by applying a trained classifier on its feature vector, and the page pointed by the hyperlink is fetched if its score is above a given threshold.

The developed focused crawler is based on a customized version of Apache Nutch[2] (version 1.9). It has been configured so that it can be set to traverse several darknets present in Dark Web, and specifically the most popular anonymous networks, namely Tor[3], I2P[4] and Freenet[5]. Necessary for supporting crawling in Dark Web, is to enable the Tor, I2P and Freenet services on the machine running the crawler.

5.2   General-Purpose Web Search Engine Querying Component

This component submits domain-specific queries to existing general-purpose search engines both on Surface and Dark Web. Currently, for Surface Web, the Yahoo! BOSS API[6] is employed, but our tool can be easily extended so as to support additional APIs (provided by Google, Bing, etc.), whereas concerning the Dark Web, Duck Duck Go[7] and Ahmia[8] search engines are supported by executing queries on their Web interface (since no API is available) and parsing the returned results. The domain-specific queries are generated in a semi-automatic, or fully automatic fashion.

The semi-automatic approach requires the availability of an initial set of seed queries that can be processed (manually or/and automatically) so as to mine abstract query patterns that can then instantiated into multiple (concrete) query instances corresponding to sequences of domain-specific keywords [2, 10]. Here, an initial set of 45 queries that was formulated by law enforcement agents and was used for the successful discovery of HME Web resources through general-purpose search engines, is used as the seed set of queries. Once the keywords appearing in all queries are mapped to discrete concepts, then in every query in the initial seed set, the keywords are replaced by the respective concepts they are mapped to; for example, the query "preparation anfo" becomes "action explosive". This results in producing a set of discrete patterns that can be used for automatic query generation (18 explosive-related patterns were produced). For example, the pattern "action explosive", where "action" corresponds to keywords such as "how to make", "preparation", etc., may be instantiated to several different queries for each of the explosives of interest. Hence, once a user expresses interest in discovering HME Web resources about a given explosive, they can select query patterns containing the concept "explosive", and these patterns will be automatically instantiated for that particular explosive, and will be submitted in parallel to the search engine; the results of all these queries will be merged before being presented.

The automatic approach aims to generate high precision and high recall queries in the HME domain. Based on machine learning techniques, it generates specific (Boolean)

---

[2] http://nutch.apache.org/.

[3] https://www.torproject.org/.

[4] https://geti2p.net/.

[5] https://freenetproject.org/.

[6] https://developer.yahoo.com/boss/search/.

[7] https://duckduckgo.com/.

[8] https://ahmia.fi/search/.

expressions (referred to as "keyword spices") [4] that aim to characterize in an effective manner the HME domain. These expressions are then used for expanding (simple) domain-related queries; these expanded queries are subsequently submitted to a general-purpose search engine with the goal of improving the effectiveness of the initial (unexpanded) queries. The methodology implemented involves splitting an annotated set of Web resources into two subsets (for training and validation respectively), constructing a decision tree based on the training set and applying a decision tree learning algorithm for discovering the keyword spices [13]. Then these initial keyword spices are iteratively simplified by removing keywords in case their removal increases the F-measure of the validation set. The completion of this process results in generating the final set of Boolean expressions (8 expansion expressions were generated), which can be used for expanding simple queries [10]. An indicative example of such an expression generated is the following: *powder OR ingredient OR explosive.*

5.3   Post-processing Classification Component

The resources discovered through focused crawling and search engine querying are then classified based on their textual content. A text-based classifier is trained on a set of Web resources annotated as relevant or non-relevant to the HME domain. Each resource is parsed, its textual content is extracted, tokenization, stopwords removal and stemming are applied, and a textual feature vector is generated using the tf.idf term weighting scheme, where tf(t,d) is the frequency of term t in sample d, normalized by the maximum frequency of any t in that sample, and idf(t) is the inverse document frequency of term t in the collection of samples. Then, an SVM [14] classifier is trained using an RBF kernel, while 10-fold cross-validation is performed for selecting the class weight parameters. At query time the classifier, if initiated by the user, is capable of classifying the search engine and/or the focused crawling results as relevant or non-relevant to the HME domain. The classifier is implemented using the libraries of the Weka[9] machine learning software.

5.4   Graphical User Interface

The three aforementioned components of our application, namely the querying, the focused crawling and the classification components, are accessible via a Web-based intuitive Graphical User Interface (GUI) with a minimalist design aiming to provide a usable, flexible and consistent environment for the user, emphasizing in their interactive communication with the application. The GUI employs a responsive tabbed design allowing both the focused crawling and the querying facility to fully adapt to the screen size, using tabs as a navigational widget for switching between them.

   Aiming to facilitate user engagement, the GUI provides a parametrized environment for running each one of these facilities. Specifically, for a focused crawling task (see Fig. 2), the following parameters can be configured: (i) the set of seed URLs constituting the starting points of the crawl, (ii) the score threshold that determines the necessary relevance

---

[9] http://www.cs.waikato.ac.nz/ml/weka/.

value that a URL needs to exceed in order to be accepted by the crawler classifier, (iii) the crawl depth (i.e. the maximum distance allowed between the seed pages and the crawled pages), and (iv) the option to perform a domain-restricted crawl (i.e. the crawler is allowed to follow hyperlinks belonging only to the same domain name(s) of the URL(s) present in the seed URL list). Additionally, for running a keyword-based query (see Fig. 3), three interaction modes are provided: (i) a free text mode for manually submitting queries, (ii) a semi-automatic mode for submitting queries taking advantage of 18 explosive-related query patterns, and (iii) an automatic mode for expanding the queries with one of the 8 available keyword spices. In both cases, a crawl or a querying run may be followed by a user-initiated post-processing classification process which re-ranks the respective returned results.

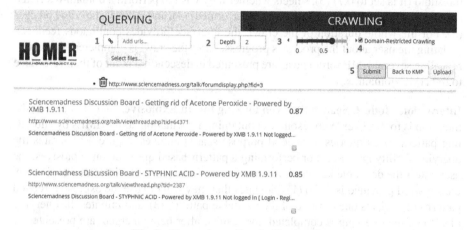

Fig. 2. Focused crawling facility interface

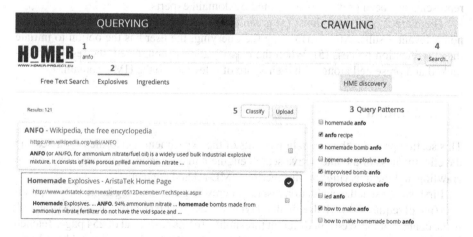

Fig. 3. Querying facility interface

6   User Interaction Modes

This section presents the modes of interaction when using the proposed search engine for performing the tasks described in the use cases discussed in Sect. 2.

Interaction Mode 1. Search a Forum Looking for HME Content. In this case, the goal is to perform a domain-restricted crawl on forums where people are discussing about HME recipes, so as to discover posts related to synthesizing HMEs. Figure 2 illustrates the crawling facility interface. For performing a crawl, the user provides the seed URL(s) (in this case, a forum[10] Web page representing a section including topics related to HMEs) (1), selects the crawl depth (it is set to 2) (2), sets the crawler classifier's threshold (it is set to 0.7) (3), selects whether they wish to perform a domain-restricted crawl or not (a domain-restricted crawl is performed) (4), and initiates the crawl process (5). For the whole duration of the crawl, the interface provides continuous feedback updating the user about the process's progress. After the crawl is completed, the results revealing several HME forum posts are presented in descending order of their relevance to the HME domain.

Interaction Mode 2. Search the Web looking for an Explosive. In this scenario, the intention is to discover Web resources containing information about HMEs by submitting pattern-based queries to general-purpose search engines. Figure 3 illustrates the querying facility interface. For performing a pattern-based querying on explosives, the user enters the desirable keyword(s) representing the explosive of interest (in this case, the keyword provided is anfo) (1), indicates that they want to use the explosive-related patterns (2), selects one or more of the available patterns (3), and initiates the querying (4). When the querying is completed, the results, after being merged, are presented to the user. A result is depicted in a colored box depending on whether the Web page it represents has been previously annotated by domain experts.

There are 2 color variations: (a) green depicts relevant results and (b) red depicts non-relevant results. After performing the querying, the user has the option to initiate the classification process (5). When the classification is completed, the results are re-ranked and presented along with their score of relevance to the HME domain.

7   Evaluation

This section provides the evaluation results of the experiments performed for assessing the effectiveness of the interactive search engine's major facilities, namely the focused crawling and the querying for discovering HME-related content.

First, we present the evaluation results for crawling emphasizing in measuring precision (recall requires knowledge of all relevant pages on a given topic, an impossible task in the context of the Web) for different thresholds. In this case, a set of 254 pages fetched by the focused crawler, when the threshold t is set to 0.5 has been assessed based on a

---

[10] http://www.sciencemadness.org/.

two-point relevance scale, characterizing the retrieved resources as being relevant (i.e. resources describing HME recipes, explosive properties etc.) or non-relevant to the HME domain. The results of the experiments for various values of threshold t at depth = 3 are presented in Table 2. As expected, precision increases for higher values of threshold t. In particular, the difference between threshold values 0.6 and 0.7 is quite significant, with precision improving significantly.

Table 2. Focused crawling evaluation results

	Threshold t				
	0.5	0.6	0.7	0.8	0.9
Precision	0.52	0.54	0.73	0.73	0.74

With respect to the query formulation module, we provide a comparison for the performance of the different techniques involved, including domain-specific keywords and enhanced queries combining keywords with patterns or keyword spices. We emphasize on mean average precision, while the recall performance is also discussed. For evaluating the querying facility, we utilized a set of 22 explosive keywords (e.g. anfo, c-4, etc.) provided by domain experts and compared the results of submitting keyword-based, pattern-based and spice-expanded queries. For the keyword-based search, 22 queries were submitted and the top 20 results were retrieved for each (i.e. 440 URLs). For the pattern-based search, we mapped the keywords to the HME patterns. Specifically 396 (22 keywords × 18 explosive patterns, Sect. 5.2) queries were submitted and the top 20 URLs for each mapped keyword were retrieved (i.e. 440 URLs) after merging the results using a linear ranking system. Finally, for the spice-expanded queries, we used the 2 best performing keyword spices during the training process (Sect. 5.2) and submitted 44 queries (22 keywords × 2 keyword spices) retrieving the top 20 results (i.e. 440 URLs) for each expanded keyword after merging the results using a linear ranking system. In total, 1320 URLs were retrieved, resulting in 720 unique URLs (after duplicate elimination), which were manually annotated. Table 3 compares the results of the three approaches.

Table 3. Querying evaluation results

	Keywords	Keyword + Patterns	Keyword + K.S.
MAP	0.70	0.87	0.71
Relevant URLs	232	233	97
Newly discovered relevant URLs	–	161	48

The improvement of the ranking results when the pattern-based approach is employed as opposed to the simple keyword-based approach indicates the significance and the usefulness of the pattern-based approach for the HME domain. Also, the "keyword spices" methodology, slightly improves the ranking when compared to the keyword-based approach. Furthermore, retrieving high recall results is of equal importance. Employing both the pattern-based and the "keyword spices" approach results in a significant increase in the number of the discovered relevant results compared to the simple keyword-based approach, which means that the recall is increased.

8   Conclusions

This work proposed an interactive search engine that was adapted in the context of the discovery and retrieval of Web resources containing HME information. It is envisaged that within such an application, which is driven by the distinctive nature of its user requirements, the tools developed provide LEAs with the technology they require to acquire more knowledge on HMEs in order to tackle the threat they pose. The application has indicated the significant adaptability of the domain-specific search approaches to the HME domain. Future work includes more extensive evaluation of the interactive search engine in terms of its usability, effectiveness, and efficiency by LEA personnel, and domain experts, in large-scale user studies that will take place.

Acknowledgement. This work was supported by the HOMER (312388) FP7 project.

References

1. Olston, C., Najork, M.: Web crawling. J. Found. Trends Inf. Retrieval **4**(3), 175–246 (2010)
2. Agarwal, G., Kabra, G., Chang, K.C.C.: Towards rich query interpretation: walking back and forth for mining query templates. In: 19th ACM International Conference on World Wide Web (WWW 2010), pp. 1–10 (2010)
3. Oyama, S., Kokubo, T., Ishida, T., Yamada, T., Kitamura, Y.: Keyword spices: a new method for building domain-specific web search engines. In: 17th International Joint Conferences on Artificial Intelligence, IJCAI-2001, pp. 1457–1463 (2001)
4. Oyama, S., Kokubo, T., Ishida, T.: Domain-specific web search with keyword spices. J. IEEE Trans. Knowl. Data Eng. **16**(1), 17–27 (2004)
5. Stenersen, A.: The internet: a virtual training camp? J. Terrorism Polit. Violence **20**, 215–233 (2008)
6. Chen, H.: Dark web: exploring and mining the dark side of the web. In: Domenach, F., Ignatov, D.I., Poelmans, J. (eds.) ICFCA 2012. LNCS, vol. 7278, p. 1. Springer, Heidelberg (2012)
7. Fu, T., Abbasi, A., Chen, H.: A focused crawler for Dark Web forums. J. Am. Soc. Inf. Sci. Technol. **61**(6), 1213–1231 (2010)
8. Chen, H., Chung, W., Qin, J., Reid, E., Sageman, M., Weimann, G.: Uncovering the dark Web: a case study of Jihad on the Web. J. Am. Soc. Inf. Sci. Technol. **59**(8), 1347–1359 (2008)
9. Kalpakis, G., Tsikrika, T., Markatopoulou, F., Pittaras, N., Vrochidis, S., Mezaris, V., Patras, I., Kompatsiaris, I.: Concept detection on multimedia web resources about home made explosives. In: 10th International Conference on Availability, Reliability and Security (ARES 2015), pp. 632–641 (2015)
10. Tsikrika, T., Kalpakis, G., Vrochidis, S., Kompatsiaris, I., Paraskakis, I., Kavasidis, I., Middleton, J., Williamson, U.: A framework for the discovery, analysis, and retrieval of multimedia homemade explosives information on the Web. In: 10th International Conference on Availability, Reliability and Security (ARES 2015), pp. 601–610 (2015)

11. Tsikrika, T., Moumtzidou, A., Vrochidis, S., Kompatsiaris, I.: Focussed crawling of environmental web resources: a pilot study on the combination of multimedia evidence. In: 1st International Workshop on Environmental Multimedia Retrieval (EMR 2014), in conjunction with the ACM Conference on Multimedia Retrieval (ICMR 2014), pp. 61–68 (2014)
12. Pant, G., Srinivasan, P.: Learning to crawl: comparing classification schemes. ACM Trans. Inf. Syst. **23**(4), 430–462 (2005)
13. Quinlan, J.R.: C4.5: Programs for Machine Learning. Elsevier, Amsterdam (1994)
14. Cortes, C., Vapnik, V.: Support-vector networks. J. Mach. Learn. **20**(3), 273–297 (1997)

Attack Tree Analysis for Insider Threats on the IoT Using Isabelle

Florian Kammüller[1]([✉]), Jason R.C. Nurse[2], and Christian W. Probst[3]

[1] Middlesex University London, London, UK
f.kammueller@mdx.ac.uk
[2] University of Oxford, Oxford, UK
jason.nurse@cs.ox.ac.uk
[3] Technical University Denmark, Kongens Lyngby, Denmark
cwpr@dtu.dk

Abstract. The Internet-of-Things (IoT) aims at integrating small devices around humans. The threat from human insiders in "regular" organisations is real; in a fully-connected world of the IoT, organisations face a substantially more severe security challenge due to unexpected access possibilities and information flow. In this paper, we seek to illustrate and classify insider threats in relation to the IoT (by 'smart insiders'), exhibiting attack vectors for their characterisation. To model the attacks we apply a method of formal modelling of Insider Threats in the interactive theorem prover Isabelle. On the classified IoT attack examples, we show how this logical approach can be used to make the models more precise and to analyse the previously identified Insider IoT attacks using Isabelle attack trees.

1 Introduction

Insider threats are notoriously difficult to prevent since the usual method of introducing a security perimeter and identifying actor's capabilities are useless: any actor possibly having privileges and access can turn into an attacker and hit organisations where it hurts most. The Internet-of-Things (IoT) denotes the combination of physical objects with a virtual representation in the Internet. It consists not only of humans but a variety of "Things" as well. From a security and privacy perspective, at this point the IoT could be perceived as a hopeless case since all prevention aspects of security (confidentiality, integrity, and availability) are inherently weak, and unwanted tracking and monitoring throws the doors wide open to privacy attacks.

The combination of IoT and insider threat thus represents a highly risky area in terms of security, privacy, and trust. This problem has been highlighted and discussed in detail in some of our recent work on the 'smart insider' [16]. The aim of this paper is to extend that work and propose a set of rigorous modelling techniques in order to provide a better understanding of IoT-facilitated insider-threat scenarios and related architectures; this would also cover related analysis methods to verify security properties of a given model and its policies. The IoT

© Springer International Publishing Switzerland 2016
T. Tryfonas (Ed.): HAS 2016, LNCS 9750, pp. 234–246, 2016.
DOI: 10.1007/978-3-319-39381-0_21

aims at integrating small devices around humans. A corresponding paradigm corresponding to the IoT might be entitled "human centric computing". Research work on insider threat on the other side has revealed that the consideration of the human aspect is crucial to arrive at useful security models. Frameworks for insider threats [15] take human aspects in consideration to provide models for a characterisation of the tipping point when an insider turns into a threat. Logical modeling and analysis techniques use such taxonomies and a three-step process of social explanation [13] to provide machine supported verification techniques of infrastructure models and their policies.

In this paper, we start by reflecting on existing research into insider threat and then consider work on attack vector models for the IoT case [16] (Sect. 2). We use a framework for modelling of Insider threats in logic with the interactive proof assistant Isabelle [13] to formalize the IoT scenarios and express these attack vectors enabling the machine supported proof of security properties (Sect. 3). The formalisation of attack vectors provides a formal underpinning that enables a stepwise refinement into given IoT insider scenarios. We demonstrate this on a real IoT insider attack case. Finally, we conclude the paper and present avenues for future work (Sect. 4).

2 Reflecting on the IoT Insider Threat Challenge

The threat that insiders pose to organisations is well-known and has been documented in industry, academic and the media. In a recent survey, globally 89 % of respondents felt that their organisation was now more at risk than before to an insider attack [22]. The key challenge with insiders is that they have an elevated level of access in order to do their jobs, but such access could easily be abused to exploit or harm their employer. In literature, three main types of insider threat are commonly acknowledged. These include insider fraud (*i.e.*, abusing one's privileges in the company for personal gain), sabotage (*i.e.*, destruction of property) and Intellectual Property (IP) theft (*i.e.*, stealing commercially sensitive enterprise data) [3]. Insiders can also be considered from the context of their attack, that is, whether it is intentional or accidental. There has been significant research on the former topic in the past, but work on accidental insiders is slowly gaining traction.

As the emphasis on the insider threat has grown, so too have the approaches to prevent and detect it. There have been proposals outlining models and frameworks for understanding and reasoning about insider threat [8,15]. Other research has focused on prevention and prediction to allow more proactive responses to the problem [6,7]. Moreover, many systems have been put forward specifically to detect behaviour of threatening insiders [1,4]. Commonly, such systems aim at areas such as monitoring activity on corporate networks (*e.g.*, emails, file accesses), analysing online activity data, and incorporating psychological information.

Possibly one of the most significant challenges with insider threats is the variety of ways in which they can attack their employers. For instance, sensitive

IP can be exfiltrated via printing, email, FTP, remote access, or pen drives. Systems can be sabotaged using several physical or electronic means (*e.g.*, deletion, malware) by insiders. Also, insiders could engage in various fraudulent activities at the expense of their employers. To add to this challenge, we are quickly progressing towards a society where every day objects (*e.g.*, phones, watches, cars) are connected in the Internet-of-Things.

While the IoT has been discussed for over a decade, only now are we starting to witness substantial progress towards technology standardisation, along with a variety of different connected products reaching businesses and homes. As these technologies enter businesses and offices more, however, each enterprises' attack surface is significantly enlarged. For instance, cameras on smart-watches worn by insiders can take discrete pictures of sensitive IP, thereby allowing exfiltration of data with no digital trace on corporate systems [16]. This lack of digital trace makes it extremely difficult for current systems to detect smart insiders, given monitoring does not currently encompass such personal devices. Having discussed the challenges faced by such insiders, next we briefly reflect on a few key attack vectors to explore the problem in greater detail.

2.1   Attack Vectors of Insiders Using IoT Devices

As mentioned above, insiders using the IoT represent a significant challenge for enterprises. In our previous work, we have assessed this problem in detail, and outlined several vectors through which insiders may attack their employers [16]. To structure that work, we drew on the VERIS 4A approach to define cyber attacks [21]. This includes understanding the *assets* at risk in the attack, the *actors* (or insiders) that launch the attack, the *attributes* (or impact) of the attack on the asset, and the specific *actions* involved in the attack. Below, we present two of the $8+8$ attack vectors (AVs) from [16] in the broad context of the VERIS approach; the first one perpetrated by a malicious insider (MI) and the second by an unintentional insider (UI) threat. Picking one AV from each group, we use them as a representative basis for analysis and discussion throughout the remainder of this paper.

MI-AV4: Using the storage system on a smart device, the insider is able to copy sensitive data (*e.g.*, IP or files) from the organisation's computers to the device and remove it from the enterprise. Bluetooth or NFC may be preferred for this attack as organisations now tend to monitor USB connections. This attack is possible with any IoT device with a storage capability.

UI-AV7: As a result of improperly configured or inadequately protected insider smart devices (*e.g.*, a smart-watch and a paired smartphone), the communications channel between them is compromised by a malicious third-party. This party then gathers enterprise data via the notifications, schedules, messages synchronised across devices. Further detail on such attacks on wearables can be found in [20]. We note that this attack could be conducted by another insider as well. This attack is possible with any device with a notification and storage capability.

3   Formal Model of Insider IoT Threats in Isabelle

Motivation of attackers and the behavioural aspects exhibited during attacks is often not considered, *e.g.*, in detection systems for cyber security (as discussed above). The challenge we approach here is to accommodate insiders' behaviour into formal models for IoT insider attacks using logical modelling and analysis techniques.

3.1   Social Explanation for Insider Threats in Isabelle

Previous work [13] uses the process of sociological explanation based on Max Weber's *Grundmodell* and its logical interpretation to explain insider threats by moving between societal level (macro) and individual actor level (micro). The interpretation into a logic of explanation is formalized in Isabelle's Higher Order Logic thereby providing a tool to prove global security properties with machine assistance [13]. Isabelle/HOL is an interactive proof assistant based on Higher Order Logic (HOL). It enables specification of so-called object-logics for an application. Examples reach from mathematical theory [10] to component based software engineering [5]. Object-logics comprise new types, constants and definitions and reside in theory files, *e.g.*, the file `Insider.thy` contains the object-logic we define for social explanation of insider threats below. We construct our theory as a conservative extension of HOL guaranteeing consistency, *i.e.*, we do not introduce new axioms that could lead to inconsistencies.

In this paper, we show how the 4A modelling approach (see Sect. 2.1) can be accommodated by this insider threat theory and a suitable extension to attack vectors. We first provide here only the elements of this Insider theory necessary as a basis for attack trees and for modelling IoT applications. For a more complete view, please refer to [13] and the related online Isabelle resources [9].

In the Isabelle/HOL theory for Insiders, we express policies over actions `get`, `move`, `eval`, and `put` representing the *Actions* category from the 4As (see Sect. 2.1). We abstract here from concrete data – actions have no parameters:

```
datatype action = get | move | eval | put
```

The next of the 4As is the *Actor* which is represented by an abstract type and a function that creates elements of that type from identities:

```
typedecl actor
type_synonym identity = string
consts Actor :: string ⇒ actor
```

Policies describe prerequisites for actions to be granted to actors given by pairs of predicates (conditions) and sets of (enabled) actions:

```
type_synonym policy = ((actor ⇒ bool) × action set)
```

We integrate policies with a graph into the infrastructure providing an organisational model where policies reside at locations and actors are adorned with additional predicates to specify their 'credentials':

```
datatype infrastructure = Infrastructure
"node graph" "location ⇒ policy set" "actor ⇒ bool"
```

These local policies serve to provide a specification of the 'normal' behaviour of actors but are also the starting point for possible attacks on the organisation's *Assets*. The assets are defined by the goals of the attacks, *i.e.*, the roots of the attack trees (see below). The `enables` predicate specifies that an actor a can perform an action a'∈ e at location l in the infrastructure I if a's credentials (stored in the tuple space `tspace I a`) imply the location policy's (stored in `delta I l`) condition p for a:

enables I l a' ≡ ∃ (p,e) ∈ delta I l. a' ∈ e ∧ (tspace I a ⟶ p(a))

3.2   Attack Trees in Isabelle

We now extend the theory Insider by Attack trees by defining the base attacks and how they constitute an attack sequence. This corresponds to combining Actions into an "insider-attack vector" (see Sect. 2.1). We represent these in Isabelle/HOL as a data type and a list over this datatype:

```
datatype baseattack = None | Goto "location"
                    | Perform "action" | Credential "location"
type_synonym attackseq = "baseattack list"
```

The following definition `attree`, defines the nodes of an attack tree. The simplest case is when a node in an attack tree is an *Asset*, *i.e.*, a base attack as defined above. Attacks can also be combined as the "and" of other attacks. The third element of type `attree` is a `baseattack` (usually a `Perform action`) that represents this attack, while the first element is an attack sequence and the second element is constituted by the fourth of the 4As, the *Attribute*. As described in Sect. 2.1, an attribute describes the impact of the attack on the asset in a variety of ways. We therefore allow a great degree of freedom in our logical model by modeling this attribute as an element of type "string":

```
datatype attree = BaseAttack "baseattack" ("𝒩 (_)") |
                  AndAttack "attackseq" "string" "baseattack" ("_ ⊕ₐ⁽˙⁾ _")
```

As the corresponding projection functions for `attree` we define `get_attseq` and `get_attack` returning the entire attack sequence or the final base attack, respectively.

The following inductive predicate `UI_AV7_intro` represents the attack vector **UI-AV7** (see Sect. 2.1) by an inductive definition. It formalizes how the attacker intercepts the traffic between the smart devices by moving into close range and getting thus the data. Logically, this is justified if an actor a can get data at location l in the extended infrastructure `add_credential I a s` in which he possesses the credential s – as is expressed by the second `enables` proviso:

```
[ enables I l a move; enables (add_credential I a s) l a get ]
⟹ UI_AV7 I s
```

$$(\texttt{get\_attackseq } ([\texttt{Goto l, Perform get}] \oplus_\wedge^{move-intercept} \texttt{Credential l}))$$
$$(\texttt{Credential l})$$

An attack tree is constituted from the above defined nodes of type **attree** but children nodes must be refinements of their parents. Refinement means that some portion of the attack sequence has been extended according to rules like the above **get_then_move**. Similar rules can be defined for all of the attack vectors for malicious insiders MI_AVi and for unintentional insiders UI_AVi [16]. Higher Order Logic allows us to define a set over the inductive predicates that we defined as attack vectors above. We can then assemble all attack vectors in the following set (we omit all but the two we illustrate here for brevity):

```
definition attack_vectors::
([infrastructure, string, attackseq, baseattack] ⇒ bool)set
where attack_vectors ≡ {MI_AV4, UI_AV7}
```

We formalize the constructor relation for the refinement of attack trees by the following inductive predicate **refines_to** syntactically represented as the infix operator ⊑. The rules **trans** and **refl** make the refinement a preorder; the rule **refineI** shows how attack vectors from the previously defined set can be integrated into the refinement process. If we replace the attack **a** by a sequence **l** of an attack vector from our predefined set of attack vectors **P**, we refine the attack sequence **A** into **A'** (the auxiliary function **sublist_rep** replaces symbol **a** in list **l** by a list, here **get_attseq A**):

```
inductive
refines_to :: "[attree, infrastructure, attree] ⇒ bool" ("_ ⊑(.) _")
where
refineI: [ P ∈ attack_vectors; P I s l a;
            sublist_rep l a (get_attseq A) = (get_attseq A');
            get_attack A = get_attack A' ] ⟹ A ⊑_I A' |
trans: [ A ⊑_I A'; A' ⊑_I A'' ] ⟹ A ⊑_I A'' |
refl : A ⊑_I A
```

The refinement of attack sequences allows the expansion of top level abstract attacks into longer sequences. Ultimately, we need to have a notion of when a sufficiently refined sequence of attacks is valid. This notion is provided by the final inductive predicate **is_and_attack_tree**. It integrates the base cases where base attacks can be directly logically derived from corresponding enables properties; it states that an attack sequence is valid if all its constituent attacks are so and it allows to transfer validity to shorter attacks if a refinement exists:

```
inductive
is_and_attack_tree :: [infrastructure, actor, attree] ⇒ bool ("_, _ ⊢ _")
where
att_act: enables I l a a' ⟹ I , a ⊢ N(Perform(a')) |
att_goto: enables I l a (move) ⟹ I, a ⊢ N(Goto l) |
att_cred: enables I l a (get) ⟹ I, a ⊢ N(Credential l) |
```

att_list: ⟦ ∀ a ∈ (set(as)). I, a' ⊢ 𝒩(a) ⟧ ⟹ I, a' ⊢ as ⊕$^s_∧$ a'' |
att_ref: ⟦ A ⊑$_I$ A'; I, a ⊢ A' ⟧ ⟹ I, a ⊢ A

The Isabelle/HOL theory library provides many list functions. We use these to define the "or" of attack trees by folding the above validity over a list of attacks:

I, a ⊢$_{G⊕∨}$ al ≡ fold (λ x y. (I, a ⊢ x) ∨ y) al False

To validate this formalisation of the attack trees, we now show how a scenario attack can be derived, based on an extended example from our previous work [16].

3.3   Example – Employee Blackmail

The insider in this case is an employee in the IT department of a manufacturing company. He has received a formal warning from the CEO because there had been reports that the employee had abused colleagues. This warning has been contrived by the CEO himself who had an extramarital liaison with one of the employees with whom the insider had been flirting with. Following that, the IT employee heard rumours that he might be dismissed, which constituted the precipitating event that made him an insider: he planned his revenge.

From a report by an online security blog, the Bitdefender Research Team [2], the insider knew that it was possible to eavesdrop on and intercept communications between a smart-watch and a smartphone. The vulnerability was described in some detail on the blog. So, when the CEO purchased a smart-watch paired with his smartphone, the insider then exploited the vulnerability using additional methods found on hacking forums. He could move freely in the offices and could thus get into close range to collect data communicated between the CEO's smartphone and smart-watch. Although the communicated data has been encrypted before being transmitted via the Bluetooth protocol, the encryption used a 6-digit PIN code as a key in addition to data obfuscation (adding redundant "padding" to the clear text). Using publicly available decryption algorithms, the insider was thus able to get the key information.

Once the encryption was broken, the Insider could use this credential to collect data on incoming phone calls, SMS and emails, and personal and work related calendar. Finally, the insider blackmailed the CEO with the stolen information that also implied the CEO's liaison with a colleague: he threatened to show it to his wife and children unless he would receive a large severance package and good references. The 4As for this case are as follows:

- *Assets*: Sensitive company and personal information;
- *Actors*: Malicious insider;
- *Attributes*: Unauthorised data access then used for blackmail and fraud; and
- *Actions*: Attack Vector UI-AV7 (where an insider is the perpetrator).

This case highlights a key weakness in IoT devices, *i.e.*, the limited security features with these devices and a clever attack building on personal knowledge helped by current reports and malicious Web forums.

3.4   Application of Insider Theory and Attack Trees to Example

For the application to the office scenario, we only model two identities, `Boss` and `Employee` representing an employee and his boss. We define the set of office actors as a local definition in the locale `scenarioOffice`. We show here in a first instance the full Isabelle/HOL syntax but in all subsequent definitions we omit the `fixes` and `defines` keywords and also drop the types for clarity of the exposition. The double quotes `''s''` create a string in Isabelle/HOL;

```
fixes office_actors :: identity set
defines office_actors_def: office_actors ≡ {''Boss''}
```

The graph representing the infrastructure of the office case study contains only the minimal structure: (1) employee's office, (2) boss's office, (3) smart-phone:

```
office_locations ≡ {Location 1, Location 2, Location 3}
```

The global policy is 'no one except office actors can get anything from the boss's office':

```
global_policy I a ≡ a ∉ office_actors ⟶
                    ¬(enables I (Location 2) (Actor a) get)
```

Next, we have to provide the definition of the infrastructure. We first define the graph representing the organisation's locations and the positions of its actors. Locations are wrapped up with the datatype constructor `NL` and actors using the corresponding constructor `NA` to enable joining them in the datatype **node** and thus creating the following **node graph** as a set of pairs between locations or actors:

```
ex_graph ≡ Graph {(NA (''Boss''), NL (Location 2)),
                  (NL (Location 2), NL(Location 1)),
                  (NL (Location 2), NL(Location 3)),
                  (NA (''Employee''), NL (Location 1))}
```

Policies are attached to locations in the organisation's graph using a function that maps each location to the set of the policies valid in this location. The policies are again pairs. The first element of these pairs are credentials which are defined as predicates over actors, *i.e.*, boolean valued functions describing, for example, whether an actor inhabits a role, or, whether an actor possesses something, like an identity or a key. The second elements are sets of actions that are authorised in this location for actors authenticated by the credentials:

```
local_policies ≡
(λ x.  if x = Location 1 then
 {(λ x. (ID x ''Boss'')∨(ID x ''Employee''),{get,put}),(λ x.True,{move})}
    else (if x = Location 2 then
      {((λ x. has (x, ''PIN'')), {get,put}), (λ x. True, {move})}
        else (if x = Location 3 then
          {((λ x. True, {get,put,move}))}
            else {})))
```

The final component of any infrastructure is the credentials contained in a `tspace`. We define the assignment of the credentials to the actors similarly as a predicate over actors that is true for actors that have the credentials:

```
ex_creds ≡ (λ if x = Actor ''Boss'' then has (x,''PIN'') else False)
```

Finally, we can put the graph, the local policies, and the credential assignment into an infrastructure:

```
Office_scenario ≡ Infrastructure ex_graph local_policies ex_creds
```

Note, that all the above definitions have been implemented as local definitions using the locale keywords **fixes** and **defines** [14]. Thus they are accessible whenever the locales `scenarioOffice` is invoked but are not axioms that could endanger consistency. We now also make use of the possibility of locales to define local assumptions. This is very suitable in this context since we want to emphasize that the following formulas are not general facts or axiomatic rules but are assumptions we make in order to explore the validity of the infrastructure's global policy. The first assumption provides that the precipitating event has occurred which leads to the second assumption that provides that Employee can act as an insider:

```
assumes Employee_precipitating_event: tipping_point(astate ''Employee'')
assumes Insider_Employee : Insider ''Employee'' {''Boss''}
```

The above definitions and assumptions provide the model for the Employee blackmail Insider attack. We can now state theorems about the security of the model and interactively prove them in our Isabelle/HOL framework. We first prove a sanity check on the model by validating the infrastructure for the "normal" case. For the boss as an office actor, everything is fine: the global policy does hold. The following is an Isabelle/HOL theorem `ex_inv` that can be proved automatically followed by the proof script of its interactive proof. The proof is achieved by locally unfolding the definitions of the scenario, *e.g.*, `Office_scenario_def` and applying the simplifier:

```
lemma ex_inv: global_policy Office_scenario (''Boss'')
by (simp add: Office_scenario_def global_policy_def office_actors_def)
```

However, since the `Employee` is at tipping point, he will ignore the global policy. This insider threat can now be formalised as an invalidation of the global company policy for ''Employee'' in the following "attack" theorem named `ex_inv2`:

```
theorem ex_inv1: ¬ global_policy Office_scenario ''Employee''
```

The proof of this theorem consists of a few simple steps largely supported by automated tactics. Thus `Employee` can get access to the data and blackmail the boss. The attack is proved above as an Isabelle/HOL theorem. Applying logical analysis, we thus exhibit that under the given assumptions the organisation's model is vulnerable to an insider. This overall procedure corresponds to the approach of invalidation of a global policy based on local policies for a given application scenario [11].

However to systematically derive the actual attack for the Employee black-mail we next apply the attack vector analysis presented in Sect. 3.2. First, we prove the following `move_intercept_lem` property:

```
lemma move_intercept_lem: UI_IV7 Office_scenario ''PIN''
  (get_attseq ([Goto (Location 2), Perform get] ⊕_∧^move intercept Perform get))
  (Credential (Location 2))
```

After reducing with the defining rule `UI_AV7_intro` (see Sect. 3.2), the proof requires solving two "enables" subgoals; the final one uses the `add_credential` for `Employee`. This lemma immediately implies the following refines property:

$$([Credential\ (Location\ 2)]\ \oplus_\wedge^{move-intercept}\ Perform\ get)$$
$$\sqsubseteq_{Office-scenario}$$
$$([Goto\ (Location\ 2),\ Perform\ get]\ \oplus_\wedge^{move-intercept}\ Perform\ get)$$

At this point we have constructed an attack tree as depicted in Fig. 1.

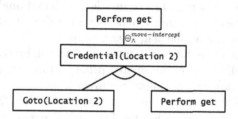

Fig. 1. Attack tree refines high level attack into base attacks.

As a final step of verification, we show that the refined attack at the leaves of the tree is valid, *i.e.*, each step in it is a possible base attack in the scenario (see Sect. 3.2):

```
lemma final_attack: Office_scenario, Actor ''Employee'' ⊢
([Goto (Location 2), Perform get] ⊕_∧^move-intercept Perform get)
```

The last lemma together with the refinement gives us finally that the top level abstract attack is a valid attack:

```
theorem office_attack: Office_scenario, Actor ''Employee'' ⊢
([Credential (Location 2)] ⊕_∧^move-intercept Perform get)
```

4 Discussion and Conclusion

In this paper we have presented an approach to characterising malicious and unintentional insider threats on the IoT by attack vectors. We added precision to a tentative taxonomy [16] by using a logic based Insider threat model [13] in Isabelle. We illustrated its use on the IoT Insider case of an employee blackmailing his boss with communication data intercepted from a smart-watch/smartphone with weak security. An extension of the Isabelle framework for insider threats to attack trees enabled the logic representation of the malicious and unintentional attack vectors. We summarized all attack vectors in a set. A notion of refinement of attack trees allows to apply the attack vectors in this set as possible refinement steps to a high level attack. The refinement serves for analysing attacks: if a high level attack can be sufficiently refined, a notion of validity of attack permits to finalise the attack analysis by proving an Isabelle theorem. The extended Isabelle framework has been introduced and illustrated on the Employee blackmail case study.

It must be clearly stated, that the attack tree generation is not a fully automated process. Isabelle is an interactive proof assistant. That is, the attack and the refinement have to be input by the user and the refinement and validity theorems have to be proved in an interactive process. However, the malicious and unintentional attack vectors provide a set of possible high level attacks that can be used as starting points for an attack tree refinement in the Isabelle Insider framework. This process supports systematic tool based analysis of infrastructures for Insider threats revealing weaknesses in policies and exemplifying the attack vectors. Furthermore, the demonstrated application to an IoT insider case shows that the proof obligations of refinement and validity can be achieved by a short series of applications of automated proof tactics that are integrated into Isabelle (for illustration see the online resources [9]).

A pioneering effort to assess insider attacks was the CMU-CERT Insider Threat project [3]. *Attack trees* as specified in [18] define the attacker's main goal as the root of a tree; this goal is then disjunctively or conjunctively refined into sub-goals until the reached subgoals represent basic actions that correspond to atomic components. Disjunctive refinements show up alternative pathways to achieving a goal, whereas conjunctive refinements visualize the attack steps leading to a goal. Automated generation of attack graphs mostly considers computer networks only [17,19]. These techniques usually start by specifying atomic attacks. By contrast, our approach is based on [12]: the attack consists in invalidating a policy, and the model just provides the infrastructure and methods for deriving the attack tree.

The presented work illustrates that the logic based approach including the human factor into insider threat modelling and analysis [13] extends also to the security critical domain of IoT Insiders. Further experimentation with the provided framework in planned projects will focus on integrating with quantitative analysis.

References

1. Ambre, A., Shekokar, N.: Insider threat detection using log analysis and event correlation. Procedia Comput. Sci. **45**, 436–445 (2015)
2. Bitdefender. Bitdefender research exposes security risks of android wearable devices (2014). http://www.darkreading.com/partner-perspectives/bitdefender/bitdefender-research-exposes-security-risks-of-android-wearable-devices-/a/d-id/1318005

3. Cappelli, D.M., Moore, A.P., Trzeciak, R.F.: The CERT Guide to Insider Threats: How to Prevent, Detect, and Respond to Information Technology Crimes (Theft, Sabotage, Fraud). Addison-Wesley Professional, Boston (2012)
4. Gavai, G., Sricharan, K., Gunning, D., Rolleston, R., Hanley, J., Singhal, M.: Detecting insider threat from enterprise social and online activity data. In: ACM CCS International Workshop on Managing Insider Security Threats. ACM (2015)
5. Henrio, L., Kammüller, F., Rivera, M.: An asynchronous distributed component model and its semantics. In: de Boer, F.S., Bonsangue, M.M., Madelaine, E. (eds.) FMCO 2008. LNCS, vol. 5751, pp. 159–179. Springer, Heidelberg (2009)
6. Hoyer, S., Zakhariya, H., Sandner, T., Breitner, M.H.: Fraud prediction and the human factor: an approach to include human behavior in an automated fraud audit. In: 45th Hawaii International Conference on System Science (HICSS). IEEE (2012)
7. Hugl, U.: Putting a hat on a Hen? Learnings for malicious insider threat prevention from the background of German white-collar crime research. In: Tryfonas, T., Askoxylakis, I. (eds.) HAS 2015. LNCS, vol. 9190, pp. 631–641. Springer, Heidelberg (2015)
8. Hunker, J., Probst, C.W.: Insiders and insider threatsan overview of definitions and mitigation techniques. J. Wirel. Mob. Netw. Ubiquit. Comput. Dependable Appl. 2(1), 4–27 (2011)
9. Kammüller, F.: Isabelle Insider framework with examples (2015). https://www.dropbox.com/sh/rx8d09pf31cv8bd/AAALKtaP8HMX642fi04Og4NLa?dl=0
10. Kammüller, F., Paulson, L.C.: A formal proof of Sylow's theorem. J. Autom. Reasoning 23(3), 235–264 (1999)
11. Kammüller, F., Probst, C.W.: Invalidating policies using structural information. In: WRIT 2013. IEEE (2013)
12. Kammüller, F., Probst, C.W.: Combining generated data models with formal invalidation for insider threat analysis. In: IEEE Security and Privacy Workshops (SPW), WRIT 2014. IEEE (2014)
13. Kammüller, F., Probst, C.W.: Modeling and verification of insider threats using logical analysis. IEEE Syst. J. PP, 1 (2016)
14. Kammüller, F., Wenzel, M., Paulson, L.C.: Locales - a sectioning concept for Isabelle. In: Bertot, Y., Dowek, G., Théry, L., Hirschowitz, A., Paulin, C. (eds.) Theorem Proving in Higher Order Logics. LNCS, vol. 1690, pp. 149–165. Springer, Heidelberg (1999)
15. Nurse, J.R.C., Buckley, O., Legg, P.A., Goldsmith, M., Creese, S., Wright, G.R.T., Whitty, M.: Understanding insider threat: a framework for characterising attacks. In: IEEE Security and Privacy Workshops (SPW), WRIT 2014. IEEE (2014)
16. Nurse, J.R.C., Erola, A., Agrafiotis, I., Goldsmith, M., Creese, S.: Smart insiders: exploring the threat from insiders using the internet-of-things. In: 4th International Workshop on Secure Internet of Things (SIoT 2015), pp. 5–14. IEEE (2015). http://dx.doi.org/10.1109/SIOT.2015.10
17. Phillips, C., Swiler, L.P.: A graph-based system for network-vulnerability analysis. In: Workshop on New security paradigms, NSPW 1998 (1998)
18. Salter, C., Saydjari, O.S., Schneier, B., Wallner, J.: Toward a secure systemengineering methodology. In: Workshop on New Security Paradigms, NSPW 1998 (1998)
19. Sheyner, O., Haines, J., Jha, S., Lippmann, R., Wing, J.M.: Automated generation and analysis of attack graphs. In: IEEE Symposium on Security and Privacy (S & P 2002). IEEE (2002)

20. Symantec. How safe is your quantified self? Technical report (2014)
21. Veris, V.: The vocabulary for event recording and incident sharing (2015). http://veriscommunity.net
22. Vormetric. 2015 vormetric insider threat report (2015). http://www.vormetric.com/campaigns/insiderthreat/2015/

The State of Near-Field Communication (NFC) on the Android Platform

Jaromír Karmazín and Pavel Očenášek[✉]

Faculty of Information Technology, Brno University of Technology, Brno, Czech Republic
xkarma06@stud.fit.vutbr.cz, ocenaspa@fit.vutbr.cz

Abstract. We analyze the Android operating system as a platform for building NFC-enabled applications. First, we briefly examine the security of NFC and provide an overview of the three modes (reader/writer, peer-to-peer, card emulation) that are exposed to developers through Android's API. Furthermore, we present some existing Android applications using NFC, such as diagnostic tools, contactless tag manipulation tools, peer-to-peer NFC applications, as well as a few uncommon use cases. We conclude with an assessment of the completeness of Android's NFC API and suggest a novel use case.

Keywords: Near-Field Communication · Mobile device · Android · Application · Communication

1 Introduction

Near-Field Communication, or NFC for short, is a somewhat new technology that allows direct wireless communication between two mobile devices, or between a mobile device and a passive tag, over a short distance.

The number of devices supporting NFC has been growing recently, including models such as the mobile phones Apple iPhone 6, Microsoft Lumia 950, and Samsung Galaxy A, as well as tablets like the Google Nexus 10 [1].

In this article, we are going to focus on the Android platform, its NFC capabilities, and existing applications for Android that utilize NFC.

2 Security of NFC

Where using NFC is an option, the very nature of the technology makes it a harder target for attacks than other technologies such as Bluetooth or Internet-based services. In order for an attacker to eavesdrop on or interfere with NFC communication, they need to establish a physical presence near the two communicating devices, at a range shorter than conventional wireless technologies. There is also no infrastructure involved, so there is no trusted third party that the attacker can spoof.

As with any method of wireless communication, eavesdropping on the physical layer is possible if the reception is good. Per [2, Sect. 7.5.1], "the distance can generally be greater than the standard reading distance" in the case of RFID tags. Haselsteiner and

© Springer International Publishing Switzerland 2016
T. Tryfonas (Ed.): HAS 2016, LNCS 9750, pp. 247–254, 2016.
DOI: 10.1007/978-3-319-39381-0_22

Breitfuß state in [3, Sect. 3.1] that for NFC, eavesdropping can be done within about 10 meters of a device communicating in active mode and within about 1 m of a device communicating in passive mode. However, they give these numbers only as rough estimates, reasoning that a "huge number of parameters" determine the radius of possible eavesdropping.

It is possible for an attacker in the vicinity of communicating devices to corrupt the transmitted data by also transmitting at the same frequencies with the correct timing and modulation. This is a Denial of Service (DoS) attack [3, Sect. 3.2].

It is also possible for an attacker to modify the transmitted data by transmitting a specific signal at the same time. Except when 100 % amplitude-shift keying (or ASK for short) modulation with modified Miller encoding is used, all bits can be modified by an attacker [3, Sect. 3.3].

An attacker may insert messages into a legitimate communication, but only if there is a long enough pause between two legitimate messages [3, Sect. 3.4].

A Man-in-the-Middle attack is considered infeasible by [3, Sect. 3.5] because of the overlapping radio fields. However, we would like to not rule out the possibility of an attack being developed in the future. For example, a sticker with two antennae and a shield separating them, placed on an NFC device, could be devised for such an attack. Applications should always provide a mechanism for verifying the other party.

For certain security-sensitive applications, such as mobile payment, the mobile device needs the level of security similar to a smart card. The application's private data should be stored in a location where other applications, and perhaps even the user, cannot read it or tamper with it.

Secure NFC exists for these purposes [4, Sect. 11.6.1]. It relies on the presence of a hardware module called the *secure element*, which can be a SIM card, a secure memory card, or a smart card chip. In this setup, the security-sensitive applet runs in the secure element and communicates directly with the NFC device. An application controller, which may run in an insecure environment, serves only administrative purposes and cannot access the secure element's data directly.

3   Android's NFC Capabilities

Android's API allows developers to use the NFC capabilities of the host device. This is documented at [5]. This section serves as a summary of these documented possibilities.

3.1   Reader/Writer Mode

Android applications can "read and/or write passive NFC tags and stickers". This uses NFC in passive mode, with the Android device as the initiator and the tag or sticker as the target. The initiator creates a magnetic alternating field, which it uses to send both power and data (using ASK) to the target. In order to send data in response, the target uses load modulation on the initiator's magnetic field.

When the Android device's screen is unlocked and NFC is not disabled in its settings, the device scans for nearby NFC tags. Once a tag is discovered, Android creates an intent (a specific type of object in Android's API), locates the application best suited to handle the given tag, and dispatches the intent to it.

Per the documentation, "Android has the most support for the NDEF standard, which is defined by the NFC Forum."

In addition, the API exposes interfaces which allow raw communication with other tag technologies. In these cases, the application must implement its own protocol for communicating with the tag.

The supported technologies are:

- NFC-A (ISO 14443-3A),
- NFC-B (ISO 14443-3B),
- NFC-F (JIS 6319-4),
- NFC-V (ISO 15693), and
- ISO-DEP (ISO 14443-4).

Optionally, Android devices may support these additional NFC tag technologies:

- MiFARE Classic and
- MiFARE Ultralight.

API level 9 (Android 2.3 Gingerbread) offers limited tag reading support. The reader/writer mode is supported comprehensively starting from API level 10 (Android 2.3.3 Gingerbread MR1). Android Application Records, which provide a stronger certainty that an NFC tag will be handled by an application, are supported starting from API level 14 (Android 4.0 Ice Cream Sandwich).

3.2   Peer-to-Peer Mode

Android offers functionality called Android Beam, which allows sending an NDEF message from one Android-powered device to another. This uses the active mode of NFC, which means that both devices take turns transmitting both power and data. In the same way as the initiator in NFC's passive mode, each device in active mode transmits data using ASK modulation.

To send data over Android Beam, the sending application must be running in the foreground of the sending device, and the receiving device must be unlocked and within a close range of the sending device. When these conditions are met, the sending device displays a "Touch to Beam" UI. If the user confirms the action using this UI, then the data is sent.

The payload of Android Beam is transmitted in one way only. The API does not provide any way to receive any payload as a recipient from the recipient.

Android Beam is supported starting from API level 14 (Android 4.0 Ice Cream Sandwich).

NFC is not suitable for the transfer of large files because of its low data rate, combined with the fact that the sender and receiver need to be in close proximity for the whole duration of the transfer. According to [7], the "sane upper bound" for data transferred using NFC is "about 1 KB (. . .), which can usually be exchanged within 300 ms".

Since API level 16 (Android 4.1 Jelly Bean), it is possible to transfer large files between Android devices using the Android Beam file transfer API [8]. Android overcomes the speed limitations of NFC by only using it for the initial setup, then silently enabling Bluetooth, temporarily pairing the two devices, and performing the actual file transfer over Bluetooth [9].

A similar approach to transferring large files was implemented in Sam- sung Galaxy S III, whose S Beam technology uses Wi-Fi Direct instead of Bluetooth to transfer large files after a connection is initiated over NFC [9].

3.3 Card-Emulation Mode

Android provides an API to implement host-based card emulation [7]. This allows Android applications to talk directly to the NFC reader without involving a secure element.

In this mode, the Android device acts as an NFC target in passive mode. This means that the Android device emulates a possibly unpowered tag and does not create a magnetic field. It only transfers data in response to an initiator (reader) using its magnetic field and load modulation.

Supported are emulated cards "based on the NFC-Forum ISO-DEP specification (based on ISO/IEC 14443-4) and process Application Protocol Data Units (APDUs) as defined in the ISO/IEC 7816-4 specification". The developer implements their own protocol stack for sending and receiving those APDUs.

Card emulation only works when NFC is enabled and the screen is on. Unlike the reader/writer mode, this can work from the device's lock screen and does not require any application to be in the foreground.

This functionality is available starting from API level 19 (Android 4.4).

3.4 Missing Features

Even though Android's API supports all modes of NFC operation, there is no public API for using NFC's secure element as of Android 6.0, so payment applications need to use host-based card emulation, which provides less protection for sensitive data.

In addition, NFC's peer-to-peer mode can only be used for Android Beam, which only allows one-shot, simplex data transfers. There is no way to obtain any payload in response to a peer-to-peer request, let alone develop a custom communication protocol, using only the public API.

4 Android Applications Using NFC

We searched for the term "NFC" on [6] in order to get an idea about how NFC is used in existing Android applications. In this section, we will analyze the many results that turned up in the search, attempt to categorize them, and point out some of the most unusual applications.

4.1 NFC Diagnosis and Management Applications

As one would expect, among all NFC applications, there are ones intended for managing and diagnosing the NFC subsystem itself, rather than making any actual use of it. These include simple applications for checking the availability of NFC on the device (e.g. NFC Enabled? by Espen "Rexxars" Hovlandsdal) and widgets for enabling and disabling the device's NFC inter- face (e.g. NFC Widget by AIT APPs).

4.2 Tag Reader/Writer Applications

The largest portion of applications using NFC focuses operations with NFC tags. Naturally, this would make use of passive NFC in reader emulation mode.

There are many applications that provide low-level support for NFC tags, such as displaying basic information about a tag (make, model, supported NFC technology, serial number, etc.), reading data from a tag, writing data to a tag, and tag cloning. It can be assumed that some knowledge of the NFC technology is required in order for the user to find any value in these applications, so average users are probably not the target audience. Examples of these applications are NFC Tools by wakdev, NFC ReTag by WidgApp Mobile Solutions, NFC Reader by Adam Nybäck, and NFC TagWriter by NXP Semiconductors.

Certain specialized applications allow extracting more information from NFC tags used in existing real-world systems:

- Credit Card Reader NFC (EMV) by Jullien Millau uses NFC "to read public data on an NFC banking card compliant with EMV [norms]", such as the contactless credit and debit cards made by Visa, American Express, and MasterCard. The application can show the card type, number, expiration date, number of remaining PIN entries, and in some cases the card's holder's name and the card's transaction history.
- Metro tickets of Moscow by Dmitriy V. Lozenko uses NFC to read information off of such tickets. The information includes the ticket's type, number, date of issue, date of expiration, the number of trips (both total and remaining), and the name of the last station (presumably the last station where the ticket communicated with a reader).
- Octopus by Octopus Cards Limited uses NFC for reading so-called "Octopus cards", which can be used for transportation, parking, retail shopping, and other facilities in Hong Kong, as well as for online payment using an NFC-enabled Android device [10].
- saldoBip NFC by YANKO uses NFC to check the balance of a "bip! card", which is a prepaid ticket used by the public transportation company Transantiago operating in Santiago de Chile [11].
- ShareMoreTransport by Share More Studio uses NFC to check the balance and transaction records on public transport cards used in various Chinese cities, such as Beijing, Shenzhen, Wuhan, Hongkong, Qingdao, and Xian.
- T-money Balance Check by RW MobiMedia uses NFC to check the balance on a South Korean contactless payment card for transportation and some convenience stores.

Another frequent use case is the use of NFC tags to trigger certain actions or change certain settings in the device that reads them. This would allow a user to place NFC stickers in certain places of interest, such as different rooms at their home, in their car, etc., and have the phone enable or disable wireless interfaces, change the ringtone volume, open certain applications, etc., based on the tag which is scanned. Examples of these applications are Trigger by Egomotion and NFC Tasks by wakdev. Another peculiar instance is NFC Alarm Clock by kamituel, which requires the user to scan an NFC tag in order to mute a ringing alarm.

A related concept is implemented in WifiTap by Andreas Rossbacher, which allows writing Wi-Fi credentials to, and reading those credentials from, a writable NFC tag. This can be useful for providing Wi-Fi access to guests at home, at an office, or at a public event.

There are a few applications which use the NFC reader mode in a novel way. For example:

- NFC Developer by Thomas Rorvik Skjolberg allows a software developer to prepare data for an NFC tag on a computer, transfer that data onto their Android phone using a QR code, and finally program an NFC tag using the phone, thus eliminating the need for a separate tag reader.
- SmartPassLock NFC by DreamOnline, Inc. adds another method of unlocking an Android device's screen, requiring a registered NFC tag to be present (the application's description only mentions support for Japanese IC cards).
- Crypto NFC by rolios allows users to write notes on their Android device, encrypt them, and keep the decryption key on an NFC tag.

4.3   Android Beam Applications

Some of the default Android applications allow sharing content, such as web pages, contacts, and YouTube videos, through Android Beam [5]. Since Android 4.1 Jelly Bean, it is also possible to share photos and videos from Gallery with the help of a transient Bluetooth connection [9].

Applications like NFC Transfer Beta by Abhinava Srivastava and NFC File Transfer by apps4u@android use Android Beam to transfer arbitrary files. SuperBeam by LiveQoS offers the same functionality but uses NFC or QR codes for pairing and Wi-Fi Direct for file transfer.

Share Tether NFC by Javi Pacheco uses Android Beam to "share tethering between two devices using NFC".

4.4   Miscellaneous NFC Applications

Applications like CardShake by Tesla System Co., Ltd. or Business Card Holder with NFC by ATSolution allow users to exchange electronic business cards over NFC.

Certain printers by HP Inc. can print content received via NFC from an Android device with the HP ePrint application installed.

NFC Porter by IMA s.r.o. uses NFC for premises access control when used together with a compatible identification system.

PassWallet - Passbook + NFC by Above Mobile Limited allows storing tickets and coupons in Apple's Passbook file format and redeeming them through NFC readers.

5 Conclusion

Android's support for NFC is quite extensive, with the most recent major update being part of Android 4.1, a version of the operating system released in 2012. Recent Android devices should, therefore, be able to use all of the features mentioned in this article, provided that their hardware supports NFC.

Without installing any applications, NFC can already be used for sharing of content between two Android devices using Android Beam. This functionality is user-friendly as well as programmable. However, developers are not given the option to extend Android Beam's capabilities too much beyond its original purpose.

The Google Play Store lists many additional applications that expand on the device's use of NFC. Enthusiasts can choose from the variety of reader/writer applications to handle NFC tags. Hardware vendors can support NFC in their products to make them easier to connect to Android devices.

Android's NFC API is the most complete in regards to card reading and writing. For manufacturers of contactless cards, this API should provide everything necessary to create an Android application to complement such cards. Some applications made for specific contactless cards have been listed as examples in Sect. 3.2.

Android provides API for host-based card emulation, but with no support for using the secure element, so applications must store all data in the phone's memory. Certain security models cannot be applied to this scenario, which disallows implementation of certain applications, especially those for contactless payment.

Although Android's support for NFC is quite extensive, we believe that the secure element and custom peer-to-peer communication are two features whose support should be added to Android to make it a mature and versatile platform for NFC applications.

We found no information about Android using encryption in its NFC communications. While security-sensitive applications will likely use an encrypted layer in their own protocol stack, developers should be aware that using Android's API for NFC may, by default, leave their communications susceptible to eavesdropping and unauthorized manipulation. In addition, the possibility of a Denial of Service attack must always be taken into account.

While the Google Play Store already provides a decent variety of NFC applications, we believe it could still be expanded upon. For instance, peer-to-peer NFC could be used for two-way synchronization of photo collections, certain types of notes, game data, etc. Moreover, we have yet to find an application that uses NFC for securely pairing two devices and exchanging cryptographic material, a use case that is also the subject of our thesis to be finalized in May 2016.

Acknowledgements. This project has been carried out with a financial support from the Brno University of Technology, Faculty of Information Technology through the specific research grant no. FIT-S-14-2299: Research and application of advanced methods in ICT.

References

1. List of nfc phones (2016). http://www.nfcworld.com/nfc-phones-list/. Accessed 28 Feb 2016
2. Oertel, B., Wölk, M., et al.: Security aspects and prospective applications of RFID systems. Bundesamt für Sicherheit in der Informationstechnik, Bonn (2005). http://www.bsi.bund.de/SharedDocs/Downloads/EN/BSI/Publications/Studies/RFID/RIKCHA_englisch_pdf.pdf?__blob=publicationFile
3. Haselsteiner, E., Breitfuß, K.: Security in near field communication (nfc). In: Workshop on RFID Security, RFIDSec 2006 (2006). http://events.iaik.tugraz.at/RFIDSec06/Program/papers/002%20-%20Security%20in%20NFC.pdf
4. Finkenzeller, K.: RFID Handbook, 3rd edn. Wiley, Hoboken (2010). ISBN 978-0-470-69506-7
5. Android developers: Near field communication. https://developer.android.com/guide/topics/connectivity/nfc/nfc.html. Accessed 11 Dec 2015
6. Google play store. https://play.google.com/store/. Accessed 01 Jan 2016
7. Android developers: Host-based card emulation. https://developer.android.com/guide/topics/connectivity/nfc/hce.html. Accessed 02 Jan 2016
8. Android developers: Sharing files with nfc. https://developer.android.com/training/beam-files/index.html. Accessed 01 Feb 2016
9. Jelly bean feature: Sending photos and videos over android beam. http://www.androidcentral.com/jelly-bean-feature-sending-photos-and-videos-over-android-beam. Accessed 02 Jan 2016
10. Octopus hong kong: Where can I use it? http://www.octopus.com.hk/get-your-octopus/where-can-i-use-it/en/index.html. Accessed 02 Jan 2016
11. Qué es la tarjeta bip! (Spanish). http://www.tarjetabip.cl/como-funciona.php. Accessed 02 Jan 2016

Towards a Usable Framework for Modelling Security and Privacy Risks in the Smart Home

Jason R.C. Nurse$^{(\boxtimes)}$, Ahmad Atamli, and Andrew Martin

Department of Computer Science, University of Oxford, Oxford, UK
jason.nurse@cs.ox.ac.uk

Abstract. The Internet-of-Things (IoT) ushers in a new age where the variety and amount of connected, smart devices present in the home is set to increase substantially. While these bring several advantages in terms of convenience and assisted living, security and privacy risks are also a concern. In this article, we consider this risk problem from the perspective of technology *users* in the smart home, and set out to provide a usable framework for modelling security and privacy risks. The novelty of this work is in its emphasis on supplying a simplified risk assessment approach, complete with typical smart home use cases, home devices, IoT threat and attack models, and potential security controls. The intention is for this framework and the supporting tool interface to be used by actual home users interested in understanding and managing the risks in their smart home environments.

Keywords: Risk modelling · Internet-of-things · Smart homes · Risk communication · Usable security · Smart cities · Tool support

1 Introduction

Technology has had an enormous impact on our world today. Amongst other things, it has greatly advanced commerce, healthcare, travel, and office and home life. The Internet-of-Things (IoT) is the next significant paradigm set to progress technology even further. It describes a reality where every day 'things' are all connected, working together towards some grander purpose. As the popularity of IoT has grown, so too has the focus on maintaining security and privacy. There have been various articles reflecting on these properties across several IoT contexts, some emphasising their need (e.g., via susceptible vulnerabilities and attacks) and open issues, and others proposing potential solutions for current and future challenges [1]. While these are excellent points of reference, their detail and perspective make them somewhat difficult to apply and use when engaging in practical security tasks, such as risk analysis. Here, we refer especially to cases where one wishes to use such topical reference points along with other information (e.g., network setups) to model the risk in a particular IoT deployment. Moreover, to engage with, and communicate that security or privacy risk to others, for instance, typical users in that environment.

© Springer International Publishing Switzerland 2016
T. Tryfonas (Ed.): HAS 2016, LNCS 9750, pp. 255–267, 2016.
DOI: 10.1007/978-3-319-39381-0_23

In this paper therefore, we aim to outline a framework, supported by a prototype interface, to allow the modelling and analysis of the security and privacy risks in IoT deployments; this framework builds on and seeks to apply previous research including our own [1,2]. A central goal of the framework is to be usable, that is, to provide a simple and intuitive way for common users of IoT technology to model the risks they may face. We scope this work especially to the context of smart homes (i.e., homes with deployed IoT devices) for two reasons. First, the prevalence of, therefore risk faced by, these homes is set to drastically increase in the future, motivated by governments (e.g., smart meters in the UK), supported living (e.g., health-related devices), and convenience (e.g., smart locks and lights). Secondly, we believe there is great value in providing a usable framework that can potentially be employed by a variety of individuals (including non-experts) to have some abstract model of the risks they may face in using IoT at home. This could even assist with issues of risk awareness (as outlined in [3]) in that environment.

To achieve the goals mentioned above, this paper is structured as follows. Section 2 will reflect on the research conducted on the smart home generally, and then from a security and privacy risk perspective. This will help to form an understanding of the current state of the art and highlight key challenges to achieving security and privacy in the smart home. Section 3 presents the core contribution of the article, i.e., the framework. Here, we motivate the need for such a framework, and introduce the modelling process which defines its. We further explain the context where it may be best used, the risk management foundation on which it is based, and the key features likely to increase its usability. Next, in Sect. 4, we apply the framework to a home scenario to exemplify how it can be used. This section also demonstrates the interface that can support individuals in the actual application task. Section 5 reflects on the framework and its goals, also considering the first impressions of prospective users; this is the important step of framework refinement. Finally, we conclude and present the next steps in this work in Sect. 6.

2   The Smart Home and its Security and Privacy Risks

Research on smart cities and smart homes has been under way since the conception of the IoT itself. While smart cities tend to be directly driven by governments and corporations (e.g., smart grids, transport and waste collection), smart homes represent a domain where public consumers have great choice and flexibility. Early research on smart homes sought to digitally engineer home life by proposing sets of adapted appliances likely to be useful [4]. These included smart pens, wardrobes, sofas, refrigerators and windows. Since that work, research in this space has specialised, and can be split into three key areas: home automation, home monitoring and security, and assisted living.

Home automation focuses on streamlined control of home devices such as adaptive lighting, heating and appliances. Whilst industry has aimed to produce clearly defined products, such as the Google Nest thermostat, Belkin's WeMo range, and Phillips Hue smart lights, research has sought to consider the full range of systems that could be implemented in the home. For instance, Han et al. [5] propose a home energy system design, using popular IoT protocols IEEE 802.15.4 and ZigBee, to provide intelligent services to home users. This includes a multi-sensing, heating and air-conditioning system and actuation application.

The domain of Home monitoring and security emphasises safety and security as key aspects in the home. Products available in this domain include WiFi cameras, motion detectors and smart door locks. Within research, some of the more noteworthy developments span smart home surveillance systems (e.g., proposals for intelligent, real-time remote monitoring tools [6]) to smart door locks with added security (e.g., two factor authentication smart lock solutions [7]). In particular, there has been a good stream of research in terms of assisted living technologies for the smart home. These aim to support individuals, such as the elderly or disabled, in a range of tasks [8].

With such a variety of technology now available for, and present in the smart home, individuals are increasingly at risk. For instance, smart locks meant to authenticate only individuals carrying certain pre-allowed devices, may fail (or be hacked remotely) thus resulting in authorised access to home properties. Moreover, as we have seen in the news, smart fridges have already been used to launch spam attacks [9], and smart TVs may be compromised to allow an attacker full remote control and access to the TV's camera and microphone [10]. Risks relating to security, privacy and dependability of smart home setups has been considered broadly in research, such as Brush et al. [11] and industry, in Kaspersky Labs [12]. While the research article highlights the issues and risks that home users face with these smart devices, the second reports on a more practical assessment of smart home devices and the serious risks that were uncovered (e.g., exposure of passwords and remote device control). These are two of the many articles discussing the range of risks facing the smart home.

In response to the risks, numerous proposals have surfaced. Busnel and Giroux [13] for example, propose a solution that uses security patterns applied to the smart home. A privacy framework is outlined in other work that seeks to support mobile health and home-care systems [14]. Furthermore, research has considered how the cloud service management principles of risk and contextualization can help solve the challenges of emerging smart home devices [15].

One area that has not received much focus however, is that of engaging with the individuals in the smart home on the risks they face through the use of smart home technology devices. This is a subtly different problem to that which is covered in existing research (e.g., [16]) on the usability of security aspects in smart home devices. This is because it is more interested in enabling users to gain an abstract model of the risks that may be present in the use of IoT in their homes. Kumar et al. propose an approach somewhat similar to this with their technique to visualise digital home safety, however, the extent to which users are involved in the process and understand the risk output presented is not clear [17]. We believe that this is a key part of research yet to be tackled and hence why we aim to explore it in this paper.

3   Framework to Support Risk Modelling in the Smart Home

A key goal our framework is to keep users in loop with regards to the security and privacy risks of smart home technologies. We appreciate that this is not a task all users will be interested in, however, for those non-experts in the home that are and have basic security and privacy knowledge, this framework could be especially useful. The framework consists of a process to model risks that draws inspiration from several risk assessment approaches [18]. As risk management and assessment are established fields with clear process and structure, we do not seek to replace them, but rather to provide thin layer between such techniques and users that could allow them to better appreciate the threats, attacks and related risks of using these home devices. Figure 1 shows our high-level modelling approach, with five tasks for home users to follow. These are **Use case definition**, **Assets and network analysis**, **Threat and attack analysis**, **Risk definition and prioritisation**, and **Control definition and alignment**.

Fig. 1. An overview of the framework process to model risks

In detail, the **Use case definition** task seeks to get users thinking about the scenarios or uses of the IoT devices in the home. This could adopt a high level or a specific usage perspective. To assist users, our approach relies on a support structure based on simple questions and the provision of several examples (or question answers) at each task level. For this level, the fundamental questions that would be placed to users are: *What scenario(s) or function(s) are the smart/IoT devices intended to support? Who are the individuals in such scenarios?* For guidance in answering these questions, there are a number of use cases with typical home users and relevant stakeholders accompanying the framework that can be referenced or selected directly. For instance, two broad use cases are Smart kitchen automation and complete Home surveillance, whilst specific cases range from Smart home security deployment to using Smart lighting. Of course, users may also decide to choose the most general use case, i.e., Smart home, and indeed we suggest this the first time the framework is applied to a smart home. Once the use cases of interest are identified, they are used to guide later tasks.

Asset and network analysis is the next task for the home user, and involves them defining the devices (assets) that are needed for the use case in focus. Additionally, here we aim to get users think about whether, and potentially how, those devices may communicate with each other to achieve their functions; this will be important in subsequent risk modelling tasks. The respective questions presented to users are: *What are the smart/IoT devices or products that support the use case? How do these devices connect or work together (or simply, what communicates with what)?*

To support individuals, the framework lists sets of devices typically used in the home, including smart TVs, door locks, alarms, lighting, thermostats, fridges, kettles, motion sensors, smoke detections, cameras, and hubs. Upon selecting relevant devices, users are asked to connect devices that may interact with each other. For instance, assuming the Smart door lock case, the devices used may include the smart lock and any smart phones that connect to it. The communication definition would include links from each smart phone to the smart lock (vendor specific app on the smart phone would define communication specifics); these are ad hoc networks, and scoped only to this use case. If the home user was interested in mapping the entire Smart home or the Smart home security features, they would also need to consider all the other devices linked to the smart phone, such as routers, PCs and other smart devices.

During this task, home users are also asked to prioritise the various IoT devices identified. Two questions that the framework poses to assist individuals are: *On which devices do the more sensitive data reside? What devices might result in the greatest harm if they were compromised (or failed to work as expected)?* Users can select from the smart devices identified earlier, and annotate them with priority details. Given the variety of users in the home, we suspect that many may not have a good understanding of the most important devices according to the questions above. To support this activity, aspects that may be relevant are listed with each device in the framework's catalogue. Therefore, for a smart TV, its microphone and camera, in addition to the fact that it may be used to enter account credentials (e.g., Amazon) or indeed, bank details for paid TV, could cause it to be considered as more important than an average device.

To keep the prioritisation simple whilst remaining useful, three stepped Likert scale levels are suggested for rating; Very important (e.g., device contains sensitive personal data such as bank details or social security numbers, or, the device allows full physical/remote access to the home), Moderately important, and Not that important (e.g., compromise of the device has little to no impact on the home or individuals in it).

With the assets and ad hoc networks identified, we then move to the **Threat and attack analysis**. The goal in this task is to define relevant threats, or specifically threat actors and map them to attacks. The question here is: *Who might seek to harm or compromise devices or individuals in the home?* Threat actors in this context are individuals that perpetrate attacks on the smart home. While there are an extensive set of actors that may be considered (both in terms of motive and capability), for ease of use the framework's initial list consists of Hackers (online), Criminals (offline), and Stakeholders/Users (Malicious/Intentional or Unintentional). The next step is to consider and link the attacks that such actors may launch, therefore; *how may the network (or part thereof) be harmed or compromised?* We support home users in this by drawing on our previous work [2]. In that research, we identify, describe and give comprehensive examples of the main types of attack on IoT devices, namely, device tampering, information disclosure, privacy breach, denial-of-service (DoS), identity spoofing, elevation of privilege, signal injection, and side-channel attacks. In addition to this, the framework provides examples of how certain threat actors may launch attacks. For instance, a hacker might conduct a DoS attack against a home router from the Internet, or a burglar may use an infected smart phone to tamper with a smart door lock. We note here that a glossary of all the security and risk terms is available with the framework.

In the **Risk definition and prioritisation** task, the framework combines output from previous tasks and aims to get users thinking about how at risk are the various home devices. Key questions here are: *What is the impact on an asset of an attack, or simply, what do home users stand to lose? How likely is the attack to occur?* For both of these, users can choose options on a likert scale from 1–3 in terms of impact and likelihood. For users, the framework highlights that level of impact can be linked to the importance levels highlighted before for assets. Therefore, if a criminal manages to compromise a front door smart lock, then the impact is very significant given they then have full access to the house. Similar to more formal risk assessment applications, likelihood is more difficult to estimate. For this, we suggest using knowledge of the number and type of individuals that may have access to the home, the neighbourhood of the home itself, and any previous attack (online or offline) information. For example, in a smart home where there are carers visiting daily to tend to the elderly, there may be an increased likelihood of device tampering (directly) or information disclosure (if they mistakenly connect an infected device to the home network).

To actually define the risk, the framework adopts a traditional approach of combining the impact and likelihood scores for attacks [18]. Therefore, for a device tampering attack on a smart lock, the impact might be very significant (3) considering what harm could result, but not likely (1) given the individuals live in a gated area. Using the straightforward metric of multiplication, the risk score would be 3 (out of a possible 9). As each attack related to the use case in focus is rated, the result would be a list of risks and respective scores. We appreciate that risks may be best perceived and interpreted in different ways [19], and therefore in addition to numeric scores also seek to use visual and verbal messages according to the score values. At present, we apply simple visuals based on colours, red, amber and green (for the main categories of high, medium and low risk); with wording such as 'These risks represent a serious area of concern for the smart home (for High risks)' also available. A future option for visuals is to integrate risk iconography [20] in the hope of being more accessible to users.

Whilst modelling risks will allow individuals to gain insight into areas of potential concern in their smart homes, it would be prudent to also supply guidance on the management of such risks. The **Control definition and alignment** task serves this purpose, by allowing home users to ask the framework: *What security controls may be applied to address the risks?* There are several different security controls that may be applied to address the various types of risk (and underlying attacks). To assist home users in identifying relevant controls, the framework draws on the OWASP Consumer IoT Security Guidance documentation [21] and aims to automatically link the guidance categories to the identified attacks. These categories outline approaches to address insecure web interfaces, physical security of devices, network services security and privacy concerns. For example, to address risks pertaining to insecure web interfaces and attacks such as identity spoofing or information disclosure, guidance is given on applying two factor authentication and engaging in network segmentation (e.g., using firewalls to segment critical devices). This process also allows users to witness how controls align to the risks present.

4   Applying the Framework

To apply the framework, users have the option of a prototype support tool, or a more manual approach using the documentation provided with each task. In this section, we describe aspects of the tool in particular, along with a simple example of its application to a risk modelling scenario. The scenario is one where a home user has installed a smart door lock to control access to their house. To commence modelling, users open the tool and create a new project. From there, they are directed to an interface for Task 1, i.e., Use case definition. In Fig. 2 we present two screenshots of the Task 1 interface.

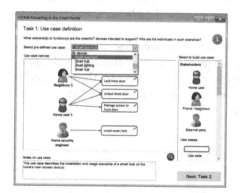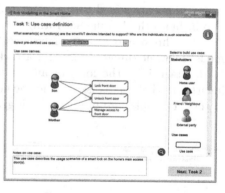

Fig. 2. Task 1 Risk modelling tool interface. The interface allows users to draw on predefined use cases, whilst also providing the graphical modelling, annotation and information-support capabilities to craft their own cases (by simple drag and drop).

As mentioned in Sect. 3 and shown in Fig. 2, users are first presented with questions setup to guiding the task. They can either select from the set predefined use cases (in the dropdown list depicted), or directly create their own by choosing relevant template items (users or use cases) from the scrollable list to the right of each interface screen. Given this scenario is similar to one in the predefined set, the user decided to select it to begin modelling. Selection automatically populates the Use case canvas (a user-editable area) centre screen with graphically depicted related scenarios and adds preliminary notes.

The scenarios added are not necessarily intended to be used as they are, but instead should (a) help users think about other pertinent individuals and activities (e.g., a home security engineer or device installation), and (b) be modified to suit specific new cases. Therefore, the system then prompts users to update the selected cases; they can rearrange, delete or add new items to the canvas as desired. In this instance, the user has modified the initial case, and created a more relevant one (with a mother and son in the home, and no other individuals involved with setup or possessing access) shown to the right of Fig. 2. If users require help or further information to assist in this task, there is an information icon in the top right of every screen.

In the Asset and network analysis task, users are presented with a similar structural interface to that in Task 1: with relevant questions and predefined IoT device options at the top, a list of device options to the right, a canvas in the middle, places to add notes, and information points. Given that the Smart lock use case was selected in Task 1, the system automatically populates Task 2's canvas with a Smart lock and two smart phones (one for each user), and creates a connection from the phones to the lock. Users are then requested to edit the canvas as necessary, to consider on which devices sensitive data resides, and what devices may lead to the greatest harm if compromised. The tool helps users by presenting potential aspects (e.g., credentials on smartphones and failure of the lock to allow entry) that may be relevant alongside each device icon shown. Annotations are added to the icons in the canvas by double clicking them; this also includes the 1–3 impact ratings.

The Threat and attack analysis task is next and involves using the tool to model relevant threat actors and attacks on IoT devices in the home. Support in this task is in the form of automated examples tailored to the previously identified IoT devices (assets) and the home's main users and stakeholders. Some of these examples are presented in Fig. 3.

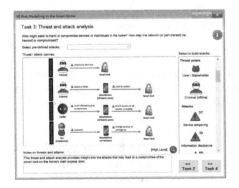
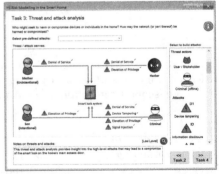

Fig. 3. Task 3 Risk modelling tool interface. This interface explores, in varying levels of detail, the threats and attacks facing the smart home.

In the screenshot to the left of Fig. 3, there are examples of preset attacks from the framework's catalogue which users can customise as they desire. For instance, a criminal could physically destroy a smart lock, potentially preventing other legitimate users from accessing it. There is also the fact that individuals without management level access (e.g., the 'Son' in this case) may use their trusted position to further elevate their or other individuals' privileges. Most importantly, these examples should give users some initial insight into the attacks they may face. As with previous tool interfaces, they can use the items (here, threat actors, attacks and IoT devices) on the right, to edit or compose additional attacks shown on the main canvas. To the right of Fig. 3, the high-level, summary of attacks, threat actors and the IoT system is presented; this is intended to be a simplified version of the low-level interface (to the left). Users can toggle between these interfaces using the 'High Level' or 'Low Level' options next to the zoom button below the canvas.

A central aim of the framework is to allow its users to better understand and model the risks which they face through the use of smart devices in the home. The Risk definition and prioritisation task is central to this. The tool's usage here is to combine user input and models previously supplied, and enable users to add further data about attack likelihood and impact to appropriately characterise the risk. This is achieved through a series of prompts for user input, where the tool asks for estimates regarding these aspects; while limited support is provided here, the tool does remind users of assets that were previously highly prioritised, as the impact on these if compromised may be greater. The result of entering this data is a Risk report; an example of which is shown in Fig. 4.

A Risk report is a list of risks, ordered in terms of their overall rating. As shown in our running example in Fig. 4, the risks along with their corresponding impact and likelihood ratings are expressed as an extension of each attack. This allows the individual modelling the risks or a user wishing to communicate those risks to others, to easily track their origin and related threat actors, whilst also

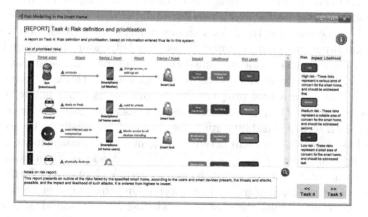

Fig. 4. Task 4 Risk report listing the risks facing the defined use case.

viewing other attack details. To support an accessible and accurate perception and interpretation of risks, we use a combination of visual and verbal messages, with colours and descriptions for risks (including impact and likelihood) [19]. Moreover, to enable users to quickly spot the most serious risks facing the use cases they initially identified, the system automatically orders risks by their levels. Given that this is a report, users are not able to edit it, but as necessary they can use the "<< Task 4" button to return to the previous screen.

The final task is Control definition and alignment. Here, the system draws on predefined mappings between attacks and respective countermeasures to suggest an initial set of security controls for the home users to consider. As highlighted prior, these controls are based on the OWASP Consumer IoT Security Guidance documentation [21]. The central tool interface is similar to Fig. 4, except for the fact that it is editable and if relevant controls have been identified for risks, they are listed next to each risk. For instance, consider the highest rated risk in Fig. 4 which involves elevation of privileges through accessing a privileged smart/mobile device. The related OWASP guidance category is 'I7: Insecure Mobile Interface', and therefore, some of the control options that would be suggested include: requiring a PIN or password; using two factor authentication (even biometrics, given its increased prevalence in smart phones); and enabling account lockout functionality. Users can decide which option(s) they wish to implement and add notes in the system if they desire. To facilitate sharing of the risk models developed in the tool, an export function is available which presents models similar to their representation in the interface.

5   Reflection on Framework and Users' First Impressions

The aim of this research was to provide a framework and supporting prototype interface to allow the modelling and analysis of the security and privacy risks in smart home deployments. We achieved this aim by considering the key components of risk analyses. In developing this framework, making the security and risk management process usable and accessible was a critical goal. This, we believe, could make understanding the risks with new smart devices much more tangible, thus potentially result in more proactive security behaviour. To achieve this, we built the framework to provide simplified guidance in the risk assessment process, and support via several predefined aspects (e.g., attacks, threats). Further support was available in a tool prototype that home users could follow the main five tasks, and model their own households and risks they face. We designed the prototype with security usability guidelines in mind, especially to be accessible, while still ascribing to the main activities in general risk management [22].

Although we believe that this is a good start at addressing a notable and increasingly relevant gap in smart home research and practice, further work needed both on the framework and prototype. One challenge yet to be tackled for example, is that whilst the abstract modelling of risks and attacks possible with the framework could help understanding, without consideration of specific vulnerabilities in different smart devices, the analysis is arguably limited. How we capture and include this information, and present it in a way that is still accessible to home users is a question for future research. A related challenge is in the mapping of security controls to risks and attacks – a high-level mapping can offer value especially for some types of users, but specific knowledge of attack details (possibly at the CAPEC level) may lead to better mappings of controls.

To gather some preliminary feedback on our framework and tool interface, we conducted informal interviews with five home technology users. The interviews involved explaining the purpose of the framework, demonstrating how it could be used, and then allowing them to apply it to any scenario they desired and ask questions. Overall, most users were able to quickly adopt the process, and they found the visual interface and support features (e.g., selection lists, automatic mapping) useful. We did notice a few issues in the framework usage however. For instance: (i) the way users modelled and linked assets, threats and attacks was not always logical or correct – e.g., a criminal stealing sensitive data from a smart light; (ii) users often disagreed on what devices should (and should not) be included in a particular use case risk assessment; and (iii) users felt that for complex use cases with a variety of home devices, the interface may not scale well. Respective resulting issues that will need to be addressed therefore include: (i) allowing flexibility but also introducing feasibility constraints on models; (ii) reviewing the pros and cons to scoping case and risk models; and (iii) testing the tool's ability to scale, and potential enhancement of interface designs. These are all aspects to be used to guide our future research.

6   Conclusion and Future Work

As technology continues to permeate the home, home users are facing a significant number of new security and privacy risks. This research aimed to provide them with some insight into those risks, via the definition of a risk modelling framework and supporting tool interface. We sought to frame these approaches as a simple and intuitive way for users of IoT technology to model the risks they may face in the home context. We also applied and reflected on our work, and highlighted some key first impressions from prospective users. These reflections identified some of the main aspects which we will seek to tackle in future work. Particularly, the question of how to include the appropriate level of detail so that our tool is highly usable and scales well, but still supplies home users with the information they need to make good security decisions. Once our next iteration of design and development is complete, we will conduct more detailed user testing to evaluate the real utility of our proposal.

References

1. Sicari, S., Rizzardi, A., Grieco, L., Coen-Porisini, A.: Security, privacy and trust in internet of things: the road ahead. Comput. Netw. **76**, 146–164 (2015)
2. Atamli, A., Martin, A.: Threat-based security analysis for the internet of things. In: International Workshop on Secure Internet of Things (SIoT), pp. 35–43. IEEE (2014)

3. Caviglione, L., Lalande, J.-F., Mazurczyk, W., Wendzel, S.: Analysis of human awareness of security and privacy threats in smart environments. In: Tryfonas, T., Askoxylakis, I. (eds.) HAS 2015. LNCS, vol. 9190, pp. 165–177. Springer, Heidelberg (2015)

4. Park, S.H., Won, S.H., Lee, J.B., Kim, S.W.: Smart home-digitally engineered domestic life. Pers. Ubiquit. Comput. **7**(3–4), 189–196 (2003)

5. Han, D.M., Lim, J.H.: Smart home energy management system using IEEE 802.15.4 and zigbee. IEEE Trans. Consum. Electron. **56**(3), 1403–1410 (2010)

6. Hou, J., Wu, C., Yuan, Z., Tan, J., Wang, Q., Zhou, Y.: Research of intelligent home security surveillance system based on zigbee. In: International Symposium on Intelligent Information Technology Application, pp. 554–557. IEEE (2008)

7. Priyadharshini, S., Nivetha, D., Anjalikumari, T., Prakash, P.: Mobile controlled door locking system with two-factor authentication. In: Padma Suresh, L., Panigrahi, B.K. (eds.) Proceedings of the International Conference on Soft Computing Systems. AISC, vol. 398, pp. 133–139. Springer, Chennai (2016)

8. Arcelus, A., Jones, M.H., Goubran, R., Knoefel, F.: Integration of smart home technologies in a health monitoring system for the elderly. In: 21st International Conference on Advanced Information Networking and Applications. IEEE (2007)

9. BBC: Fridge sends spam emails as attack hits smart gadgets (2014). http://www.bbc.co.uk/news/technology-25780908

10. Michéle, B., Karpow, A.: Watch and be watched: compromising all smart TV generations. In: Consumer Communications and Networking Conference (2014)

11. Brush, A., Lee, B., Mahajan, R., Agarwal, S., Saroiu, S., Dixon, C.: Home automation in the wild: challenges and opportunities. In: Proceedings of the SIGCHI Conference on Human Factors in Computing Systems, pp. 2115–2124. ACM (2011)

12. Kaspersky Lab: Surviving in the IoT world: Kaspersky Lab Experts Discover the Risks of Smart Home Devices (2015). http://www.kaspersky.com/about/news/press/2015/Surviving-in-the-IoT-world-Kaspersky-Lab-Experts-Discover-the-Risks-of-Smart-Home-Devices

13. Busnel, P., Giroux, S.: Security, privacy, and dependability in smart homes: a pattern catalog approach. In: Lee, Y., Bien, Z.Z., Mokhtari, M., Kim, J.T., Park, M., Kim, J., Lee, H., Khalil, I. (eds.) ICOST 2010. LNCS, vol. 6159, pp. 24–31. Springer, Heidelberg (2010)

14. Kotz, D., Avancha, S., Baxi, A.: A privacy framework for mobile health and home-care systems. In: Proceedings of the First ACM Workshop on Security and Privacy in Medical and Home-care Systems, pp. 1–12. ACM (2009)

15. Kirkham, T., Armstrong, D., Djemame, K., Jiang, M.: Risk driven smart home resource management using cloud services. Future Gener. Comput. Syst. **38**, 13–22 (2014)

16. Kalofonos, D.N., Shakhshir, S.: Intuisec: a framework for intuitive user interaction with smart home security using mobile devices. In: IEEE 18th International Symposium on Personal, Indoor and Mobile Radio Communications. IEEE (2007)

17. Kumar, P., Subramanian, N., Zhang, K.: SaViT: technique for visualization of digital home safety. In: 8th IEEE/ACIS International Conference on Computer and Information Science, pp. 1120–1125. IEEE (2009)

18. NIST: Special Publication 800–37: Guide for Applying the Risk Management Framework to Federal Information Systems (2010)

19. Nurse, J.R.C., Creese, S., Goldsmith, M., Lamberts, K.: Trustworthy and effective communication of cybersecurity risks: a review. In: Socio-Technical Aspects in Security and Trust Workshop at the Network and System Security (NSS) Conference, pp. 60–68. IEEE (2011)

20. Hosmer, H.H.: Visualizing risks: Icons for information attack scenarios. Technical report, DTIC Document (2000)
21. OWASP: Consumer IoT Security Guidance (2015). https://www.owasp.org/index.php/IoT_Security_Guidance
22. Nurse, J.R.C., Creese, S., Goldsmith, M., Lamberts, K.: Guidelines for usable cybersecurity: past and present. In: Cyberspace Safety and Security Workshop at the Network and System Security (NSS) Conference, pp. 21–26. IEEE (2011)

A Taxonomy to Classify Risk End-User Profile in Interaction with the Computing Environment

Karla Susiane Pereira, Eduardo Feitosa$^{(\boxtimes)}$, and Tayana Conte

Institute of Computing (ICOMP), Federal University of Amazonas (UFAM),
Manaus, Amazonas, Brazil
{karla.pereira, efeitosa, tayana}@icomp.ufam.edu.br

Abstract. The objective of this paper to summarize the current knowledge in Human Computer Interaction (HCI) and Information Security (IS) areas regarding the classification of the end-user profile and present a new taxonomy to classify risk end-user profile in interaction with the computing environment in the information security perspective. A systematic mapping study was performed to assess the taxonomy of end-users. From an initial set of 105 papers based on string search, we conducted and selected a total of 21 papers. After the full reading of these 21 papers, only 02 papers were selected and 01 new paper were manually added. The results obtained allowed us to identify gap profiles of end-users related to the risk they cause to the computing environment. Thus, we propose a taxonomy to classify risk end-user profile in interaction with the computing environment.

Keywords: Risk end-user · Taxonomy, Computing environment

1 Introduction

With the massive introduction of technologies in various environments, the human factor has become a major threat in the Information Security (IS) perspective. Wrong behavior, distraction, ignorance and curiosity are examples related to users and security fails in information technology (IT) area. Different studies show the real link between incidents and security flaws and the interaction of end-users with the computing environments [1–3]. To sum up, IS community has a jargon that says: "the end-user is the weakest link in any security process".

Different from Information Security area, in Human-Computer Interaction (HCI) the end-user is not blameworthy. On the contrary, all responsibility for any security flaws is the system developer. It is he who needs to worry when the end-user makes something wrong. By the way, the correct and safe use is not an end-user function. The argument is that common errors in system design, interfaces and interaction process can lead to security bugs in the operating system by end-users [4]. Thus, the identification and correction of these errors allows end-users to use safer operations.

Although both areas have different and contradictory views on the role of the end-user, the hard fact is that human being makes mistakes or failures, even in the

© Springer International Publishing Switzerland 2016
T. Tryfonas (Ed.): HAS 2016, LNCS 9750, pp. 268–276, 2016.
DOI: 10.1007/978-3-319-39381-0_24

presence of well-established processes. Thus, the following question arises: is it possibility to classify the risk end-user profiles from the information security perspective? Such an evaluation may be useful in that it allows describing the characteristics of the end-users, as the information is used and, finally, which user profiles can present a risk to the computing environment.

The objective of this paper is to summarize the current knowledge in Human Computer Interaction (HCI) and Information Security (IS) areas regarding the classification of the end-user profile and present a new taxonomy to classify risk end-user profile in interaction with the computing environment.

2 Background

This section presents the concepts of risk in both Information Security (IS) and Human Computer Interaction (HCI) areas. However, we also present some security concepts necessary for better explain risk and its analysis.

2.1 Fundamentals and Information Security Concepts

The Information Security area is governed by ISO/IEC 27000 family, whose main objective is the protection of information (data and systems) against various types of threats.

In general, the focus of these rules is to ensure three fundamental principles of information [5]: confidentiality - the information only is accessible by authorized persons; integrity - the guarantee of accuracy and completeness of information and processing methods; and availability - ensures availability to ensure reading success, of transport and storage of information.

In addition to these fundamental principles, Table 1 explains some useful and essential concepts in Information Security area.

Table 1. Concepts of Information Security area

Concepts	Definition
Security Incident	Is the occurrence of undesired and unexpected events, which has high probability of prejudice business operations and threatens the security of information [6]
Attack	Is a type of security incident characterized by the existence of an agent (attacker) that seeks to get some kind of return, reaching some asset value [6]
Attacker	Is a term used to indicate an individual or group of individuals who can make a threat [7]
Asset	Any element that has value to the organization (for example, information, physical assets, software, services and people) [5]
Threats	Are agents or conditions that, by exploiting vulnerabilities, may cause damage or loss [8]

(*Continued*)

Table 1. (*Continued*)

Concepts	Definition
Vulnerability	Is a weakness of an asset or group of assets that can be exploited by one or more threats [5]
Probability	Is the chance of a security flaw in relation to the asset vulnerabilities and the threats that may exploit this vulnerability [7]
Impact	The impact of a security incident is measured by the consequences it might cause to business processes supported by the asset [7]

2.2 Risk Concepts

In general, the term risk is defined as the possibility of danger, uncertain but predictable, that is the threat of damage to person or thing [9].

In Information Security area, the risk is understood as a condition that creates or increases the potential for damage and loss. The ISO/IEC 27005 [7] defines that the risk of information security is the ability of a specific threat exploits vulnerabilities of an asset or set of assets, harming the organization. According to ISO/IEC 31000 [10], risk is the effect of uncertainty on objectives, where an effect is a deviation from the expected behavior (positive and negative) and objectives may have different aspects (financial goals, health, safety and environmental, for example) and may apply at different levels.

In HCI area, one of the most considered risks is the communication breakdown. The best concept that assigns is the communication breakdown. It is the moment of interaction in which the end-user demonstrates not has understood the meta-communication designer or times when the end-user finds it difficult to express their intention to communicate the interface [11]. However, it is important to note that communication breakdown, even if treated, can lead to errors and, consequently, the losses and potential damage.

3   Research Method

Our systematic mapping study, to categorize end-user profiles, was performed in three steps: planning, conducting, and reporting.

3.1   Planning Step

In this step, we performed the following activities in order to establish a review protocol: (1) establishment of the research question; (2) definition of the search strategy, (3) selection of primary studies. Each of them is explained in detail as follows.

Research Question. The goal of our study is to examine the profiles of end-users from the point of view of the following research question: "*What are the classifications of end-users in computing environment context?*".

Search Strategy. We adopt three criteria in research sources selection: (i) search for papers in digital library; (ii) availability query papers; and (iii) papers available in English. For primary studies, we choose Scopus because it is the largest database indexing abstracts and citations [12]. The reviewed period include studies published from 1989 to 2012. We also manually search in journals and books available on the web.

We used a search string consists of two concepts: user computing and computing environment, according to the Table 2.

Table 2. Search String

Concept	Alternative terms & Synonyms
User Computing	("user computing" OR "user participation" OR "computer user" OR "user security risk" OR "user risk") **AND**
Computing Environment	("computing environment" or "computer environment")

Selection of Primary Studies. In the first step, called 1st filter, we evaluated only the title and the abstract of each paper to according inclusion and exclusion criteria and selecting papers that would be within the scope of the research question. In the second stage (or 2nd filter), researchers conducted a thorough reading of the selected papers from the 1st filter. And the papers were included/excluded according to the inclusion and exclusion criteria (Tables 3 and 4).

Table 3. Inclusion Criteria

#	Inclusion Criteria
IC1	Papers that discuss concepts of user profiles or category of users in computer environment.

Table 4. Exclusion Criteria

#	Exclusion Criteria
EC1	Papers in which the language is different from english cannot be selected;
EC2	Papers that are not available for reading and data collection (papers that are only accessible through paying or are not provided by the search engine) cannot be selected;
EC3	Duplicated papers cannot be selected;
EC4	Publications that do not meet any of the inclusion criteria cannot be selected.

3.2 Conducting Step

The application of the review protocol yielded the following preliminary results. The application of the review protocol yielded the following preliminary results. A total of 105 papers were returned from the search string. In the first filter, we selected 21 papers

(01 paper was doubled). In the second filter, we selected 02 papers by systematic review. We also manually added 01 paper. The search results revealed that the research papers concerning user profiles classification, based on the string round, are scarce.

4 Research Results

Based on counting the primary studies, the overall results are presented in Table 5.

Table 5. Research Question

What are the classifications of end-users in computing environment context?
Title: User Cube: A Taxonomy of End Users Keywords: End-User Computing; Morphological Analysis; Taxonomy; User Cube. Authors: Cotterman, William W., Kumar, Kuldeep. Year: 1989 Source: Communications of the ACM - Journal Metrics. Type: Paper Type of study: Morphological Analysis. Search: Automated Search
Title: Management of End User Computing. Keywords: Information Systems; Database Systems. Authors: Rockart, John F. and Flannery, Lauren S. Year: 1983 Source: Communications of the ACM Type: Paper Type of study: Exploratory Research. Search: Automated Search
Title: A Guide to Computer User Support for Help Desk and Support Specialists Keywords: Customer; User; Support. Authors: Fred Beisse Year: 2012 Source: Course Technology, Cengage Learning. Type: Book Type of study: Guide Search: Automated Search

Cotterman and Kumar [13] proposed an end-users model classification to assist managers in identifying users who operate out of function, allowing for measures to increase end-users productivity and satisfaction. The authors argue that end-users can be differentiated according to the form that interacts with a computer system within a company at: producers, those that generate results (information products); consumers, those who eat results; and producers/consumers, who produce and consume results. To understand the variety of environments and situations in which organizations provide technical support to their knowledge workers, Beisse [1] classified end-users in six categories: environment, skill level, frequency of use, software use, features used and relationship.

Rockart and Flannery [3] elaborate the first end-user classification. They argued that end-user profile is a result of the functions performed into the organization. Based on this, six distinct end-users categories were proposed: non-programming end-users, command level users, end-user programmers, functional support personnel, end-user computing support personnel and programmers.

5 Proposal of Taxonomy

As can be seen in the systematic mapping, we found the limited number of end-user taxonomies and none of them related to information security area. Thus, this work proposes a taxonomy aiming to show a more direct view of end-user, about information security perspective, using three pillars: knowledge, experience and use of information. Figure 1 shows the proposed taxonomy schema.

It is important to clarify that our classification model of the end-user profile is based on models proposed by Rockart and Flannery [3], Beisse [1], Cotterman and Kumar [13].

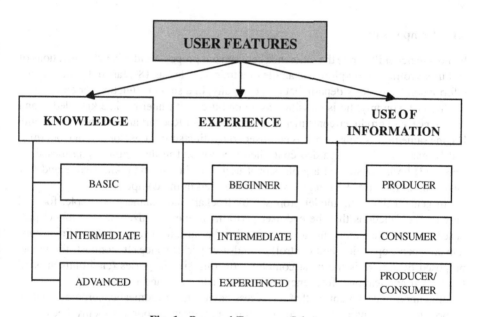

Fig. 1. Proposed Taxonomy Schema

The first pillar of our taxonomy is knowledge, whose purpose is to identify the level of information in computer area. The knowledge is divided into three levels: (1) Basic, end-user who knows the basics of computer; (2) Intermediate, end-user who knows the information technology concepts and solutions and information systems; and (3) Advanced, end-user who knows the advanced concepts of information technology and has the capacity to offer solutions for information systems.

As proof of the importance of computer knowledge, Adams and Sasse [14] applied a web-based questionnaire with 139 responses from employees of an organization.

They found that users do not understand the authentication process, confusing the user identification (ID) and password sections. In others words, users lack security knowledge.

The second pillar is **experience**, which refers to the frequency and expertise conducting daily computing tasks. Experience is divided into three levels: (1) Beginner, lay end-user, without ability to perform efficiently the tasks in information systems and/or access data through menus; (2) Intermediate, command level end-user with the ability to perform tasks in information systems as well as developing procedures for obtaining necessary data and generate simple reports; and (3) Experienced, end-user with the ability to perform efficiently the tasks in information systems as well as working with functional support, support to the end user and computer programming.

The third and final pillar is the **use of information**, used to determine the information applicability by the end-user. This group is also divided into three levels: (1) Producer, the end-user who inserts information; (2) Consumer, the end-user who consumes information; and (3) Producer/Consumer, the end-user who consumes and inserts information.

5.1   Comparison

In order to better illustrate the difference between our proposal and other classifications of end-user profiles, we explore a example of a trainee: "He has 18 years old, works in the information technology department of a company, in a support function for end-user."

In our taxonomy, he is classified as an end-user with intermediate knowledge and experience, and producer/consumer of information. For Rockart and Flannery taxonomy [1], the same user is considered as end-user computing support personnel. In Cotterman and Kumar [13], he is regarded controller/operator and in the taxonomy proposed by Beisse [3] he is considered a professional user with intermediate knowledge and low qualification that uses with regularity software used in the company.

In general lines, the model proposed by Rockart and Flannery is simple, focused only on the functions that the end-user performs in the organization. The model proposed by Cotterman and Kumar is intermediate because it focuses on three dimensions (development, operation and control) of end-user performance. In contrast, the model proposed by Beisse is the most complex, covering six categories (environment, skill level, used applications, frequency use, end-user features and relation).

It is important to mention that the access environment (domestic, corporate, public or private) is not part of the group features presented in our taxonomy because it considers that the evaluation is performed in the computing environment organizations.

5.2   Why Use the Proposed Taxonomy?

The taxonomies of Rockart and Flannery [3], Beisse [1], and Cotterman and Kumar [13] make use of knowledge, experience and use of information to build end-user profiles. However, these pillars are seen as independent elements. For instance, using only knowledge and/or experience it is possible to build an end-user profile.

Otherwise, our taxonomy allows determining the behavior of end-users regarding the computing environment, especially in an information security perspective where identify the applicability of user information is fundamental to ensure data security. For example, in November 2012, Google services were limited during 27 min in regions of Asia. The reason was the leak of Internet routes. An IT employee of Maratel Company, during maintenance of Internet routes, made a misconfiguration [15].

Analyzing the case using our taxonomy, we can assume that the IT employee has advanced knowledge and good experience with the platform (routers and Internet routes). Moreover, it is a producer user/consumer that performs system settings and maps the returned information. As result, we can suppose that although the employee has high competence, experience in implementation activities and use of information, a supervision system that evaluate the activities before the final execution could have prevented the problem.

In other words, our taxonomy allows to set an risk end-user profile, enabling the creation of prevention against future risks.

6 Conclusions

The use of technology has become increasingly present in daily life and in this scenario, from information security perspective, the end-user is a threat to computing environments. But how to identify users that can represent a security risk?

The literature research directly related to risks in computer interaction is not vast. The research on end-user profile has different point of views and uses. It is applicability depends on researcher experience and the way it performs the classification.

This work allowed us to identify the existent gap among end-users profiles, especially when they are related to risk in computing environment. For that, this paper introduced the reader in the concepts of risk in both Information Security (IS) and Human Computer Interaction (HCI) areas. Following, the research method and results of a systematic review mapping was presented, proving the low interest in to measure end-users and risks.

Finally, this study presents a new taxonomy to classify end-users profiles in computing environments. Using three pillars (knowledge, experience and use of information), our taxonomy allows to set an risk for an end-user profile, enabling the creation of prevention mechanisms against future threats.

Acknowledgment. We would like to acknowledge the financial support granted by CAPES (Coordination for Improvement of Higher Education Personnel).

References

1. Beisse, F.: A Guide to Computer User Support for Help Desk and Support Specialists, 5th edn. Course Technology Cengage Learning, USA (2012)
2. Iachello, G., Hong, J.: End-user privacy in human-computer interaction. Found. Trends Hum. Comput. Interact. 1(1), 1–137 (2007)

3. Rockart, J.F., Flannery, L.S.: The management of end user computing. ACM Commun. **26**(10), 776–784 (1983)

4. Rogers, Y., Sharp, H., Preece, J.: Interaction Design: Beyond Human - Computer Interaction, 4th edn. Elsevier Editora Ltda., London (2015)

5. ISO/IEC: ISO/IEC 27002:2005 - Information technology – Security techniques – Code of practice for information security management. Technical report (2005)

6. ISO/IEC: ISO/IEC 27000: 2009 information technology - security techniques - information security management systems -overview and vocabulary. Technical report (2009a)

7. ISO/IEC: ISO/IEC 27005:2008: Information Technology - Security Techniques - Information Security Risk Management. Technical report (2008)

8. ISO/IEC: ISO/IEC 13335-1: 2004 Information technology – Security techniques – Management of information and communications technology security – Part 1: Concepts and models for information and communications technology security management. Technical report (2004)

9. Oxford Dictionary of English. OUP Oxford, 3rd edn. (2010)

10. ISO/IEC 31000: 2009: Risk management? Principles and guidelines. Technical report (2009b)

11. Barbosa, S.D.J., de Souza, C.S., Paula, M.G.: The semiotic engineering use of models for supporting reflection-in-action. In: HCII2003 - HCI International, 2003, Creta, Human-Computer Interaction: Theory and Practice (Part I), vol. 1, pp. 18–22. Lawrence Erlbaum, Mawah (2003)

12. Kitchenham, B., Charters, S.: Guidelines for Performing Systematic Literature Reviews in Software Engineering, Version 2.3, EBSE Technical Report, Keele University, UK (2007)

13. Cotterman, W.W., Kumar, K.: User cube: a taxonomy of end users. Commun. ACM **32**(11), 1313–1320 (1989)

14. Adams, A., Sasse, M.A.: Users are not the enemy. Mag. Commun. ACM **42**(12), 40–46 (1999)

15. Paseka, T.: Why google went offline today and a bit about how the internet works. https://blog.cloudflare.com/why-google-went-offline-today-and-a-bit-about/ (2012)

Security Middleware Programming Using P4

Péter Vörös[1]([⊠]) and Attila Kiss[1,2]

[1] Department of Information Systems, Faculty of Informatics,
Eötvös Lóránd University, Budapest, Hungary
{vopraai,kiss}@inf.elte.hu
[2] Department of Mathematics and Informatics, Faculty of Economics,
J. Selye University, Komárno, Slovakia
kissa@ujs.sk

Abstract. Today's Internet requires easily manageable, and simply extensible network control systems, which we can't say about the current networks. Software-Defined Networking (SDN) [1] is an emerging architecture what aims to create a system for the upcoming needs, by offering a directly programmable, agile, centrally managed, and programatically configured way for the operators to control their network [2]. SDN decouples the network control and forwarding functions, which makes it easier to create new abstractions in networking, simplifying management and making network advancement easier.

SDN devices are programmable through a dedicated interface, with a specific protocol, from which the most known is actually OpenFlow [3]. The biggest problem with OpenFlow is that it does not support new header definitions, which is necessary for network operators to apply new packet encapsulations. To overcome these issues with OpenFlow, a new high-level language has been created: Programming Protocol-independent Packet Processors (P4) [4]. This language supports a fully programmable parser, which makes us able to define new headers without problem.

However there are a lot of opportunities to do with P4, we focused on the network security field. In this paper we introduce the first security middleware programmed and configured in P4. Our software works as a layer 3 firewall, with protocol, and port filtering, flood attack detection, and the ability to make decisions about Ethernet, IPv4, IPv6, TCP, UDP header fields.

Keywords: Software-defined networking · OpenFlow · P4 · Packet Processors · Security · Network virtualization · Programmable networks

1 Introduction

There are endless number of different network devices, with the same amount of ways to program them. Multi vendor devices, and the continuous development of new protocols makes it necessary to have a system which can respond to these

© Springer International Publishing Switzerland 2016
T. Tryfonas (Ed.): HAS 2016, LNCS 9750, pp. 277–287, 2016.
DOI: 10.1007/978-3-319-39381-0_25

changes in time. The first big step in the evolution of networks was the appearance of the Software Defined Networking. We see P4 as the next step, which is a language that supports dynamic device-, and target independent network logic describing.

In this paper we looked into the details of P4 especially in a security aspect. We studied how P4 can be used as a security middleware programming language. We created our own actions, tables, and rules to which resulted in a so called second generation firewall. It works as a packet filter which has stateful memory, but cannot yet deal with application layer things.

The paper is organized as follows. First in Sect. 2 we write about the basic background knowledge required to understand our work. After the basics we introduce some of the related works in this topic in Sect. 3 Then in Sect. 4 we present our security middleware solution and show examples how it works. At Sect. 5 we describe how we continue this project. At Sect. 6 we summarize the paper.

2   Background

The key of making long term systems is to make them able to be easily extendable, and configurable to the needs of tomorrow. Now we are going towards to an age, where everything is smart and everything is connected with everything. That's why we need to make our network systems capable of extension without too much trouble. Current networks make it impossible to change existing protocols without making infinite extra work. Which is why the development of modern networks was really slow in the past. Current networks are vertically integrated, which means the control and data planes are strongly bundled together, which is another reason why is it hard to achieve serious changes. Those systems are hard to configure, therefore it's difficult to respond to any faults or changes.

2.1   SDN

Software-defined networking (SDN) is a new computer network architecture that allows us to manage network services from a higher abstraction level. It's achieved by decoupling the control plane (the system that makes decisions) from the data plane (the system that forward packets to the destination), as it's seen on Fig. 1. SDN is an emerging architecture that is dynamic, manageable, cost-effective, and adaptable, making it ideal for today's applications [5,6].

SDN allows to use multiple different network devices for forwarding. Different vendor makes their devices programmable in different ways, but SDN ready devices have a common interface, which makes the control plane able to control the forwarding of these different devices.

OpenFlow is the most known interface. If we take a look at it's development it's conspicuous how the number of recognized header fields increased over the time. It started simply with 12 header fields in v1.0, and for v1.4 this number

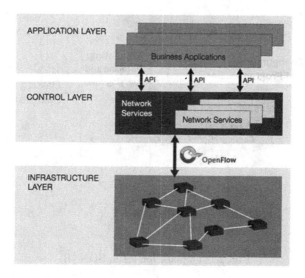

Fig. 1. The 3 layers of SDN [5]

has grown up to 41. Because of the new needs, the contiguous extensions of the protocol makes the specification too complicated. As technology goes forward there will be more and more headers, with new fields which have to be parsed as well, so in long therm a solution with the ability to define our own headers has to be presented.

2.2 P4

Programming Protocol-independent Packet Processors (P4) is a new domain specific language which raises the abstraction level for programming the network, and aims to be an interface between the controller and the network devices. In the design P4 has three main goals:

- Reconfigurability: Be able to redefine the parsing and processing of packets after deploying the switches
- Protocol independence: Be able to define new headers with new fields, with particular names and types, so packet processes can be specified with match-action tables and actions.
- Target independence: A program written in P4 is a hardware independent description, it requires specific compilers which can compile the hardware dependent binaries which is able to run on specific devices, from these hardware independent commands (Fig. 2).

P4 forwarding model (Fig. 3) is similar to OpenFlow. The incoming packets are first parsed as it is defined in the configuration. Both the ingress and the egress processing are composed of a set of match+actions, which are done by the different tables, and the parsed header fields. P4 also gives the opportunity to keep additional information between the stages, in fields called metadata.

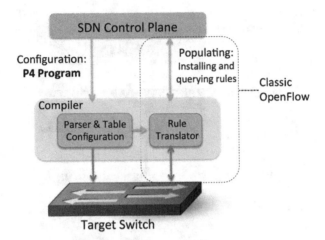

Fig. 2. The place for P4 in SDN [4]

Parsing. In the parser the different encapsulated header fields are extracted as follows in the example:

IPv4 header type in P4

```
header_type ipv4_t {
    fields {
        version : 4;
        ihl : 4;
        diffserv : 8;
        totalLen : 16;
        identification : 16;
        flags : 3;
        fragOffset : 13;
        ttl : 8;
        protocol : 8;
        hdrChecksum : 16;
        srcAddr : 32;
        dstAddr: 32;
        //options: *;
    }
    //length : 4*ihl;
    //max_length : 60;
}
```

It's the definition of an IPv4 header in P4. Due to the limitations of the behavioral model compiler variable length fields cannot be parsed yet, therefore some lines are commented out.

(Note: There is a new behavioral model generator, which is able to handle these variable length fields, but it's not fully compatible with the v1 compiler)

Parsing decisions after IPv4 header is extracted

```
parser parse_ipv4 {
    extract(ipv4);
    return select (latest.protocol) {
        0x06 : parse_tcp;
        0x11 : parse_udp;
        default : ingress;
    }
}
```

After the IPv4 parsing we make a decision about the header's protocol field. If it's 0×06 we pass it towards for TCP, if 0×11 UDP header processing. If different, then parsing stops here and, packet processing goes to the ingress pipeline.

Traffic that came from outside of the network's routers and proceeds toward a destination inside of the network is called ingress traffic. Egress is the opposite: traffic that begins inside of a network goes to a destination outside of the network.

Ingress. The current P4 specification [7] actually defines 21 *primitive actions* (e.g.: add_header, modify_field, drop, recirculate, etc.). Those primitives are the basic toolset for packet processing, the language allows new primitive definitions from the existing ones. Ingress processing usually does the most of the job, it modifies the fields, looks up the destination, makes the packet to be forwarded, replicated, dropped.

Egress. We do most of the processing in the Ingress pipeline, so basically we just send the packet out from the appropriate port. Egress for example does the modifications to the packet header for multicast copies.

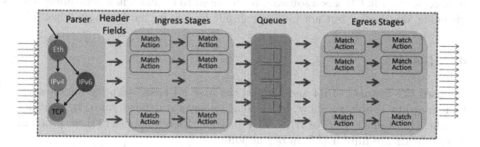

Fig. 3. P4 forwarding model [8]

2.3 Firewalls

A firewall is a network security system that monitors and controls the ingress and ingress network traffic based on different security rules. We differentiate three generations of firewalls.

First Generation: Packet Filters. The first generation is the packet filter, which makes decisions about the different header fields e.g.: IP-s, ports, protocols. These systems work with a set of rules, inspect each packet, apply the specified action for each matched rule. It works mainly with the first 3 layers of the OSI model.

Second Generation: Stateful Filters. This is where are we currently. This generation operates up to layer 4, and as it's name says it has stateful memory, which is essential for identifying attacks like DoS or portscans.

Third Generation: Application Layer Firewall. This generation understands the application protocols like HTTP, and can inspect the deep content of a package. It can identify different application level attacks. For example: if someone wants to SSH into a HTTPS port this firewall blocks the connection because the requests are not valid HTTPS requests. These inspections cannot be done without checking the content of the packets.

3 Related Work

Programmable parsing introduced by Kangaroo [9] which is also used in P4. Yadav et al. created an abstract forwarding model for OpenFlow [10], but it didn't place compiler in focus. NOSIX [11] extended the match+action table functionality, with the expense of losing protocol independence. Jeyakumar et al. propose an interface for low-latency network for network control and for data plane monitoring [12]. Sivaraman et al. propose to extend the SDN to the data plane, which results to be flexible enough to handle unanticipated application requirements [13]. Click is a software router used to evaluate new scheduling and queueing algorithms, but not able to compile binary for hardware switches [14].

4 Results

We used the features of P4 and created the first P4 based security middleware. Our program is able to allow, block, ban by several defined rules. It identifies weather the traffic is IPv4 or IPv6, TCP or UDP, therefore both of these protocol header fields are fully usable in our actions.

We can identify flood attacks, and able to block subnets or individual users from the network by checking the packet sending rate. P4 language offers meters which we use to compute the number of requests per second from a subnet or IP address.

In this section we give a detailed description how exactly our P4 firewall works. We're going through the different stages of Fig. 4:

- Parsing
- Check Ban List

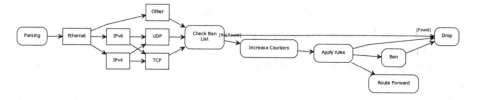

Fig. 4. The operation of our firewall

- Counters
- Rules
- Route Forward
- Ban
- Drop

4.1 Parsing

When we developed our firewall, we started out from the basic router example and extended it's functionality to make it able to work as a second generation firewall. The basic router defines the Ethernet and IPv4 headers only, which we found insufficient, so we implemented both IPv6 and UDP header parsers.

First we decapsulate the Ethernet header (we're not working with other type of packets). The Ethernet header contains a two-octet field called ethertype, which stores what's the protocol of the encapsulated payload. 0×0800 stands for IPv4, and $0 \times 86DD$ for IPv6, we handle everything else as "others".

We parse the IPv4 or IPv6 packets. The protocol field of IPv4 and the next header field of IPv6 carries the information about what is the next encapsulated protocol. We currently only accept TCP and UDP, and not handling any other protocols (eg.: ICMP, SCTP, etc.).

4.2 Check Ban List

As seen on Fig. 4 after the parsing, the next action is to check if any field of the packet in on a ban list. This ban list is one instance of stateful memory, users (MAC and IP addresses) who are breaking serious rules, or generating too significant packet rate will be added to this list. Those packets that matches this list will instantly be dropped.

4.3 Counters

P4 actually offers 3 ways to keep stateful memories: Counters, meters and registers. Counters can be used to measure the packet rate each host generates (possibility of DoS), the number of unsuccessful connection attempts (possibility of portscan, or Syn flood), or the number of bytes the host transferred.

Packet counter by source ip

```
counter packets_by_source_ip {
    type : packets;
    direct : ip_host_table;
}
```

We use direct access for the ip_host_table on this counter, which allocates a counter for each table entry. Direct counters are increased passively in the background, no more definition is required. The number of packets sent by each host can easily accessed by control plane.

4.4   Rules

The rules are defined in match+action tables, just to mention some block_protocols table contains the list of protocols which are either allowed, dropped, or banned. As it is a security software we're using a whitelist, which means by default we drop everything, so the list only contains the allowed protocols, and those which we want to ban.

Match+action Tables. As for the specification: "Tables are declarative structures specifying match and action operations, and possibly other attributes. The action specification (or action profile specification) in a table indicates which action functions are available to this table's entries [7]."

P4 differentiate 5 different match type tables: exact, lpm, ternary, range, and valid. We're mainly working with the first two. In exact match the field value must be identical with the table entry to execute the action, while lpm (longest prefix match) executes the action which table entry has the longest prefix match with the header field value.

Ingress processing

```
control ingress {
    apply(get_index);
    apply(bad_guy_check){
        miss{
            if (local_metadata.ip_type == IPTYPE_IPV4){
                apply(ipv4_lpm);
            }
            else { if (local_metadata.ip_type == IPTYPE_IPV6){
                apply(ipv6_lpm);
            }
            apply(block_protocols);
            apply(block_dst_ports);
            apply(block_src_ips);
            apply(forward);
        }
    }
}
```

We use exact matches in tables related to protocols. Lpm is used for IP-s, therefore different subnets can also be used in rules.

4.5   Route Forward

The basics of routing functionality is pretty much the same as the basic routing example. We made some extensions to be able to use IPv6, and UDP as well, but the main operation remained the same.

If a host connect to our network, it's physical address and the port where we can find it will be stored in a table, and in another table we map the IPv4/IPv6 addresses with the MAC addresses. So if the ingress processing decided to forward the packet, the MAC address and physical port is looked up (forward action).

Egress processing

```
control egress {
    apply(send_frame);
}
```

The egress processing doesn't do too much, whenever a packet arrives it is going to be sent out here. No more processing is required, because only fully processed packets can reach this point.

4.6   Ban

For keeping the stateful information about the users to ban we used registers. Registers are field similar to the ones which came from parsing. When simply set the register to 1 for the ones who we want to ban. Then drop the packet.

The ban action

```
action ban(){
    modify_field(local_metadata.bad_guy, 1);
    register_write(bad_guy, local_metadata.bad_guy, local_metadata.index);
    _drop();
}
```

This ban is easily revocable if we want to achieve time-based bans. The register can be modified back to 0 at any time both from the program, and the control plane.

4.7   Drop

Drop indicates that the packet should not be transmitted, this is a primitive action defined by the language.

4.8   Testbed

For the easiest validation of our results we used the behavioral model compiler. That compiler turns the P4 source into a Mininet configuration.

Mininet. "Mininet creates a realistic virtual network, running real kernel, switch and application code, on a single machine (VM, cloud or native), in seconds, with a single command [15]."

With Mininet it is easy to run simulations with multiple clients and routers with different topologies, therefore it was the best way to test how our network works.

To run our functional tests easier we also implemented our own test framework, that can measure how a virtual switch works with different P4 programs with specific match-action table entries.

5   Future Work

P4 is really dynamically developing, actually there are some functions that doesn't work yet, but will in the near future. The one we miss the most is that the behavioral model generator doesn't support variable length header fields, which makes it impossible for us to parse application layer information. After the update of the model generator we will start to extend the current program with the support of application level information.

With the next generation of P4 compilers will continue to implement our application level solution to interpret protocols and defend the network against even more types of malicious usage.

6   Summary

In this paper we gave a short overview of the network architectures, and firewalls. We presented P4 language, which can be the next big step forward in network device programming. It's a new and quickly developing language, that offers a protocol and device independent functionality to describe network logic. This code can actually be used to generate configuration for Mininet, but in the near future we expect several hardware compilers as well.

We used the opportunities of P4 to create a security middleware, which can act like a router with stateful packet filter functionality. We detailed how P4 works, and how we used it to implement the first version of our firewall.

Acknowledgment. Authors thank Ericsson Ltd. for support via the ELTE CNL collaboration.

References

1. McKeown, N.: Software-defined networking. INFOCOM Keynote Talk **17**(2), 30–32 (2009)
2. Kreutz, D., Ramos, F.M., Esteves, P., Verissimo, C., Rothenberg, E., Azodolmolky, S., Uhlig, S.: Software-defined networking: a comprehensive survey. Proc. IEEE **103**(1), 14–76 (2015)

3. openflow.org. Openflow definition (2015). http://archive.openflow.org/wp/learn more/
4. Bosshart, P., Daly, D., Gibb, G., Izzard, M., McKeown, N., Rexford, J., Schlesinger, C., Talayco, D., Vahdat, A., Varghese, G., et al.: P4: programming protocol-independent packet processors. ACM SIGCOMM Comput. Commun. Rev. **44**(3), 87–95 (2014)
5. opennetworking.org. Sdn definition (2015). https://www.opennetworking.org/sdn-resources/sdn-definition
6. Lopes, N.P., Bjørner, N., Godefroid, P., Jayaraman, K., Varghese, G.: Checking beliefs in dynamic networks. In: Proceedings of the 12th USENIX Symposium on Networked Systems Design and Implementation, NSDI, vol. 15 (2015)
7. P4.org. P4 latest specification (2016). http://p4.org/wp-content/uploads/2015/04/p4-latest.pdf
8. P4 language evolution (2016). http://p4.org/p4/p4-language-evolution/
9. Kozanitis, C., Huber, J., Singh, S., Varghese, G.: Leaping multiple headers in a single bound: wire-speed parsing using the kangaroo system. In: 2010 Proceedings IEEE INFOCOM, pp. 1–9. IEEE (2010)
10. Yadav, N., Cohn, D.: Openflow primitive set (2011)
11. Yu, M., Wundsam, A., Raju, M.: Nosix: a lightweight portability layer for the sdn os. ACM SIGCOMM Comput. Commun. Rev. **44**(2), 28–35 (2014)
12. Jeyakumar, V., Alizadeh, M., Kim, C., Mazières, D.: Tiny packet programs for low-latency network control and monitoring. In: Proceedings of the Twelfth ACM Workshop on Hot Topics in Networks, p. 8. ACM (2013)
13. Sivaraman, A., Winstein, K., Subramanian, S., Balakrishnan, H.: No silver bullet: extending sdn to the data plane. In: Proceedings of the Twelfth ACM Workshop on Hot Topics in Networks. ACM, p. 19 (2013)
14. Kohler, E., Morris, R., Chen, B., Jannotti, J., Kaashoek, M.F.: The click modular router. ACM Trans. Comput. Syst. (TOCS) **18**(3), 263–297 (2000)
15. mininet.org. Mininet - an instant virtual network on your laptop (2016). http://mininet.org

Author Index